NDER 'JACK' AUSTIN   RONALD JOHN BAKER   RUSSELL FRANCIS BAKER   BERNT BALCHEN   FREDERICK WALKER 'CASEY'

ELL   ARTHUR MASSEY 'MATT' BERRY   GEORGE FREDERICK 'BUZZ' BEURLING   WIL   ROSELLA

RINTNELL   HELEN HARRISON BRISTOL   FRANCIS ROY BROWN   MAURICE 'MOS   ICK BURKE

'COLLIE' COLLISHAW   WILFRED AUSTIN CURTIS   PAUL YETTVART DAVOUD   CLENNELL HAGGERSTON 'PUNCH' DICKINS

ORGE HAROLD 'MIKE' FINLAND   JAMES CHARLES FLOYD   NORMAN GLADSTONE FORESTER   ROBERT HOWDEN FOWLER

ELMER GARFIELD FULLERTON   PHILIP CLARKE GARRATT   WALTER EDWIN GILBERT   ALBERT EARL GODFREY   STUART

RY HALTON   PAUL ALBERT HARTMAN   HENRY WINSTON 'HARRY' HAYTER   ROBERT THOMAS HEASLIP   RICHARD DUNCAN

ICK WILLIAM HOTSON   CLARENCE DECATUR HOWE   ALBERT EDWARD HUTT   WILLIAM GLADSTONE JEWITT   HARRY

T LECKIE   ZEBULON LEWIS 'LEWIE' LEIGH   ALEXANDER JOHN LILLY   GEORGE BAYLISS LOTHIAN   JOSEPH HENRY LUCAS

R MACINNIS   DONALD RODERICK MACLAREN   MERLIN WILLIAM MACLEOD   WILFRID REID 'WOP' MAY   WILLIAM SIDNEY

GORDON ROY MCGREGOR   ALEXANDER DANIEL 'DAN' MCLEAN   ALAN ARNETT MCLEOD   STANLEY RANSOM 'STAN'

ONARD MICHAUD   ROBERT BRUCE MIDDLETON   JACK MOAR   ANGUS CURRAN MORRISON   RAYMOND ALAN MUNRO

ONY 'DOC' OAKS   MARION ALICE POWELL ORR   JOHN ENDER 'JOCK' PALMER   RONALD PEEL   GEORGE HECTOR REID

NDALL   BERNARD ANDERSON 'BARNEY' RAWSON   THOMAS MAYNE 'PAT' REID   JOHN HARDISTY 'JACK' REILLY   MORETTA

AY 'LINDY' ROOD   FRANK WALTER RUSSELL   WILLIAM JOHN SANDERSON   KENNETH FOSTER SAUNDERS   RAYNE DENNIS

K' SHOWLER   THOMAS WILLIAM 'TOMMY' SIERS   ARTHUR GEORGE 'TIM' SIMS   JOHN CHARLES SLOAN   ELVIE LAWRENCE

LAUDE IVAN TAYLOR   HAROLD 'REX' TERPENING   SAMUEL ANTHONY 'SAMMY' TOMLINSON   TRANS-CANADA AIRLINES

JOSEPH PIERRE ROMÉO VACHON   ARCHIE VANHEE   MAXWELL WILLIAM 'MAX' WARD   DONALD NETTERVILLE WATSON

N   JOHN ARMISTEAD WILSON   JACK FRASER WOODMAN   JERAULD GEORGE 'JERRY' WRIGHT   DENNIS KESTELL YORATH

UE OF CANADA   SOUTHERN ALBERTA INSTITUTE OF TECHNOLOGY   ONTARIO MINISTRY OF NATURAL RESOURCES

ATIONAL ORGANIZATION OF NINETY-NINES   AIR COMMAND CANADIAN FORCES SEARCH AND RESCUE / CASARA

They Led the Way

MEMBERS OF CANADA'S AVIATION HALL OF FAME

25th ANNIVERSARY — 1973 to 1998

They Led the Way

MEMBERS OF CANADA'S AVIATION HALL OF FAME

Canada's Aviation
Hall of Fame

25th ANNIVERSARY — 1973 to 1998

Copyright © 1999

Canada's Aviation Hall of Fame
P.O. Box 6360
Wetaskiwin, Alberta
T9A 2G1

Canadian Cataloguing in Publication Data

They led the way: Canada's Aviation Hall of Fame members

Edited by Mary E. Oswald

"25th anniversary, 1973 to 1998."
Includes bibliographical references and index.

ISBN 0-9684843-0-1

1. Aeronautics—Canada—Biography.
2. Air pilots—Canada—Biography.
3. Canada's Aviation Hall of Fame.

I. Oswald, Mary E.
II. Canada's Aviation Hall of Fame.

TL5349.T48 1999   387.7'092'271   C99-900117-5

Jacket and publication design by
Kennedy Lee Visual Communications, Edmonton, Alberta

Jacket photography courtesy
Kennedy Lee Visual Communications

Member portraits by Irma Coucill, Toronto, Ontario

Printed and bound in Canada by Friesens, Altona, Manitoba

Dedication

This book is dedicated to all Members of Canada's Aviation Hall of Fame and is published to bring their stories to all who are interested in knowing about Canada's aviation heritage. It also commemorates the 25th Anniversary of the Hall, 1973-1998.

The Hall of Fame began by recognizing individuals, focusing on a personality, a name and face alongside his or her accomplishments. These stories make a lasting and inspiring impression, and will encourage young people to apply themselves with distinction as they follow the leads of these pioneers.

Those who work in Canada's aerospace industry today are the Hall of Fame members of tomorrow. Their opportunities in one of the world's leading high technology sectors no longer lie in heroic open-cockpit biplane mercy flights in mid-winter over uncharted lands. They are finding other ways of being innovative, taking measured risks, facing challenges and making hard decisions. And the challenges have never been greater.

But no matter what the achievement, success depends upon contributions of many people: family members, colleagues and community. A dedication to Members is not complete without mention of the wives, husbands, families and communities who were always there, encouraging, supporting and caring for those we honour here.

Acknowledgements

I wish to acknowledge the many people who provided advice and assistance in the preparation of this special anniversary edition of the stories of Members of Canada's Aviation Hall of Fame.

For research and proof-reading:
Keri James, Jennifer Romanko, Cam Bailey, Ingrid DeLancey, Helen and Hugh Lavender, Don MacDonald, Joe McGoldrick, Brent Oswald, Byron Reynolds, Margaret Smok.

For other assistance and writing:
Jack Granatstein, Fred Hotson, Keri James, Peter Jenkins, Caren Mitchell, Jack Reilly.

For financial assistance, which allowed the project to go ahead, special thanks to: Russell Bannock, Larry D. Clarke, Douglas Matheson, and Darrel Smith; the Canada Millennium Partnership Program, the Wetaskiwin City Lotteries Board, the County of Wetaskiwin Community Lottery Board; and the assistance of McBain Cameras, and Shippers Supply, Edmonton.

For realizing the importance of this project and supporting it: the National Board of Directors of Canada's Aviation Hall of Fame, General (Ret'd) Paul D. Manson, Chairman.

For their encouragement: the Alberta Operating Committee, Brian Murphy, Chairman; and also Bill Casey, Manager of Reynolds-Alberta Museum.

For their continuing support from the beginning, I wish to especially thank: Keri James, assistant editor, whose wisdom and sense of humour were much appreciated; Jennifer Romanko, curator of Canada's Aviation Hall of Fame, who was always there and dealt cheerfully with my requests; and my husband, Gordon, whose assistance and encouragement kept me focused.

Table of Contents

Table of Contents

Foreword

Fame, by definition, is a state of being well-known and of good reputation, to which can be added, being recognized by one's peers. Canada's Aviation Hall of Fame was established to recognize all who have toiled in the building of Canadian aviation, and to record those who have made outstanding contributions to the advancement of the industry.

The Hall, with its headquarters in Wetaskiwin, Alberta, represents every branch of this industry, from business leaders and aeronautical engineers, to bush pilots and their mechanics who opened the Canadian north in the early period. There are test pilots, airline pilots, historians, scientists, writers and instructors; men and women who were outstanding in their chosen field.

This chronicle leans heavily on the peacetime conquest of air travel within Canada's geographical boundaries as it relates to the growth of the country. The names and deeds of the outstanding war heroes are also covered, including the Victoria Cross winners of both World Wars. Most early members of the Hall had military backgrounds; some continued in active service or government administration. Many went on to commercial ventures.

Despite the late opening of the Hall—it did not open until 1973—the outstanding contributors to the very early years are acknowledged. Most members will admit that fame never crossed their minds as they built their own careers. Others did not live to see their names included in the honour roll.

Canadians cannot afford to live in the past, yet the history of its aviation background should be required reading for students who aspire to a career in aerospace.

One look at a map of Canada quickly points to our unique type of aviation. Settlements bordering on the Arctic Circle were nurtured by the early bush airplane and are still maintained by its modern counterpart, the turbine transport. When new aircraft were needed in the outlying areas to replace the early Fairchilds and Bellancas, Canadian factories built those replacements.

The growth of Canadian aircraft factories has become another success story of an industry that has grown to the point where it is now the third largest civil aircraft manufacturer in the world. Canadian technology is being used in space exploration, and flight training has become a new field of leadership. We have come a long way since John McCurdy's flight in 1909. Throughout all these years of progress, the common denominator has been people.

This book is about many of these people.

Fred W. Hotson

—Fred W. Hotson, Hall of Fame Member 1998

"The Beginning"

The fragile aircraft Silver Dart shook loose
the frozen bonds of Nova Scotia's Bras d'Or
Lake in nineteen hundred nine to usher in
this fledgling nation's age of flight.

And five years later Britain's need called
forth a pride of young Canadians to serve
as airmen … all so brave and many fallen
dead from alien skies.

They served until the "war to end all wars"
was won and then a few employed their
airborne skills to probe a land that time
forgot, which lay beyond the furthest
cloud. In puny flying craft they snarled
above a million miles awesome brooding
loneliness … and vaulted battlements of
wind-swept mountain ranges yet unnamed
… tracked faultlessly the twisting turns of
brawling waterways that fed the Arctic sea
… enroute to which some stayed in
unmarked graves.

As to the south our patchworked, friendly
land was being linked more personally by
leather-suited, goggled men who strode the
earth below in flying mail vans (day and
night) and slept beneath a wing to ward
off sun or dew … while passengers were
being coaxed by other airborne crews (in
classy uniforms) to arch with them across
the sky and beat the train.

And when this nation's way of life was
challenged yet again in nineteen thirty-
nine, a thousand score and more
Canadians donned airforce blue and served
within an angry world to weave a legacy of
valour … laurel leaves for those who sleep
in foreign graves.

To honour those who gave the best they
had, unselfishly improving flight throughout
our land, a token group of aviation veterans
was chosen by their peers to represent that
whole community.

All had drunk deep at adventure's well,
their valiant efforts having stood the test of
time … but knowing others to have given
more, reserved the hallowed ground for
those as yet unnamed.

—Raymond Alan Munro, Hall of Fame Member 1974

History of Canada's Aviation Hall of Fame

Aviation notables gathered in Calgary, March 31, 1973, for the third investiture of the Order of Icarus. Among those present were C.H. 'Punch' Dickins, most Senior Companion of the Order; Captain James A. Lovell Jr., U.S. astronaut and guest speaker for the evening; and well-known, hard-working aviators like S.A. 'Sammy' Tomlinson, S.R. 'Stan' McMillan, Walter E. Gilbert, and Maxwell W. Ward.

The gathering sparked a headline in the Calgary Herald. Hall of Fame Aviators Gather in Calgary. These words set in motion an idea which gathered momentum as the year progressed. A founding Board of Directors was created with C.H. 'Punch' Dickins as Chairman, Donald N. Watson as Vice-Chairman, and H.W. 'Harry' Hayter as Secretary. Others included Z.L. 'Lewie' Leigh, P.S. 'Stan' Turner, and L. 'Lindy' Rood. Raymond A. Munro took on the bulk of the work, and served as the initial Managing Director. Canada's Aviation Hall of Fame was incorporated August 2, 1973.

This founding Board faced a momentous task. Many questions presented themselves. Who would be chosen for membership? How many would there be? Would there be adequate representation of both civilian and military aviators? By what means would their stories be told? Where would the Hall be located? How would future Members be selected?

After much discussion and debate, it was decided Members should include all who had been awarded the Trans-Canada (McKee) Trophy; all Companions of the Order of Icarus; all recipients of the Victoria Cross in aerial combat; Alexander Graham Bell and F.W. 'Casey' Baldwin for designing and building the Silver Dart; and Group Captain John E. Fauquier, to represent Bomber Command, and Flight Lieutenant George F. 'Buzz' Beurling, to represent Fighter Command, in World War II. This made a total of 79 original Members, with both civilian and military exploits well represented.

A great deal of thought was given to where the Hall should be located. Edmonton? Winnipeg? Toronto? Montreal? All these cities and more had merit. Should it be in Ottawa with the National Aviation Collection? Should it be a 'movable feast' so that all Canadians might taste our aviation heritage? Finally, Edmonton, long known as 'The Gateway to the North', was chosen as the place it would open. The entire Board of Directors, and many volunteers, worked hard to meet a deadline of July, 1974.

The stories would be told on four by eight foot panels with portraits, citations, photographs, and memorabilia. Under managing director Ray Munro, undeniably one of Canada's most colorful promoters of aviation, panels were being manufactured, medals struck, photographs and memorabilia collected, documents, certificates, stationery and the original Members Book designed and printed. Irma Coucill was commissioned to complete the Members' portraits.

Over 600 people attended the first Induction Gala on July 16, 1974, hosted by the City of Edmonton. All living Members and their families, and many of the families of the 28 deceased Members, were treated to a night they would long remember. The format of subsequent Induction Galas was set with presentation of medals and certificates of Membership in the Hall, the Order of Polaris by the Government of the Yukon, and the Order of Flight by the City of Edmonton. Unique to this first Gala were metal plaques awarding the Esteemed Brotherhood of Silver Wings to the original 79 Members by the Government of the Northwest Territories.

A Nomination Review Committee was appointed to accept nominations to Canada's Aviation Hall of Fame. This committee remains strictly confidential and looks for unselfish contributions to aviation which have been of major benefit to Canada, and which have stood the test of time. You, the reader and aviation enthusiast, play a critical role in this process. In Canada's 90 years of aviation history, there are many who have not been inducted as Members because they have not been nominated.

The Hall's display officially opened on the first day of Klondike Days, July 17, 1974, in the Sportex Building at the Edmonton Exhibition Grounds. Dismantled and moved several times in its initial years, it finally found a home in the depths of the Edmonton Convention Centre. In 1992, when the Reynolds-Alberta Museum opened at Wetaskiwin, Alberta, just 65 km south of Edmonton, Canada's Aviation Hall of Fame moved to the Aviation Hangar on the same site, with the promise of merging its exhibits with the extensive Reynolds collection of aircraft. This museum of transportation and industry is a world-class destination, and the aircraft collection is one of the most historically significant collections of vintage aircraft in Canada. Canada's Aviation Hall of Fame is proud to call Wetaskiwin home.

Each story contained in this book is just the tip of the iceberg. Each could easily be lengthened to a book in itself. These extraordinary people all made contributions to the advancement of aviation in Canada as pilots, aeronautical engineers, doctors, scientists, or administrators. In the words of Raymond Alan Munro, all have drunk deep at adventure's well, all have set permanent records for pioneering achievements ... for enterprise ... for unfailing courage ... that have stood the test of time.

Jack. Reilly

—J.H. 'Jack' Reilly, Hall of Fame Member 1974

History of the Order of Icarus

During Canada's Centennial Year, the role played by certain aviators in the advancement of Canadian aviation was brought sharply into focus.

A careful assessment of honours available to these airmen revealed that, excluding the McKee Trophy, no other superior recognition existed. To fill this void, and to honour those persons still living whose airborne skills had resulted in outstanding benefits to manned flight, the Order of Icarus was founded. In determining the requirements for admission, the founding fathers ruled themselves from membership.

They delved into Greek mythology to name the Order and selected Icarus, son of Daedalus, builder of the Labyrinth for King Minos of Crete. Legend recounts how Daedalus, to escape from a sentence of death, fashioned wings of feathers glued with wax for himself and his son. With these, they flew to freedom. Icarus, so exhilarated by flight and captivated by the spirit of adventure, flew too close to the sun, which melted the wax and collapsed his wings, plunging him to his death in what is now called the Icarian Sea. He thus became literature's first airman casualty.

The sole rank within the Order was designed as Companion, excluding those persons governing the conduct of the Order. The Senior Companions were selected by the founding group for their unique contributions to Canadian aviation and the time span and areas in which they were involved.

The decoration consists of a gilt sunburst, also representing the cardinal points of the compass, surrounding a white enameled figure of Icarus, his folded mismatched wings reminding Companions of airborne imperfections. The figure is encircled by a knight's belt, binding Companions to a common cause and on which, lettered in gold, is the Order's motto, "Despite Adversity". The insignia is suspended by

means of a golden lop ornamented with a maple leaf to denote the Order's Canadian origin.

The broad white center stripe of the ribbon defines the purity of flight across the golden sun, split by two fine blue lines signifying the companionship of airmen in adversity. The broad blue band describes the depth of yet unconquered space and the outer bars of black remind Companions of their mortality and of those who have passed before.

Companions of the Order of Icarus and the Year Invested			
1967	C.H. Dickins*	1969	H.W. Hayter*	1973	D.N. Watson*	1975	T.W. Siers*

1967 C.H. Dickins*	1969 H.W. Hayter*	1973 D.N. Watson*	1975 T.W. Siers*
1967 P.A. Hartman*	1969 M.G.M. Knox*	1974 N.J. Armstrong*	1977 J.E. Fauquier*
1967 B.W. Mead*	1969 S.R. McMillan*	1974 H.M. Bristol*	1978 J.A.M. Austin*
1967 R.A. Munro*	1969 A.M. McMullen*	1974 R. Collishaw*	1978 G.L. MacInnis*
1967 L. Rood*	1969 A.G. Sims*	1974 W.W. Fowler*	1978 B.A. Rawson*
1967 H.W. Seagrim*	1969 S.A. Tomlinson*	1974 S. Graham*	1981 A.E. Godfrey*
1967 J.C. Sloan*	1969 L.J. Tripp*	1974 Z.L. Leigh*	1981 K.L. Guthrie
1969 G.H. Finland*	1969 T.F. Williams*	1974 G.B. Lothian*	1981 W.F.S. Luck*
1969 N.G. Forester*	1973 B. Balchen*	1974 R.C. Randall*	1981 D.R. MacLaren*
1969 W.E. Gilbert*	1973 J. Moar*	1974 P.S. Turner*	1981 W.F.M. Newson*
	1973 M.F. Reilly*	1975 K.R. Greenaway*	
	1973 J.H. Reilly*	1975 H. Hollick-Kenyon*	*denotes Members of Canada's Aviation Hall of Fame
	1973 M.W. Ward*	1975 W.G. Leach*	

The Trans-Canada (McKee) Trophy

The Trans-Canada (McKee) Trophy, often referred to as the McKee Trophy, is the oldest aviation award in Canada, having been established in 1927 by J. Dalzell McKee. In 1926, McKee, of Pittsburgh, Pennsylvania, accompanied by Squadron Leader Earl Godfrey (Hall of Fame 1978) of the RCAF, flew from Montreal, Quebec, to Vancouver, British Columbia, in a Douglas MO-2B seaplane.

In appreciation of the courtesies afforded him by the RCAF and the Ontario Provincial Air Services, McKee endowed an aviation award in his name. The trophy was deeded to the Crown in the person of the Department of National Defence, which controlled all aspects of aviation at the time, both military and civil. In 1971, the administration of the McKee trophy was transferred to the Canadian Aeronautics and Space Institute.

The trophy is awarded for outstanding achievement in the field of aerospace operations, particularly in pioneering as aircrew, new areas and applications in aerospace. The achievement may be a single brilliant exploit within the past year or a sustained high level of performance in recent years. The achievement shall be of contemporary significance and the recipient shall be or have been a Canadian citizen at the time of the achievement.

From 1964 to 1983, the trophy was displayed at the National Museum of Science and Technology in Ottawa, Ontario. Since 1983 it has been on display at Canada's Aviation Hall of Fame, now located in the city of Wetaskiwin, Alberta.

Winners of the Trans-Canada (McKee) Trophy

1927 H.A. Oaks *	1945 G.W.G. McConachie *	1965 Not Awarded	1983 D.H. Rogers *
1928 C.H. Dickins *	1946 Z.L. Leigh *	1966 P.C. Garratt *	1984 G.N. Henderson (posthumously)
1929 W.R. May *	1947 B.A. Rawson *	1967 R.A. White *	
1930 J.H. Tudhope *	1948 R.B. West *	1968 Not Awarded	1985 P.Y. Davoud *
1931 G.H. Phillips *	1949 D.K. Yorath *	1969 Not Awarded	1986 T.M. Watt
1932 M. Burbidge *	1950 C.C. Agar *	1970 Not Awarded	1987 S.W. Grossmith *
1933 W.E. Gilbert *	1951 P.C. Garratt *	1971 Not Awarded	1988 Not Awarded
1934 E.G. Fullerton *	1952 K.R. Greenaway *	1972 Not Awarded	1989 G.A. Neal *
1935 W.M. Archibald *	1953 F.I. Young *	1973 M.W. Ward *	1990 B. Granley
1936 A.M. Berry *	1954 J.G. Wright *	1974 R.H. Fowler *	1991 S. Graham * (posthumously)
1937 J.R. Vachon *	1955 G.L. MacInnis *	1975 J.A.M. Austin *	
1938 P.S. Johnston	1956 R.T. Heaslip *	1976 D.C. Fairbanks (posthumously)	1992 L. Kerr
1939 M.A. Seymour*	1957 J.G. Showler *		1993 L. deBlicquy
1940 T.W. Siers *	1958 J. Zurakowski *	1977 A.E. Godfrey *	1994 B.J. Wormworth
1941 A.D. McLean *	1959 J.A.D. McCurdy *	1978 R.D. Schultz *	1995 V. Moshansky
1942 T.M. Reid *	1960 W.O. Leach *	1979 Not Awarded	1996 Not Awarded
1943 T.M. Reid *	1961 W.W. Phipps *	1980 Not Awarded	1997 Not Awarded
1944 J.A. Wilson *	1962 Not Awarded	1981 F.D. Adkins	1998 A. Dumont
	1963 F.A. MacDougall *	1982 E.N. Ronaasen (posthumously)	
	1964 Not Awarded		

* denotes Members of Canada's Aviation Hall of Fame

History of Belt of Orion

The Belt of Orion Award for Excellence was founded by Canada's Aviation Hall of Fame in 1988 to honour organizations, groups, societies or associations who have made outstanding contributions to the advancement of aviation in Canada. Descriptions of these organizations begin on page 217.

Orion, the son of Neptune, according to Greek Mythology, was a handsome and energetic hunter who possessed the power to walk through the sea and on its surface. Artemis, the Goddess of the hunt, fell in love with Orion, but her twin brother, Apollo, was jealous and sent a scorpion to kill him. In her sorrow and remorse for his death, Artemis placed him in the sky as a constellation.

Orion, the Great Hunter, is a brilliant constellation, second to the Big Dipper on the roster of major constellations. It straddles the celestial equator, and is outlined by a quadrilateral of three brilliant stars—Betelgeuse, Bellatrix and Rigel, and one of lesser magnitude. Inside the quadrilateral are three second-magnitude stars forming the Belt of Orion. The three stars of the Belt point south-eastward to Sirius, the brightest star of the heavens.

Recipients of the Award are:

1988   Canadian Air Line
         Pilots Association

1989   Air Cadet League of Canada

1990   Southern Alberta
         Institute of Technology

1991   Ontario Ministry of
         Natural Resources Aviation
         and Fire Management Branch

1992   Not Awarded

1993   Canadian Owners
         and Pilots Association

1994   431 (AD) Demonstration
         Squadron—Snowbirds

1995   Canadian Ninety-Nines

1996   Not Awarded

1997   Not Awarded

1998   CASARA/Air Command

Members

CANADA'S AVIATION HALL OF FAME

**Canada's Aviation
Hall of Fame**

1 9 7 3   t o   1 9 9 8

Carlyle Clare (Carl) Agar

(1901 – 1968)

Carlyle Clare (Carl) Agar, A.F.C., was born on November 28, 1901, in Lion's Head, Bruce County, Ontario, and moved to Edmonton, Alberta, in 1905 where he was educated. He farmed on the outskirts of the city, and by 1928 had saved enough money to pursue a long-time goal: learning to fly. He joined the Edmonton Aero Club and under the tutelage of Maurice 'Moss' Burbidge (Hall of Fame 1974), earned his Private Pilot's Licence the following year. In 1932 he accepted a position with the Department of Indian Affairs as an agricultural instructor at Wabamun, Alberta. Two years later he returned to full time farming.

At the outbreak of World War II, Agar attempted to enlist in the Royal Canadian Air Force (RCAF) as a pilot, but was rejected because, at age 38, he was over the age limit. In 1940 he reapplied to the RCAF, since the British Commonwealth Air Training Plan (BCATP) was expanding and there was increased demand for instructors. He was accepted for pilot training and posted to Moose Jaw, Saskatchewan, and Trenton, Ontario, where he graduated as a flight instructor. He was stationed at Edmonton and High River, Alberta, and Abbotsford, British Columbia. In 1944 he

Landing a helicopter in the late 1940's on a narrow mountain ledge was a skill to master. Taking off was another: the machine needed forward space to become airborne. A new, daring skill was needed. Agar learned to literally 'bump' his machine sideways off the mountain ledge, and as it fell, it picked up enough forward speed to fly.

was awarded the Air Force Cross (A.F.C.) for outstanding contributions as a flight instructor. He was discharged from the RCAF in 1945 when he reached the maximum age for aircrew.

Agar moved his family to Penticton, British Columbia, where he formed the South Okanagan Flying Club in partnership with two ex-RCAF members, pilot Barney Bent and maintenance engineer Alf Stringer. Their Club operations were limited to flight training only—no charter work was permitted. The lack of commercial flying business forced them to reassess their position, so they moved to Kelowna, British Columbia, and formed Okanagan Air Service. Their plan was to engage in instructional activities, charter flying, and crop spraying, but they were again forced to reconsider their operational activities due to high maintenance costs.

The partners learned of a Bell 47-B3 helicopter being demonstrated at Yakima, Washington, as a crop sprayer. They went to see this new machine and returned convinced of the helicopter's potential. To raise enough money to purchase one, as well as meet the costs of pilot and maintenance training, they decided to convert the Company to public ownership and sell shares. In this way, Agar was able to bring the first commercial helicopter, a Bell 47-B3, into Canada on August 9, 1947, to spray orchards in the Okanagan Valley with insecticides.

When it became evident that he needed to expand his operations to sustain his company, Agar contracted with the Government of British Columbia to spray forests affected by loop worm, and areas of the lower Fraser Valley which were infested with mosquitoes.

When not engaged in these economically crucial operations, Agar learned the secrets of helicopter flying in the remote reaches of the Rocky Mountains. Flying at high altitudes brought new challenges: the higher one goes, the less dense the air becomes, causing the rotors to provide less lift and the power of the engine to

In the rugged west coast mountains. Carl Agar at Kitimat, British Columbia, where he was flying aerial surveys for a new power transmission route.

diminish. As well, unpredictable winds created sudden up-drafts and/or down-drafts. The rugged terrain required the ability to land on a small shelf of rock and take off again. Agar practiced his theories and perfected new skills and operational techniques. When the Company needed additional pilots, he taught them the intricate mountain-flying skills himself.

When the British Columbia Government's topographical department needed a special survey of the Wahleach Mountain Range southeast of Chilliwack, Agar was ready. The operation was a complete success and his techniques for high altitude landings and takeoffs in hitherto inaccessible locations became the standard accepted world-wide.

Having conquered the altitude barrier, Agar then proved the effectiveness of using helicopters in contour flying for timber operations, and followed this successful manoeuvering strategy by transporting prospecting parties to and from remote bush areas. He accepted a contract from the Water Board of Vancouver in 1949 to airlift 400,000 pounds (181,000 kg) of construction material, equipment, and personnel to the 3,500 foot (1,067 m) level of a mountainside, and was credited with helping to complete the building of the Palisade Lake Dam on schedule. It was the first time a helicopter had been used in such a manner, and more than 2,000 takeoffs and landings were required to finalize the lift. Today the dam stands as a monument to Agar's mastery of vertical flight.

The international publicity accorded this outstanding achievement prompted industry and the military to re-think their operational transportation methods. As a result, selected commercial and military pilots were trained in mountain flying techniques by Agar's company. His expertise led to a contract in 1951 with the Aluminum Company of Canada to assist in the construction of a giant smelter complex at Kitimat, British Columbia. Engineering survey work, which formerly would have taken up to two years to complete, was finished in a matter of weeks. His firm, now renamed Okanagan Helicopters Ltd., moved its operations to Vancouver and went on to become one of the largest commercial helicopter operations in the world.

Agar received many honours and awards for his achievements. In 1950 he received Canada's highest aviation award, the Trans-Canada (McKee) Trophy, for the development of mountain flying techniques for helicopters. In 1955 he was awarded the William J. Kossler Trophy by the American Helicopter Society for his development and operation of rotary wing aircraft. This was the first time the award was given to anyone outside of the United States. In 1959 he was awarded an Honorary Fellowship in the American Helicopter Society, and in 1963 was honoured by the Helicopter Association of America.

'Mr. Helicopter', as he was dubbed, was invited to speak at many conventions and conferences, and requests for his services in a consulting capacity were increasing. In 1962 he gave up the demanding responsibilities he held with the Company. He died on January 27, 1968, at Victoria, British Columbia.

Carlyle Clare (Carl) Agar was inducted as a Member of Canada's Aviation Hall of Fame in 1974.

William Munroe Archibald
(1876 – 1949)

William Munroe Archibald, B.A.Sc., was born in Truro, Nova Scotia, on February 23, 1876. He was educated there and at McGill University, Montreal, where he graduated in 1897 with an engineering degree in mining. After graduation, he moved to Rossland, British Columbia, where he began working as a mining engineer for the British America Corporation. In 1901, following extensive experience in various mining camps, he joined the staff at Consolidated Mining and Smelting Company (Cominco) at the nearby smeltering community of Trail, British Columbia, to investigate mining properties. He soon was appointed to the position of Mining Manager.

While visiting California in 1919, Archibald became interested in flying when he saw Curtiss Jenny aircraft being used in barnstorming exhibitions. After his first flight in a Jenny, he knew he wanted to learn to fly. In 1928, as general manager of mines for Cominco, he decided that aircraft could be used to great advantage in mining exploration.

By 1929 he was determined to fly, even though he was 53 years old. He had already purchased a Gipsy Moth from the de Havilland Aircraft Company through company agents in Vancouver. These men also taught him how to fly and he became the first private aircraft owner in British Columbia. He made the first recorded flight into the interior of British Columbia

A professional mining engineer, Archibald had flown from coast to coast in Canada more often than any other pilot, and had crossed the Rockies more times than other pilots up to the mid-1930's.

In 1931, Archibald completed a coast-to-coast flight over Canada in his Puss Moth.

when he and an air engineer took off from Vancouver for Trail, a trip that took a total of four flying hours.

Archibald wasted no time in putting his plane to good use, making many flights to Cominco's operations throughout the rugged interior of the province. He moved to Creston and had an airstrip leveled on his property. He commuted to work almost daily by air, a road distance of 150 miles (240 km), but less than half that over the mountains in his aircraft. In May 1931, he completed a coast-to-coast flight over Canada in his new Puss Moth, one of many such trips he would make in the four small planes he owned during his lifetime.

He then organized Cominco Flying Service at Creston as the company's pilot training school. He staffed it with World War I aviators who were hired to train young company engineers up to flying licence standards. One of the early graduates was G. H. Finland (Hall of Fame 1974). Archibald's enthusiasm ensured that Cominco's use of aircraft for prospecting, and transporting crew and equipment would be successful. The peak period for Cominco's use of aircraft under his supervision was reached in 1932 when ten aircraft were in use almost daily.

In 1935 Archibald inaugurated the first air route in the north from Trail to Stewart, British Columbia, and to Ketchikan, Alaska. His broad interest in mining stretched from the east to west coast of Canada, south to Idaho, U.S.A., and as far north as Great Bear Lake, North West Territories. He developed routes to follow for wheeled aircraft, and made many suggestions for placement and building of suitable landing strips. He was accompanied on many of his cross-country business flights by Page McPhee, an air engineer, pilot and friend. These trips meant long days, often covering 1,500 or more miles (2,400 km) in a day.

Archibald's numerous cross-Canada flights earned him the title of 'Canada's Flying Businessman'. He was also known as 'The Father of the Yellowknife Gold Fields', since it was through his insistent efforts, shrewdness, and enthusiasm that the properties were developed.

The Trans-Canada (McKee) Trophy for service to Canadian aviation during 1935 was awarded to Archibald, who became the first person to win this award for his use of aircraft as a business tool. In 1935 alone, he had logged over 448 hours flying time, covering approximately 44,800 miles (72,000 km).

Archibald retired in 1939 after 38 years with Cominco. He became a senior mining consultant, maintaining an active interest in mining engineering from his Toronto office. He served for many years as a Director of de Havilland Aircraft of Canada. He died in Toronto, Ontario, on November 10, 1949.

William Munroe Archibald was inducted as a Member of Canada's Aviation Hall of Fame in 1974.

William Archibald with Curtis JN-4 aircraft. c. 1919.

Neil J. Armstrong
(1920 – 1994)

Neil J. Armstrong, B.A.Sc., was born in Alvinston, Ontario, on April 15, 1920. He was educated there and at Petrolia, Ontario, from where he joined the Royal Canadian Mounted Police (RCMP). He served in Ontario and Saskatchewan, and was one of the first constables assigned to Dauphin, Manitoba, when the RCMP took over the policing of that town. He enlisted in the Royal Canadian Air Force (RCAF) in 1943 and graduated as a commissioned officer and pilot at Brantford, Ontario. He served as a flying instructor at various Canadian bases until he was discharged in 1945.

The following year he began studies at the University of Toronto and graduated with an engineering degree in 1949, majoring in geology and geophysics. He worked as geologist and prospector for Eldorado Mining and Refining in the Northwest Territories and later with the International Nickel Company in Manitoba. He did well-site geology for Hudson's Bay Oil and Gas Company in the Peace River area of northern Alberta and British Columbia. He also worked as a research and project engineer with the Polymer Corporation at Sarnia, Ontario.

From 1953 to 1969, Armstrong was associated with Spartan Air Services at Ottawa and became the first known helicopter pilot/geologist in North America. He worked with the Geological Survey of

Armstrong and his wife Trudy raised a family of five children. Trudy obtained both power and glider pilot's licences. Each of their four sons and daughter became licenced pilots after soloing on their 16th birthdays.

Neil Armstrong beside a DH Tiger Moth, an RCAF basic training aircraft. c. 1943.

Canada on Operations Baker Lake and Thelon River in the Barren Lands of Northern Canada. Over a period of two years, more than 100,000 square miles (260,000 km²) were mapped geologically on a scale of one inch to eight miles. He made the first helicopter contact with the Barren Lands Inuit during this period. They had never seen a helicopter and referred to it as 'an unfinished airplane'.

In 1955 Armstrong became manager of a Spartan subsidiary, Aerophysics Ltd., specializing in airborne electronic surveys. With this firm, Armstrong pioneered the two-phase electromagnetic system for detecting mineral conductors in the earth. The system was installed in Avro Ansons, and used initially in the Knob Lake area of Quebec. It was later adapted for use in helicopters, first using the Bell 47-D1. The transmitting and receiving coils were on a twenty-foot 'bird', or catamite, towed beneath the helicopter on fifty feet of cable at 150 feet (46 m) above ground level.

Armstrong's combined knowledge of airborne devices and engineering helped him to develop and patent a helicopter hover-sight, now used world-wide as a cost-saving shortcut in airborne surveying. The instrument used a laser beam mounted on a survey tripod which was leveled vertically over the point whose coordinates were required. A circular receiver, comprised of photo-electric cells and mounted on the bottom of the helicopter, was activated when contacted by the laser beam. Hovering the helicopter and taking readings from two slave stations set up over known points gave the required coordinates through triangulation. This system cut to a fraction the man-hours required for surveying, and eliminated the need for costly towers which were normally built to obtain line-of-sight over the trees.

In 1960 the Government of Argentina hired him to head a team surveying the Province of Mendoza from the air, using a Cessna 310. This was one of the first foreign projects ever undertaken in which aerial surveys were used for evaluation purposes to determine the tax levels for the land parcels in the area.

In 1961 Armstrong and pilot Max Conrad flew across the Atlantic Ocean non-stop in a twin-engine Piper Apache, making the flight from Gander, Newfoundland, to Shannon, Ireland, in thirteen hours. Two years later he shared the pilot/navigator duties with John Stuart, flying a Piper Aztec non-stop across the Pacific Ocean, from California to Hawaii, in eighteen hours.

In 1969 Armstrong was a founding partner and President of Liftair International Ltd., a helicopter service based in Calgary, Alberta. He served as chairman of the Helicopter Committee of the Calgary Transportation and Development Authority.

His well-rounded flying career has been recorded in the numerous articles he wrote for many North American aviation periodicals. He was a strong supporter of general aviation and encouraged others to complete their pilot training and enjoy the freedom of flight. He was elected president of the Canadian Owners and Pilots Association (COPA, Belt of Orion 1993) in 1964, a position he held for three years.

Armstrong died on November 23, 1994, in the crash of a de Havilland Twin Otter in Antarctica, along with his son, Captain Corcoran 'Corky' Armstrong and two others.

Neil J. Armstrong was inducted as a Member of Canada's Aviation Hall of Fame in 1974.

Julien Joseph Audette
(1914 – 1986)

Julien Joseph Audette was born in Radville, Saskatchewan, on June 6, 1914. Following graduation from Regina's Campion College, he successively worked in his father's grocery, Canada Packers and Gray Insurance. In 1937 he began working for the Saskatchewan Government Audit Department.

In May of 1941 he joined the Royal Canadian Air Force (RCAF) and received his pilot's wings and commission at Yorkton, Saskatchewan, on February 27, 1942. He held instructor positions at Trenton, Ontario, and Saskatoon, Saskatchewan. Following operational training at Comox, British Columbia, he was posted to southeast Asia where he flew the Douglas C-47 on supply runs for the 'Canucks Unlimited' 436 Burma Star Transport Squadron until the end of the war.

Following the war, Audette assisted in the formation of the Saskatchewan Air Ambulance Service in 1946 and was its second pilot. In 1949 he became the first pilot with Kramer Air Service and eventually became General Sales Manager of a subsidiary company, Kramer Tractor Ltd. He retired in 1974 from Kramer's,

"... seeing two lenticulars still active east of my position, an easterly course was set ... the lift was quite smooth, with a rate of climb averaging 313 feet (96 m) per minute, to a maximum height of 27,300 feet (8,300 m)." That day in June 1962, Audette broke the Canadian Distance record with a soaring distance of 395 miles (635 km) in 7 hours, 55 minutes after take off.

ending a 25-year career with the company. Throughout this time he was active in the Prairie Road Builders Association, and was president of the Regina Flying Club. He was chairman of the Regina Chamber of Commerce's Aviation Committee and lobbied for improved air service, particularly for cross-border connections with North Dakota, U.S.A.

From 1976 until 1984, Audette was sales development manager for Saskmont Engineering. He was also director of the Roughriders Football Club for 27 years. Other associations to benefit from his energies were the Royal Canadian Flying Clubs Association (RCFCA), Ducks Unlimited, YMCA, Royal Canadian Legion, Air Force Association, Knights of Columbus, and the Saskatchewan Western Development Museum.

It was, however, in the field of non-powered flight that Audette made his major contribution to Canadian aviation. In 1952 he was one of three founders of the Regina Gliding and Soaring Club, and served as chief tow pilot, chief flying instructor, and president. He was instrumental in establishing a gliding scholarship for the Regina Air Cadets, and for bringing three National Soaring competitions to Western Canada.

In 1962 Audette was awarded Canada's first Diamond Badge by the Paris-based Fédération Aéronautique Internationale (FAI), #240 in the world. He was the only Canadian to earn this badge while establishing Canadian Soaring records, and was the first Canadian to break 9,144 metres (30,000 ft.) in a sailplane.

On the national level, he was the FAI Awards Chairman of the Soaring Association of Canada (SAC). He was the only Canadian to hold all eight competitive awards available, six of them simultaneously.

For the 1958 Distance to Goal, he won the Barringer Memorial Trophy of the Soaring Society of America—the only Canadian so honoured. The 1961 altitude flight earned him Canada's first Symonds Wave Memorial Plaque and Lennie pin.

With his record free distance flight on April 22, 1962, Audette became the first Canadian to combine a wave flight (27,300 ft or 8,300 m) with a thermal flight.

In 1959 and 1962 Audette was awarded the Soaring Association of Canada (SAC) President's Choice Award, and the Ball and Chain Trophy for achievement in soaring flight, one criteria for this being that he was married. In 1961 and 1962 he won the SAC's Canadair Trophy for the best five flights of the year. In 1962 he was awarded the SAC Certificate of Honour; in 1967 the FAI awarded him the Diploma Paul Tissandier Certificate of Honour for the promotion of soaring aviation, the first time a Canadian had won this award. In 1964 and 1967 he won the Alberta Soaring Council's (ASC) Carling Trophy for the best single flight of the year. In 1967 he won the Bruce Soaring Trophy; in 1977 he was inducted into the Saskatchewan Sports Hall of Fame, and in 1982 the ASC presented him with a Certificate of Achievement Plaque.

During his soaring years in the Cowley, Alberta, area, from 1960 to 1975, Audette worked closely with the Federal Meteorology Department. Recognizing that the soaring prospects in the Pincher Creek area could be enhanced by a greater knowledge of the climatology of wave clouds, he initiated a data collection program. This 'Audette Project' provided the foundation for studies by others, including the University of Calgary's Environmental Science Centre.

Audette died at Regina, Saskatchewan, in 1986.

Julien Joseph Audette was inducted as a Member of Canada's Aviation Hall of Fame in 1989.

Julian Audette's Soaring Records

1958 Distance to Goal and Return	322 km
1958 Distance to Goal	380 km
1961 Absolute Altitude	9,336 m
1961 Gain of Height	7,108 m
1961 200 km Triangle	72.6 km/h
1962 300 km Triangle	65.0 km/h
1962 Free Distance	603.8 km
1964 100 km Triangle	85.0 km/h

Audette prepares for a flight in his Schweizer 1-23G, CF-ZDO. Shown here with Air Cadets, in the early 1960's.

John Alexander (Jack) Austin
(1912 – 1984)

John Alexander (Jack) Austin, B.A.Sc., was born in Renfrew, Ontario, on September 30, 1912, attended school there and graduated from the University of Toronto in 1934 with a degree in applied science and engineering. That same year, after learning to fly at de Havilland Aircraft of Canada Ltd. (DHC), he entered a partnership with his brother Charles to form Austin Airways Limited. They were joined for a time by Leigh Capreol (Hall of Fame 1981), who was DHC's first test pilot and Austin's flight instructor.

The company began with three small aircraft, two Waco biplanes and a Tiger Moth. They operated from Toronto Air Harbour during the summer months and moved to the Toronto Flying Club field for winter operations. The following year the company was incorporated by federal charter, purchased the assets of Eclipse Airways at Chapleau, Ontario, and then opened a new base at Sudbury, Ontario. The company's first flights were made to the Little Long Lac mining area to bring prospectors into that area.

Austin obtained his Air Engineer's Licence in 1936, the year the company began flying forest fire patrols for the Government of Ontario. Also that year, they participated in the Moose River Mine rescue mission in which equipment was flown in to a gold mine in Nova Scotia where three men were trapped below

There are perhaps two main reasons why Austin Airways was successful for so long: Jack Austin's belief that his employees were entirely capable of running his airlines, and the firm belief of every employee in safety first.

Waco CF AVL of Capreol and Austin Airways, in Toronto Air Harbour, 1934.

ground. As the company expanded, a base was established at Temagami, Ontario, and a flying school opened at Sudbury, Ontario. Many of the students from this school went on to serve with the Royal Canadian Air Force (RCAF). One of their well-known students was Thurston 'Rusty' Blakey (Hall of Fame 1992), who became a long-time pilot with Austin Airways. Other sub-bases were opened at Gogama and Biscotasing, Ontario, to serve these new mining areas.

During World War II, Austin Airways' operations were restricted to essential services, such as forest fire suppression, aerial photography, timber surveys, and supplying the needs of the mining industry. The company bought larger planes and continued to expand its operations. A base was located at Nakina, Ontario, in 1943 to transport the catches from commercial fishing operations. Austin then completed an aerial survey along both shores of James Bay and Hudson Bay, which resulted in the commencement of air service to a number of isolated communities.

The next decade saw the company's fleet enlarged to include freighter aircraft, and bases were established to serve hitherto inaccessible areas. Aerial surveys were completed for mining operations, and in 1952 the company purchased Nickel Belt Airways at Sudbury.

In the mid-1950's Canada and the United States decided to build a cross-continent air defence network to guard against bomber attack from the USSR. The plan was for three radar-electronic defence lines to be strung across the country. The construction of the Mid-Canada Defence Line along the 55th parallel in 1955-56 generated a considerable amount of work for Canadian regional airlines and charter operators. Austin was named chairman of the committee which was formed to coordinate the services provided by these operators in this monumental airlift. He also assisted the Department of Transport in developing the manual which was instrumental in making the operation a complete success, proving that competitors could work together towards a common goal.

In 1958 Austin Airways took over the scheduled service from Trans-Canada Airlines between Timmins and Kapuskasing, Ontario, and then improved their own radio system to better serve communities as far north as Cape Dorset and Baffin Island in the Northwest Territories.

For a period of 20 years, from 1950 through to 1970, Austin Airways provided planes and crews flying for the Gravity Survey Division of the Dominion Observatory. Surveying for minerals was done using a device attached to an airplane which measured anomalies in gravity readings which often indicated a body of ore. These flights took them over many of the provinces and the Northwest Territories. The company was also involved in ice reconnaissance flights over Hudson and Davis Straits.

During this period, Austin Airways and Aircraft Industries of Canada Limited jointly developed the first water-bombing kit for the Canadian-built Canso aircraft, consisting of a set of tanks and water scoops which were attached to the underside of the Canso. It was very successful and was used by Canso operators for many years. Austin helped to develop the Povungnituk area in the Ungava Peninsula of northern Quebec into a viable tourist attraction. During 1966 aircraft maintenance facilities were completed at Mount Hope, Ontario, and operations were extended to Baffin Island. Ontario lakes were stocked with trout fingerlings released from Austin Airways' aircraft. Other major terminal facilities were also completed, without government assistance.

Some years earlier, Austin had been elected director of the Air Industries and Transport Association (AITA) and was named the first president of the Air Transport Association of Canada (ATAC). In 1967 he was awarded honorary life membership in ATAC.

In 1975 Austin was awarded the Trans-Canada (McKee) Trophy in recognition of his long and active service to the air transport industry. By then, Austin Airways had operated for forty years, and was Canada's oldest airline. In 1975 the company was sold to White River Air Services and Austin retired. He died in Toronto, December 1, 1984.

John Alexander (Jack) Austin was inducted as a Member of Canada's Aviation Hall of Fame in 1976.

Ronald John Baker

(1912 – 1990)

Ronald John Baker, B.Sc., was born in Yellowgrass, Saskatchewan, on March 28, 1912. He graduated with a Bachelor of Science-Engineering degree in 1934 from the University of Saskatchewan. While attending university he was commissioned as a Second Lieutenant with the Canadian Officers Training Corps.

A strong interest in radios from his early teens led to summer employment with the Province of Saskatchewan, installing radios at sites in the northern bush areas. When he became engineer in charge, it was required that he be flown from one location to another, so he left school for one year to take flight instruction at the Regina Flying School. He received his Private Pilot's Licence in November 1932, and Commercial Air Pilot Certificate one month later.

In 1936 Baker earned his Air Engineer Certificate. For two years he flew from site to site with Saskatchewan Air Service but eventually the flying was contracted to the Mason & Campbell Aviation Company (M&C). M&C's desire to set up a radio station made Baker the perfect candidate to join M&C as a pilot and air engineer. Most of the flights out of Prince Albert, Saskatchewan, were forestry surveys south of the Churchill River. In the winter the company transported fish from the northern lakes to the larger centres.

TCA test pilot, Captain Ron Baker, recalled a demonstration flight of the North Star to California: "As we checked in with various stations along the route, there were numerous remarks about our speed, as the North Star was so much faster than most transports."

"His dedication to the engineering, testing, and safe operation of commercial aircraft has been of major benefit to Canadian aviation."

—*Induction citation, 1994*

R. J Baker was on Canadair's design and testing team in the conversion of the Douglas C-54/DC-4, 'North Star.'

Early in 1939 Baker flew a Fox Moth to Winnipeg, Manitoba, and applied for a position with Trans-Canada Airlines (TCA, Hall of Fame 1974). He began working for them as a First Officer on June 15, 1939. A number of his early flights were from Winnipeg to Vancouver with Herb Seagrim (Hall of Fame 1974).

Baker was promoted to Captain with TCA in 1941. While flying with TCA he realized that the engines could be operated more efficiently, and that the time between overhauls could be extended. His new cruise control procedures were adopted immediately. In 1943, when TCA undertook the operation of the Canadian Government Trans Atlantic Service (CGTAS) using converted Lancaster bombers, the full fuel tank range was the only technical information available, until he and two young engineers were assigned the task of working out all of the data for fuel flow, rate of climb, cruise control, etc. Unfortunately, not even a change of engines, from American Packard-built Rolls Royce Merlins to British-built Rolls Royce engines, could make the Lancastrian venture successful.

Following the CGTAS exercise, Baker was sent to Canadair in Montreal to assist with the design of the cockpit and the conversion of the military C-47's to DC-3's. The small group who worked under his direction in Winnipeg wrote all the descriptive materials for the aircraft, and developed all normal and emergency operating procedures. The preparation of these manuals was approved by the

Department of Transport (DOT) and signed by the Engineering and Flight Operations Department.

In 1945 Canadair was preparing to modify the Douglas-built transport C-54/DC-4. This model would be called C-54/DC-4M or 'North Star', and would have the more powerful Rolls Royce Merlin engines. It would also be pressurized in order to overfly the weather. Baker was one of the group of pilots who set up the instrument panel on a wooden mock-up of a North Star and was on the flight test program in 1946 with Canadair Chief Test Pilot Al Lilly (Hall of Fame 1984). For pioneering technical changes and testing aircraft in California, U.S.A., prior to acceptance by the Canadian government, Baker was awarded the U.S. Air Medal.

Baker, along with several pilots from DOT's Flight Operations Headquarters, attended the ground course for the Lockheed Super Constellation, and later made trips to California to test and accept several of these aircraft for TCA. As new aircraft were added to the TCA fleet, he would test and accept each plane and ferry it to Montreal. These included Vickers Viscounts and Vanguards, DC-8's and DC-9's.

During his career, he was required to fly regularly scheduled flights while he was involved in testing and returning aircraft that had been damaged in operations. Before his retirement, Baker was very involved with the development of the auto approach-and-land features of the Boeing 747 and Lockheed 1011 aircraft.

Throughout his career, Baker maintained his interest in radios, and flew his own Cessna on floats for pleasure. In 1941 he was elected to serve as secretary to the fledgling Canadian Air Line Pilots Association (CALPA, Belt of Orion 1988). He was an active member of the Society of Automotive Engineers 7 Committee, Canadian Aeronautics and Space Institute, and Professional Engineers Association of Quebec.

After his retirement from Air Canada in March of 1972, Baker acquired an analog simulator for small aircraft and taught instrument flying procedures. He was a member and later advisor to the Accident Review Board. He passed away at Pointe-Claire, Quebec, on March 24, 1990.

Ronald John Baker was inducted as a Member of Canada's Aviation Hall of Fame in 1994.

Russell Francis Baker

(1910 – 1958)

Russell Francis Baker was born in Winnipeg, Manitoba, on January 31, 1910, where he was educated, and learned to fly at age 16. After completing two years of study at the University of Manitoba, he earned his Commercial Pilot's Licence and became a barnstorming pilot throughout the province. He moved to British Columbia in 1929 where he farmed until he joined Western Canada Airways as a pilot in 1937.

During his early years as a bush pilot, he completed numerous mercy flights resulting in the saving of human life. For several years prior to the outbreak of World War II, Baker worked with geophysical parties in the aerial prospecting of the northern British Columbia mountains, pioneering flights into areas never before entered by aircraft.

The United States military recognized his expertise and northern flying experience, and employed him for aerial survey work on the Alaska Highway. When several US bomber aircraft were forced to land in the northern mountains of the Yukon, he located them. Then, despite the difficulties of the terrain and the rigors of the winter weather, Baker flew out all of the survivors. He was awarded the United States Air Medal for this heroic and daring rescue in January 1942.

Another myth to check out in the North: during 1947 Baker flew two newspapermen into the remote Nahanni region of the Northwest Territories to debunk mysterious myths that had sprung up about an area known as 'Headless Valley.'

COURTESY JAMES A. RICHARDSON AND SONS/NATIONAL ARCHIVES OF CANADA PA-88951

Russell Baker flying a Junkers W-34 over the Nation Lakes area, 100 km north of Fort Saint James, British Columbia.

Baker became senior Captain and subsequently divisional superintendent with Canadian Pacific Airlines (CPA) at Whitehorse, working for his old friend, Grant McConachie (Hall of Fame 1974). While with CPA he saw the potential for an air charter operation in north-central British Columbia. In 1946 he left CPA and organized his own company, Central B.C. Airways, at Fort St. James. Baker had a Beechcraft seaplane, and two employees. His first major contract was with the British Columbia Forest Service. In 1947 four more planes were added to meet the forest service's growing demands.

In 1948 the company purchased the first Beaver aircraft to roll off the assembly line at de Havilland Canada's plant at Downsview Airport, Ontario. Expansion of the Company continued at a rapid pace.

In 1951 Central B.C. Airways was the air service chosen by the Aluminum Company of Canada (Alcan) to provide the necessary air services for the prime contractor handling the construction of its multi-million dollar aluminum smelter complex at Kitimat and Kemano. Baker's company handled 95% of their air transport requirements for the next several years.

From 1949 on, Central B.C. Airways began to absorb smaller airlines. Most of these found success to be elusive as they struggled with the vagaries of weather, inhospitable terrain, and marginal profits. Baker aimed to better serve the out-of-the-way points no other airline would handle. The firm subsequently acquired Kamloops Air Services, Skeena Air Transport, Associated Air Taxi, Whitehorse Flying Services, Queen Charlotte Airlines, Associated Airways, Aero Engineering Limited, and Airmotive Accessories Limited. This made his company Canada's third largest airline, after Trans-Canada Airlines and Canadian Pacific Airlines. In 1953 he changed the name of his company to Pacific Western Airlines (PWA)

and began operating a scheduled service from Vancouver to Kitimat.

In 1955, after taking over Queen Charlotte Airlines, Baker inaugurated air service to the Queen Charlotte Islands. Another event in 1955 which was important to PWA was the sub-contract signed with Associated Airways of Edmonton, owned by Tommy Fox (Hall of Fame 1983), to haul freight to Western Arctic sites on the Distant Early Warning (DEW) Line. In December of that year, PWA took over Associated Airways in order to obtain the licences necessary to service the Central Canada Section of the Line. The success of the venture was, in great measure, due to the schedules maintained by PWA despite the extended hours of darkness, inclement weather, and lack of navigational facilities.

In 1957 PWA took over the prairie service of CPA in Alberta and Saskatchewan. Baker died in Vancouver on November 15, 1958, with his dreams unfulfilled of servicing on a scheduled basis every western community which other carriers would not serve. However, before his death, he laid the groundwork for the many-times-daily airbus service between Calgary and Edmonton, and for the daily service from these centres to the rim of the Polar Sea and to the Arctic islands beyond.

Russell Francis Baker was inducted as a Member of Canada's Aviation Hall of Fame in 1975.

Bernt Balchen

(1899 – 1973)

Bernt Balchen, D.S.M. (U.S.A.), D.F.C. (U.S.A.), D. Sc. (Hon), was born at Tveit, Norway, on October 23, 1899. He was educated at the Norwegian Army Officer Training School, the Forestry Engineering School of Norway, and the Advanced Forestry Engineering School of Sweden. In 1918 he volunteered for ski patrols and the cavalry with the White Army in Finland. He graduated from the Royal Norwegian Naval Air Force Military School, and received his Pilot's Licence in 1921.

In 1926 Balchen was seconded by the Government of Norway as pilot/engineer to accompany explorer Roald Amundsen's flight over the North Pole, using a dirigible based at Spitsbergen. At the same time, American explorer Richard E. Byrd was planning to fly from Spitsbergen to the North Pole. Balchen was directed by Amundsen to repair the damaged skis on Byrd's Fokker Tri-motor, thus enabling Byrd to be the first to fly across the North Pole.

In 1927 Balchen was hired by Fokker Aircraft Corporation in the United States as chief test pilot. He was assigned to Western Canada Airways at Hudson,

The Churchill airlift operation was the first of its size in Canada's sub-arctic and marked the beginning of large scale bush flying in Canada. The flights established once and for all the importance of the airplane to the development of these regions. In recognition of this significant contribution, Balchen became the only non-Canadian to become a Member of Canada's Aviation Hall of Fame.

Ontario, to teach Canadian pilots how to handle ski-equipped planes.

At this time, the Hudson Bay Railway Co. wanted to complete its railway line from its northern end at Cache Lake, Manitoba, to an outlet on the Hudson Bay, but the best site for the terminus had not been determined. Engineers were needed to carry out critical geological tests to decide whether the railway should end at Churchill, or at an alternate site at Port Nelson. These tests had to be accomplished within a prescribed period of time so that rail crews at Cache Lake could start work on the railway in the spring.

In 1928 Western Canadian Airways, under the management of Harold 'Doc' Oaks (Hall of Fame 1974), was awarded a specific government contract to transport men, drilling equipment, explosives, and supplies from Cache Lake to Fort Churchill, a distance of about 200 miles (320 km). As one of two pilots selected for the project, Balchen flew an open cockpit Fokker aircraft during six weeks of savage winter weather across inhospitable terrain. He and his crew faced aircraft breakdowns, forced landings, frostbite, and exhaustion to successfully complete the undertaking. The experiences at Hudson and Churchill prepared them for future flights in the sub-arctic and beyond.

Investigations made by the engineers proved that a railroad could be built to Churchill. It was subsequently chosen as the ocean terminus for the Hudson Bay Railway. In paying tribute to the importance of the operation, the Government of Canada stated: "... there has been no more brilliant operation in the history of commercial aviation."

Balchen's experience and skill as pilot, engineer, and explorer was in great demand. Admiral Richard Byrd, of the United States Navy, hired him as co-pilot on a flight across the Atlantic Ocean from New York to Paris. In 1928 he piloted one of three relief planes to the crash site of the German aircraft Bremen, on Greenly

Bernt Balchen came to Hudson, Ontario in 1927 to demonstrate the use of skis on Fokker aircraft at Western Canada Airways.

Island, off the southern coast of Labrador. The following year he piloted Admiral Byrd across the South Pole, the first such flight ever made. Balchen had previously carried out cold-weather testing of Byrd's Ford Tri-Motor aircraft in Manitoba, where he had designed its skis.

In 1930 the Congress of the United States created him a citizen by special act, and awarded him a distinct medal. The following year he redesigned the aircraft Amelia Earhart used in her successful flight across the Atlantic Ocean. He was named Chief Pilot of the Lincoln Ellsworth Antarctic Expedition in 1933, and for the second time Balchen flew across the South Pole. In 1940 Balchen established Little Norway at Toronto, Ontario, as the training base for Norwegian pilots in exile.

Balchen was named Commander of Task Force Eight, and his job was to construct the world's most northern air base, on the west coast of Greenland, north of the Arctic Circle. By 1943 he had completed, and made operational, Sondre Strom Air

Base, another link in the Allied Staging Route across the North Atlantic Ocean. When an American bomber crash-landed on a remote Greenland glacier, Balchen personally led what has been called by the United States Air Force (USAF) "one of the greatest of Arctic sagas." Before it was over, six months later, five rescuers had perished, he had made three flying boat landings on the sloping ice-mass, and once had to walk fifteen days across the ice-cap to the safety of a satellite base.

As one of the chief architects of the tri-national Scandinavian Airlines System (SAS) in the early 1940's, Balchen envisioned a commercial air route linking Scandinavia with Canada, using a direct route across the North Pole, thus shortening the flying distance between the countries. As President of SAS in 1946, he helped design the navigational requirements to make such flights possible, then flew the route fifteen times to ensure its feasibility and safety. Balchen thus became the first pilot to fly across both North and South Poles.

During his career with USAF he worked on all phases of Arctic operations and commanded the first non-stop flight from Fairbanks, Alaska, to Oslo, Norway, in 1949. In 1952 Balchen was awarded the Harmon International Trophy for his significant contributions to polar flight.

Balchen logged 20,000 command hours as pilot of numerous aircraft types and was awarded the United States' Distinguished Service Medal, Legion of Merit, Distinguished Flying Cross, Soldier's Medal, and the Air Medal. He also received decorations from Norway, Sweden and Denmark for his extraordinary achievements. He was honoured with honorary Doctorate Degrees from Tufts University in Massachusetts and the University of Alaska. He died in New York City on October 17, 1973.

Bernt Balchen was inducted as a Member of Canada's Aviation Hall of Fame in 1974.

Frederick Walker (Casey) Baldwin

(1882 – 1948)

Frederick Walker (Casey) Baldwin, B.E.(B.Eng.), D.Eng.(Hon), was born in Toronto, Ontario, on January 2, 1882. He was educated at Ridley College, St. Catharines, Ontario, and at the University of Toronto, where he completed the Mechanical and Electrical Engineering course in 1906. At the age of sixteen, prior to entering university, he shipped as a deck-hand on a sailing vessel across the Atlantic Ocean.

Baldwin's inventive genius also foresaw high altitude air travel and the subsequent requirement for pressurized cabins, as well as the design and use of the variable pitch aircraft propeller.

As a university undergraduate he served in the original Second Field Company of Canadian Engineers, and during his university days met John Alexander Douglas McCurdy (Hall of Fame 1974). After graduation, he completed a summer session at Cornell University in Ithaca, New York, then visited Alexander Graham Bell (Hall of Fame 1974) at Baddeck, Nova Scotia, where he became interested in the study of aeronautics.

In 1907 Baldwin became a founding member of the Aerial Experiment Association (AEA) with Bell, McCurdy, and two Americans, Glenn H. Curtiss, a well-known engine builder and pioneer airman from Hammondsport, New York, and Lieutenant Thomas Selfridge, of the U.S. Army. They continued Bell's experiments with kites, then progressed to powered flight. For these experiments, they moved their operations to Curtiss' workshop at Hammondsport.

As chief engineer of the enterprise, Baldwin worked on the design and construction of

Members of the Aerial Experiment Association: Glenn Curtiss, J.A.D. McCurdy, Alexander Graham Bell, Casey Baldwin, and Lt. Thomas Selfridge, the men behind the Silver Dart, 1907.

their first aircraft, the Bell-conceived Red Wing, a biplane powered by a 40-hp Curtiss engine. He became the first British subject to pilot a heavier-than-air machine when he flew it at Hammondsport on March 12, 1908. The second flight ended in a crash which destroyed the aircraft. Several more aircraft were built there, each incorporating new improvements in aeronautics which had been carefully thought out and tested.

Baldwin and Bell pioneered the use of ailerons which they invented in 1908. They also used a three-wheel or tricycle undercarriage on their later experimental models. These features enabled a greater maneouverability of the airplane both in the air and on the ground. Rapid advances in flight technology were now possible.

In May 1908, Baldwin made the first flight in a new AEA machine, the White Wing, the first to use wing-tip ailerons and wheeled landing gear. The third airplane built by this group was the June Bug. Curtiss was the lead designer and first to fly it. They produced their fourth plane at this time, the Silver Dart, primarily designed by McCurdy. On December 6, 1908, McCurdy test flew the Silver Dart at Hammondsport.

Bell wanted one of the planes to fly in Canada so he shipped the Silver Dart to Nova Scotia in January 1909. The group's flying activities moved back to Baddeck, on Cape Breton Island, where Bell had an estate. There McCurdy flew the Silver Dart on February 23, 1909. This was Canada's (as well as the British Empire's) first powered airplane flight.

McCurdy also piloted the Silver Dart at Camp Petawawa, Ontario, on August 2,

1909, on demonstration flights for the Canadian Army. Baldwin joined McCurdy for rides, becoming the first Canadian passenger in an airplane.

In 1909 Baldwin and McCurdy formed the Canadian Aerodrome Company at Baddeck, and constructed two more aircraft, Baddeck I and Baddeck II, both of which flew successfully. On August 12, 1909, Baldwin and McCurdy demonstrated their own machine, Baddeck I, at Camp Petawawa, the first flight of a Canadian-built, powered airplane. In 1909, the year the AEA was disbanded, Baldwin became manager of the Graham Bell Laboratories and remained in that position until 1932, after discontinuing flying in 1911.

During his term as manager of the laboratories, Baldwin concentrated on the study of hydrofoils, and became internationally recognized for his development of devices used in aerial and naval warfare. In 1920 he became a partner in Bell-Baldwin Hydrofoils Limited at Baddeck and during this period developed methods of transmitting sound through water for navigational purposes. In 1954 a naval craft employing the hydrofoil principle, perfected by him after its conception by Bell, was christened the KC-B (Casey B).

Baldwin became interested in politics, and in 1933 was elected to the Nova Scotia Legislature for the riding of Victoria. In 1937 he became president of the Nova Scotia Conservative Association. He died at Neareagh, Nova Scotia, on August 7, 1948.

Frederick Walker (Casey) Baldwin was inducted as a Member of Canada's Aviation Hall of Fame in 1974.

Russell Bannock
(b. 1919)

Russell Bannock, D.S.O., D.F.C.*, was born in Edmonton, Alberta, on November 1, 1919. He completed his elementary and high school education there, and attended the University of Alberta night school where he studied geology. His interest in aviation began at an early age and he commenced flight training in 1937 at the Edmonton Flying Club, obtaining his Private Pilot's Licence in 1938 and his Commercial Licence the following year.

At the outbreak of World War II he joined the Royal Canadian Air Force (RCAF), and was commissioned as a Pilot Officer. On completion of his advanced training at Camp Borden, Ontario, Bannock was posted to 112 Army Co-operation Squadron in Ottawa. He was assigned to Central Flying School at Trenton, Ontario, in 1940 as a flying instructor, and was appointed Flight Commander. In September 1942, he assumed the responsibilities of chief instructor of 3 Flying School at Arnprior, Ontario.

Bannock's request for an overseas posting was granted in 1944, and he proceeded to 60 Operational Training Unit at High Ercall, Shropshire, England. He joined 418 Squadron, RCAF, in June of that year, and

Russell Bannock has had the pleasure of serving as Chairman of the Board for Canada's Aviation Hall of Fame for the years 1988 to 1995. During this time, he oversaw the relocation of the Hall to its present, permanent site in Wetaskiwin, Alberta, 65 km south of Edmonton. It stands near the excellent facilities of the Reynolds-Alberta Museum.

Casey Baldwin ready to try out 'Baddeck II' at Baddeck, Nova Scotia, October 10, 1909.

"His inspiring leadership as an instructor and fighter pilot in World War II, his unusual skills as a test pilot, and his corporate business leadership have all been of outstanding benefit to Canadian aviation." —Induction citation, 1983

The de Havilland engineering staff join pilot Russ Bannock after the first flight of the DHC-2 Beaver, August 16, 1947. From the left, R.D. Hiscocks, Aerodynamics; D. Hunter, Director of Engineering; R. Bannock, test pilot; W. Jackimiuk, Chief Engineer; J. Houston, Propulsion; and F. Buller, Design.

was engaged in flying the de Havilland Mosquito on intruder missions over Europe. He soon scored the first of many victories as an intruder pilot, and was appointed Flight Commander. Bannock was soon promoted to Wing Commander and given command of 418 Squadron in October 1944. During this period, along with his Navigator F/O Robert Bruce, he was involved in the battle against Germany's weapon of terror, the V-1 'flying bombs' that were then attacking southern England and London. On one of their missions they destroyed four 'flying bombs' within a one-hour period. For his intruder work against enemy airfields, Bannock was awarded the Distinguished Flying Cross (D.F.C.), and to this was added a Bar for his successes against the V-1s.

In November 1944, at the age of 24, Bannock was posted to 406 Squadron as Commanding Officer and was awarded the Distinguished Service Order (D.S.O.) for outstanding leadership in that command. By April 1945, he had accounted for the destruction of 11 enemy aircraft and 19 ½ 'flying bombs', had earned himself the title 'The Saviour of London', and the distinction of becoming the RCAF's leading night fighter of World War II. In May 1945, he became Director of Operations, RCAF Overseas Headquarters, London, remaining in that post until September of 1945, at which time he attended Royal Air Force (RAF) Staff College.

On retirement from the service in 1946, Bannock returned to Canada to join de Havilland Aircraft Company of Canada Ltd. (DHC) as Chief Test Pilot and Operations Manager. In 1947 he flew the de Havilland Beaver prototype, the first in a series of successful short take-off and landing (STOL) aircraft that the company was to design and manufacture. Following two fly-off competitions among major North American aircraft manufacturers, a United States Congressional decision to "promote domestic sources of supply for

aircraft" was put aside. Bannock's ability to demonstrate the Beaver's superior capabilities resulted in the sale of 978 of these aircraft to the United States Army and Air Force.

In 1950 he was appointed to the position of Director of Military Sales, followed by a promotion to Vice-President of Sales. He enjoyed continued success in the sales of the company's additional STOL entries into the market in the 1950's and 1960's, which included the Otter, Twin Otter, Caribou and Buffalo. He was a member of DHC's Board of Directors from 1956 to 1968, and then left the company to establish Bannock Aerospace Ltd., formed to carry on aerospace sales, leasing, and consulting services.

In 1975 he returned to DHC and was promoted the following year to the position of President and Chief Executive Officer. He left the company in 1978 and returned to Bannock Aerospace Ltd.

Bannock was appointed an Associate Fellow of the Canadian Aeronautical Institute in 1956. He served as chairman of the Export Committee for the Canadian Aerospace Industries Association from 1964 to 1968, and as a director of that association in 1976-1977. He has held the position of President of the Canadian Fighter Pilots Association, and has served as director for the Canadian Industrial Preparedness Association and the Canadian Exporters Association.

Russell Bannock was inducted as a Member of Canada's Aviation Hall of Fame in 1983.

Russ Bannock after completing a test flight of the first DH 'Vampire' aircraft assembled in Canada for the RCAF. Downsview, Ontario, 1948.

William George (Bill) Barker

1894 – 1930)

William George (Bill) Barker, V.C., D.S.O.*, M.C.**, was born November 3, 1894, in Dauphin, Manitoba, where he was educated. He moved to Winnipeg before the First World War, and enlisted in the First Canadian Mounted Rifles in December 1914. He arrived in England the following summer, and was given an immediate posting to France as a machine gunner. He was transferred to the Royal Flying Corps as a Lieutenant Observer, where he was awarded the Military Cross (M.C.) for completing a hazardous assignment under enemy fire.

While in England, Barker earned his pilot's wings, and returned to France flying observation aircraft. He was promoted to Captain and won a Bar to his M.C. for troop-spotting accomplishments. That summer he was wounded and returned to England, where he became an instructor. Within weeks he was back in France as a fighter pilot with 28 Squadron, scoring two victories before being shipped to Italy, where he downed two enemy aircraft on his first offensive patrol.

At the age of 24, Lieutenant Colonel Barker returned to Canada in 1919. He is Canada's most decorated soldier—not just of the First World War, but all the Wars. In fact, not only is he this country's most decorated soldier, but he ties for first place with a British officer, Major James McCudden, as the British Empire's most decorated soldier, with nine medals for gallantry, plus three Mention-in-Despatches.

"His winning of the Victoria Cross in aerial combat must be regarded as one of the most outstanding contributions possible to the military aspect of Canadian aviation." —Induction citation, 1974

Major W.G. Barker with Sopwith Camel aircraft of 28 Squadron, RAF, Italy, 1918.

During the following year, he raised his score to 33 enemy aircraft destroyed and was awarded the Distinguished Service Order (D.S.O.) and Bar, and a second Bar to his M.C. He was honoured with Italy's Valore Militare medal, and France's Croix de Guerre. He was promoted to Major, and in September 1918, was posted to England to command a flying training school.

Barker soon had a roving commission to operate at will from any squadron on the Western Front, flying a new Sopwith Snipe. On October 26, 1918, his score of victories had been confirmed at 46 enemy aircraft destroyed. On the following day, he is credited with winning one of the most astounding air battles in aviation history, for which he was awarded the Victoria Cross (V.C.).

Only rarely does an official citation describe in detail the action involved. The official War Office citation read:

> "On the morning of October 27, 1918, this officer observed an enemy two-seater over the Forêt de Mormal. He attacked this machine, and after a short burst it broke up in the air. At the same time a Fokker biplane attacked him and he was wounded in the right thigh, but

managed, despite this, to shoot down the enemy aeroplane in flames.

He then found himself in the middle of a large formation of Fokkers, which attacked him from all directions, and was again severely wounded in the left thigh, but succeeded in driving down two of the enemy in a spin.

He lost consciousness after this, and his machine fell out of control. On recovery he found himself being attacked again by a large formation, and singling out one machine, he deliberately charged and drove it down in flames.

During this flight his left elbow was shattered and again he fainted, and on regaining consciousness he found himself still being attacked; but, notwithstanding that he was now severely wounded in both legs and his left arm rendered useless, he dived on the nearest machine and shot it down in flames.

Being gravely exhausted, he dived out of the fight to regain our lines, but was met by another formation which attacked and endeavored to cut him off, but after a hard fight, he succeeded in breaking up this formation and reached our lines, where he crashed on landing.

This combat, in which Major Barker destroyed four enemy machines (three of them in flames) brought his total of successes up to 50 machines destroyed, and is a notable example of the exceptional bravery and disregard of danger which this very gallant officer has always displayed throughout his distinguished career."

Barker was promoted to Lieutenant Colonel during his extended hospitalization, and returned to civilian life in Canada in 1919. He had no formal skills other than those the military had provided, and he had no entitlements under Canadian law, being a member of the Imperial Forces. The Canadian Government was not obliged to provide a ticket home, a civilian suit, a discharge bonus, or medical care. He was not even entitled to the annual tax-free annuity of £10 given to enlisted men who had been awarded the V.C.

However, Barker was not discouraged about his prospects in civilian life. He had promised his family he would make a fortune in civil aviation after the war, and while he was in hospital convalescing, Lt. Col. Billy Bishop (Hall of Fame 1974), who had similar ideas, came to visit him. Together they started one of Canada's first commercial air services, Bishop/Barker Flying Company, using war-surplus airplanes.

After the war, Barker was commissioned as a Wing Commander in the Canadian Air Force (CAF), where he served from 1920 to 1924. In 1924 he helped found the Royal Canadian Air Force (RCAF). In January 1930, he became Vice-President of the Fairchild Aviation Corporation of Canada, but he crashed to his death near Rockcliffe Airport, Ottawa, on March 12, 1930, while test flying one of their new aircraft.

William George (Bill) Barker was inducted as a Member of Canada's Aviation Hall of Fame in 1974.

Ian Willoughby Bazalgette
(1918 – 1944)

Ian Willoughby Bazalgette, V.C., D.F.C., was born in Calgary, Alberta, on October 19, 1918. His family moved to Toronto, Ontario, in 1923, where he attended school until they moved to England four years later. He was educated at The Downs, Wimbledon, and at the outbreak of World War II was living at New Malden, Surrey. He joined the Army in 1940, and earned a commission in the Royal Artillery. The following year he transferred to the Royal Air Force where he completed training as a bomber pilot and was posted to 115 Squadron.

Promoted to Flight Lieutenant, by mid-1943 Bazalgette had completed a tour of thirty operations in Avro Lancasters and had been awarded the Distinguished Flying Cross (D.F.C.), with the following citation:

A Canadian-built Lancaster, FM 159, has been restored by the Nanton Lancaster Society, Nanton, Alberta, and at a ceremony held on August 27, 1990, it was dedicated to the memory of S/L Ian Bazalgette, V.C. The ceremony was attended by his navigator on the V.C.-winning flight, Chuck Godfrey, D.F.C., and his flight engineer, George Turner.

This is the second Lancaster that has been dedicated to the memory of a Canadian V.C. winner. The Canadian Warplane Heritage Lancaster is dedicated to the memory of P.O. Andrew Mynarski, V.C. (Hall of Fame, 1974).

A Lancaster bomber similar to the one S/L Ian Bazalgette flew on his final mission, August 4, 1944.

"This officer has at all times displayed the greatest keenness for operational flying. He has taken part in many sorties and attacked such heavily defended targets as Duisberg, Berlin, Essen and Turin. His gallantry and his record commands the respect of all in his squadron."

He was then promoted to Squadron Leader and assigned to instructional duties at an Operational Training Unit until April of 1944, when he was sent to 635 Squadron. It was with this unit that he made his final mark by performing the most outstanding deeds under the most terrible of conditions. The following citation, printed in the Sixth Supplement to the London Gazette of Tuesday, 14th August 1945, accompanied his posthumous award of the Victoria Cross (V.C.):

'The King has been graciously pleased to confer the Victoria Cross on the undermentioned officer in recognition of most conspicuous bravery:

ACTING SQUADRON LEADER IAN WILLOUGHBY BAZALGETTE, D.F.C., ROYAL AIRFORCE VOLUNTEER RESERVE, No. 635 SQUADRON (DECEASED)

On August 4, 1944, S/L Bazalgette was 'master bomber' of a Pathfinder Squadron detailed to mark an important target at Trossy St. Maximin (near Paris) for the main bomber force.

When nearing the target his Lancaster bomber came under heavy anti-aircraft fire. Both starboard engines were out of action and serious fires broke out in the fuselage and the starboard mainplane. The bomb aimer was badly wounded.

As the deputy 'master bomber' had already been shot down, the success of the attack depended upon S/L Bazalgette, and this he knew. Despite the appalling conditions in his burning aircraft he pressed on gallantly to the target, marking and bombing it accurately. That the attack was successful was due to his magnificent effort.

After the bombs had been dropped the Lancaster dived, practically out of control. By expert airmanship and great exertion S/L Bazalgette regained control. But the port inner engine then failed and the whole of the starboard main plane became a mass of flames.

S/L Bazalgette fought bravely to bring his aircraft and crew to safety. The mid upper gunner was overcome by fumes. S/L Bazalgette then ordered those of his crew who were able to leave by parachute to do so. He remained at the controls and attempted the almost hopeless task of landing the crippled and blazing aircraft in a last effort to save the wounded bomb aimer and helpless air gunner.

With superb skill and taking great care to avoid a small French village nearby, he brought the aircraft down safely. Unfortunately it then exploded and this gallant officer and his two comrades perished. His heroic sacrifice marked the climax of a long career of operations against the enemy. He always chose the more dangerous and exacting roles. His courage and devotion to duty were beyond praise".

Details of his last flight were as follows:

"Lancaster ND 811 of No. 635 Squadron, piloted by Squadron Leader Bazalgette, took off at 11.15 hours on 4 August 1944 from Royal Air Force Downham Market, Norfolk, for a raid over Trossy-St Maximin. Nothing more was heard of aircraft or crew until a telegram from the International Red Cross was received stating that the aircraft had crashed at 13.45 hours on the same day at Senantes, 20 km NW of Beauvais. S/L Bazalgette was buried in the Senantes Communal Cemetery, Department of Oise."

S/L Bazalgette was 26 years old. The four surviving crew members evaded capture and returned to England where the story of Bazalgette's last flight was recorded. In 1949 a mountain in Willmore Wilderness Park, near Jasper National Park, Alberta, was named in his honour.

Ian Willoughby Bazalgette was inducted as a Member of Canada's Aviation Hall of Fame in 1974.

Alexander Graham Bell
(1847 – 1922)

Alexander Graham Bell, D.Sc., M.D., Ph.D. (Hon), LL.D. (Hon), was born in Edinburgh, Scotland, on March 3, 1847, and educated there and in London, England. In 1870 he moved with his parents to Brantford, Ontario, where he taught speech therapy to deaf persons and began his initial experiments with voice transmission. A few years later he moved to Boston, Massachusetts, and opened a school for the training of teachers who would instruct the deaf.

Bell invented the forerunner of the modern telephone in his first successful experiment with what he called a 'speaking wire', when he transmitted his spoken message on March 10, 1876, to Thomas Watson in the next room of his apartment in Boston. He also invented a device for transmitting photographs through a beam of light, and shortly thereafter, a workable gramophone. He interested himself in the principles of mechanical flight, a subject on which he gave numerous lectures and published a number of scientific papers. He was

The Badge of 635 Squadron: In front of a roundel nebuly, a dexter gauntlet holding three flashes of lightning.

The Motto: "Nos ducimus ceteri secunter" ("We lead, others follow")

Authority: King George VI, August 1945.

The mailed fist indicates a heavy striking force while the flashes of lightning suggest the provision of light for target identification. The background of nebuly indicates the clouds in the sky.

Equipped with Lancasters, 635 Squadron formed part of the Pathfinder force (no. 8 Group) and during the period of March, 1944 to April, 1945 took part in many major bombing attacks. It was disbanded in September, 1945.

In 1876 Bell's voice was first heard being transmitted over a thin wire into the room next to where he was standing. Over the next 30 years his creative genius gave the world many new ideas and inventions which would have a great impact on the way people live. One of these was his theory of flight, and experiments testing the lifting power of plane surfaces at slow speed. Bell is unquestionably one of the world's earliest pioneers of manned flight.

named President of the National Geographic Society in January of 1898.

Bell established a summer residence at Baddeck, Nova Scotia, on Bras d'Or Lake, Cape Breton Island. He began experimenting in 1891 with rocket-powered propellers, which can now be identified with modern day helicopter rotors, and graduated to designing and flying huge man-carrying tetrahedral kites. For many years he had been conducting experiments with other kite designs in an attempt to learn which lifting surfaces were the most effective. He also introduced to aviation the hinged wing-tip aileron control.

In 1905 he saw his kite, Frost King, successfully flown, lifting into the air a total of 227 pounds (103 kg). Two years later he produced the even larger Cygnet, designed to lift the weight of a man and an engine. On December 6, 1907, it was towed to a height of 168 feet (50 m), carrying Lieutenant T.E. Selfridge of the United States army as passenger/pilot. Earlier that year, in Halifax, Nova Scotia, Bell and his wife, Mabel, had formed the Aerial Experiment Association (AEA) with two young engineers, J.A.D. McCurdy and F.W. Baldwin (both Hall of Fame 1974). This group was joined by Glenn Curtiss of Hammondsport, New York, and Lt. T.E. Selfridge. It was Curtiss' engine that powered the AEA's experimental airplanes.

The AEA group continued to experiment with Bell's kite ideas, but soon moved their activities to Curtiss' shop at Hammondsport. It was there that they built a series of four heavier-than-air machines, and in March of 1908, F.W. Baldwin became the first Canadian to fly the first of these, the Red Wing. It was a design conceived by Bell and so-named because it used red silk fabric left over from his kite-building. This airplane took off under its own power and used skis on the ice surface. A second flight ended in a crash and destruction of the aircraft.

Dr. Alexander Graham Bell explains to a group of scientists the principle of his tetrahedral kites which he believes will form the basis of successful flying machines. Baddeck, Nova Scotia, 1908.

NATIONAL ARCHIVES OF CANADA C-028214

There followed flights of other Bell aircraft: the White Wing, the June Bug, which was flown mainly by Curtiss around the Hammondsport area, and the Silver Dart, which first flew at Hammondsport on December 6, 1908. Its bamboo frame was covered in silver-gray rubber-impregnated silk. It featured a three-wheeled undercarriage, tapered wings, and small wing-tip ailerons for balance control. It also had a steerable front landing wheel which facilitated ground positioning.

Bell wanted the Silver Dart to fly in Canada and had it shipped to Baddeck in January 1909. There, McCurdy made the first flight in the British Empire, on February 23, 1909. That same year the AEA was dissolved after having reached its goal of achieving powered, manned flight.

While experimenting with airplanes, Bell applied the dynamic principles of the air foil to power boats and invented the first hydrofoil craft. In 1914 he predicted,

> "I have no doubt that in the future, heavier-than-air machines of great size, and of a different construction from anything yet conceived of, will be driven over the earth's surface at enormous velocity ... hundreds of miles an hour, by new methods of propulsion."

The United States Army sought his advice in 1919, when he was 72 years of age, to outline their policy of military aeronautics. He died on August 2, 1922, at Baddeck, Nova Scotia, after receiving numerous academic honours and awards.

Alexander Graham Bell was inducted as a Member of Canada's Aviation Hall of Fame in 1974.

Arthur Massey (Matt) Berry

(1888 – 1970)

Arthur Massey (Matt) Berry was born on June 19, 1888, on a farm at March, Ontario, near Ottawa, where he was educated. At the outbreak of World War I he was commissioned in the 30th Wellington Rifles and proceeded overseas with the 153rd Battalion of the Canadian Expeditionary Force as a Captain. In England he transferred to the Royal Flying Corps, graduated as a pilot and returned to Canada as a flying instructor with the 189th Training Squadron at Deseronto, Ontario.

In 1919, after leaving the service, Berry received his Canadian Pilot's Certificate. He worked for the Soldier's Settlement Board in Ottawa for two years, and then turned to ranching near Rimbey, Alberta. In 1924 he returned to Ottawa to work in the brokerage business. After completing a pilot refresher course with the Royal Canadian Air Force (RCAF) at Camp Borden, Ontario, in 1928, he earned his Commercial Pilot's Licence and was hired by Northern Aerial Mineral Exploration Ltd. at Hudson, Ontario, under the supervision of H. 'Doc' Oaks (Hall of Fame 1974). For the next five years he flew from company bases in northern Ontario, Manitoba, and Alberta, into the Hudson

Although Berry was forced down many times, mostly due to weather conditions, he said he was never lost, and always did find his way back. Once when he was down in the northern wilderness with a broken ski on his aircraft, he improvised a radio from a battery, a starter coil, and other odds and ends so that he could attract attention.

CANADIAN AVIATION, JUNE 1938

'Matt' Berry took this photo of his airplane snowbound on the Coppermine River more than 1000 miles (1600 km) north of Edmonton, in a blizzard with – 45° C temperatures. c. 1935.

Bay area, and throughout the Northwest Territories. He became the first pilot to land at Baker Lake, Northwest Territories. In 1929 he completed a Flying Instructor's course at Camp Borden, Ontario, and used these skills to upgrade the company's junior pilots.

In 1931, before joining Canadian Airways Ltd., he completed the first same-day return flight between Great Bear Lake in the Northwest Territories, and Edmonton, Alberta.

Berry's first assignment with Canadian Airways was to ferry two Junkers aircraft from Montreal, Quebec, to Winnipeg, Manitoba, after which he flew charter work from the company base at Tashota, Ontario. In 1932 he joined Mackenzie Air Service at Edmonton until crash injuries caused a short retirement. After convalescence, he graduated with honours from a course at the RCAF school at Camp Borden in instrument flying and radio beam work. He then returned to flying with Canadian Airways at Edmonton.

Most pioneer pilots were forced down at one time or another due to bad weather or mechanical problems, or were called upon to rescue others. Berry well depicted the courage, determination and resourcefulness

needed to save lives in the harsh northern areas. During 1935 and 1936, Berry was involved in several dramatic and difficult rescues.

In 1935, after an exhausting eleven-day aerial search of the Barren Lands for Canadian Airways pilot Con Farrell and engineer Frank Hartley, whose aircraft had been forced down in a blizzard, he located the missing men and flew them to safety.

In September 1936, he rescued two members of the RCAF, Flight Lieutenant S. Coleman and Leading Aircraftsman J. Fortey, who were overdue on a photographic mission. The two men were lost for thirty days in the Barren Lands north of Great Slave Lake before Berry, experienced in Arctic flying, was called in. This rescue won Berry the Trans-Canada (McKee) Trophy for that year. This was one of the largest and most publicized searches in Canadian history.

In December of 1936 Berry captained one of the most difficult of all recorded northern rescue flights when he and engineer Rex Terpening (Hall of Fame 1997) flew to Hornaday River on the Arctic Ocean during a period of near total darkness. They battled gale force winds and blizzard conditions to locate the isolated Roman Catholic mission and rescue Bishop Falaize and his party. After completing another short but difficult flight to bring them food, he attempted the 350 mile (560 km) return to Aklavik, Northwest Territories, but encountered blizzard conditions which necessitated a ten-day wait before he could fly them to safety. This flight established a new record as the farthest north an aircraft had been flown during the winter.

In 1937 Berry retired from professional flying to become the Edmonton-based manager of Northern Transportation Ltd., operators of freighting vessels on the Mackenzie River. He held that position until World War II, when the Canadian Government requested that he serve as second-in-command of 7 Air Observer's School at Portage La Prairie, Manitoba.

Berry's outstanding grasp of northern flying led the United States Government to seek his services in 1942 to oversee construction of airfields in the Northwest Territories and the building of the Canol Pipeline. This pipeline was built to bring crude oil from Norman Wells to the refinery at Whitehorse to supply petroleum products for the Alaska Highway and North West Staging Route.

At war's end, Berry founded Territories Air Services Ltd. at Fort Smith, Northwest Territories, and purchased Yellowknife Airways Ltd. He disposed of his interests in both companies to Associated Airways Ltd. in 1951, and concentrated his efforts on various mining ventures in northern Canada until his retirement in 1969 due to ill health. He died in Edmonton on May 12, 1970.

Arthur Massey (Matt) Berry was inducted as a Member of Canada's Aviation Hall of Fame in 1974.

George Frederick (Buzz) Beurling
(1921 – 1948)

George Frederick (Buzz) Beurling, D.S.O., D.F.C., D.F.M.*, was born on December 6, 1921, in Verdun, Quebec, where he was educated. As a youngster he built and sold model aircraft to earn money for flying lessons, and hunted game birds to improve his shooting skills. By 1939 he was a licenced private pilot and had won an aerobatics contest in Edmonton, Alberta, against civilian and military pilots.

Refused enlistment in the Royal Canadian Air Force (RCAF) at the outbreak of World War II, he sought, and was refused, enlistment in the Chinese Air Force and the Air Force of Finland. Beurling again attempted to join the RCAF as a pilot and again was rejected. This refusal caused him to join the crew of a merchant ship and cross the submarine-infested Atlantic in order to enlist in the Royal Air Force (RAF) in England. Again he was refused, this time for lack of proper documents. He promptly returned to Canada, secured the required papers, and within a week sailed back to England, where he was finally accepted for pilot training by the RAF.

After completing advanced training and graduating with his wings as a Seargent Pilot in September 1941, Beurling was assigned to 403 Squadron flying a Hurricane fighter. Within weeks he was transferred to the all-Canadian, RAF Spitfire Squadron 242, where he shot down one enemy aircraft. In June 1942, he was posted to 249 Squadron on the Island of

Beurling was originally buried in Rome. However, the Jewish people, as a gesture of respect to him, had his body exhumed and re-buried with honours in Israel.

Malta, in the Mediterranean, and by mid-July had destroyed eight enemy aircraft and won the Distinguished Flying Medal (D.F.M.). In September 1942, his score rose by 17 enemy aircraft destroyed and he was given a Bar to the D.F.M. Within four months of his posting to Malta, he had destroyed 28 enemy aircraft.

Beurling was then commissioned as a Pilot Officer and awarded the Distinguished Flying Cross (D.F.C.) for downing more hostile aircraft. On October 13 and 14, 1942, he fought his last battles from Malta and was awarded the Distinguished Service Order (D.S.O.) with the following citation:

"Since being awarded the Distinguished Flying Cross, Pilot Officer Beurling has destroyed a further six enemy aircraft, bringing his total victories to 28. During one sortie on October 13, 1942, he shot down a Junkers 88 and two Messerschmidt 109s. The following

F/L 'Buzz' Beurling in the uniform of an RCAF officer.

day, in a head-on attack on enemy bombers, he destroyed one of them before he observed his leader being attacked by an enemy fighter. Although wounded, Pilot Officer Beurling destroyed the fighter, then, although his aircraft was hit by enemy fire, he shot down another fighter before his own aircraft was so damaged that he was forced to abandon it. He descended safely into the sea and was rescued. This officer's skill and daring are unexcelled."

After recovering from his wounds in England, Beurling returned to Canada to assist in selling war bonds as Canada's leading ace of World War II. His exceptional ability as an airborne marksman was then directed to the training of new fighter pilots in Britain but he wanted to be back in the air. He was then transferred to the RCAF in September of 1943. That same month, serving with 403 Squadron, he destroyed another enemy fighter. He was transferred to 412 Squadron and promoted to Flight Lieutenant. In December of 1943 he destroyed two more enemy aircraft. He found service discipline difficult, and was released from service in October 1944 and returned to Canada, after 31 ⅓ confirmed aerial victories.

Until 1948 he barnstormed across Canada and accepted occasional bush flying assignments. But, lost in a world without air combat—"It's the only thing I can do well; it's the only thing I ever did I really liked"—he looked for an air force to join. He was refused enlistment in the Nationalist Air Force in China, but was accepted by the Israeli Air Force as a fighter pilot in the war between the Jews and Arabs in Palestine. He was killed at Rome Airport on May 20, 1948, when the aircraft he was ferrying to Palestine crashed.

George Frederick (Buzz) Beurling was inducted as a Member of Canada's Aviation Hall of Fame in 1974.

William Avery (Billy) Bishop
(1894 – 1956)

William Avery (Billy) Bishop, V.C., C.B., D.S.O.*, M.C., E.D., was born on February 8, 1894, in Owen Sound, Ontario. He was educated there and at the Royal Military College at Kingston, Ontario, from where he enlisted in the 4th Battalion, Canadian Mounted Rifles in 1914. The following year in England he transferred to the Royal Flying Corps (RFC) and was posted to France as an air observer. In March of 1917 Lieutenant Bishop was commissioned as a pilot with 60 Squadron RFC and he immediately shot down his first enemy aircraft.

On April 7, 1917, he was awarded the Military Cross (M.C.) for downing an enemy observation balloon and a German fighter, and the following day he engaged eight enemy aircraft, destroying two of them as well as a second balloon. On April 30, 1917, he battled nine times in two hours, engaging eleven different enemy aircraft in the first hour, shooting down two and dispersing the remainder. Two days later he engaged 23 enemy aircraft in three sorties and shot down three of them. The citation accompanying the award of the Distinguished Service Order (D.S.O.) read:

> "For conspicuous gallantry and devotion to duty. While in a single-seater he attacked three hostile machines, two of which he brought down, although in the meantime he

Bishop became the first Canadian airman to win the coveted Victoria Cross. He had an amazing total of 72 confirmed enemy aircraft destroyed, making him the highest-scoring 'Ace' of the British Empire in World War I.

Captain Billy Bishop, V.C., Royal Flying Corps, who had up to this date shot down 37 German aircraft. August, 1917

was himself attacked by four other hostile machines. His courage and determination have set a fine example to others."

It was before dawn on June 2, 1917, that Captain Bishop, flying a Nieuport, in a spectacular lone fight earned the Victoria Cross (V.C.) "for conspicuous bravery, determination and skill."

The words of the War Office citation read:

> "Captain Bishop flew to an aerodrome 12 miles the other side of the German lines. Seven machines, some with their engines running, were on the ground. He attacked these from about 50 feet, and a mechanic who was starting one of the engines was seen to fall. One of the machines got off the ground, but at a height of 60 feet Captain Bishop fired 60 rounds into it at very close range and it crashed.

> A second machine got off the ground, into which he fired 30 rounds at 150 yards range and it fell into a tree. Two more machines then rose. One he engaged at 1,000 feet, emptying the rest of his drum of ammunition. The machine crashed 300 yards from the aerodrome, after which Captain Bishop

emptied a whole drum into the fourth hostile machine and then flew back to his station.

Four hostile scouts were about 1,000 feet above him for about a mile of his return journey, but they would not attack. His machine was very badly shot up by machine gun fire from the ground."

In addition to this honour, he received a Bar to his D.S.O. for

"gallantry and distinguished service in the field, for consistent dash and fearlessness and for having destroyed at least 45 enemy planes within five months."

Bishop was promoted to Major and returned to Canada to aid in recruiting, but in 1918 returned to France, taking command of 85 Squadron and setting out on what authority has labelled 'a carnival of destruction'. In twelve days alone he brought down 25 enemy aircraft, bringing his total to 72. He was decorated again, receiving the Distinguished Flying Cross (D.F.C.). The French Government honoured him with the Croix de Guerre with Palm and named him a Chevalier of the Legion of Honour.

In August 1918, Bishop was relieved from operational flying, and in London was tasked as Commander of the first Canadian Air Force. It was during this period that the Maple Leaf came into use as an identification device on Canadian military aircraft. The Armistice put a temporary end to Canada's plans for an air force.

Along with William G. Barker, V.C. (Hall of Fame 1974), Bishop formed an airline serving Muskoka and Toronto, Ontario, but it was not successful. He returned to England to engage in several business operations before becoming Vice-President and Director of McColl-Frontenac Oil Company in Montreal.

Early in World War II he became Director of Recruiting for the Royal Canadian Air Force, serving with the rank of Honorary Air Marshal until 1944, when he returned to McColl-Frontenac. Bishop was named a Companion of the Order of the Bath (C.B). He died in Palm Beach, Florida, on September 11, 1956.

William Avery (Billy) Bishop was inducted as a Member of Canada's Aviation Hall of Fame in 1974.

Rosella Marie Bjornson
(b. 1947)

Rosella Marie Bjornson was born on July 13, 1947, in Lethbridge, Alberta. She was raised on her parents' farm near Champion and attended high school in nearby Vulcan. She showed enthusiasm for flying at an early age because of her father's interest. Ken Bjornson learned to fly in 1946 and took his daughter flying in his Aeronca Champ from the time she was a very young child.

Bjornson had her first flying lesson on her seventeenth birthday at the Lethbridge Flying Club and completed her Private Pilot's Licence in two months. She attended the University of Calgary where she majored in geography and geology. During this time she accumulated flying hours and studied for her Commercial Licence which she obtained in 1967. In the same year, she experienced competitive flying by entering the Alberta Centennial Air Race. She and her female co-pilot

Bjornson's husband, Bill Pratt, is a F/O on the Boeing 737 with Canadian Airlines. About once every six months, the scheduling computer pairs them together on a flight. Because of their close relationship, they enjoy working together and look forward to the times when they are booked to work the same flights. They are often asked if problems ever occur in flight deck management. It is because they are so well trained as professional pilots, and each carries out his/her specific duties, that conflicts do not arise.

Captain Rosella Bjornson aboard Canadian Airlines 737, after being promoted to Captain in late 1990.

secured a first place finish by completing the race with the exact estimate of their flight time and within one tenth of a gallon of their fuel consumption estimate.

While on campus, Bjornson was instrumental in organizing the University of Calgary Flying Club. She also devoted time to the first group of Girl Guide Air Rangers in Calgary and started the ground work which led to the formation of an Alberta Flying Farmer Teen Chapter.

In 1969 Bjornson received her Instructor's Rating and began instructing at the Flying Club in Winnipeg, Manitoba. Within a year she had earned her Class II Instructor's Rating. On May 25, 1972, she was awarded the 89th Gold Seal of Proficiency from the Royal Canadian Flying Clubs Association. While in Winnipeg, she was involved in organizing the Manitoba Chapter of The Ninety-Nines, the International Organization of Women Pilots (Canadian Sections 99s, Belt of Orion 1995). During her final year of instructing, she devoted her spare time to training a Squadron of Air Cadets.

By 1973 Bjornson had 3,500 hours flying time, an Air Transport Rating and a Class I Multi-Engine Instrument Rating, and applied to fly with the airlines. She was hired as First Officer by Transair, the fourth largest airline in

Canada. This gave her the distinction of being the first female to be hired as First Officer in North America on scheduled jet equipment, and the first female to be hired by a commercial air line in Canada. She was the first female member of the Canadian Air Line Pilots Association (CALPA, Belt of Orion 1988).

In June 1977, Bjornson married Bill Pratt, a corporate pilot flying out of Winnipeg. The onset of her pregnancy in 1979 created another first in that there had been no precedent set for a pregnant pilot. She took a personal leave of absence—sick leave was not appropriate in her case—and returned to work in 1980 as First Officer on the Boeing 737 with Pacific Western Airlines (PWA) which had purchased Transair. The family moved to Edmonton and both Bjornson and her husband flew for PWA. After a second pregnancy in 1984 she was involved in discussions with Transport Canada regarding regulations dealing with pregnant pilots. Subsequently, the regulations were changed to allow a pilot who is pregnant to fly while under her doctor's supervision. Bjornson again returned to work as First Officer on the Boeing 737 at a new airline, Canadian Airlines International, which had been formed by merging PWA, CP Air, Eastern Provincial Airlines and Nordair.

Bjornson received a number of prestigious awards in 1988. In June she was inducted into the International Forest of Friendship in Atchison, Kansas, U.S.A. A Certificate of Appreciation in recognition of her leadership in the activities of the organization was presented to her by the International Organization of Ninety-Nines in Oklahoma City, U.S.A. In October of that year, she received a Pioneering Award from the Western Canada Aviation Museum in Winnipeg.

In the winter of 1990 Bjornson became the first female Captain with Canadian Airlines International and the first woman to be promoted to Captain with a major Canadian air carrier.

Throughout her career Bjornson has made a valuable and ongoing contribution to the youth of the nation by participating in school career days. In 1990 she was featured in a poster campaign by the Alberta Government, 'Dream/Dare/Do', encouraging young people to set goals and strive towards them.

Rosella Marie Bjornson was inducted as a Member of Canada's Aviation Hall of Fame in 1997.

Thurston (Rusty) Blakey
(1911 – 1986)

Thurston (Rusty) Blakey, C.M., was born on December 12, 1911, in Ravenna, Ontario. After the death of both his parents, he lived in Bruce Mines, Ontario, with an aunt and uncle. He attended Worthington Public School and then graduated from Sudbury High School in 1930. He spent considerable time with pilots, mechanics, and airplanes on the shore of Ramsey Lake while working for the near-by Sudbury Boat and Canoe Company.

In 1932 Austin Airways, a charter service and flying school, was opened at Ramsey Lake. The owners of this charter service were Jack Austin (Hall of Fame 1976), and his brother Charles Austin, with Leigh Capreol (Hall of Fame 1981) joining them for a short while. They hired Blakey as dock and office boy in 1935. In 1937 he earned his Air Engineer's Licence, which enabled him to check out and service his own aircraft throughout his long flying career. Matt Berry (Hall of Fame 1974) gave him his first airplane ride there in 1937. Blakey became a Commercially Licenced Pilot in March of 1938.

In March 1939, Blakey opened the Biscotasing, Ontario, base for Austin Airways to serve mining ventures, and in September, Charles Austin left the company to serve with the Royal Canadian Air Force. This left Blakey with the added responsibility of meticulously photographing vast areas from the air for the Ontario provincial government. The contract was for forestry and future road

Throughout his long flying career, Blakey flew by his own rules, which he said always worked for him: "Fly in good weather", "There's always tomorrow", and "Don't overload".

building purposes. In addition, Blakey flew many rescue missions and medical evacuation flights from Hudson Bay and northern areas to the nearest hospitals. For this, he was well known in northern Ontario.

In 1940 Austin Airways purchased a Noorduyn Norseman, registered CF-BSC, which Blakey flew for twenty years. His flying experiences were wide ranging, and included freighting supplies and mail to the Inuit along the coast of James Bay. He delivered men and equipment to mines in northern Ontario. In 1948 he was the first to drop dry ice pellets from an aircraft in an attempt to cause rain, a technique that revolutionized forest fire suppression.

Throughout a career of nearly 50 years of accident free flying, Blakey flew in excess of 30,000 hours. Over 10,000 of those hours were flown in Austin Airway's Norseman, CF-BSC.

In 1978 he received an Honorary Life Membership from the Canadian Owners and Pilots Association (COPA, Belt of Orion 1993). In 1985 he was named a Member of the Order of Canada (C.M.).

Blakey's last flight was October 10, 1986. The following day he died on his way to work.

The Rusty Blakey Heritage Aviation Group erected a monument in 1988 to honour Blakey. The sculpture was unveiled on August 27 at Science North on the shore of Ramsey Lake, Ontario, and each year the Rusty Blakey Air Show takes place at this site.

Thurston (Rusty) Blakey was inducted as a Member of Canada's Aviation Hall of Fame in 1992.

Rusty Blakey handled radio communications as well as aerial photography for Ontario Department of Lands and Forests, 1939.

Ernest Joseph Boffa

(b. 1904)

Ernest Joseph Boffa was born on April 16, 1904, in Piedmont, Italy, and came to Canada with his family in 1907. They lived in Calgary until they moved to Fort William, Ontario, in 1915.

Boffa secured employment at a bicycle shop in 1915, and later, apprenticed with Canadian Car and Foundry in Fort William. During this time, he took correspondence courses in mechanical engineering and two years of drafting at night school. When the company closed, he worked as an auto mechanic and raced cars at local fairs. He built his own car, the Dreadnought, which was quite successful. He won the July 1st car race on the 60th Anniversary of Confederation in 1927 in a car with a Laurel 16 valve engine. The owner could not keep the engine running and offered the car to Boffa for the race. His winning of the race was proof of his mechanical skill.

In 1927 Boffa moved to Great Falls, Montana, U.S.A., where he decided to pursue his dream by taking flying lessons at Vance Air Services. The company had a shortage of instructors so National Parks Airlines pilots would instruct when needed. Consequently, Boffa had six different instructors in the nine hours that he needed to solo. While learning to fly, he worked at an autobody shop where he learned acetylene welding. He also worked in the hangar and was taught to do the wood and fabric work on aircraft by the

One of Boffa's interesting tasks in the early 1960's was the mapping of migration routes of ducks, geese, and caribou. This use of aircraft continues today.

Uranium prospector Ernie Boffa lands on a small northern lake to test a likely-looking rock spur for mineral content. NWT, early 1950's.

same man who prepared the wings and control surfaces on the Spirit of St. Louis for Charles Lindbergh.

In 1928 he obtained his American Aircraft and Engine Licence as well as his Private Pilot's Licence, and in 1929 he bought his first airplane. It was a badly damaged Waco 10 which he rebuilt and had licenced for export prior to moving to Lethbridge, Alberta, where he went to work for Southern Alberta Airways. When the company's Gipsy Moth was badly damaged, Boffa's Waco was used as a substitute at their flying school while he rebuilt the Moth. The employees produced the Flying Frolics, demonstrating wing-walking and parachute jumping, and barnstormed at local fairs.

After receiving his Commercial Pilot's Licence and Canadian Engineer's Licence in 1931, Boffa was kept busy flying fish from Great Bear Lake, tourists to Banff, servicing an oil well near Coutts, Alberta, and anything else that would earn income. In 1935 southern Alberta had a grasshopper plague, and he worked with an

Ernie Boffa uses a rope to whip snow and frost off the wings of his plane before taking off. Yellowknife, NWT, early 1950's.

experimental farm to develop a way of spreading the grasshopper bait, a mixture of sawdust, molasses and arsenic, from an aircraft.

In 1936 he went to Prince Albert, Saskatchewan, to fly for Mason & Campbell Aviation (M&C), forerunners of the Saskatchewan Government Airways. In 1937 he was offered a job with Canadian Airways Ltd. He worked for them until freeze up and then joined McNeal Air Services as a partner until the company was sold to M&C.

At the outbreak of World War II, Boffa completed the flight instructor's course at Trenton, Ontario, then served as Assistant Chief Flight Instructor at 6 Elementary Flying Training School at Prince Albert, Saskatchewan. In 1943, when there was a surplus of instructors, Grant McConachie (Hall of Fame 1974) asked him to fly for Canadian Pacific Airways on the Yellowknife/Port Radium run.

Boffa later flew for Yellowknife Airways and owned 20% of the company while Matt Berry (Hall of Fame 1974), held the remaining 80%. During this time he serviced mining camps, Hudson's Bay posts, and government offices throughout the Northwest Territories and Yukon.

In 1954 he served as technical advisor to the project manager of the Distant Early Warning (DEW) Line, and for the next two years he assisted in establishing radar stations throughout the far north.

From 1956 to 1963, Boffa flew contract work out of Yellowknife, servicing mining camps, prospecting parties, geological survey parties. From 1963 until he retired in 1970, he flew for a fishing lodge on Great Bear Lake, servicing the camp and flying guests to the high arctic.

Ernest Joseph Boffa was inducted as a Member of Canada's Aviation Hall of Fame in 1993.

Robert William Bradford

(b. 1923)

Robert William Bradford, C.M., was born December 17, 1923, in Toronto, Ontario. As a youth, he developed an early interest in aviation and its art. At 18, he and his twin brother Jim, enlisted in the Royal Canadian Air Force (RCAF), and trained on the Tiger Moth and Anson. Posted overseas in March 1944, Bradford was attached to the Royal Air Force as a staff pilot. He was seriously injured in a bad-weather crash, and spent several months in hospital before returning to flying. The war ended before he was posted to operational duties.

On returning to Canada, Bradford joined A.V. Roe Canada Ltd. as a technical illustrator. Four years later, in 1953, he moved to de Havilland Aircraft of Canada as project illustrator. His excellent work earned a promotion in 1956 to Chief Illustrator in the Publications Department, a position he held for ten more years.

In 1978 Bradford was commissioned by Canada's Post Office to design a series of sixteen stamps depicting important aircraft in Canadian history. The popular series was issued in groups of four and included, by year of issue:

1979—Curtiss HS-2L, Canadair CL-215, Consolidated Canso A, Canadian Vickers Vedette.

1980—Avro Lancaster, Avro Canada CF-100, Curtiss JN-4 Canuck, Hawker Hurricane.

1981—de Havilland DH-82C Tiger Moth, Canadair CL-41 Tutor, Avro Canada C-102 Jetliner, de Havilland Canada DHC-7.

1982—Fairchild FC-2W1, Fokker Super Universal, Noorduyn Norseman, de Havilland Canada Beaver.

"With enthusiasm, leadership and consummate dedication and outstanding knowledge of aviation history, he realized a vision for a national consciousness of Canada's aviation heritage, so that all Canadians may enjoy and benefit from this well-preserved heritage for generations to come." —Induction citation, 1996

In 1961 Bradford created four aviation paintings for the 1962 calendar of publisher Rolphe-Clarke-Stone Ltd., including one of the Curtiss JN-4 'Canuck' which caught the attention of Ken Molson. Molson was the first Curator of the National Aviation Museum which was formed in 1960 at the Uplands Airbase in Ottawa. Molson commissioned eighteen pieces, a series of historical aviation images in which Bradford depicts aircraft and aviation events of significance to Canada. From 1964, until the construction of a new museum building, the small collection of World War I aircraft was housed in old wooden hangars at Rockcliffe airport in Ottawa.

In 1966 Molson encouraged Bradford to join the National Aviation Museum as Assistant Curator. Thus began a twenty-three year career of dedication, perseverance and accomplishment in the preservation of our country's aviation heritage.

In Canada's Centennial year, 1967, Bradford succeeded Molson as curator. In 1970 he promoted the flying of the Museum's World War One aircraft at airshows across Canada, bringing to thousands of people the chance to see what their museum was doing.

In 1978 the National Aviation Museum Society (Friends of the National Aviation Museum) was established to bring attention to the need for adequately fireproofed housing for Canada's outstanding collection of historic aircraft. The collection was at considerable risk in the old hangars because of a significant fire hazard. As a result of Bradford's support, the Society eventually won a commitment from the Federal Government to provide a new and safer facility.

In 1982, as acting Director of the National Museum of Science and Technology, the parent museum of the aviation collection, Bradford's priority was the urgent need for improved facilities. Returning to the National Aviation Museum in 1984 as Associate Director, Bradford's persistent efforts were directly responsible for persuading the government to design

and build a new building. Bradford oversaw the acquisition of a number of artifacts of historical significance to Canadian and international civil and military aviation. Top quality restoration work has earned international renown. The collection, widely regarded as among the best in the world, is now housed in the new National Aviation Museum facility which opened to the public in 1988 at Ottawa's Rockcliffe Airport.

As soon as the commitment for a new facility was made, Bradford began to create the 'walkway of time' to represent the various eras of aviation. In this ingenious way, the visiting public is introduced to the evolution of aviation in Canada.

Throughout the years, Bradford continued to paint airplanes. Other commissioned works painted by Bradford include those to commemorate the 50th anniversary of Alcock and Brown's trans-Atlantic flight, Billy Bishop's Victoria Cross-winning aerial action, 'Doc' Oaks, the first recipient of the Trans-Canada (McKee) Trophy, and Air Canada's 50th anniversary.

In recognition of his accomplishments as an artist, Bradford was awarded the American Aviation Historical Society's Aviation Artist Award in 1974. He was the first Canadian so honoured. The Fédération Aéronautique Internationale recognized his curatorial and artistic accomplishments in the field of aviation by awarding him the prestigious Paul Tissandier Award in 1982.

Bradford was named Patron of the Canadian Aviation Historical Society in 1988, a position he continues to fill. He retired as Director of the National Aviation Museum in 1989, and continues to devote his time to painting and his life-long avocation of preserving Canada's aviation history. In 1989 he was named a Member of the Order of Canada (C.M.) for his outstanding achievements.

Robert William Bradford was inducted as a Member of Canada's Aviation Hall of Fame in 1996.

Wilfred Leigh Brintnell

(1895 – 1971)

Wilfred Leigh Brintnell, O.B.E., was born in Belleville, Ontario, on August 27, 1895. He was educated at Belleville and Kingston, Ontario, and at the Ontario Business College. In 1917 he joined the Royal Flying Corps (RFC) in Canada and received his Private Pilot's Licence at Deseronto, Ontario, where he became qualified as an instructor. He was assigned to instructional duties with the RFC at Fort Worth, Texas, and the Royal Air Force (RAF) at Camp Borden, Ontario. He was posted to the RAF's Central Flying School, Upavon, England, in 1918 to train on Sopwith Camel fighter aircraft. The war ended before he flew in combat, and he returned to Canada in 1919 to be discharged from service.

Brintnell spent the early post war years in the United States flying Curtiss JN-4's. In 1924 he joined the Ontario Provincial Air Service (OPAS, Belt of Orion 1991) as a pilot.

Western Canada Airways hired him in 1927, and the following year he was named superintendent of the company's base at Hudson, Ontario. This appointment was followed almost immediately by a promotion to manager of the line. During 1928 he piloted the first return flight from Winnipeg, Manitoba, to Vancouver, British Columbia, in a multi-engine aircraft.

Brintnell established his company in Edmonton because he saw the commercial potential of the north and realized Edmonton's strategic location. He is at least partly responsible for focusing the attention of oil companies, the mining world, and government on the north.

In 1929 Brintnell completed an historic 9,000 mile (45,000 km) return flight in a Fokker tri-motor aircraft inspecting Western Canada Airway's bases. His route took him from Winnipeg north through the Northwest Territories, to Great Slave Lake, then following the Mackenzie River to Fort Norman. From there he flew north to Aklavik, on the Arctic coast, then completed the first over-the-Rockies flight from Aklavik to Dawson City in the Yukon. Brintnell continued to Prince Rupert, on the British Columbia coast, then flew back to Winnipeg via Edmonton, Alberta.

While on this trip, he became the first person to circle Great Bear Lake by air. He took aerial photographs of ground formations in the Great Bear Lake region and as a result of these pictures, uranium prospecting and mining began. During this trip he dropped off Gilbert LaBine, a prospector with Eldorado Mining and Exploration, at Great Bear Lake. It was LaBine's preliminary exploration which later led to his discovery of a rich deposit of silver mixed with pitchblende. LaBine returned to open the mining site called the Eldorado Mine at Port Radium on Great Bear Lake. Also, while on this trip, Brintnell decided he would some day form his own commercial northern airline.

In 1931 Brintnell was appointed assistant general manager of Canadian Airways Limited, which had acquired Western Canada Airways. He resigned from this position to form Mackenzie Air Service Limited at Edmonton, Alberta, which began flying passengers into the Northwest Territories and the Arctic in 1932. On March 19, 1935, Brintnell and fellow pilot, Stan McMillan (Hall of Fame 1974) took off from the Eldorado Mine site in a Bellanca Aircruiser carrying the first shipment of radium concentrates. They brought the ore to the rail link at Waterways, near Fort McMurray.

Brintnell's company continued to expand, with more aircraft and pilots added to meet the increasing demand for services. An advancement of the 1930's was

Leigh Brintnell stands beside a Fokker Super Universal used by his company, Mackenzie Air Service. Edmonton, Alberta, 1932.

airborne communications. An aerial wireless telegraphy system, along with a network of stations from the Edmonton base to the Beaufort Sea, was pioneered by a Mackenzie Air Service engineer.

Mackenzie Air Service operated from 1932 to 1940 when the company was purchased by Canadian Pacific Railways (CPR). Brintnell stayed on with the company, assisting CPR to purchase other small companies. These were formed into Canadian Pacific Airlines (CPA) in 1942.

Brintnell left CPA to manage Aircraft Repair Limited in Edmonton, a company which had been given the task of repairing and maintaining Canada's military aircraft. He expanded Aircraft Repair and eventually formed it into Northwest Industries Limited, which he managed from 1945 until 1948. He then operated Arctic Air Lines, an aerial photographic company, until 1952.

Brintnell's outstanding services were recognized by the government, when he was created an Officer of the Order of the British Empire (O.B.E., Civil) in 1946. He died in Edmonton on January 22, 1971.

Wilfred Leigh Brintnell was inducted as a Member of Canada's Aviation Hall of Fame in 1976.

Helen Marcelle Harrison Bristol

(1909 – 1995)

Helen Marcelle Harrison Bristol was born in Vancouver, British Columbia, on December 7, 1909, and educated in England and Belgium. She began flying studies at Eastbourne, England, in 1933, earned her Private Pilot's Licence the following year, then completed a seaplane flying course in Singapore. She acquired additional instruction at Johannesburg, South Africa, before returning to England in 1935 to qualify for a Commercial Pilot's Licence. She made a total commitment to aviation in 1936 when she became one of the first women pilots to receive an instructor's rating in England. She promptly returned to South Africa.

As the first woman to hold a Commercial Pilot's Licence and Instructor's Rating in that country, Harrison Bristol taught at the Capetown Flying Club. She demonstrated such ability that the Royal South African Air Force (RSAAF) offered her an instructor's course on military aircraft at Pretoria. Because of her outstanding abilities, she was retained by the RSAAF to train reserve air

Harrison Bristol and the other women ferry pilots were given a minimum amount of training on procedures, plus a small, but important binder. This held the Ferry Pilot's notes with descriptions of all the planes they would be ferrying, instructions for take-off, cruise speed and power setting, amount of flap, and landing procedures. With this book they were expected to fly any type of aircraft even though they may not have seen one of its type before.

"The career dedication of her flying skills to instruct an almost exclusively male population of students, despite adversity, has been of substantial benefit to Canadian aviation." —Induction citation, 1974

Helen Harrison Bristol with student in floatplane, Aero Club of British Columbia, 1956.

force pilots. During this period she also qualified for the South African Commercial Pilot's Certificate as well as instructor and instrument ratings. She was employed by Central Airways at Johannesburg and Port Elizabeth until 1938.

She returned to England. In 1939 she was appointed Chief Flying Instructor at the Sheffield Aero Club. Shortly afterwards, she went to the United States to qualify for that country's Commercial Pilot's Certificate. Still upgrading her qualifications, she travelled to Hamilton, Ontario, and earned her Canadian Commercial Pilot's Licence and Class 2 Instructor's Rating. The Cub Aircraft Company at Hamilton hired her as an instructor, and within a year she was named test pilot and Chief Flying Instructor.

Harrison Bristol was involved in pilot training at Toronto, London, and Kitchener, Ontario, until February 1942, when she was accepted as the first Canadian woman ferry pilot to serve in the United Kingdom with the Air Transport Auxiliary, a civilian group under the direction of the Royal Air Force (RAF). She was part of Jacqueline Cochrane's American Group, and her job was to deliver aircraft for the RAF.

Some of the aircraft to be ferried were new, coming off the assembly lines, others were

being returned to service after repair. Harrison Bristol became qualified to ferry all types of single and twin engine aircraft. In 1943 she co-piloted a North American B-25 Mitchell bomber across the North Atlantic Ocean from Montreal, Quebec, to Scotland, and until 1944 she delivered military aircraft within the United Kingdom.

She flew a single-engined airplane across Canada in 1946 as demonstration pilot for Percival Aircraft Company. During the next 23 years she held Chief Flying Instructor positions with a number of British Columbia flying services. In 1961 she earned a United States Seaplane Instructor's Certificate, and returned to Canada to continue teaching float plane flying. In 1968 she was awarded the British Columbia Aviation Council's Air Safety Trophy, after logging 14,000 hours as pilot-in-command of 75 different aircraft types, without injury to passenger or crew.

She retired in 1969 after 34 years as a pilot, and married Donald M. Bristol. Harrison Bristol died at Blain, Washington, on April 27, 1995.

Helen Marcelle Harrison Bristol was inducted as a Member of Canada's Aviation Hall of Fame in 1974.

Francis Roy Brown
(1896 – 1960)

Francis Roy Brown was born in Stockton, Manitoba, on September 13, 1896. He attended school in Winnipeg, Manitoba, until his enlistment in the Canadian Cycle Corps at the outbreak of World War I. He served with that unit in France at Ypres, Vimy Ridge, and Passchendaele, until he joined the Royal Flying Corps in 1917. After graduating from flying training as a pilot he joined 204 Squadron in France and shortly before the November 11, 1918, Armistice, he was shot down over Belgium. He returned to Canada in 1923.

Brown was hired as a pilot by Western Canada Airways Limited in 1927, based at The Pas and Cranberry Portage in Manitoba. Typical work included hauling mining equipment, food and supplies north to Rankin Inlet, and equipment, supplies and passengers for the Churchill River Power Company.

The fall of 1929 saw one of the most spectacular aerial searches ever organized in Canada's north. On August 24 two aircraft left Winnipeg with Colonel MacAlpine,

There were many times in his life when Frances Roy Brown tried to convince others that he was not the same Roy Brown known as 'the Ace who brought down the famous Red Baron'. That momentous event on 21 April 1918 involved Captain A. Roy Brown. However, they did have something in common besides the name Roy Brown and contemporary life times: both were well known in Canada for their piloting skills in uncharted areas of this country.

"His contributions as a bush pilot, airmail pilot and World War II test pilot, coupled with his total commitment to encourage a younger generation of airmen to make substantial contributions to the development of northern flying, have been of outstanding benefit to Canadian aviation." —Induction citation, 1976

Dominion Explorer's president, leading a mineral survey project. The pilots of the two planes were Stan McMillan (Hall of Fame 1974), flying a Fairchild, and Tommy Thompson, flying a Fokker Super Universal. MacAlpine's plan was to cover over 32,000 square kilometres of land never before seen from the air. Their plan was to fly from Winnipeg into the Northwest Territories. Their route would be via Chesterfield Inlet, Baker Lake, Pelly Lake, Bathurst Inlet, Coppermine, Great Bear Lake, Fort Norman, Aklavik, then south to Fort Simpson, and return to Winnipeg via The Pas. They were to rendezvous with two other Dominion Explorer's aircraft on September 20.

The rendezvous on the Arctic coast failed to happen. When the search was organized in late September, Brown was one of nine pilots from Western Canada Airways who spent ten weeks searching in the Baker Lake and Bathurst Inlet areas of the Northwest Territories.

Members of the search parties were often in as desperate straits as the lost party themselves. Forced down on a remote Barren Lands lake, Brown spent one period of three weeks in his aircraft, with the temperature at forty and fifty below zero. The original exploration party was found, safe, at Cambridge Bay in the Arctic, although they suffered from hunger, frostbite and scurvy. It was a joyous day at The Pas on December 3rd when Brown touched down on Halcrow Lake with all the party in fair shape. All involved were brought back to Winnipeg on December 6th, but five of the rescue aircraft were damaged and had to be left in the North. They were repaired and brought out the following year.

From 1930 to 1932 Brown was superintendent and chief pilot of Western Canada Airways' prairie airmail operations with headquarters at Moose Jaw, Saskatchewan. Their routes covered the cities of Winnipeg, Regina, Moose Jaw, Medicine Hat, Calgary, Saskatoon, Edmonton and North Battleford. However, flying the mail was considered too costly during the early thirties and the service

was cancelled by the government in 1932. Brown then became Chief Pilot of the Lac du Bonnet, Manitoba, region for Canadian Airways Limited, established by James A. Richardson (Hall of Fame 1976) in 1930.

In 1934, in company with Milt Ashton, Ted Stull and Jack Moar (Hall of Fame 1974), Brown organized Wings Limited, and became President and Operations Manager.

Canadian Pacific Railway bought Wings Limited in 1941, and in 1942 formed Canadian Pacific Airlines (CPA). Brown joined CPA and later took a leave of absence to become a test pilot of all new and rebuilt aircraft for Macdonald Brothers Aircraft at Winnipeg. Brown served in that capacity until 1945, during which time he test flew some 2,500 aircraft. He then returned to CPA as Chief Pilot of the central district.

In 1947 he and Milt Ashton bought back their bush flying operation from CPA and organized Central Northern Airways, a predecessor of Trans-Air Limited of which Brown became a director.

From 1953 to 1958 Brown represented the constituency of Rupertsland in north-central Manitoba as the Liberal Member of the Legislative Assembly. He died in Winnipeg on November 30, 1960.

Francis Roy Brown was inducted as a Member of Canada's Aviation Hall of Fame in 1976.

F. Roy Brown in uniform of Canadian Cyclists Corps, Hounslow, England. c. 1914 – 1915.

Maurice (Moss) Burbidge

(1896 – 1977)

Maurice (Moss) Burbidge was born in Brough East, Yorkshire, England, on April 15, 1896, and educated at Pocklington School. He was commissioned a Lieutenant in the Royal Field Artillery at the outbreak of World War I and transferred to the Royal Flying Corps (RFC) a year later where he earned his pilot's wings.

Burbidge took the gunnery school training and served as a flying instructor until early in 1918. At that time he was sent to France with 115 Squadron, RFC, flying Handley-Page bombers. As an operational airman he flew night raids into Germany with the Independent Air Force under Lord Trenchard's command. After the war he remained with the Royal Air Force (RAF) as a Flight Lieutenant, serving in India with 63 Squadron until being transferred to No. 1 Flying Training School in England as an instructor. When the Royal Naval Fleet Air Arm was formed in 1925, it sent its student pilots to train under Burbidge's command.

He retired from the RAF in 1928, earned his British Civil Pilot's Licence and was offered three positions. Two were in India and another was as Chief Flying Instructor at the Edmonton and Northern Alberta

In December of 1939, Burbidge took a refresher course for flying club instructors at the RCAF Station at Camp Borden. The categorization of civil flying instructors at that time was still under the control of the Department of National Defence, which felt this policy was necessary in the interest of safety.

Aero Club. Burbidge accepted the latter offer and came to Canada in March 1929.

As Chief Flying Instructor, he replaced W.R. 'Wop' May (Hall of Fame 1974) who had left to form his own company, Commercial Airways Limited. During the following decade, while still employed by the club, Burbidge flew occasionally for Commercial Airways out of Edmonton. In December 1931, he became one of the pilots, with May and Cy Becker, on Commercial Airways' inaugural airmail flight to Fort McMurray, Fort Chipewyan, Fort Smith, Fort Resolution and Aklavik, following the Mackenzie River route northward through the Northwest Territories.

But it was as an instructor that Burbidge's talent was most appreciated. He was known as a born instructor with a special talent for gaining a student's confidence in the first few minutes. Hundreds of students had made their first solo flights under Burbidge's instruction by the end of 1932. One of his students was Grant McConachie (Hall of Fame 1974), who learned to fly in 1929 and who would later become President of Canadian Pacific Airlines. Another was Alf Caywood (Hall of Fame 1988), who learned to fly in 1937 and who later became President and General Manager of Eldorado Aviation.

Burbidge was awarded the Trans-Canada (McKee) Trophy for 1932 for his outstanding accomplishments in training student pilots, and the advancement of aviation in Canada. Colonel D. M. Sutherland, Minister of National Defence, announced the award and commented on the impressive work of the Edmonton and Northern Alberta Aero Club. He believed that the success of the club was entirely due to Burbidge, whose leadership, initiative and discipline made the club a model in every respect.

In April 1938, Burbidge resigned as instructor at the Edmonton Aero Club after nine years, to become associated with Trans-Canada Air Lines in Winnipeg,

Moss Burbidge, flight instructor at Edmonton and Northern Alberta Aero Club, July 4, 1929.

Manitoba. He retired from active flying in 1939, but was called back into service in 1940 as a civilian, in the post of Chief Flying Instructor with No. 16 RCAF Elementary Flying Training School at Edmonton. He left in 1942 to become the Manager of the airport at Lethbridge, Alberta.

In 1944, with H.W. Hayter (Hall of Fame 1974), Burbidge joined the staff of Transportes Aereos Centro-Americanos, an air line operating throughout Central America out of its base in Miami, Florida. He became Operations Manager of the Panama-Nicaragua section and served in that capacity until his final retirement from aviation.

During half a century of flying, Burbidge trained more than 700 students to fly, without a fatality or injury. He flew in excess of 15,000 hours and captained 32 types of aircraft, from the flimsiest pioneer trainers to modern commercial carriers. He died in 1977.

Maurice (Moss) Burbidge was inducted as a Member of Canada's Aviation Hall of Fame in 1974.

Carl Frederick Burke

(1913 – 1976)

Carl Frederick Burke, M.B.E., LL.D. (Hon), was born in Charlottetown, Prince Edward Island, on February 10, 1913, where he received his education.

While working as a hardware clerk in 1936 his desire to fly resulted in frequent journeys to St. John, New Brunswick, to take flying lessons. He obtained his Private Pilot's Licence in July of 1937, and the following year he tied for first place in the Webster Trophy competition while earning his Commercial Pilot's Licence. He purchased a de Havilland 60 Cirrus Moth which was the only privately owned aircraft on Prince Edward Island at the time. In 1939 he qualified for his Air Engineer's Certificate.

He accepted a position in May 1939, as a pilot with Canadian Airways Ltd. at Moncton, New Brunswick. At this time, he nurtured ideas of creating a Maritime regional air service, a dream shared by his flying associate, Josiah Anderson.

When Canadian Pacific Air Services acquired Canadian Airways, Burke and Anderson joined the Royal Air Force Ferry Command delivering aircraft to the British Isles. They continued to plan for a Maritime air service and in 1941, a licence was received to operate a scheduled commercial air service which included Charlottetown, Moncton and St. John. Regrettably, Burke had to

While flying with Canadian Airways Ltd., Burke used a ski-equipped de Havilland Rapide to rescue the pilot of a crashed Lockheed Hudson near Musgrave Harbour, Newfoundland. Killed in the crash were Sir Frederick Banting, co-discoverer of insulin, navigator William Bird, and William Snailman.

"His skills as a pilot, his visionary leadership as a dedicated entrepreneur, his administrative ability which guided the establishment of regional air carriers in the eastern provinces, together with his substantial contributions to the development of northern flying, have been of outstanding benefit to the Nation."

—Induction citation, 1982

carry on alone after Anderson lost his life in an airplane crash.

With the purchase of a Barkley Grow and a Fairchild 24, as well as a leased Boeing 247D, Burke's new company, Maritime Central Airways (MCA), operated its first flight on December 7, 1941. While managing the company, Burke captained many of MCA's inaugural flights.

On January 28, 1943, he made five dangerous landings on an ice floe in the Gulf of St. Lawrence to rescue four RAF crewmen and equipment from a downed Avro Anson, incurring considerable risk as it was uncertain that the ice would hold his plane. For this rescue he was named a Member of the Order of the British Empire (M.B.E., Civil).

By the end of World War II, MCA's fleet and areas serviced had greatly expanded. With the inevitable post-war slump, Burke became involved in a variety of income-producing alternatives to keep the company viable, such as seal surveys, lobster charters, and ice patrols for the federal Department of Transport, as well as forestry patrols for the Government of New Brunswick. A subsidiary company, Maritime Central Aircraft Maintenance, was formed to undertake the maintenance of C-47 Dakota aircraft at the RCAF Station Summerside, Prince Edward Island.

In 1951 MCA won the contract to provide the airlift for the eastern portions of the Pinetree Project, a chain of military radar stations. During three years of involvement, Burke provided the leadership for a successful air lift of over 10,000 tons of equipment and supplies to the eastern Arctic. The project reported some six million air miles (9,650,000 km) flown and over 100,000 passengers transported to the sites.

When Canada and the United States entered into an agreement to construct the Distant Early Warning Line (DEW Line) in November of 1954, MCA was named the prime contractor for the eastern section of the chain of stations. Burke was actively involved in the overall administration of this operation which required the

procurement of additional aircraft, spare parts and ground equipment. At its peak periods, the project needed up to 75 aircraft to meet the requirements of the contract.

In 1953 MCA acquired an interest in two small Quebec-based operations, Boreal Airways and Mont Laurier Aviation. By November 1956, the two companies became wholly owned subsidiaries of MCA and merged under the name of Nordair Ltd., which experienced a healthy growth. With the purchase of Wheeler Airlines Ltd. in 1960, MCA had an air route structure that stretched from St. John's, Newfoundland, to Windsor, Ontario, and north beyond the Arctic Circle.

During the 1960's MCA acquired trans-Atlantic range aircraft with which the airline entered the overseas passenger and cargo charter business. MCA was sold to Eastern Provincial Airlines in 1963, but Nordair was not included in the sale. In 1967, when 85% of Nordair's shares were sold to J. Tooley of Montreal, Burke continued as a Director and a member of the Executive Committee of the Board.

During his flying career, Burke was certified on 23 types of aircraft and flew a total of 10,922 hours. His community work was recognized in 1968 when Acadia University conferred upon him an Honorary Doctorate of Laws (LL.D.). He died on September 1, 1976, in Boston, Massachusetts.

Carl Frederick Burke was inducted as a Member of Canada's Aviation Hall of Fame in 1982.

Mr. and Mrs. Carl Burke and sons, Charlottetown, P.E.I. c. 1950 – 55.

Erskine Leigh Capreol

(1898 – 1963)

Erskine Leigh Capreol was born in Ottawa, Ontario, on September 17, 1898, where he attended school. On graduation he enlisted in the Canadian Army, and served in France with the 77th, 73rd and 85th battalions of the Canadian Expeditionary Force. He was seconded to the Royal Flying Corps (RFC), in which he was commissioned in December 1917, after completing cadet training at Oxford, England.

He received his flight training at Yatesbury, England, after which he was posted to the School of Special Flying as a flying instructor. At the time, instructors communicated by the Gosport System in which the instructor talked through a rubber speaking tube to a student pilot while in flight.

In March of 1918 Capreol was promoted to Flight Lieutenant and joined the staff of the RFC's Central Flying School at Upavon

In the early 1960's, Capreol accepted the position as Manager of the Dorval Airport, a new facility designed to accommodate the fast growing domestic and international air traffic into and out of Montreal. It is a credit to his managerial skills that the airport kept pace with the demands of this rapidly growing centre of aviation. In January 1963, the Minister of Transport, the Honourable Lionel Chevrier, wrote, "When Leigh Capreol became manager of the airport, things took a different turn. He was held in the highest regard at Headquarters Ottawa."

"His contributions in war and peace as a flying instructor, bush pilot, test pilot and aviation executive, coupled with his commitment to defeat all conditions of adversity, have been of outstanding benefit to Canadian aviation." —Induction citation, 1981

E.L. Capreol in cockpit of Noorduyn Norseman, with Robert Noorduyn standing on wheel. Cartierville, Quebec. c. 1943.

Downs on Salisbury Plain, Wiltshire. While instructing, he was seriously injured in an aircraft accident. After 1-1/2 years in hospital he recovered, but for the remainder of his life he needed to use a cane.

On his return to Canada in 1920, he was employed by the American Bank Note Company in Ottawa. In 1927, on receiving the encouraging news from the medical authorities that he was fit to fly, he joined the RCAF at Camp Borden, Ontario, becoming an 'A2' category flying instructor, later upgraded to category 'A1'.

In March 1932, Capreol was hired by the newly formed de Havilland Aircraft of Canada Ltd. (DHC) as its chief test and demonstration pilot. During his six years with DHC he conducted manufacturer's tests on all new aircraft, as well as demonstrating them to potential customers. He was responsible for adapting these aircraft for service in northern Ontario and Quebec under all weather conditions.

These included the Gipsy, Puss, and Fox Moths. His research and development of floats and skis contributed significantly to the development of the successful Tiger Moth in January 1930. He also gave instructor flying courses to prospective flying club instructors and Ontario Provincial Air Service (Belt of Orion 1991) pilots.

In 1934 he became General Manager and Chief Pilot of a newly formed company, Capreol and Austin Airways. This company was incorporated by Jack Austin (Hall of Fame 1976) and his brother Charles Austin, to operate charter flights into the mining areas of northern Ontario and Quebec from its seaplane base in Toronto Harbour. The company operated the first properly equipped flying ambulance in Canada with a Waco, which held a stretcher, nurse, and patient.

Capreol resigned in 1935 to accept the position of test and demonstration pilot for Noorduyn Aviation Limited, Montreal, Quebec. His experience was fully utilized in the initial flight testing of the first bush plane to be designed and manufactured in Canada, the Noorduyn Norseman. It was equipped with wheel, ski, and float capabilities to meet the demanding Canadian flying requirements and weather conditions.

In 1939 Capreol was loaned to National Steel Car, Malton Airport, Ontario, to test the first Lysander aircraft built there, and became involved in the initial flight testing of the North American Yale trainer. On completion of these assignments he returned to Noorduyn Aviation, which had been given a contract to construct Harvard trainers and Norseman aircraft. He had the responsibility of organizing the flight testing of hundreds of these aircraft.

Capreol was actively involved in aviation for 37 years. He upheld the highest standards in research, test work, development, and instructing on all types of aircraft, using wheels, skis and floats. He ignored his physical handicap, and through example led others to do likewise. He earned the certificates which permitted him to act professionally in his demanding field of endeavor: Instructor's Licences, Commercial and Transport Pilot Certificates and an Air Engineer's Certificate. Capreol died at Baie D'Urfe, Quebec, on January 7, 1963.

Erskine Leigh Capreol was inducted as a Member of Canada's Aviation Hall of Fame in 1981.

Nicholas Byron Cavadias

(b. 1929)

Nicholas Byron Cavadias, LL.D. (Hon), was born of Greek parents on February 8, 1929, in Galgaun, India. He received his high school education in Greece, and his engineering training at the University of Southampton and the London City and Guilds Institute.

From the beginning, his career was in the application of electronics to aviation. He started as a radio engineer for TAE Greek Airlines in 1946. In 1950 he moved to the U.K., and in 1953 he joined the Royal Air Force, where he became a ground radar specialist. Cavadias came to Canada in 1956 and joined the engineering department of Canadian Aviation Electronics Ltd. (CAE), a Montreal-based company, designing, manufacturing and servicing avionics equipment for the Royal Canadian Air Force. He became President of that company 18 years later.

The company entered the flight simulation field early in the 1950's when Canada purchased a fleet of Avro CF-100 all-weather fighter planes for the RCAF and needed flight simulators to train its pilots. Success there, and the cancellation of the Avro Arrow in 1959, positioned CAE to provide the simulator for the Lockheed CF-104 Starfighter in the early 1960's. Cavadias was Project Manager of the highly successful CF-104 flight simulator program, which supplied 32 systems to Canada and

The introduction of flight simulators for complex aircraft like the CF-18 Hornet, the Lockheed Aurora, and the C-130 Hercules enhanced flight safety and reduced wear and tear on valuable airframes.

"His vision and dynamic leadership in the development of flight simulation through commitment to technological innovation, excellence and total team effort for nearly forty years has significantly enhanced civil and military aviation safety and economy world wide, and has been of outstanding benefit to Canada."

—Induction citation, 1996

Byron Cavadias, left, receives a plaque from the Space Shuttle Columbia's astronauts Joe Engle and Richard Truly. CAE created the SIMFAC simulator used to develop CANADARM.

its North Atlantic Treaty Organization (NATO) allies from 1960 to 1963. In 1961 CAE established its first off-shore subsidiary simulator company in Germany, CAE Electronics GmbH.

In 1963 CAE Industries was formed, and the original company, Canadian Aviation Electronics, became CAE Electronics, the principal subsidiary of the new parent company.

Cavadias continued his rise at CAE Electronics. By 1967 he was Vice-President Operations, responsible for engineering, manufacturing, program management and quality assurance. In 1975 he was appointed President of CAE Electronics Ltd. In this role, he focused the company's efforts on simulation, and initiated a period of unprecedented growth.

In addition to the company's involvement in commercial and military aircraft flight simulation, space and air traffic applications, nuclear power station simulation, and oil field automation, other

fields of endeavour included power generation, transmission and distribution automation, machinery control systems for Naval ships, and airborne magnetic anomaly submarine detection systems.

CAE Electronics grew to become the number one force in the international commercial flight simulation business. Under Cavadias' leadership, CAE's share of the world market for commercial airline flight simulators increased from less than 3 percent to over 60 percent. CAE exports over 90 percent of its simulators, which are used to train pilots around the world by over thirty airlines in more than thirty-six countries.

In 1990 Cavadias was promoted to Senior Vice-President, Aerospace and Electronics Group of CAE Inc., the Toronto-based corporate parent. He was responsible for four companies, including the U.S.-based CAE-Link Corporation, the Germany-based CAE Electronics GmbH, CAE Electronics Ltd. in Montreal, and Northwest Industries in Edmonton. At that time, these companies were earning a total revenue of over one billion dollars annually.

Cavadias retired in 1994 after a 38-year career with CAE. His efforts resulted in many world firsts, such as the 1983 Boeing 757 simulator which was the first new simulator ever to be FAA-certified prior to aircraft certification.

Cavadias was active in the Canadian aerospace industry outside of CAE. He served as Director of the Aerospace Industries Association of Canada. He contributed to Canadian government policy as a member of the Consultative Committee on the Electronics Industry, and to New Brunswick's government while on the Advisory Board for Science and Technology. He was awarded an Honorary Doctor of Laws degree by Concordia University in Montreal in 1985, which recognized his ongoing encouragement of links between industry and the university community.

He was recognized in 1988 by the Commander-in-Chief of the USAF Military Airlift Command for significant contributions to their C-5 simulator program, and in 1990 by the National Aeronautics and Space Administration (NASA) for outstanding cooperation between government and industry on the Crew Station Research Program. In 1990 he was the recipient of the C.D. Howe Award presented by the Canadian Aeronautics and Space Institute for leadership in Canadian aeronautics and space activities.

In retirement, Cavadias lives in Brockville, Ontario, with his wife, enjoying their family, sailing, woodworking, and classical music, and, recently, golf.

Nicholas Byron Cavadias was inducted as a Member of Canada's Aviation Hall of Fame in 1996.

Alfred Beebe (Alf) Caywood
(1910 – 1991)

Alfred Beebe (Alf) Caywood was born January 22, 1910, in Oelrich, South Dakota, U.S.A. and moved with his family to Edmonton, Alberta, in 1911. After receiving a diploma from McTavish Business College in 1925 he worked up to comptroller of a mine in the Coal Branch in southwestern Alberta. Later he worked with Alberta Land Titles and Provincial Income Tax.

In 1933 he struck out prospecting in British Columbia, northern Saskatchewan, and the Northwest Territories. During this period he became impressed with the use of aircraft to reach remote areas and also to investigate favourable prospects by means of aerial observation. With this as an incentive, he received his Private Pilot's Certificate early in 1937 under the tutelage of Maurice 'Moss' Burbidge (Hall of Fame 1974). He joined the staff of Canadian Airways Ltd. as a mechanic's helper, and became one of their pilots in 1938. He was associated in those early years of flying with several well-known northern pilots who would later become Members of Canada's Aviation Hall of Fame, including W.R. 'Wop' May (1974), G.H. 'Punch' Dickins (1974), Walter Gilbert (1974) and Jack Moar (1974).

Caywood recognized the importance of both preventive and corrective maintenance for his small fleet of aircraft and his standards of excellence resulted in a very safe and efficient operation, even in severe weather conditions. Under his direction, Eldorado's per-ton and per-passenger costs were the envy of the aviation industry.

"His foresight and high standards not only benefited the company he led, but indeed the entire aviation community. In his own words, he took the romance out of bush flying and turned it into a viable business, complete with balance sheet. He played an integral role in the development of Canada's atomic age. There is no doubt that he contributed greatly to Canadian aviation."

—Induction citation, 1988

Alf Caywood at the christening of the Boeing 737 Eldorado Aviation named in his honour, May, 1980, in Seattle.

Flying regularly over unmapped country, he actually covered the area which he had walked over as a prospector. Caywood instituted the filing of sketch maps of the locations where various prospectors, trappers, etc. had been left so they could be picked up more easily at a later date. He added sketches of major routes showing predominant characteristics of the areas for the guidance of others. When Canadian Pacific Airlines was formed, he became a mainline captain on all of their routes in the Yukon, Alaska and the Northwest Territories.

On one flight in 1942, Caywood was piloting a fabric-covered, single-engine Norseman in mid-winter from Yellowknife to Coppermine on the Arctic coast. The aircraft inexplicably caught fire in mid-flight and the flames ignited boxes of ammunition which exploded, shredding the plane's skin. Caywood, barely able to control the plane, landed safely on the frozen tundra.

He and his air mechanic, Jack Rennie, escaped as the fuel tank exploded, but their friend, Paddy Gibson, had already perished in the plane. Then began their struggle to survive. They had suffered blistered faces in the fire, and the minus 40 degree weather added to their miseries by freezing the skin of their hands and feet. They had lost their gloves and their felt liner-boots were shredded. They had no tent, little food and no one knew where they were. They spent nine days huddled in shelters constructed of snow, tree boughs and airplane parts. When a search aircraft located them, they were snow-blind, had frost-bitten hands and feet and had each lost twenty pounds.

In 1944 Caywood joined Eldorado Mining and Refining on Great Bear Lake, Northwest Territories, to form their Air Division. Eldorado Aviation transported uranium for the first atomic bombs, a venture known as the Manhattan Project. Working in shifts, Caywood kept Eldorado's planes flying almost non-stop to bring supplies in to the mine site, and fly uranium ore out from Port Radium. This was of vital importance to the Allied cause.

He acquired for Eldorado the first Douglas DC-3 to be licenced commercially in Canada, from war-surplus stock, enabling him to expand what was known at that time as 'bush service'. Thus he initiated the first extensive use in Canada of the DC-3 for freight and passenger haulage. Douglas Aircraft Division called it "a saga of what dedication, determination and ingenuity can accomplish under the most dire maintenance and flying conditions." During this time Caywood broke many new records for tonnage and mileage, and initiated the use of pallets to save time loading and unloading air freight.

Caywood retired from Eldorado in 1965 to live in Victoria, British Columbia. During his retirement he served as aviation consultant for the World Bank. He died on May 23, 1991.

Alfred Beebe (Alf) Caywood was inducted as a Member of Canada's Aviation Hall of Fame in 1988.

Larry Denman Clarke
(b. 1925)

Larry Denman Clarke, O.C., LL.B., LL.D. (Hon), was born in London, England, on June 12, 1925. His family moved to Canada in 1927. During the second World War he served as an electronics technician with the Royal Canadian Navy. Following the war, he studied law at Osgoode Hall, Toronto, and was called to the Ontario Bar in 1949.

When the Korean War broke out in 1950, Clarke left his legal practice to serve as lawyer and special advisor to the Canadian government's Department of Defence Production in Ottawa as it oversaw the military procurement operations as a member of the United Nations force in Korea.

When the Korean War ended in 1953, Clarke joined de Havilland Aircraft of Canada (DHC) as contracts administrator, and began his career in the aviation industry. He soon demonstrated his business acumen as an organizer, planner and negotiator. He served as President of a joint venture with CAE Electronics and Ferranti Packard Canada called DCF Systems, where he set up the contract with the Canadian government to install

The success of the Canadarm program led to Spar being chosen to head up a cross-Canada industrial team to provide Canada's participation in the American Space Station Program, developing the station's Mobile Servicing System. Spin-off technologies from this will continue to benefit Canada's economy in the fields of mining, forestry, environmental clean-up and nuclear energy.

"The opportunities he created for thousands of young Canadian engineers and technicians to contribute at home to the development of the world's space business testify to his vision, entrepreneurial capacity and tenacity as a businessman who, despite adversity, recognized and realized the potential of the space industry to the outstanding benefit of all Canadians."
—Induction citation, 1996

Bomarc missile bases. Later, as corporate secretary and Vice-President of Administration and Planning for DHC, he arranged for the company to manufacture the wings and tail for the Douglas DC-9. He also arranged the subsequent sale of the former Avro plant at Malton Airport in Toronto to Douglas Aircraft.

Clarke also assisted the small research and development group within DHC known as the Special Products and Applied Research Division (S.P.A.R.). The S.P.A.R. Division was started in 1953, the year Clarke joined DHC, to work on the missile program for the Canadian government. At this time he had been working with infrared technology and components primarily for defence applications. When the government scrapped the Avro Arrow in 1959, S.P.A.R. lost the related Sparrow missile development work, and was left practically productless. Its team of engineers began moving S.P.A.R. into non-military and space-related applications, developing the 'storable tubular extendible member' (STEM) from an abandoned National Research Council concept. This was the extendible antenna credited with launching S.P.A.R.'s abilities in space.

Canada's Alouette Scientific Satellite Program, conceived by Dr. John Chapman of the Defence Research Board, provided S.P.A.R.'s entry into the satellite business. For the Alouette 1, Canada's first, and the world's third, satellite, the research team at S.P.A.R. designed and built the satellite structure and provided the STEM's, with RCA in Montreal providing the electronics. At this time, however, DHC decided to concentrate on its specialized line of short take-off and landing (STOL) aircraft, and in

Larry Clarke receives his appointment as an Officer of the Order of Canada (O.C.) from Governor-General Jeanne Sauvé, January, 1989.

1967 decided to find a buyer for the S.P.A.R. Division.

Clarke had studied the business of S.P.A.R. since its inception and felt confident that it had the talent there to expand within the emerging space industry. Believing that unless Canada developed its own space business, it would become dependent on other countries for its space communications. He approached DHC with an offer to purchase S.P.A.R.

By the end of 1967 Clarke had assembled a team of investors and directors, raised the finances and launched his new company under the name of Spar Aerospace Products Limited. From this humble beginning, with few contracts and little cash flow, he built not only a company, but laid down the roots for an entire business sector in this country.

Clarke began a campaign to enhance Spar's profile in Ottawa, and within the plant he was a highly visible CEO, working long hours alongside the staff. He led the take-over and turnaround of York Gears, merged it with Spar and added space mechanisms to its line of jet engine and helicopter gear boxes.

In the mid 1970's, it became apparent that to become a prime contractor and leader in developing Canada's space manufacturing capability, Spar needed electronics expertise. He persuaded his board of directors to take a risk and purchase RCA Canada Ltd.'s Aerospace Division, and Northern Telecom's Space Division. The company was then renamed Spar Aerospace Limited. These acquisitions put Canada's satellite program firmly in Canadian hands and preserved high technology expertise in this country that otherwise would undoubtedly have been lost to the United States.

With its design and manufacturing capability successfully tested on subcontracts to American satellite builders, Spar won the Canadian contract to build the Anik D satellites, and became one of the few companies world-wide capable of supplying commercial communications satellites. This was reinforced by winning the contract for Brazil's first communications satellite, a contract that provided nearly 3,000 person-years of employment for Canadians.

Few people have the foresight to press ahead with such vigor as Clarke did in the face of huge odds. In the early 1970's, when Canada had no formal national space policy, Spar led a team of Canadian companies that conceived the world's first space robot. Spar was chosen by the National Research Council as its prime contractor for NASA's shuttle Remote Manipulator System (RMS) which became known as the Canadarm, Canada's most recognizable technological achievement.

Today, Canada is among world leaders in satellite communications with the Spar-built Anik E satellites and the first Mobile Communications satellites, called Msat. These sophisticated and powerful systems provide video, voice and data services for television, cellular phones, computers and navigation over all of North America. With the launch of RADARSAT, Spar put Canada in the forefront as the first nation in space with a commercial microwave radar satellite for remote sensing and monitoring the world's environment and natural resources.

For his patriotic vision and drive, Clarke was appointed an Officer of the Order of Canada in 1987 (O.C.). He served as Chancellor of York University in Toronto, and holds honorary degrees from Athabasca University in Alberta, Ecole Polytechnique in Quebec, Ryerson Polytechnic University in Toronto, and York University. He has been the honorary Chairman of the Canadian Foundation for the International Space University, and the Chairman of the Advisory board of the same institution. He is also a member of the Corporate Higher Education Forum.

Clarke retired as CE of the Board of Spar Aerospace in 1989 and remained Chairman until the spring of 1993.

Larry Denman Clarke was inducted as a Member of Canada's Aviation Hall of Fame in 1996.

Raymond (Collie) Collishaw
(1893 – 1976)

Raymond (Collie) Collishaw C.B., D.S.O.*, O.B.E.*, D.S.C., D.F.C., was born in Nanaimo, British Columbia, on November 22, 1893, and received most of his schooling there. At age 15 he joined the Royal Canadian Navy's Fishery Protection Service. He served on several patrol ships operating along the British Columbia coast, and rose to First Officer. In 1915 he joined the Royal Naval Air Service (RNAS) and, at his own expense, briefly attended the Curtiss Flying School at Toronto, Ontario. In January of 1916 he embarked for England.

On completion of fighter training Collishaw was posted to No. 3 (Naval) Wing, formed to fly long range bombing attacks on German industrial targets from bases in France. After five months of escorting RNAS bombers to enemy targets he was awarded the French Croix de Guerre for gallantry in action. In 1917 he was posted to 3 (Naval) Squadron attached to the Royal Flying Corps (RFC) on the Somme. He scored his first confirmed aerial victories with this squadron but during the winter suffered severe frostbite and was sent to England to recover.

Collishaw returned to the Ypres front in France a month later and was posted to 10 (Naval) Squadron, a fighter unit, equipped with the Sopwith Triplane, and led the famous 'Black Flight' throughout the spring and summer of 1917. While serving with this squadron, he was credited with shooting down 27 German aircraft and was

During a three month period, May – July, 1917, Major Ray Collishaw claimed 33 victories, and by war's end, Collishaw was the highest scoring pilot in the Royal Naval Air Service, with 60 victories, the third highest total of all British Empire pilots.

Squadron-Commander Raymond Collishaw on left, with
Lieutenant A.T. Whealy seated in Sopwith F.1 Camel
Aircraft. No. 203 Squadron, RAF, Allonville, France.
July, 1918.

awarded both the Distinguished Service
Cross (D.S.C.) and the Distinguished Service
Order (D.S.O.). He was then granted leave to
Canada.

He returned to duty in November 1917,
as Flight Leader in the Seaplane Defence
Squadron, based near Dunkirk, France.
Its main duties were to provide the aerial
protection of Royal Naval vessels off the
French and Belgian coasts, carrying out
fighter sweeps and escorting RNAS bombers.
In December he took command of the
squadron and during the next two months
was able to add to his score of enemy
machines destroyed.

Collishaw was made Commanding Officer
of his old squadron, 3 (Naval). It eventually
became 203 Squadron, RFC, and he was
promoted to Major. When he led the
squadron on patrols into enemy territory, his
score of victories mounted steadily and more
decorations followed: the Distinguished
Flying Cross (D.F.C.) in July 1917, and a Bar
to his D.S.O. in September 1918. The
citation accompanying the latter award
referred to his being credited with destroying
51 enemy machines as of August 1, 1918.
Under his command, 203 Squadron was
credited with shooting down some 125
enemy aircraft, with fewer than 30 of its own
pilots being killed or taken prisoner of war.

During his World War I flying career, he was
Mentioned in Despatches on four occasions.

At war's end, he accepted a permanent
commission in the RAF. During 1919 and
early 1920's he commanded 47 Squadron
which flew in south Russia in support of
Denikin's White Russian Forces fighting the
Bolsheviks. In late 1920 Collishaw was sent
to Iraq to command 30 Squadron in further
actions against the Bolsheviks in north
Persia. Collishaw was named an Officer
of the Order of the British Empire (O.B.E.,
Military) and three Imperial Russian orders
were added to his list of decorations.

Three years later he returned to England
and attended the RAF Staff College. More
commands of squadrons and stations
followed. In 1929, as Wing Commander,
he was appointed senior RAF Officer aboard
HMS Courageous, an aircraft carrier in the
Mediterranean Sea. In 1932 he returned
to England to take command of the RAF
station at Bircham Newton. In 1935, as
Group Captain, he took command of the
RAF station at Upper Hayford.

As war with Germany became increasingly
imminent, the RAF forces in the Middle East
were strengthened. In 1939 a new
operational formation known as the Egypt
Group came into being. Collishaw was
promoted to Air Commodore in 1940
commanding this group which ultimately
became known as the Desert Air Force.

When Italy entered the war in 1940,
Collishaw's group was badly outnumbered.
He was able to maintain the offensive, and
his crews destroyed some 1,100 Italian
aircraft. He managed to fly operations in
Hurricanes before being grounded. He was
considered too valuable to lose and knew
too much to be captured by the enemy.
His inspirational leadership was recognized
in March 1941, when he was created a
Companion of the Order of the Bath (C.B.).

In 1942 Collishaw was posted to Fighter
Command Headquarters in England.
He was promoted to Air Vice-Marshal and
given command of 14 Fighter Group in
Scotland. He retired from the RAF in 1943,
but until war's end served as liaison officer
with the Civil Defence Organization.

Collishaw returned to Canada in 1945.
In 1946 he was created an Officer of the
Order of the British Empire (O.B.E., Civil).
He died in Vancouver, September 29, 1976.

Raymond (Collie) Collishaw was inducted
as a Member of Canada's Aviation Hall of
Fame in 1974.

Wilfred Austin Curtis
(1893 – 1977)

Wilfred Austin Curtis, C.B., C.B.E., O.C.,
D.S.C.*, E.D., C.D., LL.D. (Hon), D.Mil.Sc.
(Hon), was born in Havelock, Ontario, on
August 21, 1893. He was educated in
Toronto and in 1915 joined the infantry of
the Canadian Army. He requested transfer
and returned from overseas to take flying
lessons at the Curtiss Aviation School in
Toronto at his own expense. He graduated
August 11, 1916, and returned overseas,
joining the Royal Naval Air Service (RNAS)
as a fighter pilot.

In 1917 Curtis was promoted to Captain and
awarded the Distinguished Service Cross
(D.S.C.) for his skill and courage. In 1918 he
was awarded a Bar to the D.S.C. He proved
his worth as a highly successful fighter pilot
by shooting down 13 enemy aircraft,
confirmed, and 3 probables. He transferred
to the Royal Air Force (RAF) in April of 1918,

**Air Marshal Wilfred Austin Curtis was
looked upon as the 'Father of Canada's
Post War Air Force'. Through his drive,
interpersonal skills, sense of humour,
understanding of aviation and effective
leadership, the RCAF became a well-knit,
effective and efficient fighting force.**

Pilot Officer John G. Magee receiving his wings from Group Captain W.A. Curtis. Magee wrote the poem 'High Flight'.

but relinquished his commission because of ill health in June of 1919.

On his return to Canada Curtis maintained his interest in military as well as civil aviation. During the late 1920's and early 1930's, he served as an officer in the Toronto Scottish Regiment Reserve. For some time there were no non-permanent military aviation positions available. However, when the opportunity presented itself in 1933, he became involved in the formation of 110 (Army Co-operation) Squadron. He became Officer Commanding in 1935 and initiated experimental air operations in mid-northern Ontario. In 1939 he founded and organized the Canadian National Air Show at Toronto.

Wing Commander Curtis was called to active duty in the Royal Canadian Air Force (RCAF) on September 1, 1939, and served with distinction in many capacities throughout World War II. In 1939 he was assigned to select air field locations in Canada for the British Commonwealth Air Training Plan (BCATP). He was named Commander, Order of the British Empire (C.B.E.) in 1943 for his outstanding work in promoting working relationships between the RCAF and RAF in the development of the BCATP.

He was, for a period, Deputy Commander of the RCAF overseas, headquartered in London, England. As a member of the RCAF Air Council, and as the Canadian member of the joint Canada-U.S. Air Council, he displayed his knowledge of air command and strategy. He received the Efficiency Decoration (E.D.) in 1945, and was named Companion of the Most Honourable Order of the Bath (C.B.) in 1946.

In 1947 Curtis was appointed Chief of Air Staff, and at this time guided the RCAF through the difficult stages of reorganization which followed the war and through the expansion of Canada's participation in the Korean conflict and the North Atlantic Treaty Organization (NATO). He received French, American and Italian decorations in recognition of his contributions.

Air Marshal Curtis had a great interest in the development of the Canadian aircraft industry. During his term of office, he continually and successfully directed his efforts to secure money for experimental work on and production of a jet trainer and twin-engine fighters, the CF-100 and the CF-105, suitable for interception operations in the northern Canadian climate. Early in the Cold War, he convinced the federal cabinet that the RCAF should make a major contribution to the North Atlantic Treaty Organization (NATO). This resulted in a force of twelve F-86 Sabre jet squadrons being dispatched to Europe. This contribution of 300 front line aircraft was part of the principal air defence force against the Soviet threat on that continent during the 1950's. He remained Chief of Air Staff until his retirement in January of 1953.

On his retirement from the RCAF, Curtis accepted the position of Vice-Chairman of Hawker Siddeley Canada, where he continued to have a substantial impact on the development of aviation in Canada. He was appointed to the Board of Directors of A.V. Roe Canada Ltd. in June 1953, and served until the demise of the Arrow in February 1959.

He devoted time to other aviation interests. He was President, and later, Grand President of the RCAF Association, and was appointed the Honorary Wing Commander of 400 (City of Toronto) Squadron, the old 110 squadron he had commanded in the late 1930's. He was Chairman of the committee which formed York University and was elected its first Chancellor in 1960.

Honorary Doctor of Laws degrees (LL.D.) were conferred on him by Western University (1948) and York University (1968). He received an Honorary Doctor of Military Science degree from Royal Military College, Kingston, Ontario, in 1963. In 1967 he was named Officer of the Order of Canada (O.C.). Curtis died in Toronto, Ontario, on August 14, 1977.

Wilfred Austin Curtis was inducted as a Member of Canada's Aviation Hall of Fame in 1984.

Paul Yettvart Davoud
(1911 – 1987)

Paul Yettvart Davoud, O.B.E., D.S.O., D.F.C., was born in Provo, Utah, U.S.A., on November 25, 1911. Upon his father's death, his mother moved the family to her home in Kingston, Ontario. Davoud attended Royal Military College at Kingston from 1928 to 1932. During the summers of 1929 through 1931 he trained at Royal Canadian Air Force (RCAF) Station Camp Borden, Ontario. At the conclusion of the summer of 1931 he became a Provisional Pilot Officer and was awarded the Sword of Honour as the best all-round cadet.

The RCAF was not offering many permanent commissions in the early 1930's so Davoud went to England and obtained a permanent commission with the Royal Air Force (RAF), where he remained until 1935. In that year he received an offer from James A. Richardson (Hall of Fame 1976) of Winnipeg, Manitoba, to join Canadian Airways Ltd. He returned to Canada and flew for that company from 1935 to 1938. In 1938 he joined the Hudson's Bay Company as a bush pilot and organized and operated an air transport service for the fur trade department throughout the Canadian north until 1940.

Davoud joined the RCAF in 1940 and was posted to Trenton, Ontario, as Assistant Chief Flying Instructor. He proceeded to the United Kingdom in June of 1941 and was assigned the rank of Squadron Leader to form 410 Night Fighter Squadron. One month later, as Wing Commander, he was appointed Commanding Officer of 409

In 1971 the Canadian Forces honoured Paul Davoud by naming their public school on the base at North Bay, Ontario, the 'Paul Davoud School.'

"The application of his exceptional skills as a pilot in peace and war and as an outstanding leader in military and civil aviation have been of superior benefit to Canadian aviation." —Induction citation, 1985

Night Fighter Squadron which operated Bristol Beaufighter and later de Havilland Mosquito aircraft. He destroyed his first enemy aircraft, a Dornier 217, over the North Sea in November of 1941. In February 1943, he crashed due to sudden engine failure while landing a Beaufighter. He was badly burned on his face and hands but was able to return to operations four months later.

In June of 1943 Davoud was the first Canadian to command 418 (City of Edmonton) Squadron, which had just been equipped with de Havilland Mosquitos. When Davoud left the squadron in January 1944, it was becoming the top scoring fighter squadron, night and day, in the RCAF. During the time he commanded night fighters he was awarded the Distinguished Service Order (D.S.O.) and the Distinguished Flying Cross (D.F.C.). One citation reads:

> "a forceful and courageous leader whose personal example and exceptional ability have been reflected in the fine fighting qualities and efficiency of the squadron he commanded."

Davoud's squadron became known for saving countless lives in Britain by shooting down V-1 'buzz-bombs'. They also succeeded in pursuing and altering the direction of many more of these weapons.

In February 1944, Davoud was promoted to Group Captain and given command of 143 Fighter Bomb Wing, comprising three squadrons of Hawker Typhoons. The Typhoon, with its four 20-mm cannon, plus either eight 60 lb. rockets or two 1,000 lb. bombs, proved to be the most formidable fighter/bomber in the allied air forces and provided effective close support to the allied armies in Normandy and across northwestern Europe. In April 1944, Davoud gave a demonstration of the Hawker Typhoon to General Dwight Eisenhower, Supreme Commander of the Allied Expeditionary Force, 1943-45, who was so impressed with its enormous

Wing Commander Paul Davoud, Commanding Officer of 409 Squadron, RCAF, meeting King George VI and Queen Elizabeth at Digby, U.K. Summer of 1942.

firepower that he wrote a letter of appreciation to Davoud.

Just prior to leaving the RCAF, Davoud was made an Officer of the Order of the British Empire (O.B.E. Military). The Dutch government made him a Commander of the Order of Orange Nassau and the French awarded him the Croix de Guerre with Palm Leaf, and the Legion of Honour.

In 1945 Davoud, Gordon McGregor (Hall of Fame 1974) and Earnest Moncrieff, were chosen by C.D. Howe (Hall of Fame 1976) for senior positions with Trans-Canada Airlines (TCA, Hall of Fame 1974) because of their distinguished records in the RCAF. Davoud was named assistant to John Tudhope (Hall of Fame 1974), who was Operations Manager for TCA at Winnipeg. In 1948 he was employed by the Canadian Breweries/Argus Corporation to establish their extensive air service. In 1951 he became General Manager of Field Aviation and its associated company, Kenting Aviation. In 1954 he became Vice-

President, Sales and Service at Orenda Engines Ltd., at that time Canada's leading aircraft engine manufacturer. Five years later, the cancellation of the Avro Arrow, which was to use the new Orenda Iroquois engine, put him out of work.

In 1959 the Federal Government selected him to be Chairman of the Air Transport Board for a five year term, 1959 to 1963. Upon completion of his term he joined de Havilland Aircraft as Vice-President of Sales, a position he held for the next seven years. In 1971 Davoud was hired by the government of Ontario as the Director of Aviation Services for the Ministry of Transportation and Communications. He held this position until he retired in 1978. He died on March 24, 1987.

Paul Yettvart Davoud was inducted as a Member of Canada's Aviation Hall of Fame in 1985.

Clennell Haggerston (Punch) Dickins

(1899 – 1995)

Clennell Haggerston (Punch) Dickins, O.C., O.B.E., D.F.C., LL.D. (Hon), was born in Portage la Prairie, Manitoba on January 12, 1899. His family moved to Edmonton, Alberta, in 1907. He attended the University of Alberta until enlistment in the Canadian Infantry in World War I. In 1917 he transferred to the Royal Flying Corps, earned his pilot's wings and a commission and was posted to 211 Squadron where he served until 1919. He was awarded the Distinguished Flying Cross (D.F.C.) for persistence and gallantry in completing aerial assignments under fire.

At war's end Dickins returned to Canada, joined the Canadian Air Force and then became one of the original officers of the Royal Canadian Air Force (RCAF) when it was formed in 1924. He conducted cold weather, high altitude experiments in the Siskin fighter aircraft at Edmonton for two years, proving that cold-weather flying was possible. He flew forest patrol duties and completed special aerial photographic survey flights in Alberta and Saskatchewan. He left the RCAF in 1927.

He joined newly formed Western Canada Airways Ltd. in 1927 and began a career which added up an impressive number of aviation firsts. Collectively, these helped unlock the secrets of Canada's north.

Throughout his life, Punch Dickins was proud to call himself 'a Bush Pilot'. He was also called one of the most outstanding Canadians in this nation's first century, and was christened by native groups 'The Snow Eagle' and 'Canada's Sky Explorer'.

Mr. Wilkin hands a package to C.H. 'Punch' Dickins for air delivery. On the far right is John Michaels.

In November 1928, Western Canada Airways, formed in December 1926 by James A. Richardson (Hall of Fame 1976) of Winnipeg, won the contract to carry mail on the prairie circuit of Winnipeg, Regina, Calgary, Edmonton, Saskatoon, and Winnipeg. Dickins made the first airmail flight in a Fokker Super Universal. It was successful and within a few months, airmail service became a regular feature in these areas.

In August 1928, Western Canada Airways was contracted by Dominion Explorers Limited to fly their President, Charles MacAlpine, on an exploratory flight to visit prospective mining sites across Canada's unmapped Barren Lands of the Northwest Territories. Dickins was selected to fly the group in a new Fokker Super Universal float plane, G-CASK. The expedition's route was from Winnipeg through Fort Churchill, up the west coast of Hudson Bay to Chesterfield Inlet, inland to Baker Lake, southwest to Stony Rapids, and return to Winnipeg, covering some 4,000 miles (6,400 km). Dickins described the many difficulties of navigating over this desolate

area. First of all, the only map available to him had the word "unexplored" printed across much of the area. While he expected to pick out large lakes and main rivers, as time went on all he could see were lakes and bare rock with little vegetation. There was no radio communication beyond Fort Churchill, and from there on, they were completely out of radio contact. He flew by the sun most of the way because his compass, affected by magnetic interference, went round in circles in several places and couldn't be trusted. A result of the twelve-day trip was that large areas of the region were mapped. Dickins was awarded the Trans-Canada (McKee) Trophy for 1928 because of his outstanding contribution to Canadian aviation made during this trip.

On March 6, 1929, Dickins flew to Fort Good Hope on the Mackenzie River to collect furs on the first aerial shipment to traders in Winnipeg. In July 1929, Dickins became the first pilot to fly the full length of the Mackenzie River, some 2,000 miles (3,200 km) in two days, from Edmonton to Aklavik on the Arctic Ocean. On this trip he became the first pilot to cross the Arctic Circle. In September he flew the first prospectors into Great Bear Lake where pitchblende was discovered.

Dickins felt both the agony of defeat and the thrill of success in dangerous searches for lost companions. In late September 1929, word was received that the MacAlpine party, which had been flown north for some serious prospecting, was overdue and possibly lost. Dickins and engineer W.S. Tall made three searches over an area of the North West Territories for two weeks, without incident, but to no avail. The total search took place over ten weeks and involved nine aircraft, before the party was found at Cambridge Bay and flown out to Winnipeg on December 8, 1929.

Western Canada Airways was taken over by Canadian Airways Ltd. in November 1930. Dickins was named Superintendent of the Mackenzie River district for the new company, which was based in Edmonton. In recognition of his outstanding aerial work in the development and expansion of flying routes in northwestern Canada, Dickins was named an Officer of the Order of the British Empire (O.B.E., Civil) in 1936. That same year he was appointed General Superintendent of Canadian Airways at Winnipeg and completed an historic 10,000 mile (16,000 km) air survey flight of northern Canada.

Canadian Pacific Railways named Dickins assistant to the President in 1941, then appointed him operations manager of the wartime Atlantic Ferry Service which had the responsibility of delivering by air up to 150 aircraft per month across the North Atlantic to the United Kingdom. In 1942 this operationally successful service was then handed over to the RCAF Ferry Command.

Dickins' unequaled grasp of northern Canadian aviation, with its diverse problems, resulted in his appointment in 1942 as Vice-President and General Manager of Canadian Pacific Airlines. His task was to amalgamate several small, scattered airlines into one cohesive, air transportation network serving western Canada. During this same period he was to oversee the management of six of the many British Commonwealth Air Training Plan (BCATP) schools, which trained approximately 130,000 air crew for the Allied air offensive.

In 1947 Dickins joined de Havilland Aircraft at Toronto, Ontario, as a Director and Vice-President. The company had just unveiled a new design called the 'Beaver', an aircraft that would revolutionize bush flying. During the following two decades he developed a world wide sales organization, second to none in the aviation industry, which sold Canadian-designed and built aircraft in over 60 countries.

Dickins retired from professional flying in 1966 after 45 years in the business and more than one million miles across the uncharted north, often in weather unforgiving of human error. In 1968 he was appointed an Officer of the Order of Canada (O.C.) for his over-all services to the nation in introducing the air age to northwestern Canada. His legendary exploits as a Canadian air pioneer were recognized by the University of Western Ontario and the University of Alberta which conferred upon him Honorary Doctor of Laws Degrees.

Dickens played a major role in establishing Canada's Aviation Hall of Fame in 1973. He was elected by his peers to become the first Chairman of the Board of this prestigious organization. Dickins died at the age of 96 in Toronto, on August 3, 1995.

Clennell Haggerston (Punch) Dickins was inducted as a Member of Canada's Aviation Hall of Fame in 1974.

C.H. 'Punch' Dickins looks at a 600 pound (272 kg) boulder containing about 2,400 ounces (68 kg) of silver. Great Bear Lake, July 1932.

Robert Leslie (Bob) Dodds
(1921 – 1986)

"His sincerity, dedication and persistence to the cause of improving the medical licencing problems in the air line industry have been of major benefit to Canadian aviation."

—Induction citation, 1994

Robert Leslie (Bob) Dodds was born in Stratford, Ontario, on November 19, 1921, and was educated there and at the University of Toronto. He held a Commercial Pilot's Licence prior to World War II, and flew for Dominion Skyways Air Observer School at Malton Airport during much of the war. He joined the Royal Canadian Air Force (RCAF) in 1944, and in order to get an opportunity to see action at that late date, he transferred to the Royal Navy Fleet Air Arm (RNFAA). He retired at the end of the war with the rank of Sub-Lieutenant. In 1946 he joined Trans-Canada Airlines (TCA, Hall of Fame 1974) and flew his entire career out of their Toronto base.

He became Chairman of the Canadian Air Line Pilot's Association (CALPA, Belt of Orion 1988) Aeromedical Committee in 1966. At that time the industry's attitude toward medical re-certification was very restrictive. A pilot had to meet all of the medical standards or he would be grounded; no debate or appeal was allowed. Throughout his career, Dodds

Robert Dodds fought hard to change a rule which prevented Canadian pilots, who were grounded for medical reasons, from regaining their licences, even if they could later pass a medical examination.

had always been dedicated to aviation safety but he found that the medical requirements were grossly over-restrictive. He felt that flexibility could be granted in many instances without risk, and licencing authorities should not maintain standards that were outdated, but seek to broaden them as prudently as experience and new knowledge allowed.

Dodds became dedicated to improving the medical licencing situation and from 1966 until he retired in 1981, spent most of his time working toward change. It was a long uphill struggle as the official attitude was well entrenched. However, with a quiet persistence, he began to change the official thinking. He found precedents from the practices in other countries, and learned that where preventive medicine, rather than mere examination for fitness, was employed, fewer pilots were grounded. He attended many medical meetings, sought support for his views from the medical profession and enlisted help from a number of distinguished physicians whose views were the same as his. The eventual success of the crusade was due, to a considerable extent, to the active assistance that he was able to obtain from medical experts.

Dodds wrote many papers and presented them to medical meetings, the Minister of Transport, airline management, the International Federation of Air Line Pilots Association (IFALPA), and the International Civil Aviation Organization (ICAO). He frequently went to Ottawa to confer with senior personnel in Transport Canada and the Department of Health and Welfare. He was made the Chairman of the IFALPA Medical Study Group in 1973, and became influential internationally, as well as in Canada. For a number of years he was away from home several days per month, usually on his own time, attending meetings or representing pilots. He was always well prepared.

Dodds' sincerity, dedication and persistence began to show results. An Aeromedical Review Board was established in Canada, and some pilots who had been medically grounded were re-certified following reviews. This was the case most often when the individuals had the support of their airline. A degree of flexibility was introduced to the regulations. Major airlines such as Air Canada began to apply preventive medicine principles. On Dodds'

recommendation, incapacitation training which enabled crews to recognize, and to act, when one of their members became subtly incapacitated, was begun using simulators.

Largely on his recommendation, CALPA organized Pilot Assistance Committees at all pilot bases to assist pilots who were having job-threatening problems. These committees developed procedures and skills useful in assisting pilots who were suffering from drug or alcohol abuse. Dodds consistently emphasized the costs to the airlines and the industry of unnecessary groundings, since by the time a pilot becomes a senior captain, his airline has invested heavily in his training and competency.

Dodds was a recognized world authority on pilot medical problems. Both IFALPA and CALPA presented him with their respective Scrolls of Merit for his outstanding contributions to flight safety, and in 1981 he was awarded CALPA's prestigious Founder's Flight Safety Award. He was among the first group of Air Canada employees to be presented with the Award of Excellence.

In 1981, when he retired as chairman of the Aeromedical Committee, the committee had expanded to include representatives from every pilot base across the country. The major beneficiaries of Dodds' life's work were the pilots whose careers were threatened by minor medical disability, and the airlines which were spared the expense of terminating pilots unnecessarily.

Dodds was one of the first pilots to be re-certified after learning he had cancer in 1980. He was reinstated and was able to return to the line on the L-1011 for two months prior to his normal retirement from Air Canada in 1981. He died in Toronto in October of 1986.

Robert Leslie Dodds was inducted as a Member of Canada's Aviation Hall of Fame in 1994.

John Talbot (Jack) Dyment
(b. 1904)

John Talbot Dyment, C.M., B.A.Sc., LL.D., was born in Barrie, Ontario, on November 23, 1904. He moved to Toronto in 1912 and was educated there. His deep interest in aviation began at the age of nine while watching a Wright biplane fly near Daytona, Florida. He attended the University of Toronto, graduating with a degree in mechanical engineering in 1929. During his university years he learned to fly at the Royal Canadian Air Force (RCAF) Station at Camp Borden, Ontario, during the summer. He was awarded the Sword of Honour as top cadet at the time he received his wings. He was also very active in the field of sports, winning 36 medals in various athletics, including track, wrestling, shooting, and Canadian championships in fencing. In 1927 he performed the first delayed parachute jump in Canada, free-falling 1,000 feet (305m) before opening the parachute.

Following graduation from university he learned his trade by working for the Aviation Division of the Ford Motor Company in the United States, as well as the Aeronautical Engineering Division of both the Department of National Defence and the newly formed Department of Transport. It was during this period he gained invaluable knowledge and experience in the fields of stress analysis, aerodynamics, propulsion and air worthiness approval. He also assisted

TCA was re-named Air Canada in 1965. Under Jack Dyment's guidance the engineering department gained a reputation for serviceability and reliability, in addition to conceiving and introducing over one hundred firsts in the world of air transportation.

"His fifty years of dedicated service applied with superior knowledge and determination for the advancement of commercial aviation in the land of his birth and around the world have substantially benefitted Canadian aviation." —Induction citation, 1988

Bob Noorduyn on the original performance calculations for the Norseman aircraft.

In 1938 he was appointed Chief Engineer of Trans-Canada Airlines (TCA, Hall of Fame 1974), a position he held for 30 years. During this time the airline grew to become the sixth largest in the world and saw great advances in the technology used to operate aircraft.

Dyment's team of engineers at TCA faced many challenges in adapting airplanes designed in warmer climates to fly effectively in the colder weather zones in Canada. A few of the problems they dealt with were: preventing ice build-up on leading surfaces, protecting propeller blades against icing, redesigning carburetor intake systems to prevent or reduce icing, and preventing condensation of moisture which affected electrical controls. Additional projects included the development of lubricants which would not congeal, and flexible hoses which would not harden and crack in extreme cold.

Dyment's knowledge and practical application of aeronautical technology has been recognized world wide. He has been chairman of a number of prestigious international symposiums. Three of these were: 1950, Chairman of the first international conference on turbine powered air transports; 1953, Chairman of the International Air Transport Association's first international symposium on helicopters; and in 1961, Chairman of the first international meeting on supersonic air transports.

Up to the time of his retirement from Air Canada in 1968 he had been invited to present some 70 scholarly papers in Canada, the United States, England and Europe. These dealt with such topics as air transport design and operations, airline organization, and engineering education. He is the only non-American to be appointed as a consultant by the government of the U.S.A. to recommend civil aviation research and development programs for that country. In 1964 he was elected President of the U.S. Society of Automotive Engineers, the only non-American so elected.

In 1973 Dyment received an Honorary Doctor of Laws Degree at the Centenary Convocation of the University of Toronto, and in 1981 he was inducted into the University of Toronto's Engineering Hall of Distinction. He is a Fellow of several organizations and societies, including: the Royal Aeronautical Society, the Canadian Aeronautics and Space Institute, the Society of Automotive Engineers, and the Canadian Academy of Engineering. He is a life member of the Engineering Institute of Canada, the Order of Engineers of Quebec and a number of alumni associations. He is also an Honorary Member of the Canadian Air Line Pilots Association (CALPA, Belt of Orion 1988). In 1991 Dyment was named a Member of the Order of Canada (C.M.) for his service to Canadian aviation.

John Talbot (Jack) Dyment was inducted as a Member of Canada's Aviation Hall of Fame in 1988.

Maurice D'Arcy Allen Fallow
(1913 – 1971)

"His dedication to the flight and safety training of young pilots and the growth of the Edmonton Flying Club was of great benefit to Canadian aviation"

—Induction citation, 1992

Maurice D'Arcy Allen Fallow was born on September 5, 1913, in Vermilion, Alberta. In 1937 he received his Private Pilot's Licence under the direction of Maurice 'Moss' Burbidge (Hall of Fame 1974) at the Edmonton and Northern Alberta Aero Club.

In 1942 he joined the Royal Canadian Air Force (RCAF). When he had completed his training, he became an instructor and served at Nos. 9, 16, and 6 Service Flying Training Schools.

At the end of the war in 1945, Fallow returned to Edmonton, Alberta, and founded Western Aero Motive which offered flying training and aircraft maintenance. The next year he established a flying school at Vermilion and barnstormed the country fair circuit in eastern Alberta.

In February 1967, a disastrous fire destroyed the Edmonton Flying Club. Fifteen aircraft and all of the Club's assets were lost— everything the Club had built up since it was formed in 1928 as the Edmonton and Northern Alberta Aero Club. Fallow's leadership qualities showed when he was able to have the Club back in operation within a few days, operating out of a trailer and using borrowed training aircraft.

Left to right: W.W. Fowler, F.I. Young, J.T. Dyment (seated in model's cabin), W.W. Stull, J.T. Bain, F.M. McGregor, M.B. Barclay, J.H. Tudhope with mock-up of 'North Star'. Winnipeg, 1944.

In 1948 Fallow joined the Edmonton Flying Club as its Secretary-Manager, and served the club with great distinction until his death in 1971. During this period he was awarded the Yorath Trophy eight times in the period from 1950 to 1958. The Yorath Trophy was originated and sponsored by Dennis K. Yorath (Hall of Fame 1974) while he was President of the Royal Canadian Flying Clubs Association (RCFCA) during 1947 – 1949. Its purpose was to stimulate, at the management level, active competition among flying clubs across Canada. The trophy was presented annually by the RCFCA to the Flying Club Manager who best utilized the facilities of his club.

As proof of Fallow's administrative ability, the Edmonton Flying Club's membership grew from 154 to 1,500 members, becoming the largest flying club in Canada. He won the RCFCA Best Club Bulletin Shield ten times in the period from 1950 – 1967 for the Edmonton Flying Club's 'Slipstream' publication, judged most effective in communicating with club membership.

As well as excelling in the field of administration, Fallow remained a top flight instructor, setting the standards for the training of Air Cadets on scholarships from the Air Cadet League of Canada (Belt of Orion 1989). He was also capable of leading prospective pilots from ab initio training to Airline Transport Ratings. He maintained his Senior Commercial Pilot's Licence up to the time of his death.

In 1951 Fallow became the first Canadian to be elected President of the International Northwest Aviation Council (INAC). His promotion of flight training and safety was recognized when he was awarded the RCFCA Gold Medal in 1959.

Fallow died suddenly in Edmonton on May 22, 1971. In 1975 he was posthumously named one of the first recipients of INAC's Roll of Honour Award for his promotion of the field of aviation, and particularly the public's understanding and acceptance of aviation's value to the community.

Maurice D'Arcy Allen Fallow was inducted as a Member of Canada's Aviation Hall of Fame in 1992.

John Emilius (Johnny) Fauquier
(1909 – 1981)

John Emilius (Johnny) Fauquier, D.S.O.**, D.F.C., was born in Ottawa, Ontario, on March 19, 1909, educated at Ashbury College and then entered the investment business in Montreal, Quebec, where he joined a local flying club. After earning his Commercial Pilot's Licence he formed Commercial Airways at Noranda, Quebec. Prior to World War II, he had flown some 3,000 hours as pilot-in-command on bush operations.

Fauquier joined the Royal Canadian Air Force (RCAF) in 1939 as a Flight Lieutenant, completed an advanced course and served until mid-1941 instructing a group of British Commonwealth Air Training Plan (BCATP) instructors. After a short period in England at a glider and paratrooper training centre, he was posted to 405 Squadron and by February, 1942 had been promoted to Wing Commander and given command of the squadron. He was awarded the Distinguished Flying Cross (D.F.C.) for gallantry.

Shortly afterwards, Fauquier was seconded from operations to the RCAF's Overseas Headquarters for staff duties. He then served a short term with No. 6 Bomber Group, RCAF, before once again taking command of 405 Squadron. In 1943 he

In 1940 Fauquier was one of many civilians who were contacted by Canada's Minister of National Defence to teach instructors at the RCAF Military Base at Trenton, Ontario, through the BCATP. He left behind a charter operation in the lower St. Lawrence region, and then went on to become one of the RCAF's outstanding bomber pilots.

Maury Fallow (on right), Manager of the Edmonton Flying Club, receives the Yorath Trophy from Dennis K. Yorath. 1954.

"His exceptional abilities as an airman and wartime operations commander set the highest standard of leadership and dedication to purpose and caused those whom he led to excel themselves, resulting in outstanding contributions to Canadian aviation." —Induction citation, 1974

was promoted to Group Captain for his leadership of that squadron, which had become a member of 8 Pathfinder Group.

On the night of August 17, 1943, Fauquier led an epic raid on the German rocket base at Peenemunde on the Baltic coast. He acted as deputy master bomber, making 17 passes over the target, guiding the waves of bombers to it. The base was destroyed, which delayed the use of these rockets by a full year. He was awarded the Distinguished Service Order (D.S.O.) with the following citation:

"This officer is a first-class leader whose skillful and courageous example has proved most inspiring. His sterling qualities were well illustrated during an operation against Peenemunde one night in August and again a few nights later in an attack on Berlin. Group Captain Fauquier has displayed boundless energy and great drive and has contributed, in large measure, to the high standard of operational efficiency of the squadron he commands."

During January 1944, Fauquier completed his second tour of operations with 405 Squadron after flying 38 sorties. He was then awarded a Bar to his D.S.O. with the accompanying citation:

"This officer has commanded the squadron with notable success during the past nine months. He has frequently taken part in sorties against distant and well-defended targets, including several attacks on the German capital. He is a forceful and gallant leader whose outstanding ability and unswerving devotion to duty have been reflected in the fine operational work performed by the whole squadron. Group Captain Fauquier has set an example of the highest order."

In June 1944, after promotion to Air Commodore, which rank precluded his flying on operations, Fauquier voluntarily reverted to Group Captain so that he might begin a third tour of operations.

This time he served as Commanding Officer of 617 (Dambuster) Squadron, Royal Air Force, which he led from December 1944. Subsequently he led them on raids against submarine pens, viaducts and the last of the German battleships, the Tirpitz. Under his command 617 Squadron dropped the first 22,000 pound (9,980 kg) 'Grand Slam' bombs from Lancaster bombers. To conserve the bombs, Fauquier developed the tactic of flying low near the target while the squadron released several bombs. As soon as the target was hit, he signaled the remaining bombers to return to base, with their bomb loads intact.

At the end of the war in Europe, Fauquier was awarded a second Bar to his D.S.O., the equivalent of three D.S.O.'s. He was the only Canadian officer to be so decorated, receiving the following citation:

"Since assuming command of 617 Squadron in December 1944, this officer has taken part in almost all of the aerial sorties to which the formation has been committed.

Early in February 1945, Group Captain Fauquier led the squadron in an attack on the U-boat pens at Poortshaven. Photographs obtained showed that the bombing was accurate and concentrated. Since then, this officer has participated in a number of sorties, during which the railway viaduct at Bielefeld, a railway bridge over the river Weser at Bremen, and a viaduct, were all rendered unusable to the enemy. By this brilliant leadership, undoubted skill and iron determination, this officer played a good part in the successes obtained. He has rendered much loyal and valuable service."

The government of France awarded Fauquier the Croix de Guerre with Palm and named him a Chevalier of the Legion of Honour. At war's end he returned to private business. He died in Toronto on April 3, 1981.

John Emilius (Johnny) Fauquier was inducted as a Member of Canada's Aviation Hall of Fame in 1974.

Group Captain J. Fauquier sits atop a 22,000 lb. (9,980 kg) 'Grand Slam' bomb which was used during the closing days of WWII. Targets were submarine pens, viaducts and bridges. 1945.

both the CF-100 and CF-105 projects, two outstanding first-line fighters, designed and built in Canada. In the same year he was invited by the Royal Aeronautical Society to give the Fourteenth British Commonwealth Lecture in London, England, where he presented a paper on the design and development of the Arrow.

Following the cancellation of the Arrow project in February 1959, Floyd went to England and was appointed Chief Engineer of an elite group of British and ex-Avro Canada engineers to undertake studies in state-of-the-art aeronautical and space projects at Hawker Siddeley Aviation's Advanced Project Group in England. One of these studies led to the British government's funding of the Concorde project. For his work, and papers on the problems of designing supersonic passenger aircraft, he was awarded the Royal Aeronautical Society's George Taylor Gold Medal in 1961.

In 1962 he formed his own aviation consulting firm of J.C. Floyd and Associates, serving international aviation interests, including a number of major Canadian companies. He was retained by the British government as a consultant on the Concorde project during the eight years of its development from 1965 to 1972.

After his retirement in 1980, he and his family returned to Canada. Since that time he has dedicated himself to encouraging young Canadians to re-light the flame of technological enthusiasm which will once again put Canada among the leading nations in aerospace technology.

For many years Floyd was Patron of the Aerospace Heritage Foundation of Canada and a director of the International Hypersonic Research Institute in the United States. In 1988 he was presented with a Lifetime of Achievement Award by the Aerospace Industries Association of Canada. Other awards include Fellowships in the Royal Aeronautical Society, the Canadian Aeronautics and Space Institute, and the American Institute of Aeronautics and Astronautics.

James Charles (Jim) Floyd was inducted as a Member of Canada's Aviation Hall of Fame in 1993.

Norman Gladstone (Norm) Forester

(1898 – 1975)

Norman Gladstone (Norm) Forester was born in Oakville, Ontario, on March 21, 1898. He was educated there and in Vernon, British Columbia, where his family moved when he was ten years old. He joined the Canadian Army Medical Corps in 1916 and served in England until the following year when he transferred to the Royal Flying Corps. He completed his aerial training and graduated as a commissioned officer, then flew as a pilot with the Royal Air Force. He returned to Canada in 1919 and turned to other pursuits until 1928, when he accepted a temporary commission with the Royal Canadian Air Force (RCAF). He proceeded to Camp Borden Military Base, Ontario, for a refresher course. He reported to Squadron Leader R.S. Grandy (Hall of Fame 1988) and learned to fly seaplanes. He also studied navigation and aerial photography.

Forester's first base of operations in 1929 was at Senneterre, Quebec, when the RCAF was mapping the province extensively from the air. The following year he resigned his commission after an offer by Leigh Brintnell (Hall of Fame 1976), General Manager of Western Canada Airways, to join this company as a commercial pilot. He reported to Don MacLaren (Hall of Fame 1977), who was Superintendent of the company's Vancouver base.

Forester wanted to become a doctor, but World War I intervened. In 1917, while serving with the Medical Corps in France, he saw an enticing recruiting poster, and immediately volunteered for flying training with the Royal Flying Corps. For the next 40 years, his career involved flying.

"The application of his superior skills in aerial mapping and his mercy flights to aid others, despite adversity, have been of outstanding benefit to Canadian aviation."

—Induction citation, 1974

Norman G. Forester beside Junkers of Canadian Airways Ltd. At Carcross, south of Whitehorse, Yukon. 1929.

Forester's first duty was the spraying of Stanley Park at Vancouver, British Columbia, with fellow pilot Jack Moar (Hall of Fame 1974), to destroy a severe caterpillar infestation. His next assignment was to fly the coastal and fisheries patrols of that province. When the fisheries work was completed for the season, he was transferred to Winnipeg, Manitoba, where his duties included flying the night mail run to Regina and Moose Jaw, Saskatchewan, air freighting ore concentrates from Manitoba mines, and flying forestry patrols.

During the winter of 1931-1932, Forester was based at Norway House at the north end of Lake Winnipeg. He flew supplies to Hudson's Bay posts in northern Manitoba and brought out ore concentrates from northern mines, using a Fokker Super Universal monoplane. In 1932 he was sent to Carcross, Yukon, to transport passengers and supplies into isolated areas. He carried out a number of mercy flights that resulted in the saving of human lives.

After a Canada-wide series of temporary postings, Forester was assigned to Western Canada Airway's Sioux Lookout base in Ontario, in 1934, flying equipment, supplies, and passengers throughout northern Ontario. In 1935 he was moved to flying operations in northern Manitoba. In 1936 Forester was assigned to carry out a high-altitude photographic survey in northern British Columbia. Operating for extended periods of time at altitudes up to 17,000 feet (5,200 m) in a specially outfitted Fairchild 71, he and Bill Sunderland, air engineer and camera operator, completed the task and returned to Sioux Lookout.

Forester's skills as a high-altitude photographic pilot were used extensively throughout Canada, mostly in northern regions. This was mostly seasonal work, interspersed with operational flying assignments. In 1938 Forester was asked to work full time in aerial photography, and was transferred to Montreal, Quebec, with Bill Kahre as his air engineer and camera operator, again using a Fairchild 71. This team also completed photographic surveys in the Maritimes.

After the outbreak of World War II Forester was seconded to instruct young student pilots in navigation at No. 2 Air Observer School at Edmonton, Alberta, a school managed by W.R. 'Wop' May (Hall of Fame 1974). A year later he returned to aerial survey duties in Quebec and Newfoundland with Canadian Pacific Airlines (CPA), which had absorbed Canadian Airways Limited, which earlier had taken over Western Canadian Airways.

In January 1943, Forester was called by the United States Army to rescue the crew of an American Army C-87, a cargo variant of the B-24 bomber, which had been forced to land on a snow covered lake in northern Quebec almost three weeks before. The American Army did not have the capability of rescuing this crew although many planes were involved in the search. A US Army C-47, which had tried to rescue the bomber crew, was unable to take off on its wheels and was stuck in the deep snow. Those requiring rescue now included the crew of the C-47. Forester and his engineer, Norman Crewe, flew to the site in a Barkley Grow on skis and rescued the twenty men in two difficult flights. For this successful mission they were awarded the United States Air Medal.

During the next six years Forester continued in his role as an aerial photographic pilot throughout eastern Canada, until he was offered a Captain's position with CPA. From 1949 until his retirement nine years later, he flew DC-3's on scheduled airline flights throughout eastern Canada and Alberta. Forester died in Edmonton, October 4, 1975.

Norman Gladstone Forester was inducted as a Member of Canada's Aviation Hall of Fame in 1974.

Robert Howden (Bob) Fowler
(b. 1922)

Robert Howden (Bob) Fowler, O.C., was born in Toronto, Ontario, on September 19, 1922, where he received his education. He was employed at Maclean Hunter Limited from 1939 to 1942, and during that time he learned to fly in a J-3 Cub at Barker Field, Toronto.

He joined the Royal Canadian Air Force (RCAF) in July 1942. After graduating from training as a Pilot Officer at Moncton, New Brunswick, in 1943, he was posted to England. There he served with 226 Squadron in the 2nd Tactical Air Force (TAF) of the Royal Air Force and completed 48 missions flying B-25 Mitchell bombers. Before returning to Canada in 1945 to receive his discharge, he ferried aircraft and instructed at the 2nd TAF Support Unit in the United Kingdom.

Fowler enrolled in the University of Toronto as a law student, but returned to full time flying the following year. He received his Commercial Pilot's Certificate in May 1946, and became Chief Pilot for Dominion Gulf Company of Toronto, carrying out magnetic surveys over northern Quebec and Ontario. Three years later he joined Spartan Air Services at Ottawa, Ontario, and spent the following three years in the Arctic and other

The role of a test pilot carries much responsibility. He is involved with a new aircraft from the moment it has begun as an idea, right on through its early design stages until the moment it is certified to be flown by its purchasers. He is the one who makes sure that nothing has been overlooked in the development of the aircraft before it is certified safe to fly.

"His ability as a pilot, together with his knowledge of flight engineering, has enabled him to provide major contributions to the engineering, flight testing and subsequent development of a family of short take-off and landing aircraft, which has brought his company to world leadership in that specialized field, and which contributions have been of significant benefit to Canadian aviation and to the nation." —Induction citation, 1980

Captain R.H. (Bob) Fowler, right, with Inuit visitor beside DHC-4 'Caribou' aircraft on demonstration tour, Frobisher Bay, N.W.T., February 1961.

parts of Canada engaged in high-altitude photo surveys, flown at 35,000 feet (10,700 m). He carried out airborne geophysical explorations using the magnetometer developed by Dominion Gulf. Fowler flew modified Lockheed P-38's in both of these operations. A photograph taken at 35,000 feet (10,700 m) covers exactly 100 square miles (258 square km).

In 1952 Fowler went to work as a test pilot for de Havilland Aircraft of Canada Limited (DHC). He was involved in flight testing all of the aircraft models manufactured by that company, commencing with the final certification of the last piston-engined aircraft they produced, the Caribou, a twin-engined short take-off and landing aircraft (STOL).

The Trans-Canada (McKee) Trophy, Canada's highest award in aviation, was presented to Fowler in 1974. The citation reads, in part,

"... this work was followed by an extended period of research flight testing, in which the aerodynamic and human factors of fixed-wing, steep gradient approaches and landings were explored, in a research aircraft utilizing modulated jet thrust. The work marked the means by which DHC embarked on the development of its turbine-powered aircraft. He performed the first flight of the prototype PT-6A turboprop engine. He also carried out the first flight and initial development flight testing of the prototype General Electric YT 64 turboprop engine. He also performed the first flight tests and much of the subsequent development testing and certification of the Turbo Beaver, Buffalo and Twin Otter aircraft, all of which have found wide acceptance in world markets."

On March 27, 1975, Fowler carried out the first flight testing of the DHC Dash 7 aircraft and performed much of the subsequent development flight testing. On June 20, 1983, Fowler performed the first flight testing of the first DHC Dash 8/100 airliner and again was involved in much of the follow-up development flight testing. Four years later he took part in the first flight of the Dash 8/300, the 50-passenger stretched version.

Fowler's prominent position in the development of de Havilland's aircraft was not confined solely to experimental flying.

He had a keen interest in, and made significant contributions to, the development of flight controls and propeller systems, helping DHC to become a world leader in the design and production of STOL aircraft.

Between 1972 and 1974, Fowler worked with the United States National Aeronautics and Space Administration's Ames Flight Research Center at Mountview, California. Here he and Seth Grossmith (Hall of Fame 1990) were involved in the creation and flight testing of the Augmentor Wing Jet Research Aircraft. They were two of the Canadians who flew the augmentor wing Buffalo at the Ames Center. The new wing design used an augmentor flap through which air was blown. It also had leading edge slats, and rotatable, thrust-vectoring ducts on the engines. Tests on the Buffalo proved that steep approaches could be made at speeds as low as 55 knots (100 km/h), and takeoffs using as little as 350 feet (106 m) of runway.

During a 49-year career as a professional pilot, mainly in the area of flight testing, Fowler has flown more than 15,000 hours as captain-in-command of some 60 aircraft types. He is a Fellow of the Canadian Aeronautics and Space Institute. In 1975 he was created an Officer of the Order of Canada (O.C.) for his service to the nation. Fowler retired in September of 1987 after 35 years of test flying at de Havilland.

Robert Howden Fowler was inducted as a Member of Canada's Aviation Hall of Fame in 1980.

Walter Warren (Walt) Fowler
(1906 – 1986)

Walter Warren (Walt) Fowler was born in Sackville, New Brunswick, on September 8, 1906. In 1928 he earned a Commercial Pilot's Certificate at the Jack Elliot Flying School in Hamilton, Ontario, under the instruction of Len Tripp (Hall of Fame 1974). International Airways in St.-Laurent, Quebec, hired him as a mechanic in 1929 and transferred him to Windsor, Ontario, attending to air mail service aircraft and supplying hourly weather reports over teletype. Fowler's desire to become a professional pilot led him to undertake two additional jobs that summer: instructing students, and working as night mechanic for the Windsor Flying Club.

Fowler always said that bush flying was the most interesting type of flying he ever did, particularly flying on floats. "Fuel would be cached at various locations, and each lake was like landing at a new airport. We had to study from the air any ridges, rocks and reefs under the surface of the water which would make landings and takeoffs hazardous. Calm waters presented their own problems, and there were many tricks of the trade in getting off with loaded aircraft, and of landing under various conditions. The pilot is on his own, and an aircraft would have to be overdue for three days before a search would be started. Each had his emergency rations and equipment, and was left very much on his own."

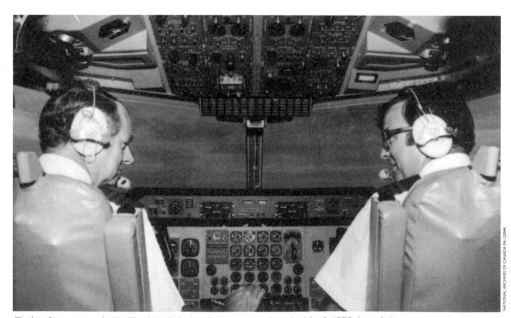

Testing the prototype de Havilland Dash 7 aircraft, Downsview, Ontario, March 1975. In cockpit are Captains R.H. (Bob) Fowler (left), and Tom Appleton.

In 1929, when International Airways merged with Canadian Airways Limited, Fowler was assigned to Detroit, Michigan, the terminus of Canadian Airway's air mail service to Detroit-Windsor. The following year he was moved to Moncton, New Brunswick, as pilot mechanic for the Magdalen Island and Prince Edward Island air services and given operational command of the Moncton Flying Club.

His exceptional flying abilities qualified him to attend an instructor's course with the Royal Canadian Air Force (RCAF) at Camp Borden Military Base, Ontario. On graduation in 1930 he was named Superintendent of the Maritime Region for Canadian Airways, and instructor for the Moncton Flying School. Two years later he was based at Charlottetown, Prince Edward Island, a time in which the company's Maritime routes were upgraded to daily service. During this period he flew scheduled passenger flights between Montreal, Moncton and Charlottetown, and earned his Air Engineer's Licence. Again, Fowler's abilities were recognized by his appointment to the first civilian instrument flying course offered by the RCAF at Camp Borden in 1933.

Bush flying operations out of Senneterre, Quebec, for Canadian Airways were placed under his command in 1937, when he took over the base from Paul Davoud (Hall of Fame 1985). This base was used to provide service to northeastern Ontario and northern and central Quebec. A considerable number of emergency flights were carried out from this base. In October 1937, Fowler resigned his position after ten years with the company. He then applied for a position with Trans-Canada Airlines (TCA, Hall of Fame 1974). He reported to TCA in Winnipeg, Manitoba, and was one of the first six pilots to take flight training. His first line flight was in a Lockheed Electra on November 9, 1937.

With TCA, Fowler flew every Canadian route, including a number of inaugural flights, one being their first scheduled

Walter W. Fowler, one of the first Captains hired by Trans-Canada Airlines, stands beside a Lockheed Electra. 1938.

passenger flight between Montreal and Moncton. Named Flight Superintendent of TCA's Atlantic region 1939, he was transferred to Moncton and became familiarly known as 'Mr. TCA'. In 1942 he inaugurated the Moncton-St. John's, Newfoundland, air service, linking Canada with that island.

In June 1940, he was assigned to TCA's war-time ferry service, flying aircraft into Canada from various American manufacturers to be used at the RCAF training base at Trenton, Ontario. At this time as well, he used his exceptional skills in instrument flight to train American pilots who were scheduled to ferry aircraft across the North Atlantic to the United Kingdom. During this same period he continued his regular scheduled flights with TCA.

In March 1944, Fowler was transferred to Winnipeg as Assistant General Manager and gradually eased himself out of professional flying. The senior appointments that followed utilized his superior knowledge of air operations in the Maritimes, until he became General Manager of the Atlantic region in August 1969.

He retired in 1971 after logging some 10,000 pilot-in-command hours in 41 aircraft types, from World War I trainers to four-engine airliners, without injury to passenger or crew. Fowler died in Moncton on January 19, 1986.

Walter Warren (Walt) Fowler was inducted as a Member of Canada's Aviation Hall of Fame in 1974.

Thomas Payne (Tommy) Fox
(1909 – 1995)

Thomas Payne (Tommy) Fox was born December 24, 1909, in Vancouver, British Columbia, where he attended school. He started his own trucking business and operated a wood and coal supply company. He learned to fly in Vancouver, receiving his Private Pilot's Licence in 1930. The following year he constructed a Pietenpol Air Camper from plans published in a home mechanics magazine, and flew it for several years. It was considered to be one of the first successful 'homebuilts' to be constructed and flown in western Canada.

In 1939 Fox joined Canadian Airways Limited which operated No. 2 Air Observer School in Edmonton for the British Commonwealth Air Training Plan (BCATP). In 1940 he became Assistant Operations Manager, responsible for the supervision and training of pilots. Three and a half years later, he joined No. 45 Group, Royal Air Force Transport Command (RAFTC) as an aircraft ferry pilot. He completed 30 trans-Atlantic crossings, delivering Consolidated B-24 Liberators and Boeing B-17 Flying Fortresses, mostly to the Middle East and India.

At the end of the war, Fox returned to Canada and formed Associated Airways Limited at Edmonton, Alberta, with his partner, David C. Dyck. They had two aircraft, a de Havilland Dragonfly and a Tiger Moth. Fox obtained his Air Engineer's Licence and was Associated Airway's sole aircraft mechanic. In the first few years of operation, the company provided passenger flights, charter flights, and flight instruction, and started a regular flight service to northern Alberta communities.

During the search for oil in Alberta in 1950, Fox saw the potential value of the helicopter to the exploration and surveying phases of the oil industry. Associated Helicopters Limited was formed as a wholly-owned subsidiary, and a Bell 47-D1 was purchased and put into immediate service in the Lesser Slave Lake area in northern Alberta. Additional helicopters were acquired and used in the transport of survey crews and equipment into otherwise inaccessible regions.

In 1951 he purchased Territories Air Services Limited and Yellowknife Airways Limited in the Northwest Territories from Matt Berry (Hall of Fame 1974). By the end of the year Associated Airways had charter bases at Edmonton and Peace River in Alberta, and Fort Smith, Hay River, and Yellowknife in the Northwest Territories.

Fox made a major move in 1952 and bought his first Bristol Freighter, using it to transport heavy equipment into remote mining and oil drilling sites. In 1955

JOHN DAVIES COLLECTION

T.P. 'Tommy' Fox's Bristol Freighter during unloading demonstration at a Convention held in Great Falls, Montana. About 1952 – 53.

Associated Airways was designated the prime contractor to supply the western Arctic section of the Distant Early Warning (DEW) Line. Four Avro Yorks were acquired to undertake the massive airlift of men and materials to the Arctic radar construction sites.

Fox joined the Air Industries and Transport Association (AITA) in 1947 and distinguished himself there with his consummate diplomacy. He was elected to the Board of Directors in 1949, and after serving as Western Vice-President for a number of years, was elected President in 1954. In an unprecedented move, he was re-elected for the 1955 term and under his leadership, the Association played a major role in ensuring that air transport requirements for the construction of the DEW Line would be handled by Canadian civilian operators. The Association's successful efforts in obtaining this agreement added many millions of dollars to the industry at a critical time in its development.

As the company's fleet of aircraft grew, Aero Engineering was acquired as a subsidiary in Edmonton to undertake major overhauls of engines, propellers and airframes, and to perform similar work for other aircraft owners.

In 1956 Associated Airways was sold to Pacific Western Airlines (PWA), and as a director and vice-chairman of the new Board of Directors of PWA, Fox played a leading role in the acquisition of jet aircraft for that company. Fox sold Associated Helicopters to Neonex Group in 1969, but remained with the company

In January 1947, one of Associated Airways' pilots damaged a wing of an Anson aircraft on a flight to Fort Chipewyan, 360 miles (580 km) north of Edmonton. When Fox arrived at the site anxious to recover one of his company's major assets, he saw that nine feet (2.6 m) was broken off one wing. He knew that to save it he would have to fly it out, or it would sink into the lake at spring thaw. After draping a tarpaulin shelter over the undamaged wing tip to provide some shelter from the –50°F (–45°C) temperature, he set to work to equalize the wing balance by cutting nine feet (2.6 m) off that wing. He then patched both wing tips with materials he brought with him. He was able to get the plane airborne and could maintain altitude by keeping the throttles wide open. Near Fort McMurray, Fox was forced to land due to a frozen cross-feed fuel line which prevented him from using the fuel from another tank. For three nights in extremely cold temperatures, he huddled inside his plane until fuel was flown in from Edmonton. He was able to fly to Fort McMurray, switch from skis to wheels and then fly to Edmonton safely. However, the authorities took a dim view of Fox's innovations, and demanded both his pilot's and mechanic's licences. Both were returned to him from Ottawa the following week.

as Chairman of the Board until his retirement in 1971.

Fox was a director of the International Northwest Aviation Council (INAC) for a number of years and was elected Vice-President in 1950. He served as chairman of the Aviation Committee of the Edmonton Chamber of Commerce. He was a Life Member of the Air Transport Association of Canada (ATAC) and the Edmonton Flying Club, of which he was a long-time director. For many years he provided leadership for several community-minded associations and societies in Edmonton. Fox died in Edmonton on September 14, 1995.

Thomas Payne ('Tommy) Fox was inducted as a Member of Canada's Aviation Hall of Fame in 1983.

T.P. 'Tommy' Fox, President of Associated Airways, stands in front of a newly acquired Bristol Freighter. Edmonton, 1952.

James Henry Foy
(1922 – 1974)

James Henry Foy, D.F.C., was born in Brantford, Ontario, on August 8, 1922. With Robert Fowler, (Hall of Fame 1980) he attended Vaughan Road Collegiate in Toronto, Ontario, where he planned to enter university to study international law. On October 24, 1940, he enlisted in the Royal Canadian Air Force (RCAF), trained as a pilot and was posted to England in June of 1941, where he served with Bomber Command of the Royal Air Force (RAF).

Following operational training, Foy flew with 405 and 419 Squadrons, RCAF. He was promoted to commissioned rank in 1942, and within a few months, had completed 31 operational flights on Vickers Wellington bombers. He was awarded the Distinguished Flying Cross (D.F.C.) with the following citation:

> "Flying Officer Foy now on his second tour of operational duties has participated in a large number of operational sorties including the 1,000-bomber raids on Cologne, the Ruhr and Bremen. On two occasions he successfully flew his aircraft home on one engine. On completion of his first operational tour, this officer served for

One of Foy's most memorable flights was in 1973 when he was in command of the Royal Flight from London, England, to Toronto, carrying Her Majesty, Queen Elizabeth II and Prince Philip for a 10-day royal tour. He and his crew were responsible for providing a safe, seven and three-quarter hour flight in a specially styled DC-8 chartered by the Canadian government.

"His exceptional abilities as an aviator in both war and peace, coupled with his exemplary qualities of leadership and dedication to purpose, brought credit to his chosen profession and to the organizations for which he labored, resulting in the advancement of aviation in Canada." —Induction citation, 1980

some time as a pilot instructor. His operational record as a deputy flight commander has been of the highest order."

Foy was seconded from operations and trained as an instructor. He later returned to 405 Squadron which had, in his absence, become a unit of 8 Pathfinder Group, and completed another 15 missions on Halifax bombers.

His Halifax bomber was shot down on July 16, 1943, on his 47th operational sortie while engaged as a 'target lighter'. He and his crew parachuted into German-occupied France, where he spent eight months working with the French underground resistance movement. They convoyed other downed allied air crew members to safety from Paris across the Pyrenees Mountains and Spain, to Gibraltar. He used the same route to make his own escape. On his return to England in April 1944, he was promoted to Flight Lieutenant and was Mentioned in Despatches on two occasions. His work with the French precluded his return to operational flying and he was released from service.

Foy was hired by Trans-Canada Airlines (TCA, Hall of Fame 1974) in August of 1944 as a co-pilot. Two years later he was promoted to Captain. During a 30-year career with TCA and Air Canada, Foy flew all of the fleet's aircraft, from the Lockheed 14 to his final assignment on the DC-8, on all domestic and overseas routes. His total pilot-in-command time exceeded 21,000 hours.

Foy's flying abilities were coupled with numerous contributions to the development of aviation in Canada through organizational work. He served with distinction on a number of committees of the Canadian Air Line Pilot Association (CALPA, Belt of Orion 1988). He was elected President of that organization in 1957, an office he held for five years. He then accepted the position and responsibilities of Deputy-President of the International Federation of Airline Pilots Association (IFALPA) from 1962 to 1964. He was appointed President and served an additional three years. He became the only Canadian elected to head this group, which represented the pilot associations of 65 countries. He took on a number of challenges while serving with CALPA and IFALPA, including work on training standards, medical problems, and remuneration standards. For his contributions to IFALPA he was awarded the Clarence N. Sayen Award in 1969, to recognize outstanding contributions within the Federation.

Foy died in Toronto on April 28, 1974. Two years later he was posthumously awarded CALPA's Ken Wright Memorial Trophy for "outstanding airmanship and professional performance, contributing to the enhancement and image of airline pilots."

James Henry Foy was inducted as a Member of Canada's Aviation Hall of Fame in 1980.

Air Canada Captain J.H. Foy, right, was awarded a Life Membership in the Canadian Air Line Pilots Association in 1962 by CALPA President Captain A.D. Mills.

Wilbur Rounding Franks
(1901 – 1986)

Wilbur Rounding Franks, O.B.E., C.D.*, B.A., M.A., M.D., was born in Weston, Ontario, on March 4, 1901, and received his elementary and secondary education in Regina, Saskatchewan. He graduated from the University of Toronto with a Bachelor of Arts Degree in 1924, his Masters Degree in Physiology in 1925, and three years later he graduated with a Bachelor of Medicine. He then took a rotating internship at the Toronto General Hospital and assisted Dr. Frederick Banting with research projects. During 1930-31, while on sabbatical leave, he undertook post-graduate studies at the University of Zurich, Switzerland, and the University of Munich, Germany.

Upon his return to Canada in September 1931, he resumed his career as a research associate with the Banting and Best

Dr. Wilbur Franks, called 'the father of aviation medicine', has been credited with saving the lives of thousands of fighter pilots. His G-suit, developed in 1942, has been worn by every air force pilot in the world, as well as the astronauts and cosmonauts. He designed the first human centrifuge, and was interested in research to improve the efficiency of oxygen masks worn by pilots at high altitudes, and in the effects on the body during rapid climbs in unpressurized aircraft. While he gained renown around the world for his accomplishments, Franks has been virtually unrecognized in his own country.

"His invention of the Franks Flying Suit and the human centrifuge, which have been accepted throughout the aerospace industry, and his significant contributions to research in aerospace medicine have been of outstanding benefit to Canadian aviation."

—Induction citation, 1983

Department of Medical Research at the University of Toronto, and specialized in cancer research. In 1937 he was appointed an associate professor at the University. During the period 1939-41, he performed defence medical research with Dr. Frederick Banting, and because of the highly secret nature of his work, he was commissioned a Lieutenant in the Royal Canadian Army Medical Corps. When the Royal Canadian Air Force (RCAF) formed its own medical branch, he was transferred to it with the rank of Flight Lieutenant.

Military doctors who studied aviation medicine were aware that the newest fighter and bomber aircraft of the time had exceeded the physical capabilities of the pilots and crews who operated them. Pilots were experiencing G-forces many times the pull of gravity, and were temporarily losing consciousness from the effects of centrifugal force. Dr. Banting was approached to provide assistance, since his fame as co-discoverer of insulin would be certain to result in funding for research.

Franks was a senior researcher on Banting's team, and he began active medical research into solving the problems related to high altitude flying and high G-force manoeuvers. During his cancer research experiments in 1938 he had discovered that he could prevent small test tubes from breaking while being accelerated if he immersed them in larger, stronger, laboratory centrifuge tubes filled with water. He concluded that a similar immersion should protect pilots who are subjected to high radial accelerations and de-accelerations. He designed a protective suit consisting of durable non-stretch fabric containing water filled bladders which fitted over a person's abdomen and legs. The suit automatically exerted counter-pressure by hydrostatic force during high G-force loadings, and proved that the principle was practicable. Franks was the first person to be protected from radial

This photo of the human centrifuge designed by Dr. W.R. Franks, shows the control deck and the gondola at the end of the boom.

acceleration in an aircraft during tests while wearing the Franks Flying Suit.

During this time, Franks was instrumental in procuring facilities for the RCAF No. 1 Clinical Investigation Unit. As early as 1939 he had sketched out the fundamental design for a man-rated centrifuge, consisting of a gondola at the end of a rotating boom. Once Franks' concepts had been laid out, the over-all design and engineering was carried out by members of the Engineering Faculty at the University of Toronto. The end result was the RCAF human centrifuge, the first machine of its kind on the Allied side in the Second World War. The centrifuge was used to produce various G-forces at high speeds, simulating the effect of manoeuvers in combat aircraft. The basic design is still used to train astronauts.

Franks was appointed Director of Aviation Medical Research, RCAF, Overseas, and in March 1941 he proceeded to RCAF Headquarters at London, England. He served with the Royal Air Force (RAF) Physiological Laboratory, and the Royal Aeronautical Establishment at Farnborough. He also served with the Air Fighter Development Unit at Duxford, RAF Fighter Command, and the Fleet Air Arm in connection with the further development and introduction of the G-suit. This was the first G-suit to be used operationally anywhere in the world.

Franks returned to Canada as a Squadron Leader in 1943, and until 1945 he served as Director of the Investigation Section of the RCAF Headquarters Directorate of Medical Services in Ottawa. That appointment was followed by attachment to the RCAF Institute of Aviation Medical Research, National Research Council, Ottawa, correlating the work of both civilian and military research projects being carried out in Canada.

He retired from the RCAF in 1946, but retained his association with the air force in the capacity of Scientific Advisor in Aviation Medicine with the RCAF Institute of Aviation Medicine. He also returned to the Banting and Best Department of Medical Research to continue cancer research on a part-time basis. The remainder of his time was absorbed in the area of aerospace medicine. He published several articles related to his research. He retired from the department in 1969.

For his contributions to the advancement of aerospace medicine, Franks was made an Officer of the Order of the British Empire (O.B.E.) in 1944, and received the United States Legion of Merit in 1946. The Aerospace Medical Association (USA) awarded him the Theodore C. Lyster Award in 1948 for outstanding research in aerospace medicine, and the Eric Liljencrantz Award in 1962 for outstanding research in problems of acceleration and altitude. He was made a Fellow of the Aerospace Medical Association in 1950 and the Canadian Aeronautical Institute in 1960. He was appointed Honorary Physician to the Queen in 1966 and Honorary President of the Canadian Society of Aviation Medicine in 1974.

Franks' interest in the field of aviation continued and in 1976, he co-fostered the development of the Universal Language of Air and Space Operations known as UNIGEN. The Aerospace Linguistic Foundation is developing the language as a response to linguistic problems encountered by modern-day air traffic controllers and air crew on a world-wide basis. He died in Toronto on January 4, 1986.

Wilbur Rounding Franks was inducted as a Member of Canada's Aviation Hall of Fame in 1983.

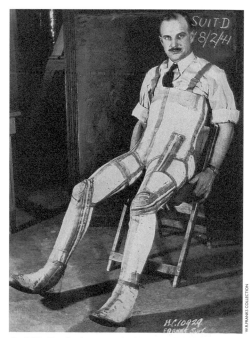

Dr. W.R. Franks demonstrates his design of the Franks Flying Suit in 1941. It was particularly important to prevent the pooling of blood in the abdomen and lower limbs during high G-force manoeuvers, which caused blackouts.

Douglas Cowan Fraser

(1904 – 1990)

Douglas Cowan Fraser, LL.D. (Hon),
was born in St. John's, Newfoundland,
on August 21, 1904, while that island
was still a colony of Britain. His early
education took place at Bishop Field
College in St. John's and following
graduation he attended Framlington
College in Suffolk, England. While there
he made his first flight at Cricklewood
Airport. In 1927 Fraser returned to Canada
and began to work for Curtiss-Reid Aircraft
Manufacturing Company at Cartierville,
Quebec. He earned his Private Pilot's
Licence in 1928 and a Commercial
Licence the following year.

**Douglas Fraser's last flight for Imperial
Airways was with Group Captain D.C.T.
Bennett to locate the crash site of the
aircraft in which Sir Frederick Banting
was killed on February 18, 1941.
Dr. Banting was aboard a Lockheed
Hudson bomber which was being ferried
from Gander to Ireland when it went
down in bad weather near Musgrave
Harbour, south east of Gander.
Dr. Banting, co-discoverer of insulin,
was doing research related to physical
stresses of high G-forces experienced by
pilots in the war. At the crash site, Fraser
recovered Banting's briefcase containing
research papers on his findings. The pilot
of the downed aircraft was rescued by
Carl Burke (Hall of Fame 1982) who was
employed by Canadian Airways Ltd.**

SHELDON LEGROW PHOTO

*D.C. Fraser reminisces at home in St. John's, Newfoundland. Surrounded by souvenirs of the Gipsy Moth era and aerial
surveys, he learns that he has been selected to be inducted as a member of Canada's Aviation Hall of Fame. 1987.*

With the assistance of several St. John's
businessmen, Fraser formed Old Colony
Airways in 1931. During the early 1930's,
facing some of the most difficult and
treacherous flying weather, and with little
financial support, he promoted aviation
throughout Newfoundland. Except in the
cases of mercy flights, there was little
public support for his work, and
government assistance was not
forthcoming.

Using a Curtiss Robin on floats, Fraser
was involved in forestry patrols and
aerial location of squid, capelin and seals
for the Department of Fisheries. He flew
surveying parties, geological expeditions,
mercy flights and aerial searches
throughout Newfoundland.

Fraser began flying for Imperial Airways
in 1934. At the time, the company was
making an aerial survey of Newfoundland
to establish triangulation points for the
Geodetic Survey of Canada. He was
instrumental in the successful completion
of this project. In 1936 Imperial Airways
transferred him to England where he flew
as co-pilot on routes between England,
France, Belgium, Italy and Ireland. He
returned to Newfoundland to prepare for

the trans-Atlantic flying boat operations at
Botwood on the northern shore, and the
subsequent operation of British Overseas
Airways Corporation (BOAC) and Pan
American Airways at Gander,
Newfoundland.

Fraser was responsible for the calibration
of the wireless direction-finding stations at
Botwood and Gander. At the same time he
conducted daily upper air meteorological
flights in support of the trans-Atlantic
operations while stationed at Norris Arm,
near Botwood. His aerial surveys resulted
in the establishment of large military
airports at Stephenville, on the west coast,
and Argentia, on the south coast of
Newfoundland. On his recommendation,
Gander airport, which he had surveyed
with Lord Snowdon Gamble of the British
Air Ministry, was built and he was the first
to land there after its completion.

In 1982 Memorial University of
Newfoundland awarded Fraser an Honorary
Doctor of Laws Degree. He died in
St. John's in 1990.

Douglas Cowan Fraser was inducted as a
Member of Canada's Aviation Hall of Fame
in 1987.

During World War I the need for service men grew more rapidly than living space, and camps like the one pictured here at Rockcliffe, Ottawa, were used as temporary housing. 1916.

Elmer Garfield Fullerton

(1891 – 1968)

Elmer Garfield Fullerton, A.F.C., C.D., was born in Pictou, Nova Scotia, on October 29, 1891, was educated there before attending Royal Military College at Kingston, Ontario. He enlisted in the Royal Canadian Signal Corps in 1915 and spent a year in France before transferring to the Royal Navy Air Service (RNAS) where he learned to fly. Until the end of the war he served as a flying instructor and a fighter pilot, then attended Royal Naval College. On his return to Canada, he became an instructor with the Canadian Air Force (CAF) at Camp Borden, Ontario. While there, he qualified for his Commercial Pilot's Certificate and Air Engineer's Licence.

In 1920 Imperial Oil geologists discovered oil at Fort Norman, near the Mackenzie River in the Northwest Territories. At that time it took weeks or months to reach this far north by railway, then by steamboat or dogsled. The company decided to try the new concept of air transport and purchased two Junkers aircraft. In 1921 Fullerton left the service to join Imperial Oil Limited as a pilot. Almost immediately, the company assigned him to pilot aircraft G-CADP, known as 'Vic', with George Gorman flying G-CADQ, or 'René', on a pioneer flight

Fullerton flew in the Northwest Territories for two years on operational flights and in 1922 was selected to accompany the Norwegian explorer Roald Amundsen as a pilot on a proposed air expedition to the North Pole. Unfortunately, another pilot severely damaged their aircraft in Alaska, forcing cancellation of the flight.

into the Mackenzie River district. They became the first airmen to penetrate that area of Canada. Unfortunately, Gorman suffered two mishaps on attempted take-offs in deep snow, using first one plane and then the other, at Fort Simpson. Skis were damaged during these attempts, but much worse, the propellers of both aircraft were broken beyond repair, stranding the expedition for a possible five months until the Mackenzie River became navigable.

Air engineer William Hill, with the assistance of Walter Johnson, the Hudson's Bay Company carpenter at Fort Simpson, decided to make a propeller for 'Vic'. They found several oak sleigh boards which they laminated with glue made from boiled dried moose hides. After the glue was dry, the wood was carefully carved and sanded to the exact shape that was needed. The process took eight days, and became an internationally-publicized engineering feat which has never been duplicated. Fullerton tested the propeller with the plane on the ground and then made a successful six hour, nonstop flight to the company's southern base at Peace River, Alberta.

In 1923 Fullerton rejoined the CAF as a Flight Lieutenant engaged in airborne fire patrols out of High River, Alberta. Later he was ordered to Vancouver, British Columbia, as a flying-boat pilot for the Canadian Customs and Fisheries Departments. In 1926 he returned to Camp Borden, and after completion of a senior RAF program in England, was named Chief Flying Instructor. His outstanding abilities were recognized by the RAF in 1931 when he was asked to instruct their Fleet Air Arm pilots in carrier deck operations. A posting to the RAF Central Flying School in England was followed by a tour of duty in Egypt grading pilots who were instructing there. He again returned to Camp Borden as Chief Flying Instructor and completed the Royal

Canadian Air Force (RCAF) Staff College course.

Fullerton commanded 7 General Purpose Squadron at Rockcliffe, Ontario, in 1934, teaching both military and civilian pilots the art of instrument flying. In 1935 he was awarded the Trans-Canada (McKee) Trophy for his contribution to Canadian aviation during the preceding year. He was the first permanent member of the RCAF to be so honoured. Until 1938 he served in staff positions before taking command of 1 Fighter Squadron at Trenton, Ontario. He was the first pilot in Canada to test-fly the Hawker Hurricane fighter.

At the outbreak of World War II, Fullerton was assigned to 15 Auxiliary Fighter Squadron, Montreal, Quebec, as instructor in air fighting tactics, then named Senior Air Staff Officer, No. 3 Training Command. From 1941 to 1945 he was Commanding Officer of No. 9 Service Flying Training School at Summerside, Prince Edward Island. During the time he was at Summerside, he was instrumental in developing the familiar blue, maroon and white RCAF tartan which was officially registered on August 15, 1942.

Fullerton was awarded the Air Force Cross (A.F.C.) for meritorious contribution to the British Commonwealth Air Training Plan (BCATP) in training large numbers of air crew. He also received the Canadian Forces Decoration (C.D.). Until his retirement as Group Captain in 1946, he commanded the RCAF Station at Trenton, Ontario. He died in Calgary, Alberta, on March 6, 1968.

Elmer Garfield Fullerton was inducted as a Member of Canada's Aviation Hall of Fame in 1974.

"The application of his exceptional abilities as a pilot and instructor, and his unswerving demand for perfection in flight during a distinguished and dedicated career, have been of outstanding benefit to Canadian aviation." —Induction citation, 1974

Philip Clarke (Phil) Garratt

(1894 – 1974)

Philip Clarke (Phil) Garratt, C.M., A.F.C., was born on Friday, July 13, 1894, in Toronto, Ontario, where he was educated. He left the University of Toronto in 1915 to undertake basic training with the Curtiss Aviation School in Toronto as one of its first students. He earned his pilot's wings with the Royal Flying Corps (RFC) a year later in England. He served for some months with 70 Squadron, RFC, in France as a reconnaissance pilot, before being posted to the Gosport Flying School in England as an instructor, serving in that capacity until the end of the war. He was awarded the Air Force Cross (A.F.C.) for his services.

When W.G. Barker and W.A. Bishop (both Hall of Fame 1974) formed a commercial flying service in 1920, Garratt obtained a Civilian Aviator's Licence and was hired as a pilot. He did some barnstorming with the company, but the firm was not successful. He joined the Canadian Air Force as an instructor at Camp Borden, Ontario, but left the service the following year to enter the chemical business. He maintained his flying interest with a part-time job as test and ferry pilot for de Havilland Aircraft Canada (DHC) at Toronto until 1936, when he became Managing Director of the company.

For many years Phil Garratt had dreamed of producing the ideal bush plane—one that would be built for the Canadian operator's requirements. Bush pilots were canvassed from coast to coast and their recommendations tallied closely with his own. He incorporated their opinions, and the result was the prototype Beaver, which became an unqualified success.

"His fathering of a series of short take-off and landing aircraft, each of which gained world-wide acceptance, has been of outstanding benefit to Canadian aviation." —Induction citation, 1974

P.C. (Phil) Garratt, left, Chairman of the Board of de Havilland Canada, shown handing over logbooks of the first DHC-3 'Otter' aircraft delivered to the Indonesian Air Force. Downsview, Ontario. 1958.

Quick to recognize the value of opening up Canada's northland for the exploration and development of natural resources, Garratt concentrated DHC's efforts on modifying their production aircraft to operate in this new environment. The Moth series had already been adapted for float operations. Under his direction, the Dragonfly and Dragon Rapide were successfully put to use as sturdy and rugged bush planes. Then he turned his attention to re-tooling the British parent company's highly successful training plane, the Tiger Moth, for use by the Royal Canadian Air Force (RCAF). DHC produced 1,747 of these training aircraft during the Second World War. As well, he managed to produce more than 1,000 Mosquito fighter-bombers, and assemble 375 Avro Anson aircraft.

During the post-war period, the demand for a modestly-priced bush aircraft led Garratt to order the design and construction of a modified Fox Moth. He promoted production of the Chipmunk trainer, which served the air forces of many countries and remained the basic training aircraft of the RCAF for two decades.

In 1947 his foresight led to de Havilland's construction of the Beaver, the most successful work aircraft in Canadian history. More than 1,600 were built and, under the direction of C.H. 'Punch' Dickins and Russ

Bannock (both Hall of Fame 1974), sold to 65 countries for both civil and military use. This success was followed by production of the Otter, Caribou, Buffalo, Twin Otter, and the 4-engined Dash-7, all short take-off and landing aircraft (STOL), which earned DHC a world-wide reputation.

Garratt received many honours and awards for his dedication and effort towards the improvement of aviation in Canada. He was chosen to receive the Trans-Canada (McKee) Trophy for 1951 for his distinguished aviation accomplishments. In 1960 he received the Canadian Aeronautics and Space Institute's McCurdy Award, and in 1966 he was named recipient of the Trans-Canada (McKee) Trophy for the second time, in recognition of his fifty years' contribution to aviation in Canada.

He retired as Chairman of the Board of de Havilland Aircraft Company in 1965, retaining a seat as Director until his full retirement in 1971, after a half-century as a pilot and aviation executive. In 1971 he was made a Member of the Order of Canada (C.M.). Garratt died in Toronto on November 16, 1974.

Philip Clarke Garratt was inducted as a Member of Canada's Aviation Hall of Fame in 1974.

Walter Edwin Gilbert

(1899 – 1986)

Walter Edwin Gilbert was born in Cardinal, Ontario, on March 8, 1899, and was educated there. In 1917 he enlisted in the Royal Flying Corps (RFC) at Toronto, Ontario, received his pilot's wings and was posted to the RFC's Central Flying School in England. At the height of the German offensive in 1918, he was sent to France as a front line fighter pilot with RFC Squadrons 56 and 32, and was invalided back to Canada the following year with disabilities.

During the next seven years Gilbert flew only occasionally, updating his skills with the Canadian Air Force at Camp Borden, Ontario. He co-founded the International Air Force Club at Vancouver, British Columbia in 1923, which became the Aero Club of B.C. and an original unit of the Royal Canadian Flying Clubs Association (RCFCA). In 1927 he flew forestry patrols in Manitoba and aerial mapping assignments in northern Saskatchewan as a pilot with the newly created Royal Canadian Air Force (RCAF).

Gilbert was invited to join Western Canada Airways, formed in 1926 by James A. Richardson (Hall of Fame 1976). He was the youngest pilot in the company. His first posting was to Cranberry Portage, Manitoba, then to Vancouver for a year on charter work, fishery patrols, and freighting equipment into the mountainous areas of Alaska.

Gilbert's wife, Jeanne, was the first woman to receive her Private Pilot's Licence in British Columbia, successfully completing her tests on December 6, 1929. The Gilberts were believed to be the only husband and wife to hold pilot's licences at that time.

"His challenging flights into the high Arctic under the most primitive conditions, to explore and record unmapped areas, despite adversity, have been of outstanding benefit to Canadian aviation." —Induction citation, 1974

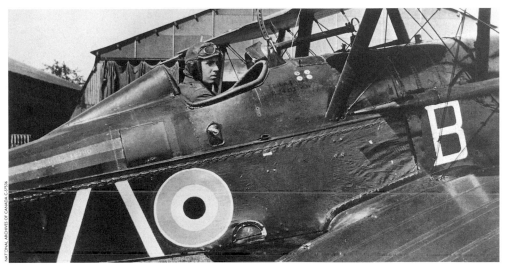

W.E. Gilbert, in his late teens, seated in an SE 5a aircraft of the Royal Air Force. The SE 5a was built by Royal Aircraft of England, and vied with the Sopwith Camel for the title of the most successful British fighter of World War I. c. 1916.

Fort McMurray, Alberta, was Gilbert's base of operations for the next five years. He flew the first freight into the Great Bear Lake radium discovery site with C.H. 'Punch' Dickins (Hall of Fame 1974), and subsequently flew out the radio-active concentrates that would later be used in nuclear fission experiments. He became a seasoned northern pilot with a surveyor's eye for topographical detail.

In the summer of 1930 Gilbert was named pilot of a government-sponsored aerial expedition to the high Arctic, flying Canadian Airways' Fokker G-CASK with Major L.T. Burwash as the leader of the expedition. They accomplished several tasks: recording the magnetic properties near King William Island, checking the location of the North magnetic pole, finding old campsites of the ill-fated Franklin expedition that had vanished 80 years earlier, and photographing and mapping a major stretch of the Arctic coastline.

For his survey and photographic work, as well as flying to the North Magnetic Pole, Gilbert was honoured with a Fellowship in the Royal Geographic Society and was named a Fellow of the Royal Canadian Geographic Society in 1932. He was also made a member of the Explorers Club.

At Aklavik, Northwest Territories, in 1931, Gilbert met Mr. and Mrs. Charles Lindbergh during their flight to the Orient. He was able to help them get their heavily loaded

Lockheed float plane off the glassy waters of the Mackenzie River by using his Fokker Super Universal to roughen the water. That same year Canadian Airways Ltd. expanded by absorbing Western Canada Airways. In 1934 Gilbert piloted the first airmail flight from Cameron Bay on Great Bear Lake, to Coppermine on the Arctic coast, opening the first post office on the Arctic Ocean. In March 1934, it was announced that Gilbert would receive the Trans-Canada (McKee) Trophy for 1933 in recognition of his exploratory flights in northern Canada.

Prince Albert, Saskatchewan, was his next base of operations until 1938, the year he was transferred to Vancouver as District Manager of Canadian Airways. When Canadian Pacific Airlines was formed in 1942 by the absorption of a number of smaller companies, among them Canadian Airways, Gilbert was appointed Superintendent of the Edmonton district in 1943. A year later he retired from northern aviation service, took an extended holiday and in 1951 moved to Washington State to supervise an aerial spraying company until his retirement.

During his aviation career he flew 37 aircraft types and penetrated deeper into the unknown Arctic than any Canadian airman before him. Gilbert died on October 18, 1986.

Walter Edwin Gilbert was inducted as a Member of Canada's Aviation Hall of Fame in 1974.

Albert Earl Godfrey

(1890 – 1982)

Albert Earl Godfrey, M.C., A.F.C., was born in Killarney, Manitoba, on July 27, 1890. He grew up in Vancouver, British Columbia, where he attended school, and joined the 6th Regiment, Duke of Connaught's Own Rifles in 1902 as a drummer boy and bugler. Godfrey enlisted in the 11th Canadian Mounted Rifles in 1915 and was soon transferred to the 1st Canadian Mounted rifles. He was transferred to the 1st Canadian Pioneer Battalion to embark for England, and the following year was commissioned as a Lieutenant Observer with the Royal Flying Corps (RFC). He was assigned to combat in France with 10 Army Co-operation Squadron and 23 Fighter Squadron, RFC, and shortly after was credited with downing two enemy aircraft.

Pilot training in England followed in 1917 with W.G. Barker (Hall of Fame 1974). Godfrey then joined 40 Squadron, RFC, and within nine months had destroyed 13 ½ enemy aircraft and two observation balloons. For these victories he was awarded the Military Cross (M.C.).

In accordance with strict military rules and the legalities of government responsibility, A.E. Godfrey had to go on leave from the RCAF and take part in the McKee trans-Canada flight as a civilian. That in itself held implications, for if the project were to come to grief, it would be damaging to his already established and promising military career. Godfrey realized the full implications but pressed forward with the plans to demonstrate the feasibility of a seaplane route across Canada.

"His record can be matched only by those airmen of high endeavor and professional calling, who have devoted their lives and skills to the benefit of the free world, despite adversity, and whose contributions have substantially benefitted Canadian aviation."

—*Induction citation, 1978*

While serving with this unit he designed a mounting for twin machine guns on his Nieuport aircraft, the first single-seater fighter to be so equipped in France. His last operational flying assignment was in September 1917, as a night fighter pilot with 44 Squadron, the Home Defence Unit of the RFC in England. In this role he flew a Sopwith Camel against enemy zeppelins and bombers attacking London.

Promoted to the rank of Squadron Leader in 1918, Godfrey was named Commander of the School of Aerial Fighting at Beamsville, Ontario. For meritorious service he was awarded the Air Force Cross (A.F.C.). At war's end he retired from the service and joined the Civil Aviation Branch of the Government of Canada. He flew fishery patrols along the Pacific Coast, and as a civilian pilot, earned both an Air Engineer's Certificate and Commercial Pilot's Licence in 1921. In 1922 he was recalled to service in the newly formed Canadian Air Force, and took command of the Vancouver unit as Squadron Leader when the RCAF came into being two years later.

While serving with Air Force Headquarters at Ottawa, Ontario, Godfrey was assigned in 1926 to accompany an American sportsman, J. Dalzell McKee, on the first flight of a seaplane across Canada. Using the fueling and servicing facilities of the RCAF bases spaced across the nation, and the Ontario Provincial Air Service (Belt of Orion 1991), the flight in McKee's Douglas seaplane began September 11 in Montreal, Quebec, and was completed September 19 in Vancouver, British Columbia. In nine days Godfrey and McKee covered 3,000 miles (4,800 km), in 35 flying hours. They established three Canadian flight records: it was the first time one aircraft of any type had flown all the way across Canada; it was the first time a seaplane made such a flight; and it was the first time an airplane of any type had flown nonstop across the Rockies from Edmonton to Vancouver.

In appreciation for the service rendered to him by the RCAF, Mr. McKee presented and endowed the Trans-Canada Trophy. This award was created in 1927 to honour airmen who were considered by a panel of judges to have contributed most substantially to the advancement of Canadian aviation in any given year. The first recipient of the trophy was H.A. Oaks (Hall of Fame 1974) for the year 1927.

In September 1928, Godfrey flew a Fairchild seaplane carrying the first official trans-Canada airmail from Ottawa to Vancouver, making the trip in three days. He served in various posts until the outbreak of World War II, when he was promoted to Air Commodore and given command of Western Air Command. As Deputy Inspector General of the RCAF in 1942, he inspected the force's facilities. He brought to that command a full grasp of international military aviation affairs, having been schooled at both the RAF Staff College and the Imperial Defence College in England. The following year he was promoted to the rank of Air Vice-Marshal. He retired from the service in 1944.

It is significant to note that Godfrey was named winner of the Trans-Canada (McKee) Trophy in 1977, the 50th anniversary of the award. In presenting this honour, the Canadian Aeronautics and Space Institute, custodians of the trophy, stated:

> "Godfrey's dedication to the advancement of flying in Canada was not confined to a singular or spectacular feat. His service to Canadian aviation was invariably performed behind the scenes and always as a participant out of the public eye."

Godfrey died in Kingston, Ontario, on January 1, 1982.

Albert Earl Godfrey was inducted as a Member of Canada's Aviation Hall of Fame in 1978.

A/V/M A.E. Godfrey accepting the Trans-Canada (McKee) Trophy for 1977, during the awards dinner of the Canadian Aeronautics and Space Institute, Quebec City, May, 1977.

Stuart Graham

(1896 – 1976)

Stuart Graham, O.B.E., A.F.C., was born in Boston, Massachusetts, U.S.A., on September 2, 1896. He moved to Canada and received most of his education in Nova Scotia. He enlisted in the Canadian Army in 1915 and was sent to France with the 5th Canadian Mounted Rifles. He transferred to the Royal Naval Air Service and received pilot training in France. He was assigned to patrol the Allied shipping lanes in flying boats and seaplanes until war's end, and was awarded the Air Force Cross (A.F.C.) for his actions against two enemy submarines.

Graham returned to Canada in 1919, convinced of the potential of air operations in Canada. He learned of a group of pulp and paper companies in the St. Maurice River Valley of Quebec who were interested in air patrols for fire protection purposes and aerial surveying of their timber limits. With his assistance the St. Maurice Forest Protective Association completed a loan agreement with the Canadian government, purchased two Curtiss HS-2L flying boats, and hired him as pilot. His first assignment was to fly

In 1994 the Royal Canadian Mint produced a coin showing the image of the first bush plane and a cameo in gold of the first bush pilot, Stuart Graham. The inscription "the world's first bush plane" is based on the accomplishments of 1919, at which time the plane bore the original civil markings consisting of 'La Vigilance'. The letters 'SM' in a circular design was the logo of the St. Maurice Forest Protective Association Inc.

"His vision, foresight and application of airborne skills, despite adversity, during the birth of civil aeronautics, have been of outstanding benefit to Canadian aviation."

—Induction citation, 1974

Curtiss MF Seagull flying boat and Curtiss HS-2L flying boat, of Laurentide Co. Ltd. Taken at Lac à la Tortue (Grand'Mère), Quebec. The HS-2L was the type of flying boat first brought to Quebec by Stuart Graham, when he flew 'La Vigilance' for the St. Maurice Forest Protective Association in 1919.

both aircraft from Halifax, Nova Scotia, to Lac à la Tortue (Grand'Mère), Quebec. His wife, Madge, sat up front in what was the gunner's cockpit, protected from the spray by a canvas cover. Aviation historians recognize him as the nation's first professional peacetime pilot, and this operation as the beginning of bush flying in Canada.

He was the sole pilot of this extensive operation during the first two years, and was involved with forest fire patrol, forest inventory, aerial mapping and survey, and transportation. In 1920 he and air engineer Walter 'Bill' Kahre flew a forestry engineer into an isolated area of Quebec to stake Canada's first mining claim using an aircraft for transportation. In 1920 Graham and Kahre went to Long Island, New York, to pick up a Curtiss Seagull, which proved to be a more economical flying boat to operate. From 1921 until 1923 he represented Curtiss Aeroplane and Motor Company in Canada.

While engaged as a pilot, Graham designed a sectional canoe which could be carried aboard an aircraft, a remote control landing-direction indicator for use at airports, and an automatic view-finder camera control, all of which were commercially successful. The view-finder camera control was not further developed by the Canadian Government but instead, the patent was taken over by Fairchild Camera Corporation in exchange for use of the camera in survey activities.

For two years Graham worked with Canadian Vickers Limited at Montreal, Quebec, on aircraft construction, in particular, the production of the Vickers Vedette flying boat. In 1926 he served with the Royal Canadian Air Force (RCAF) as aircraft acceptance test pilot and on aerial mapping. From 1928 to 1939, Graham worked with the Air Services Division of the Canadian government as one of two District Inspectors, who between them supervised air operations throughout Canada. He was in charge of accident investigations, and one of his primary duties was the testing of pilots for licences. His keen interest in aviation history led to the recovery and preservation of numerous Canadian aeronautical treasures now in the National Aviation Museum in Ottawa.

Stuart Graham, Canada's first 'bush pilot'. Photo taken at Wolfville, Nova Scotia. 1942.

During World War II, Graham planned airports and facilities across Canada for the British Commonwealth Air Training Plan (BCATP). In 1945 he was named an Officer of the Order of the British Empire (O.B.E.) for his services. After the war he became technical and safety representative to the International Civil Aviation Organization (ICAO), and Chairman of their Air Navigation Committee. He contributed significantly to the drafting of standards, regulations and operating procedures for both national and international civil aviation.

From 1951 to 1963 he was aviation advisor for ICAO to various underdeveloped countries in the Middle East, Latin America, East Africa, Haiti and Rwanda-Burundi. He was decorated with the Star of Menelik by Emperor Haile Selassie for organizing the Civil Aviation Department of Ethiopia. He retired from active flying in 1963 to research and write the history of northern Canadian aviation.

Graham died on July 17, 1976. In 1988 the National Aviation Museum opened in Ottawa with a memorial honouring him. The Curtiss HS-2L flying boat, La Vigilance, with which he pioneered bush flying in 1919, has been restored and is part of the aircraft collection.

In 1991 Graham was awarded the Trans-Canada (McKee) Trophy with the following citation:

"Aviation in Canada has been significantly enriched by this talented and inventive man whose devotion to the advancement of aviation in this country is so well recorded in the footsteps he has left behind him. He was a Canadian of whom we can all be proud."

In 1997 the Community Cablevision Company of Grand'Mère, Quebec, produced a documentary film depicting the story of Graham's career.

Stuart Graham was inducted as a Member of Canada's Aviation Hall of Fame in 1974.

Roy Stanley (Bill) Grandy
(1894 – 1965)

Roy Stanley (Bill) Grandy, O.B.E., was born in Bay L'Argent, Newfoundland, on March 5, 1894. By the age of 16 he had already sailed around the world and earned the nickname 'Sailor Bill' because of his heavy Newfoundland accent. The name 'Bill' stuck with him. Although he came to love flying, he never lost his love for the sea, which undoubtedly contributed to his expertise as a flying boat and seaplane pilot. He once said that aerobatics was much like being atop the mast in a sailing boat during rough weather.

In 1912 Grandy joined military reserve unit No. 96 Lake Superior Regiment. At the outbreak of World War I, he joined the Royal Newfoundland Regiment, where he became a Signals Officer. He saw active service in France and Gallipoli. In 1916 he was seconded to the Royal Flying Corps (RFC) where he earned his Royal Flying Club Certificate at Central Flying School, Uphaven, Wilts. He served as a fighter pilot with Sopwith Camels on the western front and was Mentioned in Despatches. He was later assigned to the prestigious instructor school in Gosport. He left the Royal Air Force in 1919.

Grandy earned the reputation for being both a precision pilot and able instructor after joining the Canadian Air Force in 1920. At Camp Borden Military Base he

Group Captain Grandy loved teaching young pilots, and soon after retirement, he was instructing at the Halifax Aero Club where among his many students were young Air Cadets. He was back in his favourite element, that of imparting his knowledge of airmanship to young pilots.

was noted for his skills in landing his Avro 504K, which had no brakes, and stopping almost exactly where he wanted it. By 1921 he was issued his Air Engineer's Certificate and Commercial Pilot's Licence. He left the Canadian Air Force (CAF) in 1923 to enter civil aviation.

Grandy joined Laurentide Air Services where he pioneered aerial surveying, mapping, and fire patrolling in eastern Ontario and Quebec. He was the pilot on the first regular airmail service in Canada to Rouyn, Quebec.

In 1924 Grandy made two unprecedented flights. The first made a remarkable improvement to the centuries-old seal hunt in his native Newfoundland. Until that time, the sealers relied on their own instincts to find the herds of seals, and they were not eager to change their ways until Grandy proved that the use of an airplane to spot the herds would be very effective. In the spring of that year, he flew an Avro 'Baby' biplane off the ice beside the sealing ship S.S. Eagle. After spotting the seals, Grandy pointed the sealers in the right direction. Had he not intervened, a large herd of seals would have been missed as the ships were actually sailing in the opposite direction.

Later that year, Grandy made a flight which was to prove a rare accomplishment for that period in aviation: he flew a Vickers Viking flying boat 900 miles (1,450 km) over a period of 12 days to pay treaty money to Natives on various reserves in Northern Ontario. He followed the Albany River to Fort Albany on James Bay, and flew northward from there.

In 1925 Grandy rejoined the RCAF where his exceptional skills were used in all phases of service flying. He was one of a very few pilots certified to test and qualify both civilian and military pilots as flight instructors. He was also the testing pilot for the Webster Trophy contests. He was actively involved in the early attempts to develop an airmail route from the Atlantic coast where mail was transferred from ocean vessels to a flying boat, thus speeding the mails to central Canada. In 1934, in recognition of his work on mail routes, RCAF Headquarters recommended Grandy be installed as an Officer in the Military Division of the Most Excellent Order of the British Empire (O.B.E., Military).

When World War II broke out Grandy was Commanding Officer at RCAF Station Dartmouth, Nova Scotia. He was promoted to Group Captain in 1940, and when the Battle of the Atlantic developed, he was appointed Commanding Officer of the RCAF base at Torbay, Newfoundland. He was rewarded again during World War II by being Mentioned in Despatches.

One of Grandy's most challenging and rewarding postings was to Camp Borden as Commanding Officer while the British Commonwealth Air Training Plan was in full operation. He was an inspiration to hundreds of young airmen who passed through his base. He retired from the RCAF in 1946. Grandy died in Toronto in 1965.

Roy Stanley (Bill) Grandy was inducted as a Member of Canada's Aviation Hall of Fame in 1988.

Aboard the S.S. Eagle, with Avro 'Baby' aircraft used for seal-spotting flights. Pilot R.S. Grandy, H.E. Wallis, Air Engineer, and Jabez Winsor, Observer. St. John's, Newfoundland. March 1924.

Robert Hampton Gray
(1917 – 1945)

"His winning of the Victoria Cross in aerial combat must be regarded as one of the most outstanding contributions possible to the military aspect of Canadian aviation."

—Induction citation, 1974

Robert Hampton Gray, V.C., D.S.C., was born in Trail, British Columbia, on November 2, 1917, and received his early education at Nelson, British Columbia, graduating from high school there in 1936. The following year he enrolled at the University of British Columbia and had completed three years of an arts course by 1940 when he offered his services to the Royal Canadian Navy Volunteer Reserve (RCNVR).

After reporting to HMCS Stadacona, Halifax, Nova Scotia, Gray was sent, with the rank of Ordinary Seaman, to HMS Victory at Portsmouth, England, in September 1940. From there he reported to HMS St. Vincent at Gosport to train for his commission in the Fleet Air Arm. Following promotion to Sub-Lieutenant, RCNVR, in December 1940, he was given

In August 1989, a rock garden and memorial plaque were erected in Sakiyama Peace Park, overlooking Onagawa Bay on Northern Honshu Island, in honoured memory of Lieutenant Robert Hampton Gray. This memorial is the only one ever erected by the Japanese to an Allied officer or serviceman on Japanese soil.

six months of operational training at Collins Bay, Kingston, Ontario. He returned to England to serve in 757 Squadron at Winchester and then sailed for a tour of duty in Kenya, where he was attached to 795, 803 and 877 Squadrons, part of the time being spent aboard HMS Illustrious.

Gray was promoted to Lieutenant in December 1942. In August of 1944 he joined 841 Squadron aboard the aircraft carrier HMS Formidable and on the 24th and 29th of that month led a section of Corsair fighters in attacks against heavy anti-aircraft positions surrounding Alten Fjord, Norway, where the German battleship, Tirpitz, lay at anchor. Returning from the raid on the 29th with most of his aircraft's rudder shot away and the aircraft badly damaged, he had to circle the Formidable for 45 minutes before making a successful landing. For these actions Lieutenant Gray was Mentioned in Despatches for undaunted courage, skill and determination.

HMS Formidable was detached from the Home Fleet and assigned to the British Pacific Fleet. Her aircraft took part in many strikes against the enemy in the Far East. By the middle of July 1945, the Japanese were receiving tremendous punishment in their homeland. On July 18th Gray led a flight of Corsairs on an airfield strafing raid. On the 24th and the 28th he was the leader of successful

Robert Hampton Gray with his family. When his Victoria Cross was awarded posthumously in 1945, the acceptance ceremony was attended by his parents and sister.

bombings of bases along the Japanese Inland Sea.

Twelve days after his death on August 9, 1945, he was awarded the Distinguished Service Cross (D.S.C.) for leadership in the July strikes, and was gazetted with a citation which simply read: "For determination and address in air attacks on targets in Japan." But on the morning of August 9th, as he led his Corsair bomber group away from HMS Formidable, Gray had no knowledge of the recommendation for the award. Nor did he know that just hours after this raid, a second atomic bomb would be dropped on a Japanese city (Nagasaki), and that the war would be over five days later.

As the pilots approached the naval base at Onagawa Bay, they could see five Japanese warships at anchor. The combined anti-aircraft barrage from the ships and shore batteries steadily increased in intensity and accuracy. Selecting a ship, the Amakusa, Gray set his Corsair into a bombing attack. Gray's heavily damaged plane could not save him and it plunged into the waters of the Bay.

Lieutenant Gray was killed on August 9th, 1945, the last Canadian killed in action in World War II. He was awarded the Victoria Cross (V.C.), the only V.C. awarded to a pilot in the Royal Canadian Navy during World War II. The citation, published in the London Gazette of November 13, 1945, posthumously awarding him the highest decoration for gallantry, describes the incident and pays tribute to his steadfast conduct to the end. It reads:

> "The King has been graciously pleased to approve the award of the Victoria Cross to the late Lieutenant Robert Hampton Gray, D.S.C., RCNVR, for great valor in leading an attack on a Japanese destroyer in Onagawa Wan on the 9th of August, 1945. In the face of fire from the shore batteries and a heavy concentration of fire from five warships, Lieutenant Gray pressed home his attack, flying low to ensure success and, although he was wounded and his aircraft in flames, he obtained at least one direct hit, sinking the destroyer. Lieutenant Gray has consistently shown a brilliant fighting spirit and most inspiring leadership."

Robert Hampton Gray was inducted as a Member of Canada's Aviation Hall of Fame in 1974.

Keith Rogers Greenaway
(b. 1916)

Keith Rogers Greenaway, C.M., C.D.*, D.Mil.Sc., (Hon), was born on a farm near Woodville, Ontario, on April 8, 1916. He was educated in Toronto and joined the Royal Canadian Air Force (RCAF) in May, 1940. After graduating as a wireless operator in 1940, he served as an instructor for two years until he transferred to the navigator-wireless operator branch of the RCAF. On completion of his navigation training, he was sent first to No. 8 Air Observer School at Ancienne Lorette, Quebec, and then to the Central Navigation School at Rivers, Manitoba, as a staff instructor. In 1944 he was promoted to Flying Officer.

For the next two years Greenaway worked with the United States Navy (USN) and the United States Air Force (USAF) participating in experimental pressure pattern flights over the North Atlantic, and carrying out experimental flights over the polar regions testing a low frequency navigation system, using bases in Edmonton, Alberta, and Fairbanks, Alaska. In the spring of 1946,

In the vicinity of the Magnetic Pole, magnetic compasses are of little use due to the weakness of the horizontal component of the earth's magnetic field. Also, aurora borealis and magnetic storms induce large errors in magnetic compasses, making them unreliable within a distance of 500 miles (835 km) of the Magnetic Pole. Greenaway's goal was to develop a way for pilots to steer accurate courses by some means independent of magnetic influences.

Greenaway, now a Flight Lieutenant, was one of the navigators aboard a B-29 Superfortress, the first U.S. military aircraft to fly over the North Geographic Pole.

Greenaway is an internationally recognized authority on aerial navigation, with particular reference to polar flying. In 1947, in association with Mr. J.W. Cox, a Defence Research Board scientist, he developed the RCAF's Twilight Computer, a navigation aid for use in extreme northern latitudes. The computer, perfected in 1952, was adopted by the RCAF and Royal Air Force for use in northern flying.

Late in 1948, Greenaway was seconded to the Defence Research Board, Ottawa, to work on high latitude navigation problems, serving in this capacity until 1954. During this period, he prepared numerous reports on polar navigation and continued to carry out experimental flights in the arctic regions, extending to the North Geographic Pole.

In 1956, after serving for two years with the USAF, Greenaway was promoted to Wing Commander and transferred to RCAF Headquarters, Ottawa, for duty in the Directorate of Plans and Programs. During August 1958, he was loaned to the USN to assist in navigating a USN ZPG-2 Airship on its polar flight to 'Ice Island T3', which he had discovered in April 1947, and now was found to have shifted its geographic location. He was transferred to Winnipeg, Manitoba, in August 1959, to take the post of Officer Commanding the RCAF Central Navigation School. While at the school he developed the Canadian Forces Aerospace Systems Course and perfected the Earth Convergency Grid Technique for measuring direction in the polar regions. In August 1963, Group Captain Greenaway was appointed Commanding Officer of RCAF Station Clinton, Ontario.

From 1967 to 1970, Greenaway was again seconded to the Department of External

K.R. Greenaway with a map of northern Canada demonstrating the use of his Twilight Computer. August 1953.

Affairs and appointed Air Advisor to the Chief of Air Staff of the Royal Malaysian Air Force (RMAF). In this position, Brigadier General Greenaway advised on organization, management, and training for the RMAF.

Greenaway retired from the Canadian Forces as a General in March of 1971. During his military career, he flew as crew member on 26 aircraft types, accumulating some 8,000 hours of which nearly one third were north of the Arctic Circle. Following retirement, he assisted the Advisory Committee on Northern Development.

Greenaway is an accomplished author. A partial list of his books include: *The Arctic—Choices for Peace and Security* (1989), *From MacKenzie King to Pierre Trudeau— 1945 – 1985* (1989), *The Arctic Environment and Canada's International Relations* (1991), and *No Day Long Enough—Canadian Science in WW II* (1997).

He has received numerous awards, including the Trans-Canada (McKee) Trophy in 1952 in recognition of his development of new methods of aerial navigation in the

Arctic regions. He was awarded the Massey Medal in 1960 for outstanding personal achievement and contributions to the development of Canada. In 1952 he was awarded the Canadian Decoration (C.D.) and in 1962 received the Clasp to this decoration. In July of 1970 he was awarded the Johan Mangku Negara by the Malaysian Government. In 1976 he was made a Member of the Order of Canada (C.M.), and in 1978 he received the honorary degree of Doctor of Military Science from the Royal Military College, Kingston, Ontario.

Greenaway is a Fellow of the Canadian Aeronautics and Space Institute (CASI), the Royal Institute of Navigation, the Explorers Club and the Arctic Institute of North America. In 1996 he was made a member of the College of Fellows of the Royal Canadian Geographic Society. In 1984 Greenaway was elected Chairman of the Board of Canada's Aviation Hall of Fame.

Keith Rogers Greenaway was inducted as a Member of Canada's Aviation Hall of Fame in 1974.

Seth Walter Grossmith

(b. 1922)

Seth Walter Grossmith, C.D., B.Eng., was born on January 5, 1922, in Montreal, Quebec, where he received his education. At the age of 18, he joined the RCAF. He received his wings and then performed instructional duties until 1942. He spent a year as Flight Examination Officer, then proceeded overseas until 1945. He instructed at Instrument Flying School until 1946, then was released to further his education by attending the refresher course for veterans at Sir George Williams University. He received a Bachelor of Engineering (Honours) from McGill University in 1951. He then participated in a technical training course at Westinghouse Co., Hamilton, Ontario, and worked for them as a design engineer on transformers, motors and generators before re-enlisting for military service.

While with the Royal Canadian Navy (RCN), Grossmith completed the Empire Test Pilot's Course in 1954 at Farnborough, England, where emphasis was placed on flight evaluation techniques of new aircraft and preparation of flight and technical reports. He also conducted experimental flying on the English Electric Canberra and Hawker Hunter aircraft programs. His career with the RCN included work with the United States Navy (USN) development

From 1957 to 1966, Grossmith was a test pilot with Experimental Squadron 10 evaluating new aircraft and equipment such as the doppler decca radar, and sonar, and gained extensive experience in flight simulator development. Doppler radar is important in the detection of low-level windshear.

"During his long and distinguished career, his dedication to research and experimental flying had improved the future of Canadian aviation."

—Induction citation, 1990

test centre, and a tour of duty with a USN Helicopter Anti-submarine Warfare Squadron. His training with the U.S. forces included nuclear weapons safety and delivery systems.

Grossmith served as Executive Officer of RCN Squadron VX-10 with a staff of 75 officers and men whose tasks ranged from operational research to proposing operational doctrines for front line use. The squadron won two safety awards and was officially commended by the Board of the Royal Canadian Navy and the United States Chief of Naval Operations. He also did a tour with the USN HSS-2 Helicopter Anti-Submarine Squadron No. 10 and was Naval Air Technical Liaison Officer with United Aircraft of Canada Limited for helicopter system development CHSS-2 program. He then became a test pilot for United Aircraft which later became known as United Air Lines following several mergers with other airlines.

From 1967 to 1970 he was a test pilot with Canadair Ltd. on the CF/NF 5 and the Canadair CL-215 water bomber, planning flight test programs, and safety and emergency procedures.

In 1970 he joined the Department of Transport, Airworthiness Project Group, as a test pilot, and was involved in certification programs in Canada, U.S.A. and Europe on more than 25 fixed and rotary wing aircraft as well as glider certification programs in Poland and Finland.

In 1972 he was seconded to the National Aeronautics and Space Administration (NASA) Ames Research Centre in California, as research pilot on the Augmentor Wing Jet Research Aircraft. Here, he and R.H. Fowler (Hall of Fame 1980) tested the de Havilland Canada (DHC) Buffalo fitted with the augmentor wing and found it greatly enhanced the short take-off and landing (STOL) performance. Grossmith also served on the Advanced STOL Project. Much of the research was concerned with handling

qualities and evaluation of airworthiness certification criteria pertinent to propulsive-lift STOL aircraft. Grossmith also participated in studies using the Lockheed C-141 Transport High Altitude Infra-Red Observatory. He also took part in Zero 'G' studies using the Lear Jet 23.

From 1981 to 1983 he served with the Department of Industry, Trade and Commerce engaged in the planning, development and implementation of policies to promote the growth of Canada's aerospace industry. As test pilot for DHC he worked on and demonstrated the Augmentor Wing Research Aircraft at RCAF Station Mountain View, Ontario.

In 1983 Grossmith became Project Leader, Design, for the Airworthiness Manual Project at Transport Canada, where he was in charge of formulating Canadian Aeronautics Code Chapters 527 and 529, Normal and Transport Category Rotorcraft. He was the air worthiness representative to the working group on Aircraft Operating Regulations and Commercial Operations and also participated as flight specialist for briefings on the Lockheed Hercules C-130 PL at USAF Systems Command. Grossmith retired in 1986.

Since earning his wings in 1940, Grossmith has flown in excess of 12,400 hours in 170 types of aircraft and had many of his research papers published. In 1987 he was awarded the Trans-Canada (McKee) Trophy for "outstanding achievement in the field of air operations in recognition of his significant contribution to aeronautics in Canada as an Engineering Test Pilot." In 1988 he was made a Fellow of the Canadian Aeronautics and Space Institute.

Seth Walter Grossmith was inducted as a Member of Canada's Aviation Hall of Fame in 1990.

S.W. Grossmith participated in the Augmentor Wing Research Program in 1982 and 1983. This photo shows the de Havilland research Buffalo taking off at the NASA Ames Research Centre, California.

Harry Halton

(b. 1922)

Harry Halton, B.Sc., was born in Pilsen, Czechoslovakia, on January 24, 1922. He emigrated to England in 1938 where he attended technical school at Walthamstow, earning his diploma in Mechanical and Electrical Engineering. He attended Northampton Polytechnic, earning a Bachelor of Science degree in 1944.

Throughout World War II, while pursuing his formal education, he also worked for the Bell Punch Co. Ltd. of Uxbridge, Middlesex, first as a machinist and then as an assistant in design and component development of hydraulic and electrical equipment for many aircraft. These included the Avro Anson, the Hawker Hurricane, Tornado and Typhoon, the Supermarine Spitfire and Vickers Wellington, the Airspeed Oxford, Blackburn Botha, Short Stirling, and the Handley Page Halifax. He also did component work on the de Havilland Mosquito, Fairey Swordfish and Barracuda, and the Avro Lancaster. In 1946 Halton was appointed Chief Design Engineer at D & H Designs Ltd., London, England.

In 1948 Halton moved to Canada to join Canadair Ltd. in Montreal as a design engineer working on the North Star

In September 1975, shortly after becoming Executive Vice-President of Canadair, Harry Halton emerged as a paraplegic following routine surgery for a small tumor. In spite of this tragic accident and the subsequent limitations to his mobility, he pursued his career to the full, achieving the highest honours his company and peers could grant to him.

"His exceptional abilities in aircraft design and development together with his outstanding personal and leadership qualities have all been of outstanding benefit to Canadian aviation." —Induction citation, 1984

Harry Halton (centre) is presented with the Royal Canadian Air Force Association's Gordon R. McGregor Memorial trophy for his "outstanding contribution to Canadian civil and military aviation" in 1981.

conversion and the Royal Canadian Air Force (RCAF) C-5. He became Test Engineer in 1950 and moved up to Group Leader, Functional Test Group. He became Program Manager for the CL-89 Surveillance Drone in 1967. He was next appointed Program Manager for the CL-215 Water Bomber, being responsible for all activities including design, development, certification and production.

In 1971 Canadair Ltd. appointed Halton as Director of Engineering responsible for the engineering on all programs. In 1972 he was appointed Vice-President, Engineering, and three years later he became Executive Vice-President. In the latter position he was responsible for all engineering quality control, procurement, program management, manufacturing and industrial engineering, and product support activities on all Canadair programs. He was specifically responsible for the establishment and operation of the Canadair/Urban Transportation Development Corporation Intermediate Capacity Transit System Development and Test Facility in Kingston, Ontario.

As Program Manager, Halton was responsible for the total development of the Challenger, a wide-bodied corporate jet. Responsibilities included everything from the preliminary design, definition, detail design, planning, tooling, prototype manufacture, flight tests, obtaining certification by the Department of Transport (Canada) and Federal Aviation Authority (U.S.), to production and final deliveries of the CL-600 Lycoming ALF-502 powered aircraft. As well, he was responsible for the definition and initial detail design for the CL-601 GE CF-34 powered Challenger. Halton established the Surveillance Systems as a Canadair product line by initiating the CL-289 Long Range Drone and CL-227 Remotely Piloted Vehicle programs.

Halton is a Past President and Fellow of the Canadian Aeronautics and Space Institute, Senior Member of the Instrument Society of America, Senior Member of the American Institute of Aeronautics and Astronautics, Senior Life Member of the Institute of Electrical and Electronics Engineers, and an Honorary Life Member of the Aerospace Industries Association of Canada.

Aviation Week and Space Technology, an aviation journal, awarded Halton 'Laurels for 1978' for outstanding leadership in the development of the Challenger. The Governor General of Canada awarded him the Organization for Rehabilitation and Training Centennial Medal for "exemplary contribution to technical education". In 1981 he received the RCAF Association Gordon R. McGregor Memorial trophy for "outstanding contribution to Canadian civil and military aviation". In 1984 he received the General A. McNaughton Gold Medal from the Institute of Electrical and Electronics Engineers for "outstanding service to the Canadian aerospace industry".

Halton retired from Canadair Ltd. in 1983.

Harry Halton was inducted as a Member of Canada's Aviation Hall of Fame in 1984.

Paul Albert Hartman

(1918 – 1990)

Paul Albert Hartman, D.F.C., A.F.C., C.D.*, was born in Grafton, Massachusetts, U.S.A., on November 25, 1918, and moved with his family to South Portland, Maine, in 1933. He attended school there and learned to fly, obtaining his Private Pilot's Licence in 1938. He enlisted in the Royal Canadian Air Force (RCAF) in 1941, and was commissioned a Pilot Officer that same year. After completing a navigational reconnaissance course with the RCAF at Charlottetown, Prince Edward Island, he was posted to the Royal Air Force (RAF) Ferry Command at Dorval, Quebec. He ferried a Lockheed Hudson across the North Atlantic Ocean to Scotland in April 1942.

On arrival in the United Kingdom, Hartman completed his operational

Some of Hartman's exceptional memories of flying include piloting six vintage aircraft from the National Aeronautical Collection in Ottawa, Ontario, for Canada's Centennial Celebrations in 1967. These included reproductions of the Nieuport 17 and Sopwith Triplane, a restored Sopwith Snipe and an original Avro 504K. Two other originals he flew were the Aeronca C-2 and Fleet Finch. Flying these at the end of his long career emphasized the amount of progress that has been made in the world of aviation, and the change that this progress has made in the relationship that exists between the pilot and the aircraft he or she is flying.

training in Northern Ireland, then joined 69 Squadron, Royal Air Force, in 1942, flying Vickers Wellington bombers on night torpedo runs off the coast of Malta. He was awarded the Distinguished Flying Cross (D.F.C.) later that year for sinking an enemy vessel by torpedo, despite intense anti-aircraft fire from protecting enemy destroyers. He was then promoted to Flying Officer.

In 1943 he returned to Canada where he served as a Flight Lieutenant Instructor with No. 6 Operational Training Unit, RCAF, before taking command of 3 Training Squadron and Glider Training Detachment at Cassidy, British Columbia. For his services to this command he was awarded the Air Force Cross (A.F.C.).

At the end of the war, Hartman was appointed to serve at the Test and Development Establishment at Rockcliffe, Ontario, where he was named Staff Test Pilot. In 1948, after completing a specialist course, he was posted to Farnborough, England, where he completed the Empire Test Pilot's Course. He then returned to his post at Rockcliffe.

Hartman became a Canadian citizen in 1951, and in 1952 completed the RCAF Staff College course as a Squadron Leader. He was promoted to Wing Commander and assigned to RCAF Headquarters at Ottawa, Ontario, where he held several senior staff positions in training, transport and air defence commands. He served three terms as a test pilot at the RCAF's Central Experimental and Proving Establishment. In 1961 he was named Commanding Officer of the unit and the following year became Senior Test Pilot. Because of his extensive flying experience in all RCAF aircraft, Hartman was appointed test pilot of the Avro CF-100 and Canadair F-86E Sabre acceptance trials.

In commemoration of the fiftieth anniversary of manned flight in Canada, Hartman was invited to fly the RCAF-built replica of the Silver Dart. The flight took place at Baddeck, Nova Scotia, on February 23, 1959, on the same site where J.A.D.

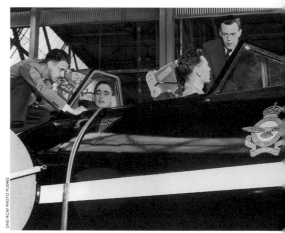

In 1961, Wing Commander P.A. Hartman was test pilot of the Avro CF-100 acceptance trials. Here he is shown, seated left, with S. Badaux, receiving flying tips from A.V. Roe's test pilots.

McCurdy (Hall of Fame 1974) first flew the original aircraft in 1909. Some 13,000 people, McCurdy included, witnessed the historic flight on the ice of Bras d'Or Lake.

In 1964 Hartman served with the United Nations Emergency Force as Commanding Officer of No. 115 Air Transport Unit, based at El Arish, Egypt. The following year he was named Base Operations Officer of Canadian Forces Base Uplands, Ontario.

Hartman retired from the service in 1968 after having flown 120 different aircraft types and logging over 7,000 hours of flight time. Following his retirement, he served as a test pilot with Canadair Limited at Cartierville, Quebec, on the CL-215 water bomber project. In 1971 he formed his own aeronautical consulting firm, Triple-A Aero Service, in Ottawa, and worked as a freelance test pilot.

His contribution to manned flight was recognized by the Royal Aeronautical Society which named him an Associate Fellow. He was awarded the Canadian Forces Decoration (C.D.) and Clasp for his years of service. Hartman died in Ottawa on January 30, 1990.

Paul Albert Hartman was inducted as a Member of Canada's Aviation Hall of Fame in 1974.

Left: Hall of Fame Member 'Jack' Reilly shows a pioneer-pilot's helmet to a young visitor and her family. This is one of the items that interest visitors who come to learn about the Members of Canada's Aviation Hall of Fame.

Below: Canada's Aviation Hall of Fame Membership Medal, which is presented to the Inductees, or their representatives, at the Induction Ceremonies. The medal depicts a seven cylinder radial engine and the Hall's motto —"Liberaliter viam monstrabant" or "Unselfishly they showed the way".

Members gathered for a group photo at the Induction Gala held in Toronto in 1996. They are, standing: Seth Grossmith, Bob Fowler, Jerry Wright, Angus Morrison, Dick Richmond, Keith Greenaway, Don Watson, Byron Cavadias, Larry Clarke, Max Ward, Eugene Schweitzer. Seated are: Bob Heaslip, Jim Floyd, Archie Vanhee, Al Lilly, Elvie Smith, Russ Bannock, Lindy Rood, Robert Bradford.

Meeting old friends is high on the list of social activities during Induction Galas. Here, Neil J. Armstrong, Tommy Williams and Jack Reilly pause in their conversation to pose for the camera. All three were inducted in 1974.

Following the Investiture of the Order of Icarus, Calgary, Alberta, March 31, 1973. Standing are: Lindy Rood, Jack Reilly, Max Ward, Archie McMullen, Stan McMillan, Don Watson, Mel Knox, Walter Gilbert, Mike Finland, and Norm Forester. Seated: Harry Hayter, Captain James Lovell, Jr., U.S. astronaut and special guest, Punch Dickins, Molly Reilly, Sammy Tomlinson, Tommy Williams, Ray Munro, Jack Moar. Those who were unable to attend were: Bernt Balchen, Paul Hartman, Bert Mead, Herb Seagrim, Tim Sims, Jaycee Sloan, and Len Tripp.

Jennifer Romanko, Curator for Canada's Aviation Hall of Fame, with Robin Gale, WO 1 of the 52 (City of Calgary) Squadron RCAC. The Cadets served as hosts during the reception and formed the guard of honour prior to the Gala Dinner held in Calgary, 1997.

Lieutenant Governor of Alberta, the Hon. Gordon Towers, presents the Membership Medal of Canada's Aviation Hall of Fame to Mrs. Woodman, who accepts on behalf of her late husband, Jack Woodman. Looking on is Mrs. Towers. The ceremony was held at Government House in Edmonton, 1995. On the right are Chairman Russ Bannock and Jennifer Romanko.

Keith Greenaway takes a moment to share his own thoughts on being selected to Membership of Canada's Aviation Hall of Fame. Edmonton, 1974.

MC Jack Boddington toasts Piper Jeff McCarthy at the opening of the Induction Gala held in Montreal, 1998.

Above: Rex Terpening shares his most memorable experiences as an air engineer at a time when northern Canada was coming alive with exploration and development. Calgary, 1997.

Left: The Hon. Gordon Towers, Lieutenant Governor of Alberta, and Mrs. Towers, enter the dining hall for the Gala Dinner held in Edmonton, 1995.

Above: Donald Rogers stands beside his Hall of Fame panel, which describes his accomplishments and contributions to aviation. Induction Gala, Montreal, 1998.

Left: Stan McMillan (1974), Archie Vanhee (1987), and Bob Randall (1974), obviously glad to see each other again as they swap stories during the reception.

Clockwise from top:

Noorduyn Norseman CF-BDG of Canadian Airways Ltd., gets its annual change-over from floats to wheels under the hoist at Cooking Lake, Alberta.

Roméo Vachon repairing the engine for a HS-2L flying boat at Lac a là Tortue, Laurentide Air Service. He designed this engine-testing stand to facilitate his work. 1919.

Super Fokker G-CASK changing from wheels to floats at Cooking Lake, Alberta. Spring, 1931.

Left: This Waco aircraft of Starratt Airways Ltd. was damaged during a wind storm at Pickle Lake, Ontario, in 1938. Supporting hoists had to be built on the spot before repairs could be done.

Below: Hitting ice ridges or snow drifts had devastating results. This crash of a Commercial Airways Bellanca CH-300 occurred at Fort Resolution, N.W.T., in March, 1930.

Imperial Oil's Junkers F-13, G-CADQ, 'René', following the rough landing in which the propeller was shattered. At Fort Simpson, N.W.T., March, 1921.

MGen Ray Henault, Canadian Forces Search and Rescue, accepts the Belt of Orion Award on behalf of all SAR personnel across Canada. Presenting the award is Chairman Elvie Smith. Induction at Montreal, 1998.

Above: Rosella Bjornson stands beside her Hall of Fame panel following her induction as a Member of Canada's Aviation Hall of Fame. Calgary, 1997.

Left: N. Byron Cavadias accepts his framed Membership from Chairman Elvie Smith during the Induction ceremony, Toronto, 1996.

Fred Hotson, newly inducted Member, talks to guests at the Gala Dinner in Montreal, 1998.

Mrs. Monica Dodds receives the Membership certificate from Chairman Russ Bannock on behalf of her late husband, Robert Dodds, at the Induction Ceremony held in Edmonton, 1994.

Doug Matheson, QC, a long-time member of the Board for Canada's Aviation Hall of Fame, salutes the Hall during ceremonies held in Edmonton, 1994.

Air Industries and Transport Association Directors Meeting at Quebec, 1954.
Standing are: D.N. Kendall, P.Y. Davoud, C.H. Dickins, E. Moncrieff, J. Drummond, D.A. Newey, F.L. Trethewey.
Seated are: A.L. Michaud, B.W. Pitfield, T.P. Fox, Chairman, R.W. Ryan, P. Wood.

W/C Jack Showler demonstrates the SHORAN Trilateration Net Chart devised for the survey of the Canadian Arctic. 1956.

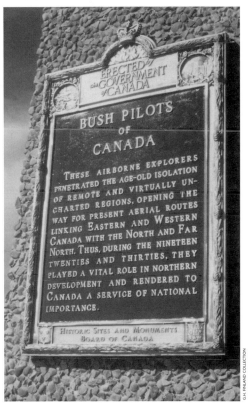

Left: W.R. 'Wop' May helped the ground searchers track Albert Johnson, known as the 'Mad Trapper', from the air. May's knowledge of northern flying contributed to the success of the hunt for the killer. 1931.

Below: A Memorial Plaque was unveiled as a Canada's Centennial Project at Yellowknife, N.W.T., in 1967. Many bush pilots and guests attended the unveiling ceremony. The citation reads: "These airborne explorers penetrated the age-old isolation of remote and virtually uncharted regions, opening the way for present aerial routes linking Eastern and Western Canada with the North and Far North. Thus, during the nineteen twenties and thirties, they played a vital role in northern development and rendered to Canada a service of national importance."

In August, 1970, a reunion of the men who flew the Northwest Territories during the 1920's and 1930's was organized. The flight left Edmonton on a Pacific Western Airlines DC-6B, and followed a route through Hay River, Fort Simpson, Yellowknife and Inuvik and return. Bush pilots and air engineers who are shown in this photo include, standing: Don Ferris, Al Brown, Bert Burry, K.M. Guthrie, A/V/M ret'd, Jim Dick, Fred Meilicke, Gordon Latham, Herb Hollick-Kenyon, Rex Terpening, Mike Finland, Pep Innes-Taylor, Jack Bowen, Jack Moar, Max Ward, John Davids, Norm Forester, Gordon Cameron, Bud Potter. Seated: Bert Field, Stan Knight, Stan McMillan, Scotty Moir, Bob Randall, Sammy Tomlinson, Earle Jellison, A/V/M ret'd, Phil Lucas, Bill Jewitt, Ralph Oakes, Harry Hayter. Those also on the trip, but missing from the photo: Joe Irwin, Harold Miller, Tellef Vaasjo.

Enjoying the company of friends at an Induction Dinner reception are Mr. and Mrs. Bob Randall, Neil Armstrong and Sheldon Luck.

Jean and Bob Heaslip meet Irma Coucill, centre, portrait artist for Members of Canada's Aviation Hall of Fame. Induction Dinner reception held at Toronto, 1996.

Max and Marjorie Ward, centre, happy to be a part of the festivities, with members of their family. Induction at Toronto, 1996.

Rex Terpening with his wife and family, following his Induction held at Calgary, 1997.

His Honour, Lieutenant Governor Gordon Towers and Mrs. Towers, seated centre, join newly inducted Member Dick Richmond, seated, left, with members of his family. The ceremony was held at Government House, Edmonton, in 1995.

Byron and Juliet Cavadias, fifth and sixth from the left, are joined by their proud family prior to the Induction ceremonies in 1996.

Left: The Victoria Cross Winners' Circle: Eight panels form an octagon, one showing the story of the Victoria Cross and the others highlighting the lives of the seven Members of the Hall who were awarded this medal.

Below: The Victoria Cross. Members of the Hall who won this medal were: William Avery Bishop (1917), William George Barker (1918), Alan Arnett McLeod (1918), Andrew Charles Mynarski (1944), David Ernest Hornell (1944), Ian Willoughby Bazalgette (1944), and Robert Hampton Gray (1945).

Medals awarded to Paul Yettvart Davoud. Among them are the Distinguished Service Order, the Order of the British Empire, Distinguished Flying Cross, France's Legion of Honour and Croix de Guerre, and the Netherland's Commander of Orange Nassau.

Above: A group of aviation pioneers and bush pilots who attended the Alberta Aviation Council annual convention held in Edmonton, November 1966.
From the left are: A.N. Westergaard, Norm Forester, Archie McMullen, Leigh Brintnell (in aircraft seat), W. McFarlane, Stan McMillan, Jack Moar, G. 'Mike' Finland.

Right: Commercial Airways Limited aircraft preparing to leave Fort McMurray on their inaugural air mail flight to Aklavik, Northwest Territories. December 10, 1929.

Below: A Douglas DC-4 of Maritime Central Airways. c. 1960's.

Left: Dennis K. Yorath, Chairman of Calgary's Second Annual Air Show, is shown receiving a message from Air Vice-Marshal K.M. Guthrie, Air Officer Commanding, North West Air Command. The message, delivered by RCAF helicopter, officially opened the Air Show. c. 1947.

Below: Jan Zurakowski is hoisted to the shoulders of his colleagues after the first flight of the Avro CF-105 'Arrow', which he piloted, on March 25, 1958. Malton Airport, Ontario.

Carl Agar of Okanagan Air Services, lifts off in his company's first helicopter, with spray booms attached. Its side hoppers have just been filled with insecticide to apply against the Hemlock Looper, which was destroying large stands of B.C. forests. The pilot is unprotected from toxic materials. July, 1948.

Clockwise from top:

The Canadair Assembly Plant, showing the Challenger in various stages of assembly. Montreal, 1980.

Air Cushion Vehicle SBN-6 at Churchill, Manitoba. The craft was demonstrated with passengers during Expo '67 at Montreal, Quebec.

The Air Cushion Vehicle SBN-6 during cold weather trials over the Hudson Bay, out of Churchill, Manitoba. 1967 – 68.

Henry Winston (Harry) Hayter

(1900 – 1974)

Henry Winston (Harry) Hayter was born in Murray River, Prince Edward Island, on October 29, 1900. He joined the Canadian Light Infantry at age 15 and served with the 26th Battalion in France until October 9, 1918, when he was wounded. While recovering, he completed his secondary education by correspondence before attending three more years at veteran's college.

Hayter worked at Jacksonville, Florida, for the Buick Motor Company in 1924 as a special tool maker, and worked nights and weekends repairing small aircraft in exchange for flying lessons. In 1927 he moved to St. John, New Brunswick, where he completed his flight training and qualified for his Transport Pilot's Certificate and Air Engineer's Licence. During this time, Hayter flew every available aircraft type in the Maritimes as a barnstormer and charter pilot. He also flew as seal-spotter for the Boston fleet from a base in the Magdalen Islands (Iles de la Madeleine, Quebec), near Prince Edward Island.

In 1932, having read about the uranium find at Great Bear Lake in the Northwest Territories, he flew his own aircraft from St. John across Canada to Fort McMurray, Alberta, where he organized his own air operation carrying passengers and freight northward into the sub-Arctic. He established a base at Cameron Bay on Great Bear Lake, and worked closely with Mackenzie Air Service in providing a life-line for the inhabitants of the area.

Harry Hayter brought his wife with him in 1933 to establish their home at Cameron Bay. They learned soon after that she was only the fifth white woman to live in the Arctic up to that time.

"The unselfish application of his airborne skills and his personal determination in the operation of his own aeroplane, despite adversity, over isolated areas for sustained periods of time in the service of others, have been of outstanding benefit to Canadian aviation." —Induction citation, 1974

A semi-permanent shelter in the sub-Arctic, made from caribou skins. c. early 1930's.

He became nationally known in the fall of 1933 when a freighter and barge were caught in a severe storm on Great Bear Lake and the eleven men aboard were presumed lost. In preparation for freeze-up, Hayter was changing his plane from floats to skis at Cameron Bay, on the east end of the lake. During this period, neither floats nor skis are useful, since a trip which begins in the frozen north with skis will need floats to land on water further south. Hayter knew the dangers of flying his plane over the waters of Great Bear Lake, but he also knew that an air search must be started immediately in order to find and save the crew of those two vessels.

In one of the greatest mercy flights of the north, he began his search on October 29. With snow and ice carpeting the shoreline, Hayter flew his unheated, single-engined, ski-equipped aircraft over the freezing 12,000 square mile (31,200 sq. km) body of water, often at wave-top height, for 11 consecutive days until he finally located the nine survivors and flew them to safety.

Fortunately, only one of the men, Vic Ingraham, desperately needed hospitalization for treatment of severely frozen limbs. Hayter had only one choice of hospital, Aklavik, where he could land with skis. On December 2nd, W.R. 'Wop' May (Hall of Fame 1974) flew to Aklavik to bring Ingraham to hospital in Edmonton, Alberta. Ingraham survived his ordeal, and returned to live in the north.

In 1934 Hayter's extraordinary talents as a pilot and air engineer were recognized by W.L. Leigh Brintnell (Hall of Fame 1976), owner of Mackenzie Air Service, who hired him as his company's General Manager. At the same time, Hayter was recognized for his exemplary service to the Northwest Territories by being appointed Commissioner for that area. Among many of his notable 'firsts' was piloting the inaugural passenger flight from Dawson City in the Yukon, to Edmonton, Alberta. He went on to become a near-legend to the adventurous trappers and prospectors whom he flew into remote regions, leaving them isolated for months at a time, but never failing to pick them up on the appointed day.

He remained with McKenzie Air Service until World War II was declared in 1939. The Royal Canadian Air Force commissioned him as a Flying Officer, but the government diverted his services almost immediately to organize and manage Aircraft Repair Limited in Edmonton. This job took him to one of the largest maintenance plants in Canada, working with W.L. Brintnell. It was important to the war effort that this plant be kept open to maintain military aircraft.

In 1944 Hayter and M. 'Moss' Burbidge (Hall of Fame 1974) were invited to Miami, Florida, to work with Transportes Aereos Centro-Americanos, an airline operating out of Miami and flying throughout Central America. Hayter became Operations Manager of the airline, and organized the first routes across uninhabited jungle. He also organized the first airmail flights from all of the Central American countries to Miami. Soon after returning to Edmonton in 1945, he responded to a request from Aero Transportes in Mexico to set up an administration office for that company. He was Captain on that country's first transcontinental flight, from Tampico on the east coast to Mazatlan on the west.

Hayter retired from professional flying in 1950. During his career he logged more than 20,000 command hours in numerous aircraft, including the renowned Bernelli Flying Wing. He died on March 17, 1974, in Edmonton, Alberta.

Henry Winston (Harry) Hayter was inducted as a Member of Canada's Aviation Hall of Fame in 1974.

H.W. Harry Hayter with an Inuit friend, dressed in winter clothing. c. early 1930's.

Robert Thomas (Bob) Heaslip

(b. 1919)

Robert Thomas (Bob) Heaslip, A.F.C., C.D.*, was born in Uxbridge, Ontario, on June 26, 1919. After graduating from Oshawa Collegiate in 1936, he joined the Oshawa Times-Gazette where he remained until he enlisted in the Royal Canadian Air Force (RCAF) in 1941. He received his pilot's wings the same year and was assigned to 122 Squadron at Patricia Bay, British Columbia, on army co-operation and transport flights. Two years later he was posted to 166 Squadron at Sea Island, British Columbia, as a communications and transport pilot. He was awarded the Air Force Cross (A.F.C.) in 1945 for his part in rescue activities.

At war's end Heaslip completed the RCAF's first pilot/navigator course at Summerside, Prince Edward Island, and was posted to 435 Squadron at Winnipeg, Manitoba, as a Flight Lieutenant. During 1947 he was trained as one of the RCAF's first helicopter pilots at Trenton, Ontario, and then was ordered to Rivers, Manitoba, to command the helicopter section of the RCAF Light Aircraft School. He instructed helicopter pilots until 1951, was then appointed

The Continental Air Defence System was built on the theory that an attack would be launched by the U.S.S.R. across the north by conventional bombers. However, nuclear weapons, advances in radar-jamming methods, warning devices, and missiles made the system obsolete. The western half of the line was shut down in January 1964, the eastern half from Hudson Bay to Labrador ceased operations on March 31, 1965.

"The application of his exceptional abilities as a military helicopter pilot, and his perfecting of new operating techniques for rotary wing aircraft, have been of outstanding benefit to Canadian aviation."

—Induction citation, 1974

Piasecki H-21 helicopter with S/L R.T. Heaslip, on Mid-Canada Defence Line Operations.

Commanding Officer of the RCAF recruiting unit at Fort William, Ontario, promoted to Squadron Leader and posted to command the Hamilton, Ontario, recruitment centre. As the RCAF's most experienced helicopter pilot, he was named commander of the force's first all-helicopter unit, No. 108 Communications Flight at Bagotville, Quebec, in 1954.

In April of 1954, the Canadian and United States Governments jointly announced plans for continental air defence. Four links emerged in the planning: the northern Arctic link was known as the Distant Early Warning (DEW) Line, the Mid-Canada Line was built along the 55th parallel of north latitude, the Pinetree Line was located along the Canada-U.S. border, and the fourth link was the line of radar towers which extended down both flanks of North America.

The Mid-Canada Defence Line was an electronic warning network with no tracking facilities. It consisted of a series of stations linked by multi-channel communications at intervals along the line. The system used an electronic device which sent a beam straight up to detect all types of airborne objects moving through the electronic 'fence', from ground level to heights above the ceiling of any bombers of that day. It received electronic warnings from the DEW Line, confirming the direction of any attack. It would give a minimum of 60 minutes warning to the closest North American targets against any bombers or other aircraft flying at speeds up to 700 miles (1,126 km) per hour. The Pinetree Line would control the interceptor forces.

At Bagotville, Heaslip organized and trained a 200-man unit to provide air transport for the construction phase of the Mid-Canada Line. In February 1956, Heaslip's unit, using up to 22 helicopters, carried out the major lift of the materials required to build and furnish the sites.

Heaslip was awarded the Trans-Canada (McKee) Trophy for his work in 1956, in recognition of his contribution to helicopter operations during the construction of the Mid-Canada Line. The helicopter flight he commanded had flown in excess of 9,000 hours airlifting 14,000 personnel and 10,000 tons (9,072 tonnes) of electronic and construction equipment over rugged terrain, often under hazardous conditions. He personally piloted many of these flights and he evolved unique airlift techniques for a large variety of load configurations, including bulky antenna assemblies, large diesel engines, steel towers, and other equipment peculiar to the needs of the Mid-Canada Line operation. He was responsible for the evolution and perfection of many new cold-weather operating techniques, which allowed the operation to proceed smoothly under extreme climatic conditions

in the north. His command was then moved to Rockcliffe, Ontario, and later disbanded.

After completing the RCAF Staff College course at Toronto, Ontario, in 1957, Heaslip was selected to remain on the college's directing staff for three years and was promoted to Wing Commander. A senior staff officer's posting followed at Trenton, where he supervised a selected staff in the development of military plans concerned with transport operations, including those related to United Nations (UN) requirements in foreign lands.

This comprehensive background in air operations led to his appointment in 1965 as Commanding Officer of No. 117 Air Transport Unit in Lahore, West Pakistan, operating in support of the UN mission to that country. The 100-man unit operated from the Himalayan Mountains near the Chinese border to the Arabian Sea, a frontier of some 1,200 miles (1,931 km).

The following year he was named Base Operations Officer and Second-in Command of Canadian Forces Base, Trenton, in charge of flying activities, support services, flight planning, air traffic control, weather services and air movement. He retired from the service in 1968 to become Military Marketing Manager in North America for de Havilland of Canada Ltd. at Downsview, Ontario. He received the Canadian Forces Decoration (C.D.) and Clasp for his service.

Robert Thomas (Bob) Heaslip was inducted as a Member of Canada's Aviation Hall of Fame in 1974.

Richard Duncan (Dick) Hiscocks
(1914 – 1996)

"His dedication and expertise in the area of aircraft design helped to foster a line of Canadian-built aircraft that continue to be highly successful around the world, and his ability to impart knowledge and encouragement to others, is of lasting and significant benefit to Canada." —Induction citation, 1998

Richard Duncan (Dick) Hiscocks, M.B.E., B.Eng., LL.D. (Hon), was born in Toronto, Ontario, on June 4, 1914. He had determined to pursue an aviation career by the age of ten. While in high school he won first prize for both scale and flying model aircraft at Canadian National Exhibition competitions. His early education was received at Winchester Public School and Jarvis Collegiate in Toronto.

Hiscocks graduated from the University of Toronto's inaugural class in Engineering Physics in 1938. While attending university, he obtained summer employment at de Havilland Aircraft Company of Canada Ltd.

R.D. (Dick) Hiscocks published nearly fifty papers on aircraft design, airworthiness, engineering education, and industrial research. In 1995 he published "Design of Light Aircraft", which is in widespread use by students and engineers across Canada. He contributed two stories, "The Ubiquitous Beaver" and "Whither STOL?", both of which are published in *De Havilland, You STOL My Heart Away.*

Air Vice-Marshal C.R. Dunlop (left) and Frank Piasecki meeting S/L R.T. Heaslip, who brought the first H-21 Piasecki/Vertol into Canada. 1954.

Richard 'Dick' Hiscocks receives the first McCurdy Award in 1954, from John McCurdy, who flew the Silver Dart in Canada in 1909. The Award was created by the Canadian Aeronautics & Space Institute.

(DHC), working on the assembly of the Rapide and the Dragonfly. Following graduation, he was hired by DHC and sent to the de Havilland (U.K.) main design office at Hatfield, England.

In 1940 Hiscocks returned to Canada to accept an offer from the National Research Council (NRC) in Ottawa, Ontario, where he was assigned to the structures laboratory. He led a group that responded to wartime metal shortages, concentrating on wood replacement projects. He had a major role in designing wooden parts for the Harvard that never went into production, and wooden parts for the Anson Mark V that did go into production and saw substantial service.

In 1945, with a group of scientists, he was sent to Germany to examine German technological advances, and returned with insights that would be put to good use in the design of post-war Canadian aircraft. In 1947 he was made a Member of the Order of the British Empire (M.B.E.) for his work with the NRC.

Hiscocks returned to DHC in 1946, and joined Chief Designer Fred Buller on the Beaver project. His main contribution to the Beaver was the design of the wing geometry, including an airfoil curve of his own calculations. He became Chief Engineer at DHC in 1949, and continued working with Buller to develop the Otter, Caribou, Buffalo, and Twin Otter. All of these aircraft utilized the rugged short-field performance associated with the Beaver, which became a distinctive de Havilland Canada feature.

Hiscocks fostered research and development work in aerodynamics, structures, rough field landing gear, and other technologies that helped to establish DHC's place as the world's largest manufacturer of aircraft with short take-off and landing (STOL) capabilities. These aircraft needed the ability to operate safely from rudimentary, short airstrips, and required full international civil airworthiness approvals to enable world wide sales.

In 1968 he rejoined the NRC as Vice-President of Industry, a post he held until 1976. In this position he was charged with assisting Canadian industry, including aerospace, to make the best possible use of the facilities and expertise available at the NRC. At the same time, he was President of Canadian Patents and Development, which was associated with the NRC. In 1976 he rejoined DHC as Vice-President of Engineering, until his retirement in 1979. During that period he was involved with the development of the Dash 7 and Dash 8 aircraft.

During his career, Hiscocks delivered lectures on aeronautical subjects at the University of Toronto and its Institute for Aerospace Studies. Following retirement and a move to Vancouver, British Columbia, he was appointed adjunct professor at the University of British Columbia where he resumed his aeronautical lectures. He applied for and received appointment as a Design Approval Representative for Transport Canada, empowering him to approve various aspects of aircraft design or design changes. He acted as a consultant to several Canadian and American companies.

Between 1990 and 1995 he was involved with Murphy Aircraft Manufacturing Ltd. of Chilliwack, British Columbia, working on aerodynamic design and stress analysis for a high-wing, bush-type aircraft, the Rebel, and a larger, four-seat high-wing aircraft, the Super Rebel, for the homebuilder's market.

In 1954 Hiscocks was the first-ever recipient of the Canadian Aeronautics and Space Institute's McCurdy Award. He was awarded honorary doctorate degrees by McMaster, McGill and Carleton Universities. Hiscocks took an active part in the development of his profession outside the design office as is shown by his years of work with the Canadian Aeronautics and Space Institute where he was president in 1964-65. He died in Vancouver, British Columbia, on December 13, 1996.

Richard Duncan (Dick) Hiscocks was inducted as a Member of Canada's Aviation Hall of Fame in 1998.

Basil Deacon Hobbs

(1894 – 1963)

Basil Deacon Hobbs, D.S.O., O.B.E., D.S.C.*, was born in Arlington, Berks, England, on December 20, 1894. His family moved to Canada where he obtained his education and developed a life-long love for flying boats, ships and the sea. In 1915 he took flying training at the Wright Flying School, Dayton, Ohio, U.S.A., and after receiving his wings joined the Royal Naval Air Service as a Flight-Lieutenant. At his posting to Felixstowe, Norfolk, England, he flew the F-3 and H-12 flying boats on anti-submarine patrols.

Hobbs was awarded the Distinguished Service Cross (D.S.C.) in 1917 for sinking a German submarine. Later that year, in his four-engine flying boat, he destroyed a German Zeppelin, following which his aircraft was severely damaged by fighters, forcing him to land in the sea. He taxied across the Channel to England where he beached the flying boat. He was awarded the Distinguished Service Order (D.S.O.) for this action. The letter from Their Lords Commissioners of the Admiralty announcing the D.S.O. award also contained a second letter, a reprimand for "taking one of H.M. aircraft away from its allotted training area without permission, and, thereby, causing serious damage to said aircraft." In November of the same

In order to complete the long trans-Canada trip in 1920, pilots and crews had to overcome almost insurmountable difficulties, such as the lack of weather reports, airfields, communication, refueling stations, and other facilities. Good planning and persistence kept them focused on their goal.

"This man truly reached for the stars and through his flying achievements and ability in peace and war brought honor to the aviation fraternity of Canada." —Induction citation, 1987

year he was awarded a Bar to his D.S.C. for sinking another submarine and was Mentioned in Despatches. Hobbs became the only Canadian on record who was directly involved in the destruction of two U-boats. In 1919 he returned to Canada.

He joined the Canadian Air Force (CAF) in 1920 and was employed by the Canadian Air Board as a 'Certificate Examiner' for civil aircraft and pilot licencing. In October 1920, Hobbs was one of the pilots on the first trans-Canada flight, under the leadership of LCol Robert Leckie (Hall of Fame 1988). Conducted by eight men with six different aircraft of the CAF, the undertaking began on October 7, 1920, from Halifax, Nova Scotia. Hobbs was in charge of the first leg, from Nova Scotia to Winnipeg, Manitoba. He shared the flying duties with Leckie, who was the first Director of Flying Operations with the Air Board of Canada. Flying boats were used on this section of the trip, and were replaced by single-engined, wheel-equipped, two-seater de Havilland biplanes on the leg from Winnipeg through to Vancouver, British Columbia. Mail was also carried on this cross-country flight. In all, the trip took ten days, with a flying time of 49 hours, covering 3,265 miles (5,250 km).

The following year Hobbs was appointed Superintendent and Commanding Officer of the Winnipeg Air Station where the main responsibilities included forestry work and fire control operations. Prior to World War II, fighting forest fires was an almost hopeless task. Canoe patrols would often miss seeing a blaze only a short distance back from the lakeshore. It was the men of the newly founded Canadian Air Force who soon proved that aircraft were an effective way to spot and fight forest fires. The airplane originally purchased for the job was the Curtiss HS-2L flying boat, followed later by the more powerful Vickers Viking, which was not only useful for spotting fires but also served very effectively as a photographic machine. The camera was mounted on the

A Vickers Viking flying boat, used by B.D. Hobbs in his aerial photographic survey work. The camera was mounted on the front, giving the cameraman a clear view to the front and sides.

nose of the flying boat like a machine gun, away from the structure of the airplane itself, and the cameraman had a clear view for miles around at an operating altitude of 5,000 feet (1,500 m).

Hobbs made his greatest contribution to Canadian aviation as a peacetime pilot. In 1924 he was the sole pilot on the crew of a Vickers Viking assigned to carry out the first long range aerial photographic survey undertaken in Canada. The route, beginning at the southern tip of Lake Winnipeg, was over the northern regions of Saskatchewan and Manitoba. The flight was accomplished in one month and covered nearly 3,000 miles (4,800 km). The geodetic trilateral survey of the Canadian Arctic Islands, a project begun in 1924 by Hobbs, was completed in 1957.

In 1924 he became a Squadron Leader in the newly formed Royal Canadian Air Force (RCAF). A year later he became the Director of Air Operations, Ottawa. Following his resignation from the RCAF in 1927, he established his own business, Basil D. Hobbs and Sons, Wine & Spirit Merchants in Montreal.

At the beginning of World War II, Hobbs was re-commissioned into the RCAF with the rank of Group Captain. His skills and flying ability were put to use in anti-submarine warfare training and operations as Commanding Officer at Dartmouth, Nova Scotia, and later at Patricia Bay, British Columbia. He was named an Officer of the Order of the British Empire (O.B.E., Military). Hobbs died in Montreal, Quebec, in 1963.

Basil Deacon Hobbs was inducted as a Member of Canada's Aviation Hall of Fame in 1987.

Herbert (Bertie) Hollick-Kenyon

(1897 – 1975)

Herbert (Bertie) Hollick-Kenyon was born in London, England, on April 17, 1897, moved to British Columbia as a youth and worked locally until 1914 when he joined the Canadian Army as a trooper and was sent overseas. He was wounded at both the Somme and Ypres in France during 1916 and was returned to Canada and medically discharged.

Following his recovery, Hollick-Kenyon joined the Royal Flying Corps (RFC) in Canada in 1917 and attended the School of Aeronautics at the University of Toronto. He enrolled in flight training at the RFC's winter training facility at Fort Worth, Texas, and returned to Camp Borden, Ontario, where he graduated as a commissioned pilot. He was retained there as an instructor for the balance of that year, then was assigned to service in the United Kingdom in 1918 immediately preceding the war's end. He served in England with the Royal Air Force (RAF) until his unit was disbanded, and for the next two years was an officer with the Royal Irish Constabulary.

In 1922 he rejoined the RAF as a flying instructor, and during this tour of duty he helped to pioneer the early British sound detection system which warned against incoming aircraft. He resigned from the RAF and returned to Canada in 1928 and went to work as a pilot with Western Canada Airways Limited.

During his extended career Hollick-Kenyon flew 45 aircraft types as pilot-in-command for 14,000 hours. He became one of only a few airmen to pilot an aircraft across areas adjacent to both the North and South Poles.

"The long-range flights he captained during the Antarctic expedition and the Levanevsky search allowed the mapping of hitherto uncharted areas, which contributions have proven of great benefit to the international fraternity of aviators, and of outstanding benefit to Canadian aviation." —Induction citation, 1974

NATIONAL ARCHIVES OF CANADA C-062298

H. Hollick-Kenyon at the South Pole with the Lincoln Ellsworth Expedition, 1935 – 36. He is shown at top of photo, tending to the Northrop 'Gamma' aircraft Polar Star, which he flew.

When the MacAlpine Expedition was marooned in the Canadian Arctic during the fall of 1929, he was one of several pilots who spent weeks on the lengthy and difficult search. A major problem which caused delays was that during the time of freeze-up, it was unsafe to fly with either skis or floats, and this was complicated by the differences between freeze-up times in the south and northern regions. When the MacAlpine party, including pilot Stan McMillan (Hall of Fame 1974) was eventually located at Cambridge Bay, Hollick-Kenyon assisted in flying them from the Arctic Ocean to The Pas, Manitoba.

In 1930, when Western Canada Airways merged with Canadian Airways Limited, Hollick-Kenyon was assigned to the night Prairie Airmail Service on the Winnipeg-Regina route. In 1933 he was assigned to fly the Edmonton-Great Bear Lake route and with W. E. Gilbert (Hall of Fame 1974) inaugurated the airmail service to Cameron Bay.

Hollick-Kenyon left Canadian Airways in 1935 to work for explorer Lincoln Ellsworth on his Antarctic expedition. He had been selected to pilot Ellsworth's single-engined Northrop Gamma monoplane across a major area of the continent from Dundee Island to Little America, a flight of some 2,250 miles (3,620 km) over a land never before seen from the air. The actual flying time of the trip was 20 hours, during which they encountered numerous mechanical and weather problems, forcing them to remain on the hostile terrain for two months. The flight called for him to fly the ski-equipped aircraft across 300 miles (480 km) of open water of the Weddell Sea and over 12,000 foot (3,660 m) mountains, with only basic navigational aids and without the benefit of weather science.

In tribute to his outstanding achievement, a major land area on the Antarctic continent was named the Hollick-Kenyon Plateau and the Royal Canadian Air Force named him honorary Air Commodore. On his return from Antarctica he was employed as a pilot with Skylines Express, owned by Jack Moar (Hall of Fame 1974).

In 1937 Hollick-Kenyon became involved in one of aviation's greatest aerial searches, covering the western Arctic from Siberia through Alaska and the Yukon. Australian explorer Sir Hubert Wilkins was asked to head a rescue expedition to locate the Russian pilot, Sigismund Levanevsky and his five companions, missing on a trans-polar flight from Moscow, Russia, to Fairbanks, Alaska. Hollick-Kenyon was selected to pilot Sir Hubert's long-range aircraft during the search, which he flew on dangerous search patterns from Point Barrow, Alaska, to Coppermine, Northwest Territories, and then to within 120 miles (190 km) of the geographic North Pole. He flew almost five months of the eight-month long search during the hours of polar night. Also participating in the search was A.M. 'Archie' McMullen and R.C. 'Bob' Randall (both Hall of Fame 1974).

When Trans-Canada Air Lines (TCA, Hall of Fame 1974) was formed in 1937, Hollick-Kenyon was hired as dispatcher in Winnipeg, Manitoba. He was transferred to Lethbridge, Alberta, and became Operations Superintendent of the pilots who pioneered the Rocky Mountain Route to Vancouver, British Columbia. As a tribute to complete mastery of his craft, the airport at Lethbridge was named Kenyon Field.

In 1942 he joined Canadian Pacific Airlines (CPA) and served in flying capacities in Western Canada, Yukon and Northwest Territories, beginning as Superintendent at Whitehorse, Yukon, and rising through Check-Pilot to become the line's first Chief Pilot. He eventually took command of all CPA's pilot training at Vancouver, retiring from the company in 1962. He died in Vancouver on July 30, 1975.

Herbert (Bertie) Hollick-Kenyon was inducted as a Member of Canada's Aviation Hall of Fame in 1974.

Herbert Hopson
(1909 – 1993)

Herbert Hopson was born in Blandford, Dorset, England, on December 2, 1909. His family moved to Calgary in 1912 and in 1929 he commenced flying training at Great Western Airways, operated by F.R. McCall (Hall of Fame 1978) and J.E. Palmer (Hall of Fame 1988).

On April 4, 1930, he obtained his Commercial Pilot's Certificate and began instructing as well as barnstorming with an OX5 Waco. In 1932 he attended an instrument flying course at Camp Borden Military Base, Ontario, and later helped J.E. Palmer train Chinese students to fly so they could join the Cantonese forces to help to defend their homeland.

Until 1937 Hopson continued with occasional flying jobs but had to make a living by working in an engine-rebuilding firm. That year he renewed his Instructor's Certificate and received an 'A' rating, rare in Canada at that time. Leigh Brintnell (Hall of Fame 1976) offered him a position with his firm, Mackenzie Air Service, based in Edmonton, Alberta. Hopson spent two years with Mackenzie Air flying Fairchild 71's and 82's and Noorduyn Norseman aircraft.

In March 1939, he joined Trans-Canada Airlines (TCA) and within four months was

In 1947 Herbert Hopson became one of TCA's 'Million Milers', pilots who have flown over 1,000,000 miles (1.6 million km) at the controls of company aircraft. This adds up to some interesting figures: it's roughly equal to 40 times around the equator, or more than 6,000 hours in the air.

promoted to Captain. In September he was transferred to Toronto flying Lockheed 14's and 18's and helped set up new routes to Moncton, New Brunswick, to London and Windsor, Ontario, and to New York.

Hopson was promoted to Check Pilot in 1943 and to Chief Pilot a year later. In 1945 he introduced the Douglas DC-3 to TCA service. From 1946 to 1952, he was on loan, part-time, to the Department of Transport (DOT) to assist in the implementation of the Instrument Landing System (ILS). TCA provided a DC-3 and a radio engineer to assist the DOT technicians. They covered all major airports to be commissioned with ILS, from Victoria, British Columbia, to St. John's, Newfoundland. With this experience, Hopson became a member of the International Air Transport Association (IATA) Flight Technical Committee to define requirements for instrument landing systems. The standards they set became the International Civil Aviation Organization (ICAO) International Standard.

With the adoption of ILS it became imperative that High Intensity Lighting be developed. As a member of IATA and Technical Advisor to ICAO, Hopson helped to establish International Standards for High Intensity Approach, Threshold, and Runway Lighting Systems. This was followed by work to develop the In-Runway Lighting Systems used with Category 2-ILS and Category 3-ILS.

From 1947 to his retirement in 1969, Hopson filled the position of Technical Assistant, Test Pilot and, eventually,

Director of Flight Operations, Technical Development for TCA/Air Canada. He was responsible for the coordination of company recommendations to the government regarding construction of runways, aprons, lighting and navigation aids. He assisted in selection of new aircraft, flight deck layouts, etc., during the era of the Lockheed Super Constellation, Vickers Viscount and Vanguard, Douglas DC-8 and DC-9, Boeing 747 and Lockheed 1011. During this time, he was responsible for all of Air Canada's Route and Airplane Operating Manuals and Route Operating Certificates. He flew TCA's first Viscount on cold weather trials at Churchill, Manitoba, and also flew the first Vickers Vanguard.

With the proposed introduction of supersonic aircraft, Hopson became a member of the IATA Supersonic Operations Requirements Committee. In the final development stages within ICAO, he was accredited to the Canadian delegation and given freedom to act on behalf of Canada in final decision making.

After retirement from Air Canada at the end of 1969, he spent several years consulting for an air planning services firm working on Short Take-Off and Landing/Vertical Take-Off and Landing (STOL/VTOL) with Jack Dyment (Hall of Fame 1988), and for a manufacturing firm developing area navigation systems, fibre optic instrumentation, weight and balance systems, etc. Hopson died on August 25, 1993.

Herbert Hopson was inducted as a Member of Canada's Aviation Hall of Fame in 1989.

David Ernest Hornell
(1910 – 1944)

"His winning of the Victoria Cross in aerial combat must be regarded as one of the most outstanding contributions possible to the military aspect of Canadian aviation."

—Induction citation, 1974

The 'David Hornell, V.C.'—the last PB2B-2 Catalina to be built by Boeing Aircraft of Canada. Christened by Air Vice-Marshall F.V. Heakes, C.B., then officer commanding Western Air Command (1945), this particular aircraft was diverted for use by the Royal Australian Air Force.

David Ernest Hornell, V.C., was born in Lucknow, Ontario, on January 26, 1910, and educated in Toronto. He worked for the Goodyear Tire and Rubber Company from 1927 to 1940. He enlisted in the Royal Canadian Air Force on January 8, 1941, was commissioned to serve as a pilot on Canada's west coast and posted to 162 Squadron at Reykjavik, Iceland, on January 2, 1944.

On June 24, 1944, Flight Lieutenant Hornell was captain of a Canso flying boat on anti-submarine patrol operations from Iceland. A German U-boat was sighted in waters north of the Shetland Islands, fully-surfaced and travelling at high speed. At once Hornell turned to attack. The U-boat's Captain decided to fight on the surface, and opened up with fierce and accurate anti-aircraft fire. The Canso was hit hard. Big holes were torn in the wing and the fuselage, and the starboard engine caught fire.

Ignoring the enemy fire, Hornell carefully manoeuvered for the attack. Oil poured from the starboard engine which was on fire, as was the starboard wing, endangering the fuel tanks. Meanwhile the aircraft, hit again and again by enemy fire, was vibrating and difficult to control. Despite his precarious position, Hornell brought his aircraft in low to the target and released depth charges in a perfect pattern. The bow of the U-boat rose out of the water, toppling some of its crew overboard before plunging beneath the surface.

Hornell contrived, by superhuman effort at the controls, to gain a little height. The fire in the starboard wing had grown

David Hornell joined the RCAF in January 1940. He was 30 years old, and had he delayed joining for three weeks more, he would have been too old for air crew under the regulations then in existence.

more intense and the vibration had increased. Then the burning engine fell off. The plight of the crew was now desperate. With the utmost coolness Hornell took his aircraft into the wind and despite the manifold dangers, brought it safely down on the heavy swells. Badly damaged and blazing furiously, the aircraft settled rapidly.

After ordeal by fire came ordeal by water. With only one serviceable dinghy, the crew of eight took turns going into the icy water, holding onto the sides. Once, the dinghy capsized in the rough seas and was righted again only with great difficulty. An airborne lifeboat was dropped to them from a search aircraft, but it fell some 500 yards (460 m) down wind. The men struggled vainly to reach it and Hornell, who throughout had encouraged them by his inspiring courage and leadership, proposed to swim to it, although he was nearly exhausted. He was restrained with great difficulty. After 21 hours in the sea, during which time both flight engineers died from exposure, they were picked up by a rescue launch. Hornell, blinded and completely exhausted, died shortly after being rescued.

Hornell had completed 60 operational missions involving 600 hours of flying time; he well knew the dangers and difficulties attending attacks on submarines. By pressing home a skillful and successful attack against fierce opposition, with his aircraft in a precarious condition, and by fortifying and encouraging his comrades in the subsequent ordeal, this officer displayed valour and devotion to duty of the highest order.

For this display of "valour and devotion to duty of the highest order", Flight Lieutenant David Hornell was awarded the Victoria Cross (V.C.)—the first such award to a Canadian airman in the Second World War—for service with the squadron on June 24, 1944. He died the following day and was buried in the Shetland Islands.

David Ernest Hornell was inducted as a Member of Canada's Aviation Hall of Fame in 1974.

Frederick William (Fred) Hotson
(b. 1913)

Frederick William (Fred) Hotson was born in Toronto, Ontario, on December 29, 1913. He received his early education at Fergus, Ontario. In 1934 he entered the aircraft engineering course at the Central Technical School in Toronto.

Hotson was chosen from the graduating class of 1935 for a position with the de Havilland Aircraft Company of Canada Ltd. (DHC). He gained valuable experience in all departments at the time, particularly during the introduction of the Canadian Tiger Moth.

He obtained his Pilot's Licence from the Toronto Flying Club in 1938 and during the same year, test flew his home-built Heath Parasol sport plane. He completed the Department of Transport's Engineer's Licence, A and C, in 1939. He stored the Parasol and continued as foreman of DHC aerodrome service during the first nine months of the war.

In 1941 Hotson left DHC to join the British Commonwealth Air Training Plan (BCATP) as instructor at No. 1 Air Observers School, Toronto, and pilot-instructor and operations manager at No. 9 AOS, St. Jean, Quebec. He served as duty pilot, chief instructor and assistant operations manager as the school grew under Canadian Pacific Airlines (CPA). In 1944 CPA was asked to assist the Royal Air Force Transport Command (RAFTC) in delivering aircraft to Britain. A ferry flight department was quickly put together by CPA with captains from the western lines

Hotson's interest in history, and his careful documentation and writing style have left a legacy and treasure of written words about Canada's aviation heritage.

"His lifetime in aviation has been highlighted by his contribution to corporate aviation and the 70-year history of de Havilland in Canada. His ability to relate his extensive career to the writing and preservation of the country's aviation history has been of lasting value to Canada."

—Induction citation, 1998

and first officers from the AOS schools. Hotson was chosen to join the group in March 1944, and completed a total of twenty Atlantic flights to Europe and Africa. He spent the last six months of the war in service with 231 Communications Squadron, RAFTC.

At war's end Hotson obtained his Public Transport Licence and Instrument Rating. He made several aircraft deliveries to South America in the employ of Aircraft Industries Ltd. He flew a Fairchild Husky as a bush pilot in northern Ontario and Quebec until 1948. At that time he became personal pilot for Major A.P. Holt, flying a Grumman Mallard. He then moved with the same aircraft to become Chief Pilot for the Ontario Paper Company. He continued in that capacity for 18 years and added a DC-3 to the company fleet in 1955. In 1958 he was a founding Director of the Canadian Business Aircraft Association (CBAA) and served as its President in 1964.

In 1966 he was granted a leave of absence to conduct a two month study in Afghanistan for the International Civil Aviation Organization (ICAO) on the technical and economic use of short take-off and landing (STOL) aircraft in the remote areas of that country. After studying its history, geography, economics, and culture, Hotson realized the challenge of introducing any modern airplane into a country of such rugged and inhospitable terrain. There were very few landing strips, navigation aids or weather stations. There were few locally trained pilots, mechanics or other specialists needed to run an airline. Nor were there hotels, taxis or fuel in the back country.

He travelled extensively within Afghanistan and, on completion of his report, rejoined DHC in 1967 in the flight test department, primarily as a Twin Otter flight instructor. He returned to Afghanistan with their first aircraft and instructed pilots on how to fly it. Similar flight instructor assignments were carried out in Norway, the United States and Canada. He joined DHC's product support department in 1969, and acted as Sales Engineer until his retirement in 1978, with a total of 13,000 flying hours on 25 types of aircraft.

Hotson has had a continuing interest in preserving Canada's aviation history. In 1969 he became President of the Canadian Aviation Historical Society (CAHS), an office he held for 15 years. In 1977 he received the Aircraft Owners and Pilots Award from the Canadian Owners and Pilots Association (COPA, Belt of Orion 1993) for the promotion of Canadian aviation history. Hotson has written over 25 meticulously researched history-related articles for the CAHS Journal and publications in Canada, the U.S. and the U.K. During 1983 he edited and published a 325-page CAHS chronology, *125 Years of Canadian Aviation*, earning him the 1986 Ninety-Nines' Canadian Award in Aviation.

On the occasion of the 50th anniversary of DHC, Hotson wrote a 65-page book on the history of that company in 1983, *The de Havilland Canada Story*. This book received the Aviation Writer's Association

Citation of Merit. In 1988 he completed a long-standing personal research project, the story of the first east to west air crossing of the Atlantic. The crew of two Germans and an Irishman, flying from Ireland to New York, were far north of their intended course and were forced to land during a snowstorm on Greenly Island off the southern tip of Labrador, Newfoundland. Hotson's book about this adventure, *The Bremen*, earned him the AWA non-fiction award for that year.

In 1980 he was made an Associate Fellow of the Canadian Aeronautics and Space Institute (CASI) and four years later, raised to Fellow. He took an active role in the formation of the National Aviation Museum Society with the objective of providing fireproof accommodation for the national aviation collection at Rockcliffe Airport, Ottawa. The Society remains active as an advisory group.

In 1985 Hotson retired as the President of CAHS and was made Chairman. Returning to his CBAA interests in 1991, Hotson wrote and published *Business Wings*, a 30-year history of the Association and received the CBAA Award of Merit in 1994.

Frederick William (Fred) Hotson was inducted as a Member of Canada's Aviation Hall of Fame in 1998.

Clarence Decatur Howe
(1886 – 1960)

Clarence Decatur Howe, P.C., B.Sc., D.Sc. (Hon), LL.D. (Hon), was born in Waltham, Massachusetts, U.S.A., on January 15, 1886. He graduated with a B.Sc. degree from the Massachusetts Institute of Technology in 1907 and remained on the faculty as an Assistant Professor of Engineering. The following year he came to Canada and served as Professor of Civil Engineering at Dalhousie University, Halifax, Nova Scotia, from 1908 to 1913. He became a Canadian citizen in 1913.

In 1916 he formed C.D. Howe and Company, consulting engineers, at Port Arthur, Ontario. This firm designed grain terminals, wharves, factories and other works in Canada, the United States and later, in Argentina. During that period he also designed the Howe Car Dumper to replace the unloading of grain from railway cars by hand. Howe became Chief Engineer for the Board of Grain Commissioners of Canada and in that capacity designed most of the government's largest grain elevators.

In 1935 Howe was elected to the House of Commons representing the constituency of Port Arthur and was immediately named to Prime Minister Mackenzie King's cabinet, being appointed Minister of Railways and

Fred W. Hotson with his Aircraft Owners and Pilots Association Award presented to him by COPA (Canadian Owners and Pilots Association) in 1977.

During more than two decades in government, C.D. Howe served in many Cabinet posts, often concurrently, earning him the nickname 'Minister of Everything'. He was considered to be one of the most powerful people in the government at that time.

Canals, and Minister of Marine. He united both departments into one Department of Transport in 1936, reorganized the administration of Canadian National Railways, and established the National Harbours Board. He fashioned the Canadian Broadcasting Corporation from the former Canadian Radio Commission.

In 1937 Howe established Canada's first transcontinental airways system, Trans-Canada Airlines (Hall of Fame 1974). On July 30th, he was one of the government officials who were passengers on the first pre-inaugural inspection flight of Trans-Canada's Airlines' routes, checking airport sites selected by J.H. Tudhope (Hall of Fame 1974) and Bob Dodds. This was known as the 'Dawn to Dusk' flight on a Lockheed 12A piloted by Tudhope. The flight took 14 hours of actual flying time and followed the route from Montreal to Vancouver, British Columbia, a distance of some 2,550 miles (4,103 km). The purpose of this flight was to show that the airway was a practicable proposition, and could be developed in the near future.

At the outbreak of World War II, Howe was made responsible for the War Supply Board, which was subsequently replaced by the Department of Munitions and Supply, which he headed with the title of Minister.

The chain of airports that Howe had established across Canada to support the services of TCA proved invaluable to the British Commonwealth Air Training Plan (BCATP), which, beginning in 1940, helped train many thousands of Allied air crew for World War II. During the wartime period he also undertook the construction of Dorval International Airport at Montreal, and established the Canadian Government Trans-Atlantic Air Service (CGTAS).

Participants in the 'Dawn-to-Dusk' transcontinental flight, Montreal to Vancouver, July 30, 1937. Left to right: J.H. Tudhope, pilot; Hon. C.D. Howe; J.D. Hunter, copilot.

During the war, the production of aircraft increased from 250 a year to 4,000. At war's end, government-owned companies were turned over to private enterprise to ensure the viability of the Canadian aircraft industry. After the war Howe assumed the title of Minister of Reconstruction and led Canada's wartime industry into a prosperous peacetime era. In 1948 he was named Minister of Trade and Commerce, followed by appointment as Minister of Defence Production in 1951.

Howe's numerous honours include appointment to the Imperial Privy Council (P.C.) in 1946, the Medal of Merit awarded by the American government in 1947, the Award of Merit of the American Institute of Consulting Engineers, the Hoover Medal, the Daniel Guggenheim Medal for contributions to aviation progress. In 1960 he was awarded the gold medal of the Royal Canadian Flying Clubs Association for meritorious service to the flying club movement. From 1957 until his death, Howe was Chancellor of Dalhousie University. He died in Montreal, Quebec, on December 31, 1960.

Clarence Decatur Howe was inducted as a Member of Canada's Aviation Hall of Fame in 1976.

The Rt. Hon. C.D. Howe, on the cover of TIME Magazine, as 'Man of the Year', February, 1952.

Albert Edward Hutt

(1901 – 1990)

Albert Edward Hutt was born January 30, 1901, in Halton, Ontario, and in 1917, at the age of 16, he joined the Royal Flying Corps in Canada as an engine mechanic. As heated hangars and instructional facilities were lacking, the squadron was transferred to Texas for initial training. When the war ended in 1918, a number of the early airmen were absorbed into a Canadian Government body called the Canadian Air Board, which in 1920 administered three sections: Civil Aviation, Flying Operations, and the Canadian Air Force (CAF).

In the early 1920's the CAF was carrying out aerial surveying and mapping of the Rocky Mountain areas west of Calgary, Alberta. Hutt was one of the survey camera operators on these flights. While serving as an engine mechanic on their Rolls-Royce powered de Havilland DH-4 aircraft, he designed and built one of the earliest engine test stands.

The Ontario Provincial Air Service (Belt of Orion 1991) was formed in 1924, and Hutt joined them as a mechanic/aerial photographer, doing aerial survey work and fire patrols with Leigh Brintnell (Hall of Fame 1976) and T.W. Tommy Siers

Albert Hutt's career (1928-1966) with Western Canada Airways and CPA spanned the transition from the floats and skis of the early years to a smoothly-run airline operation. His expertise was such that he, too, made a smooth transition in maintaining the airlines' aircraft, from the piston-driven era to the jet age.

"A pioneer in the field of aircraft maintenance and engineering at a time when there was only his knowledge and integrity for guidance, his lifetime of excellence provided an example for all who followed, thus benefitting Canadian aviation."

—Induction citation, 1992

SOURCE UNKNOWN

A.E Hutt was one of the highly-skilled and indispensible air engineers who accompanied pilots on their northern flights. The big Junkers was part of the Canadian Airways Limited fleet.

(Hall of Fame 1974). In Curtiss HS-2L flying boats, they carried out survey flights over unmapped territory as far afield as Hudson Bay.

In 1928 Hutt was hired by James A. Richardson (Hall of Fame 1976) for his company, Western Canada Airways. He worked as manager of the company's Brandon Avenue Shops at Winnipeg, under Tommy Siers, who was the Superintendent of Maintenance. Hutt was responsible for the repair and overhaul of a fleet of 45 aircraft comprised of 14 different types that used 9 different makes or models of engines. His solutions to complex problems became legendary. When the Junkers JU-52 Flying Boxcar was introduced into Canadian bush flying, an engine vibration problem rendered it virtually unusable until he diagnosed and corrected the problem.

In 1939 Hutt and Rex Terpening (Hall of Fame 1997) started work on the development and installation of the first oil dilution system on one of the company's Junkers aircraft, to make it more adaptable to the cold weather in Canada. This was considered the most significant

engineering development of its day in Canada. They provided valuable assistance to Siers in refining and finalizing the system to the operational stage.

During WW II, when several smaller aircraft-operating companies were amalgamated to form Canadian Pacific Airlines (CPA), Hutt was transferred to New Westminster, British Columbia, to become manager of the repair plant there. Under his direction, the company's overhaul shops became the most highly rated aircraft maintenance organization in Canada.

At war's end Hutt was transferred to Edmonton as Regional Maintenance Manager. He applied his expertise to the only equipment available—ex-military aircraft. When CPA established their headquarters in Vancouver, British Columbia, Hutt was appointed Director, Maintenance Engineering, and placed in charge of the shops and overhaul facilities. He held this position until his retirement in 1966. Hutt died in Langley, British Columbia, on April 27, 1990.

Albert Edward Hutt was inducted as a Member of Canada's Aviation Hall of Fame in 1992.

William Gladstone Jewitt
(1897 – 1978)

William Gladstone Jewitt, B.Sc., LL.D. (Hon), was born in Marton, England, on May 15, 1897. The family moved to Calgary, Alberta, in 1908 where he completed his elementary and secondary school education. In 1915 he enlisted in the 3rd University Company of the Canadian Army and after training in England he served in France with the Princess Patricia's Canadian Light Infantry until 1917. Commissioned a Lieutenant, he transferred to the Royal Flying Corps and commenced flight training at Stamford, England.

On graduation as a pilot, Jewitt completed an instructor's course at Gosport, England, then returned to Stamford as an instructor until 1918, when he was assigned to ferry repaired aircraft to France. When he returned to Canada, he enrolled at the University of Alberta from where he graduated in 1923 with a Bachelor of Science degree in mining engineering.

In 1927 he joined the Consolidated Mining and Smelting Company Limited

Pilots flying aircraft on skis learned to avoid taxiing in narrow channels of rivers, where the ice would often not thicken sufficiently to bear the load. On one trip, Jewitt's Fairchild dropped through the ice at Fort Rae even though the temperature was 40 degrees below zero. No long timbers were available and they had to build an A-frame on a mat of poles frozen together with water poured over them—all of this done at minus 40 degrees.

"His pioneer flights over unmapped territory under adverse conditions during three decades, established new aviation procedures and bases that have substantially benefitted Canadian aviation."

—Induction citation, 1978

at Trail, British Columbia. Two years later, W.M. Archibald (Hall of Fame 1974) asked him if he would be interested in flying aircraft on mining exploration in the Northwest Territories. He obtained his Commercial Pilot's Licence as well as his Air Engineer's Licence, and was assigned to explore for potash in northern Alberta and the Northwest Territories. The Cominco fleet at that time consisted of three Fairchild 71's, one Fokker Super Universal and three Gipsy Moths. The Moths were used for reconnaissance trips, the larger aircraft supplied camps and moved prospectors.

Archibald established a small flying school at Creston, British Columbia, early in 1930, and Jewitt's next assignment was to train company engineers as pilots for northern exploration work. When he returned to explorations flying, he personally flew the furthest-ranging and most difficult flights, some into the Arctic islands where no aircraft had previously ventured. These flights resulted in the development of such mines as Echo Bay, Con, Box, Thompson Lundmark, Ptarmigan and Pine Point.

In these hitherto unexplored and unmapped regions, he pioneered new methods of aerial prospecting, utilizing aircraft to transport men, equipment and supplies. During his extended civil aviation career, which ended in 1954, he carried out a number of emergency air ambulance flights, often through difficult weather conditions.

His resourcefulness as a bush pilot was proven in 1930 on Prosperous Lake, an uninhabited area near what is now Yellowknife, Northwest Territories. A hole blew through a piston of his Curtiss Robin's engine on take-off, reducing the power below what was required to fly. Using only hand tools, he and his mechanic, Jim Fox, disassembled the engine, then repaired the damage with sheet metal cut from the gas filter, and flew

W.G. Jewitt fuels his aircraft, a de Havilland Gipsy Moth. Pilots in the late 1920's and early 1930's were very much exposed to the weather in the open cockpits.

the aircraft to Yellowknife Bay where another pilot located them. Another trip later in 1930 was to the north side of Victoria Island to investigate a reported occurrence of native copper. It was believed to be the furthest north an aircraft had been flown in Canada at that time.

As a result of his aerial prospecting ventures, many new flight techniques were discovered, to be eventually incorporated as standard civilian procedures. All northern-flying pilots had to learn, mostly by experience or unpleasant incidents, that various precautions had to be taken in order to keep flying. For example, frost on the wings virtually destroyed their lift, ice accumulating on leading edges in flight had the same effect, ski-equipped aircraft had to be taxied onto cross poles to prevent the skis from freezing to the snow or ice. They learned the desirability of carrying as light a load as possible, but to include adequate survival supplies.

A second result of these pioneer flights was the mapping of vast stretches of terrain, information which was disseminated among aviation personnel, both civil and military. Over a period of 30 years, Jewitt's airborne teams established hundreds of cache sites and aerial bases as far north as the Arctic Ocean that have proven valuable to commercial aviation.

In 1953 Jewitt was awarded an Honorary Doctor of Laws degree by the University of Alberta for his contributions to northern exploration. He died in Victoria, British Columbia, on June 20, 1978.

William Gladstone Jewitt was inducted as a Member of Canada's Aviation Hall of Fame in 1978.

Harry Marlowe Kennedy
(1904 – 1989)

"He gave full measure of his airmanship to all tasks set to him, as a first generation bush pilot, a wartime military aviator and a peacetime military commander, which resulted in outstanding benefit to Canadian aviation."

—Induction citation, 1979

Harry Marlowe Kennedy, A.F.C., C.D.*, was born on August 27, 1904, in Winnipeg, Manitoba, where he was educated. In 1925 he joined the Royal Canadian Air Force Officer Cadet Program and during three summer periods earned his pilot's rating and a Commission as a Flying Officer. This was followed by an advanced flying course at Jericho Beach, Vancouver, British Columbia.

In 1928, while flying for the Canadian Air Board, Civil Air Operations, out of Winnipeg, Kennedy made aerial photographs of many landing facilities in northern Ontario and Manitoba and aerially mapped large sections of Canada for the proposed prairie night-airmail routes. When personnel numbers in the Royal Canadian Air Force (RCAF) were reduced in 1932, he joined the Manitoba Government Air Service carrying out forestry patrol flights and fire suppression missions.

Western Canada Airways hired him in the fall of 1932, and he flew airmail along the Winnipeg-Pembina route before transferring to bush operations in the north. In this role he was involved in

H.M Kennedy's Junkers CF-AQW which he flew for Canadian Airways Ltd. At Norway House, near the northern tip of Lake Winnipeg, Manitoba. 1933.

a number of mercy flights, resulting in the saving of human lives. Northern bush float-flying usually came to a halt in late October, and all personnel were involved in the maintenance program of aircraft repair and engine overhaul in the operational base hangar. Floats were exchanged for skis to be ready for winter flying conditions.

In 1934 Kennedy went to work for Mackenzie Air Service at Edmonton, Alberta, operating from bases in the

Northwest Territories. There he was involved with Matt Berry (Hall of Fame 1974) in the lengthy, but successful search for two RCAF members, Flight Lieutenant Sheldon Coleman and Leading Aircraftsman J.A. Fortey, downed in an inoperable aircraft during a photographic survey mission to Fort Reliance on the northeast point of Great Slave Lake, Northwest Territories.

On New Year's Day, 1937, Kennedy made a trip to Eldorado Mines on Great Bear

In February 1933, Marlowe Kennedy was ordered to fly a welder and his equipment to Lac du Bonnet, the Western Canada Airways base operated by F. Roy Brown (Hall of Fame 1976). It had been snowing all morning, but eased up in the afternoon sufficiently for him to attempt the trip. However, the snowfall thickened, forcing him to use the power-line as his guide. The snow storm rapidly worsened, resulting in limited visibility, causing him to miss picking up the Lac du Bonnet shore line. While trying to find a shore line to land by, he found himself completely without visual references at low altitude over the middle of the frozen lake. He crashed onto the ice about a half mile out from the base, completely wrecking the plane. After being treated for their injuries, both Kennedy and his passenger were back working again less than a month later.

P/O H.M. Kennedy, newly commissioned as Pilot Officer, Camp Borden, Ontario. Fall of 1927.

Lake, Northwest Territories, flying men and supplies into their camp and bringing radium concentrate out to the railhead at McMurray. When Lord Tweedsmuir, Governor General of Canada, scheduled a visit to Coppermine on the Arctic Coast in August of 1937, Kennedy was selected as pilot because of his extraordinary airmanship and knowledge of the North.

He became one of the first pilots to join Trans-Canada Air Lines (TCA, Hall of Fame 1974), where he served until 1940. At that time he obtained leave for war service to re-join the RCAF as a Flight Lieutenant with 12 Communications Squadron at Rockcliffe, Ontario. When he was named Squadron Commander, he envisioned an Aerial Transport Service for the RCAF which eventually became the RCAF Air Transport Command. Kennedy was appointed its deputy commander under the leadership of Z.L. Leigh (Hall of Fame 1974). These organizational undertakings, coupled with his piloting of the Duke of Kent on a wartime Canadian coast-to-coast tour, resulted in his being awarded the Air Force Cross (A.F.C.) in 1942.

At Pennfield Ridge, New Brunswick, Kennedy helped to create the RCAF's Air Transport Instrument and Night Flying School, and graduated from Staff College. At the end of the war, he was recalled to TCA and remained an airline pilot until he was offered a permanent commission in the RCAF in 1946 with the rank of Wing Commander.

In his new role Kennedy was assigned to the International Civil Aviation Organization (ICAO) and subsequently was named Deputy Director of Air Intelligence for the RCAF. Later, he was assigned to the Canadian Embassy in Brussels, Belgium, to establish the new post of Air Attaché. In 1949 he was appointed Commanding Officer of RCAF Sea Island Air Station at Vancouver.

Three years before his retirement, he was promoted to the rank of Group Captain, and given command of the largest fighter base in Air Defence Command, at St. Hubert, Quebec. He was awarded the Canadian Forces Decoration (C.D.) and Clasp. Kennedy retired in 1956, and died in Vancouver on June 11, 1989.

Harry Marlowe Kennedy was inducted as a Member of Canada's Aviation Hall of Fame in 1979.

Wilbert George Melvin (Mel) Knox

(1911 – 1996)

Wilbert George Melvin (Mel) Knox was born in Howich, Ontario, on March 12, 1911. As a child he moved with his family to Tuxford, Saskatchewan, where he was educated. In 1929 he gained his Private Pilot's Licence at the nearby Moose Jaw Flying Club, and eventually joined Prairie Airways as a commercial pilot, barnstorming throughout Saskatchewan and Manitoba. During this period he also qualified for his Air Engineer's Licence and Instructor's Rating. He graduated from a specialized course given by the Royal Canadian Air Force (RCAF) for civilians after the outbreak of World War II, and he returned to work at the Moose Jaw Flying Club training student pilots for the RCAF .

In 1941 he began instructing at No. 3 Air Observer School. The following year he re-joined Prairie Airways flying the Regina, Moose Jaw, Saskatoon, Prince Albert and North Battleford routes in Saskatchewan until Canadian Pacific Airlines (CPA) absorbed Prairie Airways in 1942. When

When Mel Knox began flying in 1929, he flew a one-passenger Gipsy Moth with a gross weight of 1,800 pounds (816 kg) and top speed of 80 miles-per-hour (128 km/h). His sole navigation equipment was a compass. Forty-two years later, on his final flight, he commanded a 240-passenger DC-8 jet with a gross weight of 355,000 lbs. (161,000 kg), and cruising speed of 580 mph (930 km/h). Its control panels included the sophisticated Inertial Navigation System equipment.

NATIONAL ARCHIVES OF CANADA PA-088407

W.G.M. Knox with CPA's first Barkley Grow. Vancouver, 1943.

he was transferred to Edmonton, Alberta, he gained his first northern flying experience flying into northern British Columbia and the Yukon. The next year he was moved to Vancouver, British Columbia, and flew the Yukon to Alaska route until he was transferred to Regina as Flight Superintendent in 1947.

When CPA designed its Asian routes in 1949, Knox was one of nine captains to proceed on the first overseas survey flight to Shanghai, China, by way of Alaska and the Aleutian Islands. The initial flight took 14 days, in an unpressurized Canadair North Star aircraft. For the first time, Canada and the Orient were linked by commercial transport, as envisioned by CPA's president, Grant McConachie (Hall of Fame 1974). Knox operated two additional charter flights to Hong Kong via Tokyo, Japan, before regular service began in 1949.

He became captain on the South Pacific Ocean routes to Hawaii, Fiji, New Zealand and Australia. In 1958 he was named

Check Pilot for all overseas routes, testing the competency of the flight crews. In this role he flew to Mexico, Peru, Chile, Argentina, Portugal, Spain, Italy and Holland.

Knox was named Chief Pilot Overseas in 1968, attesting to his outstanding abilities, and when the technology was created for the Inertial Navigation System (INS), he was chosen as one of its flying evaluators. This equipment, manufactured by the same company which was responsible for the navigation equipment that accurately guided the astronauts to the moon and back, displayed the aircraft's present position (latitude and longitude), the distance to the destination, the course to fly to reach that destination, and other data. Upon Knox's recommendation, the Carousel IV INS was adopted by CPA, and he became responsible for operational and training procedures, pilot qualification flights and the composition of flight manuals. On March 21, 1971, he captained the first flight without a navigator, using the INS, from Vancouver to Hawaii.

As an airline captain he flew all of CPA's routes to five continents. As Pilot-In-Command during 43 years of flight, he logged 26,000 hours in 28 aircraft types for a distance of 7,000,000 miles (11,265,000 km), equal to circling the globe 280 times at the equator, without injury to passenger or crew. Included in this mileage are 204 flights across the Pacific Ocean, 84 flights across the Atlantic Ocean and 56 flights across the Arctic Ocean between Vancouver and Amsterdam, Holland.

On retirement from CPA in 1971, Knox joined the Ministry of Transport at Vancouver, as an air carrier inspector for the Douglas DC-8 and DC-9 aircraft. Knox died in Vancouver, British Columbia, on November 13, 1996.

Wilbert George Melvin (Mel) Knox was inducted as a Member of Canada's Aviation Hall of Fame in 1974.

Thomas Albert Lawrence
(1895 – 1992)

Thomas Albert Lawrence, C.B., C.D.*, was born in Creemore, Ontario, on June 11, 1895. He was educated at Cookstown Continuation School and Barrie Collegiate Institute in Ontario. After graduation in 1912, he worked for the Ford Motor Company at Windsor, Ontario, to earn his university tuition fees.

He joined the Canadian Expeditionary Force on August 25, 1915, and served with the 4th Infantry Battalion in France from May 1916 until January 1918, when he transferred to the Royal Flying Corps as a flight cadet. On completion of training in England he was brevetted as a pilot and posted to 24 Fighter Squadron, Royal Air Force (RAF) in France, flying SE-5A aircraft.

Lawrence returned to Canada in July 1919, and in April 1920, joined the Canadian Air Board as an air engine fitter. In July of the same year he was reclassified as Air Pilot Navigator, receiving Commercial Air Pilot Certificate No. 101. His flying duties with the Air Board involved forestry timber cruising and fire patrols, aerial photography, mapping and other civil government air operations. He served in the Non-Permanent Canadian Air Force from May 22, 1922, until the birth of the

"His organizational and leadership abilities, initially directed to the early development and use of aviation in Canada, and latterly to the effective employment of aviators and their equipment, have been of outstanding benefit to Canadian aviation."

—Induction citation, 1980

Royal Canadian Air Force (RCAF) on April 1, 1924, as a Flying Officer with Regimental No. C7.

During 1926 the Canadian government planned the development of an ocean port on Hudson Bay in response to the need for a new shipping route to Europe that would be shorter than the Great Lakes via the St. Lawrence River. An important question needed to be answered: how many days of each season were safe for conventional freighters to move in and out of Hudson

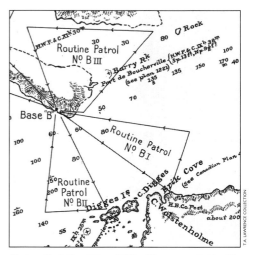

Hudson Strait Expedition, 1927 – 28, commanded by S/L T.A. Lawrence. Aerial mapping of the geographic features of the Strait was a requirement. This map shows some of the markings made from one of the stations that were set up by the expedition.

The Canadian Air Board was established in Ottawa in 1919 as a separate department of government to organize, administer, operate and control civil aviation in Canada. This was largely a result of a large post-war donation of air stations, surplus aircraft and other equipment, from the British Munitions Board and the United States, both of whom had operated in Canada during World War I. The government adopted a policy of providing air services for government departments and the provinces by way of aerial photography, forest fire and customs patrols, timber surveys and mapping, in order to subsidize the overall Air Board operations. Since some 20,000 Canadians had served in the British Air Services during W.W. I, trained personnel were readily available.

Bay through the Hudson Strait? The Hudson Strait Expedition of 1927-28 was authorized to find the answer.

In 1927 Lawrence, now a Squadron Leader, was selected to organize and command the air operations of the Canadian Government Expedition to the Hudson Strait over a period of sixteen months. This expedition was commissioned to make a visual and photographic survey of the ice conditions as related to marine navigation of the Strait from freeze-up to break-up and was associated with the project of developing an ocean port at Churchill, Manitoba. It also served to test aircraft as an aid to marine navigation, locate air bases and report on the feasibility of detached air operations in sub-Arctic conditions. Despite the obstacles presented by the generally hostile environment, inadequate navigation and communication equipment, and other operational facilities, the operation provided much-needed information.

Among air operations conducted by Squadron Leader Lawrence following the expedition, was a six week experimental air mail service between Ottawa, Ontario, Montreal, Quebec, St. John, New Brunswick, and Halifax, Nova Scotia. This was completed in January and February 1929, in association with A.D. McLean (Hall of Fame 1974).

Lawrence was appointed RCAF Liaison Officer to the RAF Air Ministry in 1932 in London, England. On his return to Canada he was given command of a number of Squadrons, at Camp Borden and Trenton, Ontario, and later at Ottawa. In 1938 he was commanding 2 Army Cooperation Squadron, and when war in Europe seemed to be inevitable, led that

Fokker G-CAHE of the Hudson Strait Expedition at Wakeham Bay, 1927 – 28. Using a portable slip-way worked, but it was still a difficult task to get the float equipped aircraft either up or down. From high tide to low tide the difference in water line was 140 yards (128 m).

squadron to an operational base at Halifax, preparing for submarine patrol off Halifax harbour.

During World War II Lawrence held a number of senior air force appointments, rising in rank to Air Vice-Marshal. From June 1942, he was Air Officer Commanding, 2 Training Command of the British Commonwealth Air Training Plan (BCATP), with headquarters in Winnipeg, Manitoba. He was then appointed to organize and command the North West Air Command at Edmonton, Alberta, in May 1944. In this role he was responsible for coordinating, with the United States Air Force, the movement of aircraft and supplies over the North West Staging Route in Canada, following the route of the Alaska Highway. As well, he provided liaison with the American forces on the Canol Pipeline Project between Whitehorse, Yukon, and Norman Wells, Northwest Territories.

In 1945, for his contributions to aviation, Lawrence was named a Companion of the Most Honourable Order of the Bath (C.B., Military). He was also awarded a King's Commendation for valuable services in the air. Later the same year he was awarded the Legion of Merit of the United States in the degree of Commander for his services to that country while with the RCAF in World War II.

Fokker G-CAHE gets an equipment change as the season changes. Crews were prepared to carry on without the aid of hoists.

Lawrence retired from the RCAF in April 1947. From 1950 to 1954 he served as Director of Civil Defence for Toronto and York County, Ontario. In 1956 he was appointed Manager, Maintenance and Operations of the Eastern Region of the Distant Early Warning (DEW) Line, a position he held for two years. From 1958 to 1962 he served as the Ottawa representative for International Telephones and Telegraph of Canada. Lawrence considered himself fully retired in 1962. He died in Toronto on February 19, 1992.

Thomas Albert Lawrence was inducted as a Member of Canada's Aviation Hall of Fame in 1980.

Fokker G-CAHI of the Hudson Strait Expedition at Wakeham Bay, 1927 – 28. Bringing the aircraft in to shore after a flight was a hazardous and cold task because of winds and rocky beach. The sea water never got over +40°F (+3°C).

Wilson George Leach

(b. 1923)

Wilson George Leach, C.M.M., C.D.**, B.A., M.D., was born on September 28, 1923, in Chalk River, Ontario, where he was educated. He held a variety of jobs until 1942 when he enlisted in the Royal Canadian Air Force (RCAF) with the hope of becoming a pilot. After pilot training in Quebec and Ontario he received his wings in 1943 and a commission the following year. He was assigned through the British Commonwealth Air Training Plan (BCATP) to instructional duties at several Canadian bases until war's end.

A desire to become a medical doctor resulted in enrollment at Pembroke Collegiate, Ontario, to complete Grade 13 examinations before accepting his military gratuities to assist him with higher education. In 1946 he was accepted at the University of Western Ontario in London, in the general science course, and two years later he qualified for the medical program.

An interest in research being conducted on wound healing techniques influenced his decision to return to the RCAF Reserve in 1949 as a Flying Officer, and for two summers Leach worked as a technical assistant on these animal experiments. In March 1952, he accepted a permanent

Dr. Leach's work was primarily directed towards the protection of air crew against the hazards of their hostile environment. This included such concerns as oxygen equipment, escape devices, survival equipment, and man's performance under adverse environmental conditions.

commission in the RCAF. When he graduated with his Bachelor of Arts and Doctor of Medicine degrees in May 1952, he had already been elected to the Honour Society of the medical school and received a gold key from the Hippocratic Society for his services to that Council.

He completed his junior internship at Victoria Hospital in London, Ontario, and remained for an additional year of post graduate studies in the biophysics department at the University of Western Ontario. Among his studies during that year were thermal conductivity of skin, and muscle physiology in a cold environment. In 1954 he was posted to the Institute of Aviation Medicine at Toronto, Ontario, where he spent the next twelve years, totally involved with aviation medicine, and was project officer in respiratory physiology.

With the advent of the Avro CF-105 Arrow fighter aircraft, a great deal of time was devoted to the development of partial-pressure breathing equipment to counteract the effects of loss of cabin pressure at extremely high altitudes. From these experiments, techniques and procedures were developed for the extensive trials conducted in the high altitude chamber on the effects of rapid decompression that might occur with the loss of cabin pressurization in transport aircraft such as the Yukon and DC-8. These experiments included trials with both service and civilian flying personnel.

In 1959 Leach received the Canadian Forces Decoration (C.D.) for service to the military. In 1960 he was awarded the Trans-Canada (McKee) Trophy for his contributions to manned flight through medical research. He was promoted to Wing Commander in 1961, and appointed Officer Commanding, Flying Personnel Medical Establishment. He was promoted to Group Captain in 1966 and transferred to Canadian Forces Headquarters at Ottawa as the Director of Staffing and Training in the Surgeon General Branch. For the next three years he was actively involved in the

career management of medical personnel for the Canadian Forces Medical Services.

A posting to the National Defence College, Kingston, Ontario, followed in 1969. On completion of this course, Leach was promoted to Brigadier General and named Deputy Surgeon General (Operations). He was also appointed Honorary Physician to Her Majesty Queen Elizabeth II. In 1969 he received a clasp to his C.D. In 1971, when the government decided that the Surgeon General Branch would have only one deputy, he was appointed Deputy Surgeon General.

In 1976 Leach was promoted to Major General and appointed Surgeon General of the Canadian Forces Medical Services. As well, in 1976 he was promoted to Commander in the Order of St. John of Jerusalem (C.St.J.). In 1978 he was awarded the Order of Military Merit with the rank of Commander (C.M.M.). In 1979 he received a second clasp to his C.D. MGen Leach retired from the Canadian Forces in 1980.

Wilson George Leach was inducted as a Member of Canada's Aviation Hall of Fame in 1974.

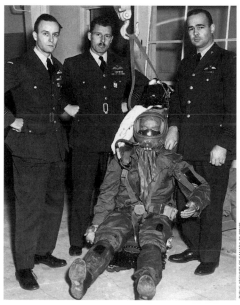

Left to right: S/L R.A. Stubbs, W/C L. Jervais, and S/L W.G. Leach with 'friend' outfitted for trial run on the high speed rocket sled, to test the ejection seat and high altitude oxygen equipment. Hurricane Mesa, Utah. c. 1956.

Robert Leckie

(1890 – 1975)

Robert Leckie, C.B., D.S.O., D.S.C., D.F.C., C.D., was born in Glasgow, Scotland, on April 16, 1890, and at the age of sixteen, immigrated to Toronto, Ontario. In 1915 he joined the Royal Naval Air Service (RNAS) after learning to fly at the Curtiss Aviation School in Toronto, at his own expense. On completion of his training he was commissioned and following further flight training in the United Kingdom, was posted to RNAS Station Great Yarmouth where he flew Curtiss HS-2L flying boats for the duration of the war.

For three years Leckie flew out of Great Yarmouth, attacking Zeppelins and flying anti-submarine patrols into the enemy stronghold of Helgoland (Heligoland), a small island in the North Sea off the coast of Germany. He had a reputation for being able to fly in the worst North Sea weather. His first Zeppelin kill, the L22, was made on May 14, 1917, a particularly dangerous operation from a slow flying boat. On August 5, 1918, during a Zeppelin raid, he

As Director of Canada's Air Board in the early 1920's, Wing Commander Leckie directed the start of forest fire and anti-smuggling patrols, treaty money flights to Indians in isolated areas, and general communications and transport flights. His work was considered to be the beginning of Canada's civil air operations, which laid the ground work for the future development of a mail and passenger service across Canada.

"His dedication to the development of civil and military aviation together with his exceptional organizational skills and desire for perfection have been of outstanding benefit to Canada." —Induction citation, 1988

Preparations for the first trans-Canada flight, starting from Halifax, Nova Scotia. LCol Robert Leckie in cockpit of Fairey Seaplane, with co-pilot Basil Hobbs on ladder. 1920.

was flying a de Havilland DH-4, and on this sortie shot down Zeppelin L70, which had on board the Commander of Germany's Zeppelin fleet, Peter Strasser.

Following an anti-submarine mission on February 20, 1918, Leckie carried out a daring rescue after sinking one of two German submarines involved in the attack. He saved the lives of the crew of a DH-4, a land plane which had to put down in the North Sea because of heavy enemy damage. Leckie, who was accompanying the DH-4 on this raid, decided to land alongside it, knowing he would be unable to take off in his Curtiss H-12 flying boat because of heavy seas. After picking up the two crew men, he taxied towards England until he ran out of fuel, then drifted for sixteen hours before they were taken in tow by a naval vessel. For these actions, he was awarded the Distinguished Service Order (D.S.O.), Distinguished Service Cross (D.S.C.), and Distinguished Flying Cross (D.F.C.).

In 1919, with the rank of Wing Commander, Leckie was loaned to the Canadian government where he worked for the Canadian Air Board as Director of Flying Operations. In 1920 he organized and led the first trans-Canada flight starting from Halifax, Nova Scotia, in a Fairey Seaplane. His co-pilot on this trip was Basil Hobbs (Hall of Fame 1987). From Halifax to Winnipeg, Manitoba, the airplanes used were flying boats. From Winnipeg, wheeled aircraft were used to complete the flight to Vancouver. The flight took ten days with an actual flying time of 49 hours. This was the first time that mail had been carried from coast to coast by air.

When the Canadian government decided to organize the defence forces into a single division under the Canadian Army, Colonel Leckie returned to the Royal Air Force (RAF). After a tour with Coastal Command Headquarters, he took over the flying command of HMS Hermes, one of

Britain's early aircraft carriers. He served in various other capacities, and in 1935 he was made Director of Training of the RAF. He was responsible for the training of many of the men who would soon fight in the Battle of Britain. In 1938 he was posted to Malta as Air Officer Commanding of the Mediterranean area with the rank of Air Commodore.

Leckie made a number of representations to the RAF to establish flying training schools in Canada. In 1940 he was seconded to the Royal Canadian Air Force (RCAF) and given the responsibility of organizing the British Commonwealth Air Training Plan (BCATP). At its conclusion, the BCATP had trained 131,553 air crew from 11 countries, a great achievement for Canada. In 1942 Leckie transferred to the RCAF with the rank of Air Vice-Marshal. In 1944 he was promoted to Air Marshal and appointed Chief of Air Staff, a position to which he gave dedicated service and unexcelled leadership during the final year of the war and the immediate post-war years. He received the Canadian Forces Decoration (C.D.). He retired from the RCAF on September 1, 1947.

During his career he was named a Companion of the Most Honourable Order of the Bath (C.B.). He was awarded the Commander of the Legion of Merit by the United States, Commander of the Legion of Honour by France, Grand Officer of the Order of the Crown by Belgium, Grand Commander of the Order of the White Lion by Czechoslovakia, Grand Commander of the Order of Polonia Restituta by Poland, and the King Haakon VII's Cross of Freedom by Norway. Following his retirement, he was appointed special consultant to the Air Cadet League of Canada (Belt of Orion 1989). He died at the age of 84, in Ottawa, Ontario, on March 31, 1975.

Robert Leckie was inducted as a Member of Canada's Aviation Hall of Fame in 1988.

Zebulon Lewis (Lewie) Leigh
(1906 – 1996)

Zebulon Lewis (Lewie) Leigh, O.B.E., C.M., E.D., was born in Macclesfield, England, on June 19, 1906, and came to Lethbridge, Alberta, at the age of three. He learned to fly there and became a barn-storming pilot and instructor for Southern Alberta Airlines in 1928. A year later he formed his own flying school in Medicine Hat, Alberta. In 1931 he left to become Chief Pilot for Maritime and Newfoundland Airways at Sydney, Nova Scotia. His area of operations included the Gulf of St. Lawrence and Newfoundland. When a Heinkel seaplane, catapulted from the German liner 'Bremen', was reported lost in the Bay of Fundy, Leigh located the wreck and rescued the surviving pilot, who later died of exposure.

Before accepting the job of Chief Pilot with Explorer's Air Transport of Sydney, Nova Scotia, in 1932, Leigh completed an instrument flying course with the Royal Canadian Air Force (RCAF) at Camp Borden, Ontario. His first assignment began with a flight from the Maritimes to Edmonton, Alberta, to commence northern operations. An instructor's job with the Brandon Flying Club in Manitoba followed until 1934, when he joined Canadian Airways Limited at Edmonton as pilot, with C.H. 'Punch' Dickins and Walter Gilbert (both Hall of Fame 1974). The Barren Lands and the Mackenzie River district of the Northwest Territories were his areas of operation. In December 1935, his piloting skills were used to locate John Harms, a wanted killer, and earned him a

Group Captain Leigh was involved in the purchase of two de Havilland Comets in 1953, the first military purchase and operation of jet transports in North America.

S/L J.A. Anderson, Mr. Lloyd of de Havilland, and G/C Z.L. Leigh, with DH Comet. 1953.

commendation from the Royal Canadian Mounted Police.

Canadian Airways sent Leigh to the Boeing School of Aeronautics at Oakland, California, in January 1936, to complete instrument flight, navigation and airline operation courses. With these qualifications he operated Canadian Airways' instrument flight school, training pilots to airline standards. He was Canada's first instrument-rated airline pilot. In 1937 Trans-Canada Airlines (TCA, Hall of Fame 1974) hired him as one of their first pilots. On April 2, 1939, he flew the first official westbound TCA flight from Winnipeg, Manitoba, to Vancouver, British Columbia.

Leigh resigned in 1940 to join the RCAF. As a Flight Lieutenant he served on east coast maritime patrols until given command of 13 Operational Training Squadron at Patricia Bay, British Columbia. In June 1942, he was promoted to Wing Commander and posted to Air Force Headquarters, Ottawa, Ontario, to help organize an RCAF Air Transport Command. These operations linked all Canadian military establishments, and included regular military mail service across the

Atlantic to the United Kingdom, North Africa and Italy. During this time they completed 688 crossings. His success was recognized by his promotion to Group Captain.

After D-Day, June 6, 1944, when the Allies had established a foothold in Europe, aircraft under his command evacuated large numbers of casualties from the war zone. Leigh personally flew with the first transport aircraft into Normandy. In 1944 he was named an Officer of the Order of the British Empire for his services (O.B.E. Military). He was appointed Commanding Officer of No. 9 Transport Group the following year and in 1946 was awarded the Efficiency Decoration (E.D.).

When Field Marshal Montgomery of Alamein visited Canada in 1946, Leigh was named air commander of the tour. He then took over the RCAF base at Goose Bay, Labrador, where he completed a number of rescue missions. The Trans-Canada (McKee) Trophy for 1946 was awarded to Leigh for outstanding contributions to Canada's air operations.

During the devastating Fraser River floods in the spring of 1948, Leigh was commander of No. 12 Group, RCAF Vancouver, which provided assistance. In September of that year, he became searchmaster of 'Operation Attaché', which involved a 13-day search for an aircraft missing in northern Manitoba. For the rescue of the crew and the British and American Naval Attachés aboard, he was decorated with the United States Legion of Merit.

In 1950 Leigh completed the National Defence College course at Kingston, Ontario, and was posted to Ottawa as Director of Air Operations for the RCAF. In the following several years, he served as Commanding Officer of the Air Transport Command at Lachine, Quebec, senior planner of the Korean airlift from Canada to Japan, and finally as Commander of No. 2 Air Defence Group, Toronto, Ontario.

He retired in 1957. He then served as Director of Operations of the Canadian National Exhibition Air Show at Toronto until 1966. In 1989 Leigh was made a member of the Order of Canada (C.M.). He died at Grimsby, Ontario, on December 22, 1996.

Zebulon Lewis (Lewie) Leigh was inducted as a Member of Canada's Aviation Hall of Fame in 1974.

Alexander John (Al) Lilly

(b. 1910)

Alexander John (Al) Lilly was born in Moose Jaw, Saskatchewan, on July 19, 1910. He commenced flying lessons in the late 1920's and dropped out of university to pursue a career in aviation.

In 1932 he joined the Royal Canadian Mounted Police (RCMP) and while posted to the detachment at Meadow Lake, Saskatchewan, he advocated the use of ski or float equipped aircraft to replace dog-teams and canoes. He was successful in his advocacy, leading the RCMP and others to increase their use of the bush plane. Although he attempted to continue his flying training while at Meadow Lake by scheduling his holidays to take lessons, the shortage of Department of Transport inspectors to give him his test frustrated his efforts.

He welcomed a transfer to Moncton, New Brunswick, but the Moncton airport was inactive when he arrived, forcing him to drive 100 miles (160 km) to St. John for lessons. Because of frequent fog at St. John, he arranged to hire a de Havilland Moth in order to fly out of the Moncton Airport and Flying Club. This move led to the reopening of the Moncton Flying Club, which remains operational today. Lilly obtained his Commercial Pilot's Licence while in Moncton. The RCMP transferred

On August 8, 1950, Al Lilly flew the first Canadian-manufactured F-86 Sabre Jet at Dorval, Quebec. On this flight he became the first in Canada to exceed the speed of sound. He accomplished this by putting the F-86 into a steep dive, an act which was considered very dangerous at the time.

"The application of his superior skills in test flying, leading to vital improvements in many aircraft during war and peace, have been of outstanding benefit to Canadian aviation."

—Induction citation, 1984

Al Lilly in cockpit of a 'North Star'. He delivered all twenty-two of these aircraft purchased by British Overseas Airways, which renamed them 'Argonauts', and set up a pilot training program for BOAC. c. 1949.

him to headquarters in Ottawa, but since this removed him from flying opportunities, he resigned and went to England to join Imperial Airways, the predecessor of British Overseas Airways Corporation (BOAC).

When World War II broke out, Lilly returned to the Moncton Airport as the Chief Flying Instructor at the British Commonwealth Air Training Plan (BCATP) station. After teaching instructors and ab initio students for a year, he was persuaded to join Ferry Command in Montreal. He was the first on Ferry Command to deliver six Lockheed Hudson aircraft to Prestwick, Scotland. He was among the first to fly supplies in North Africa in a stripped down Consolidated B-24 Liberator. The route took him to West Palm Beach, Florida, across the South Atlantic from Brazil to Liberia, south to Accra and north from there to Cairo. The latter part of the trip was flown over thousands of miles of unmapped desert. Lilly was appointed Chief Test Pilot for Ferry Command, a job which required the flying of Lockheed Hudsons and Venturas, Douglas A-20 Bostons, North American B-25's, Douglas C-47 Dakotas, B-24 Liberators, Consolidated Catalinas, Boeing B-17's, Avro Lancasters and de Havilland Mosquitos.

In June of 1946 Lilly was hired by Canadair in Montreal, Quebec, as a test pilot. On September 14th he and co-pilot R.J. Baker (Hall of Fame 1994) flew a 'North Star' from Montreal to Vancouver to test its long distance performance. The North Star was modified from the Douglas-built C-54 transport, and it became known as the DC-4M. Their passengers included the Hon. C.D. Howe (Hall of Fame 1976), founder of Trans-Canada Airlines (TCA, Hall of Fame 1974). R.J. Baker was test pilot for TCA on loan to Canadair as part of the conversion design team on this aircraft. Lilly was test pilot on this aircraft for a year, demonstrating it in the United Kingdom, Switzerland, Czechoslovakia, Holland, and Denmark. BOAC purchased twenty-two North Stars, renaming them Argonauts.

In 1950 Lilly was sent to North American Aviation's plant in California for familiarization flights on the F-86 Sabre fighter which Canadair was to build under licence. Canadair was successful in selling this aircraft to several countries in addition to sales of more than 300 within Canada. Lilly was responsible for the training and checking out of pilots on the F-86 in Columbia, South Africa and West Germany.

Lilly's final appointment at Canadair was Assistant to the President, and he continued to be in charge of test flying. He later worked as a consultant until he retired in 1976 and moved back to Moncton.

Lilly had an unblemished career of over 35 years as instructor, test pilot, transport pilot and aviation executive. As Chief Test Pilot for Ferry Command, his development of fuel control procedures and the correction of mechanical snags on many types of aircraft saved many lives. As Chief of Flight Operations and Test Pilot he was responsible for the successful testing of several thousand Canadair-produced aircraft.

Alexander John (Al) Lilly was inducted as a Member of Canada's Aviation Hall of Fame in 1984.

George Bayliss Lothian
(b. 1909)

"His inspired leadership in ocean flying despite adversity, the sharing of his exceptional aviation skills with others willing to learn, his unswerving demand for perfection in all who served under his command, bred a most superior grade of airman and resulted in outstanding benefit to Canadian aviation." —Induction citation, 1974

J.A.D. McCurdy and Captain George Lothian. March, 1960.

A life-long ambition was satisfied in 1968 when George Lothian chose an early retirement from Air Canada to accept the post of chief of the International Civil Aviation Organization (ICAO) mission to Katmandu, Nepal, and flight operations advisor to that government. He returned to Canada in 1973 with a record of 21,000 flying hours as pilot-in-command of numerous aircraft types. He then served as a consultant for the Canadian government in Indonesia and Nepal.

George Bayliss Lothian was born on November 20, 1909, in Vancouver, British Columbia, where he attended school. He commenced flying at the Aero Club of British Columbia in 1929, then joined the staff at the newly-opened Vancouver airport for a year. Until 1936 he flew locally as a commercial pilot and instructor, and with Canadian Airways Limited as a flying-boat pilot and crew member on scheduled flights between Vancouver and Seattle, Washington.

When Trans-Canada Airlines (TCA, Hall of Fame 1974) was formed in 1937, Lothian was hired as one of their first pilots and became a member of a small group who flew the Rocky Mountain route between Lethbridge, Alberta, and Vancouver. In 1941 he was seconded from TCA to North Atlantic Ferry Command, delivering bombers from Montreal, Quebec, to the United Kingdom. A year later he transferred to the Trans-Atlantic Return Ferry Service, carrying priority passengers and cargo between Scotland and Canada aboard operational aircraft. He became the first pilot to complete one hundred air crossings of the North Atlantic.

Lothian's wide experiences in the piloting of Liberator bombers, which he flew on the North Atlantic route, led to his transfer to 10 Squadron, Royal Canadian Air Force (RCAF) at Gander, Newfoundland, to train coastal command pilots on these operational aircraft for service during the Battle of the Atlantic. When this difficult task was completed, he joined the Canadian government Trans-Atlantic Mail Service operated by TCA, carrying troop mail and high priority passengers overseas. He then became Check Pilot and finally Chief Pilot of this unit.

Because of his extensive air management experience, TCA assigned him to the position of Superintendent of Flying, system wide, in 1952, a position which was later named Director of Flight Standards. As a pilot on the North Atlantic route to Europe, he set the trans-Atlantic speed record on three different occasions between 1943 and 1968.

During the period from 1952 to 1968, Lothian made the first deliveries into Canada of five of TCA's largest aircraft, the Lockheed Super Constellation, Vickers Viscount and Vanguard, Douglas DC-8 and DC-9. (In 1965 TCA was renamed Air Canada.) Lothian was responsible for pilot introduction, training, and flight deck procedures on these aircraft as well as on the Bristol Freighter. He was active in the development of the use of flight simulators for the advancement of airline flight technique, training and checking.

A superior knowledge of sustained high-altitude flight resulted in his leadership of the Air Canada team during rapid decompression experiments at the School of Aviation Medicine at Downsview, Ontario. These tests had considerable influence on the setting of international standards for all air lines. He was named a member of the international flight-deck committees for the British and French-developed Concorde, Boeing 747 and the experimental Boeing swept-wing supersonic aircraft. He was named deputy chairman of the International Air Transport Committee for pilot standards and flight training.

George Bayliss Lothian was inducted as a Member of Canada's Aviation Hall of Fame in 1974.

Joseph Henry Lucas
(1912 – 1961)

Joseph Henry Lucas was born in Toronto, Ontario, on June 14, 1912, and completed his matriculation at Riverdale Collegiate. He became interested in aviation and spent many hours at the Leaside airport where the Toronto Flying Club was operating. He enrolled in a newly formed aviation school in a downtown Toronto garage but the school was short lived. He finally got his start at age 16 with National Air Transport apprenticing under S.A. 'Bill' Rouse, working towards an Air Engineer's Licence. He quickly passed his A & C exams which covered routine servicing responsibilities, with authority to declare an aircraft or engine fit for flight. Then he proceeded to complete the requirements for the B & D Certificate allowing sign-out privileges for both airframe and engines after major overhaul. This achievement made him the youngest B & D engineer in Canada.

By this time National Air Transport had moved to Barker Field, named after Major W.G. Barker, V.C. (Hall of Fame 1974).

In the late 1950's, Joe Lucas was approached by Austin Airways' chief pilot, Jim Bell, about the feasibility and engineering possibilities of attaching water tanks to a Canso to make a more effective water bomber. He soon had two removable tanks, each holding 350 gallons (1,325 L) designed and fastened onto the sides of a Canso's body, and tests proved this invention to be a success. A few years later, improvements in design had the water scoops built into the underside of the Canso.

The first Canso water bomber designed and built by Aircraft Industries of Canada, Ltd. Photo shows the port tank with water pick-up probe and conical tail cap.

Here Lucas met pilot Tom Higgins and spent most of 1932 accompanying him on 'bush' flights and servicing aircraft in Sudbury, Chapleau and Gogama. He then returned to work at the National Air Transport's hangar until it burned on November 12, 1935. After an interview in Montreal with H. Molson, he was hired for a position in charge of maintenance for Dominion Skyways at Senneterre, Quebec. His previous bush experience helped in his promotion to Maintenance Superintendent and a move to Rouyn, Quebec, by 1937.

In late 1937, when a report of an untouched food cache reached headquarters of the Quebec Forestry Department, pilot Ralph Spradbrow and Lucas were asked to conduct an aerial search for a group of missing surveyors. On New Year's Eve, shortly before dark, the party of fifteen men was spotted on an island 13 miles from the Ontario-Quebec border. They had missed the food cache due to deep snow and had subsisted on fourteen rabbits over a period of 39 days. Early on New Year's morning the airlift of the weakened, hungry men began. Flying a Noorduyn Norseman, Spradbrow first flew the weakest of the group to hospital while Lucas remained behind and prepared food for the others. Three more trips were made to complete the rescue.

For a brief time in 1938 Lucas joined de Havilland Aircraft of Canada Ltd., which was beginning to manufacture Tiger Moths, but by the end of the year he returned to Dominion Skyways in Noranda, Quebec. At this time initial plans were being made for the British Commonwealth Air Training Plan (BCATP) and the Dominion Skyways proposal for Air Observer Schools (AOS) was accepted. Lucas was placed in charge of all maintenance at No. 1 AOS in Toronto when it opened on May 27, 1940. In order to use No. 1 AOS as a model, W.R. 'Wop' May (Hall of Fame 1974) flew his senior staff to Toronto for training prior to opening No. 2 AOS in Edmonton. Lucas' responsibilities grew with the opening of each new school, for he was in charge of all Dominion Skyway's maintenance.

In 1942 Lucas moved to St. Jean, Quebec, and took on the additional job of assistant general manager until the end of the war when he was contacted by the War Assets Corporation and subsequently set up an office in Montreal where he became chief of demolition and inspector, Aircraft Division, for one year.

He joined Aircraft Industries of Canada Ltd. in 1946. Although sales of war surplus aircraft was the original intent of the company, overhaul services under Lucas soon drew the attention of operators. When a Douglas DC-3 went down during a search in 1947, Aircraft Industries Ltd. got the salvage contract. This led to other government contract work with Canso conversions. Lucas then became Vice-President/General Manager at St. Jean, Quebec, and the company grew rapidly. Overhaul orders for the North American Harvard, DC-3 and Canso PBY aircraft, along with seasonal calls for engine changes, radio installations and overhaul work necessitated an increase in staff and space.

In 1954 the Babb Company bought Aircraft Industries and made Lucas President/General Manager. He was also asked to head the first Airworthiness Council under Transport Minister George Hees. He held these positions until February 13, 1961, when he suffered a fatal heart attack.

Joseph Henry Lucas was inducted as a Member of Canada's Aviation Hall of Fame in 1991.

William Floyd Sheldon Luck
(b. 1911)

William Floyd Sheldon Luck was born in Kingston, Ontario, on January 26, 1911. He attended school in Edmonton and Calgary, Alberta, and as a youth became interested in flying, against the wishes of his family. He persevered, won the confidence of his parents and commenced flying at Rutledge Air Services at Calgary. For the next forty seven years, Sheldon Luck was actively involved in and contributed to the development of aviation in Canada.

After receiving his Private Pilot's Licence in June of 1931, Luck participated in barnstorming activities and for four years was engaged in charter flying in Alberta and northern British Columbia for a number of companies. He flew fish out of northern Alberta and pioneered the establishment of commercial scheduled services from the Yukon to Vancouver, British Columbia. In 1936 he joined United Air Transport, which became Yukon Southern Air Transport. He was appointed Chief Pilot of Yukon Southern in March

"For nearly five decades he has displayed resourcefulness with the highest order of professionalism in his devotion to the advancement of aviation, which together with his qualities of leadership, have been of outstanding benefit to Canadian aviation." —Induction citation, 1981

1941, and retained that responsibility with Canadian Pacific Airlines (CPA) when it absorbed Yukon Southern in January 1942.

It was during the early portion of this period that he was engaged in a number of 'firsts'. Two of these included participation with Grant McConachie (Hall of Fame 1974) in August 1938, on the first official mail run from Vancouver, to Whitehorse, Yukon, through Fort St. John, British Columbia, and in November 1939, he pioneered the first weekly air service to Whitehorse via Fort St. John from Kamloops, British Columbia.

In 1942 Luck took a leave of absence from CPA to join the RCAF Transport Command where he served for the duration of World War II. Assigned to 231 Squadron, Royal Air Force, he was involved in ferrying aircraft across the Atlantic, which he accomplished 78 times, along with other airborne activities. He was the courier pilot for British Prime Minister Winston Churchill and his delegation to the Atlantic Conference in August 1941, when Churchill, United States' President Roosevelt, and Canada's Prime Minister Mackenzie King met aboard a cruiser off the coast of Quebec to discuss

A copy of Sheldon Luck's commendation from King George VI, signed by Prime Minister Winston S. Churchill. June 1944.

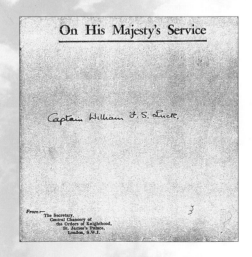

plans for post-World War II peace. In August 1942, Luck flew emergency supplies to El Alamein, Egypt, and between December 1944, and May 1945, he flew Coronado flying boats to and from Lagos, Nigeria. At the conclusion of his service with the RAF Transport Group, he was honoured with a King's Commendation for his valuable services to the war effort.

In October 1945, Luck returned to the domestic operation of CPA to resume the position he left in 1942. In 1946 he resigned to join Flota Aerea Mercante Argentina in Buenos Aires, Argentina. This returned him to overseas flying as a captain on Sandringham flying boats and Douglas DC-4's to the United Kingdom and New York, U.S.A. In 1948 he left Argentina to return to Canada. For five years he flew out of Vancouver, and operated over large areas of Canada and the United States. In 1953 he joined Maritime Central Airways based at Mont Joli, Quebec, and Moncton, New Brunswick, flying Bristol Freighters and DC-4's in the Maritimes, Newfoundland and Labrador.

In 1958 he started a cattle ranch near Fort St. James, British Columbia, and supported the enterprise by flying charter flights throughout the Yukon and British Columbia. It was during this period that he became interested in the aerial suppression of forest fires and was appointed Chief Pilot of the Flying Firemen which accomplished outstanding results in forest fire detection and prevention. From 1970 to 1974 he was Chief Pilot and Operations Manager of TransProvincial Airlines, Instrument Flight Rule operations, located at Terrace and Prince George, British Columbia. In 1975 he flew water bombers for Conair at Abbotsford, British Columbia, and in 1977 he flew the same duties for Avalon Aviation out of Thunder Bay, Ontario.

During his career in aeronautics Luck has had an unusually wide experience of flying. He was intimately involved as an aviation administrator and in all phases of flying activities. He was a bush pilot and aerial fire fighter; he flew charter operations and as an airline pilot. After 51 years as an active pilot, he has flown over 26,000 hours as Pilot-in-Command of 57 types of aircraft.

William Floyd Sheldon Luck was inducted as a Member of Canada's Aviation Hall of Fame in 1981.

Frank Archibald MacDougall
(1896 – 1975)

Frank Archibald MacDougall, B.Sc.F., was born in Toronto, Ontario, on June 16, 1896, and received his primary and secondary education at Carleton Place, Ontario. He attended Queen's University at Kingston, Ontario, during 1915, but left to enlist in the Royal Canadian Artillery. He served in France as a signaler and was injured by chlorine gas at Vimy Ridge. He returned at war's end to attend the University of Toronto, where he graduated in 1923 with a degree in forestry.

Following the war he worked on the temporary staff with the Ontario Provincial Forestry group and in 1922 took part in the James Bay survey which operated from a base near Kapuskasing. This was the summer of ravaging forest fires in northern Ontario, as well as the disastrous fire at Haileybury on the shore of Lake Timiskaming, with its devastating losses. That event made a distinct impression on MacDougall and had much to do with shaping his future career.

Until 1924, when the Ontario government set up an air service, forest fires had been detected from ground patrols and from boats or canoes. They were fought by conventional methods, using shovels and axes. The use of aircraft in the forestry service opened up other important uses of the airplane, including wildlife surveys and enforcing game regulations. The incidence of poaching, which during the 1930's had been a major problem, was practically wiped out.

"His practical development of aircraft modifications and utilization, in the protection and preservation of forested areas and wilderness parks, has been of outstanding benefit to Canadian aviation." —Induction citation, 1974

Frank MacDougall with the Trans-Canada (McKee) Trophy, 1963.

The government of Ontario employed MacDougall in their forest survey branch during the summers of his university years, and following his graduation named him Assistant Forester of the Pembroke and Sault Ste. Marie district. In 1924 he was named district forester of the Sault St. Marie district, the same year the Ontario Provincial Air Service (OPAS, Belt of Orion 1991) was formed. It was during this period he became convinced of the usefulness of aircraft in the protection of forests and in the administration of the province's parks. G.H.R. Phillips (Hall of Fame 1974) encouraged him and became his flying instructor. MacDougall gained his Commercial Pilot's Licence in 1930, eventually logging some 6,000 hours as pilot-in-command. He also obtained his Air Engineer's Certificate that same year.

From 1931 to 1941 MacDougall served as Superintendent of Algonquin Park and Chief Forester of the Pembroke district. With his broad spectrum of knowledge and experience, he was appointed Deputy Minister of Lands and Forests. The Department of Game and Fisheries was added to this portfolio in 1946.

MacDougall immediately became involved in the expansion and development of air services, with particular application not only to the detecting of forest fires, but in suppressing them by means of water-bombing from the air. His department was directly responsible for developing the water-bombing tanks to equip the fleet, and this method of combating forest fires has since been adopted by numerous other forestry protection air services. In addition, he developed the use of department aircraft for the administration of game and fish regulations, wild life surveys, and the movement of inspectors and other officers on forest management duties. The restocking of lakes and streams with game fish fingerlings dropped from aircraft was another function assumed by his department.

MacDougall's lengthy experience as a pilot, flying across unmapped and uninhabited areas, led him to take active steps in developing the Canadian-designed and built de Havilland Beaver and Otter aircraft to meet northern bush requirements. He gave both stimulus and initiative to the development of these world-famous aircraft by placing orders for them even before they had flown. The first OPAS Beaver was delivered in April 1948, and over the years the department owned 45 Beavers and 28 Turbo Beavers. It was through his foresight and decisions that the Ontario Department of Lands and Forests operates the world's largest fleet of government-owned aircraft on forest protection services. For these contributions to aviation he was awarded the Trans-Canada (McKee) Trophy for 1963. MacDougall retired from government service in 1966, on his 70th birthday. He died in Toronto on June 27, 1975.

Frank Archibald MacDougall was inducted as a Member of Canada's Aviation Hall of Fame in 1974.

Elizabeth Muriel Gregory (Elsie) MacGill

(1905 – 1980)

Elizabeth Muriel Gregory (Elsie) MacGill, O.C., B.Sc., M.Sc., D.Sc.(Hon.), LL.D.(Hon.), was born in Vancouver, British Columbia, on March 27, 1905. She received her education in Vancouver and then attended the University of Toronto. In 1927 she became the first woman to graduate from that university with an Electrical Engineering Degree. This was followed by graduate study at the University of Michigan, where, in 1929, she became the first woman to receive a Masters Degree in Aeronautical Engineering.

While MacGill was at the University of Michigan, she was stricken with acute infectious myelitis, a form of polio. She wrote her final exams from her hospital bed, determined that her disability would not stop her pursuit of a career in engineering. In 1933 she enrolled at the Massachusetts Institute of Technology to further her post-graduate work. In 1934 she was hired as an engineer at Fairchild Aircraft Limited at Longueuil, Quebec. During her time with the company she worked on stress analysis of the prototype Fairchild Super 71, which had the first stressed-skin, all-metal fuselage designed and built in Canada.

In 1938 she left Fairchild to become Chief Aeronautical Engineer at the Fort William (Thunder Bay) plant of Canadian Car and Foundry Company Limited. It was there

Elsie MacGill was the author of many technical aviation articles and a biography, *My Mother the Judge*, which is about her mother, Judge Helen Gregory MacGill, who was Judge of the Juvenile Court in Vancouver for 22 years.

"Her contribution to Canadian and international design and engineering, her high honours, her resolve that led her to the top of her profession, have been of outstanding benefit to Canadian aviation."

—Induction citation, 1983

Members of the Lakehead Branch of the Engineering Institute of Canada. Left to right: P.G. Doncaster, Elsie MacGill, Gordon O'Leary. Fort William, Ontario, 1938.

that she became the first woman to work on the over-all design of an airplane, the Maple Leaf II, a two-seat, single-engine biplane designed as a primary trainer for use on wheels, skis or floats. This trainer received its certificate of airworthiness, aerobatics category, within eight months of the commencement of design, an outstanding achievement.

A few weeks after the beginning of World War II in 1939, she was informed that the plant would be involved with large-scale production of military aircraft. She was put in charge of all engineering work related to the Canadian production of the British-designed Hawker Hurricane fighter. Within a year the old railway car plant was producing three fighters a day with a staff of 4,500. A total of 1,450 Hurricanes were produced in just two years. When this contract was completed, MacGill was responsible for the production of 835 Curtiss Hell Divers for the U.S. Navy.

In 1937 she became the first woman to be admitted to corporate membership in the Engineering Institute of Canada and received the Institute's Gzowski Medal in 1940 for her paper on "Factors Affecting the Mass Production of Aeroplanes." In 1943 she married E.J. (Bill) Soulsby, Assistant General Manager of Victory Aircraft Limited, and established her own business in Toronto as an aeronautical engineering consultant.

In 1946 MacGill became the first woman to serve as Canadian Technical Advisor to the International Civil Aviation Organization (ICAO), where she helped draft the international air worthiness regulations for the design and production of commercial aircraft. In 1947 she served as chairman of the stress analysis committee at ICAO, the first woman to hold this position.

MacGill held Fellowships in the Canadian Aeronautics and Space Institute, the Royal Aeronautical Society, and the Engineering Institute of Canada. She was a member of the American Institute of Aeronautics and Astronautics, and the first woman member of the Association of Professional Engineers of Ontario.

MacGill's contributions and accomplishments earned her wide recognition and many honours. The American Society of Women Engineers honoured her in 1953 and presented her with the Society's medal, the first time these distinctions were granted to someone outside of the United States. The Canadian Government, recognizing her substantial contributions, appointed her an Officer of the Order of Canada (O.C.) in 1971. She received the Engineering Institute of Canada Julian C. Smith Memorial Medal in 1973. The Ninety-Nines International Organization of Women Pilots awarded her the Amelia Earhart Medal in 1975. Four Universities conferred Honorary Doctorates on her: Toronto (1973), Windsor (1976), Queens (1978) and York (1978).

In addition to her aeronautical pursuits, she had a concern for the legal rights and status of women, became active in women's organizations throughout Canada, and was highly respected for her thoughtful and constructive views. In 1967 she was one of the seven appointees to the Royal Commission on the Status of Women. Just prior to her death she had accepted an appointment to the Canadian Organizing Committee for the 1981 International Year of the Disabled. She died in a car accident at Cambridge, Massachusetts, U.S.A., on November 4, 1980, before she could participate on this committee.

Elizabeth Muriel Gregory (Elsie) MacGill was inducted as a Member of Canada's Aviation Hall of Fame in 1983.

Gerald Lester (Gerry) MacInnis

(1914 – 1991)

Gerald Lester (Gerry) MacInnis was born in Amherst, Nova Scotia, on June 2, 1914. He was educated there, at Point Pleasant, Prince Edward Island, and Montreal, Quebec. The Royal Canadian Air Force (RCAF) accepted him for air crew training in 1941. He graduated as a commissioned officer and air observer and was posted to 116 Squadron at Dartmouth, Nova Scotia, on anti-submarine patrols during the Battle of the Atlantic. The following year he transferred to 117 Squadron on aerial patrols over the Gulf of St. Lawrence, under Wing Commander S. R. McMillan (Hall of Fame 1974).

In 1943 he was selected for pilot training and at graduation, became one of the few members of the RCAF qualified to wear both observer and pilot wings. He returned to 117 Squadron until 1944 when a transfer placed him with No. 45 Group, Royal Air Force Transport Command, based at Dorval, Quebec, where he was promoted to Flight Lieutenant. He completed a number of long-range ferry flights.

Drifting snow and reduced visibility were constant hazards, and made the problem of locating the advance party on the second and third flights to each DEW Line site almost as difficult as spotting the sites initially. Although the Arctic regions do not usually receive large volumes of snow, the incessant winds cause the snow to drift and the surfaces to become extremely rough and hard, adding to the problems of landing aircraft in that region during the darkness of winter.

Gerald MacInnis receives the Trans-Canada (McKee) Trophy from A/V/M. M.M. Hendricks, who presented it on behalf of the Minister of National Defence. October, 1956.

MacInnis was seconded to British Overseas Airways Corporation (BOAC) as an Instrument Flight Instructor and Check Pilot on the North Atlantic Ocean route in 1945. At the end of World War II, BOAC offered him a permanent position and he subsequently qualified for both British and American Senior Pilot's Licences, Instrument Ratings and Navigator's Certificates. In 1948 he qualified as Captain on the Constellation. He resigned in 1950 to become a full-time farmer on Prince Edward Island.

In 1951 the Distant Early Warning (DEW) Line, a chain of radar stations, was under construction in the eastern Arctic as part of the Canada-United States northern defence line. Maritime Central Airways, operated by C.F. Burke (Hall of Fame 1982), was the prime airlift contractor for the eastern sector of the DEW Line. Burke offered MacInnis a position as a pilot, which would take him to a setting very different from the idyllic farm life of the Maritimes.

MacInnis was given the responsibility of landing the advance parties at each of the sites in the Arctic region, set 50 miles (80 km) apart and extending over a total distance of 900 miles (1,450 km), from St. John's, Newfoundland, along the coast of

Labrador, to Frobisher Bay, Northwest Territories. He personally carried out the initial aircraft landings at all but one of these points, enabling camps to be set up preparatory to construction work. The task of locating the sites was a serious problem in itself. While the sites had been chosen by advance aerial surveyors and marked on maps, there were few, if any, geological features to facilitate their identification from the air. Moreover, for the initial flights, navigational aids were non-existent.

MacInnis' aerial operation was considered one of the most difficult in the history of Canadian commercial aviation. Long distance flights in ski-equipped Douglas DC-3/C-47 aircraft through brutal winter storms to unmapped areas were a constant requirement. Due to the distances involved, aircraft had to leave the main base on almost every flight with full tanks of fuel, thus reducing the payload. After landing the advance party, it was necessary to complete a second and sometimes a third flight to each site to deliver supplies, and equipment for setting up navigational aids for further flights.

During this 29-month period in the north, MacInnis flew 2,455 hours, of which 540 hours were completed at night. He was awarded the Trans-Canada (McKee) Trophy for 1955. His abilities as a pilot and navigator were cited as one of the greatest single factors in the success of the DEW Line venture.

In March of each year from 1952-1954, MacInnis was assigned to lead seal surveys. Patrol flights were made over the Atlantic Ocean north of Newfoundland to chart the movement of the sea ice to help in predicting the locations of seal herds. During these periods he also completed a number of emergency missions in that region.

Work on the DEW Line was completed in 1957, and for the next two years, MacInnis flew long-range charter flights. In 1959 he joined the Ministry of Transport (MOT) as an Air Carrier Inspector. He was transferred to Ottawa, Ontario, in 1965, and named Supervisory Pilot for the MOT fleet of fixed-wing aircraft. When he retired from MOT on June 1, 1979, he had flown 21 different aircraft types and spent over 21,000 hours in the Captain's seat, which is equivalent to almost 2.5 years off the ground. He died in Ottawa on March 6, 1991.

Gerald Lester (Gerry) MacInnis was inducted as a Member of Canada's Aviation Hall of Fame in 1974.

Donald Roderick MacLaren
(1893 – 1989)

Donald Roderick MacLaren, D.S.O., M.C.*, D.F.C., was born in Ottawa, Ontario, on May 28, 1893. His family lived for some years in Calgary, Alberta, and Vancouver, British Columbia. In 1914, after two years at McGill University in Montreal, Quebec, he accompanied his father and brother to northern Alberta, where they opened a fur-trading post at Keg River, about 200 miles (320 km) north of Peace River Crossing.

In early 1917 MacLaren joined the Royal Flying Corps (RFC) in Canada, completed his flying training at Camp Borden, Ontario, and was brevetted a pilot that same year. After operational training in England as a 2nd Lieutenant, he was posted to 46 Squadron in France. He remained with that unit during his entire tour of combat flying, becoming Commander of the squadron within a year.

D.R. MacLaren was among the most brilliant of the many Canadians who distinguished themselves as fighter pilots with the RFC. He did not get into action until late November 1917, and his first aerial victory did not come until early March 1918. His operational career ended in October 1918. Yet in less than eight months, he was credited with 54 aerial victories, having brought down 48 enemy aircraft and six observation balloons, becoming the fourth-ranking Canadian fighter ace of the war. He was also credited with more aerial victories in the Sopwith Camel than any single pilot of World War I.

His first aerial victory came in March of 1918, and from that time on, except for two brief periods of leave, his name was featured almost daily in military communiqués. In April he was promoted to Captain, awarded the Military Cross (M.C.) and named Flight Commander. During one sortie behind enemy lines he disabled a long-range gun and shot down one balloon and two enemy aircraft. Three months later, when his score of hostile aircraft destroyed stood at nine, he was awarded a Bar to the Military Cross. Only a few weeks later, having by then shot down thirty-seven enemy aircraft in combat, he was awarded the Distinguished Flying Cross (D.F.C.). He was promoted to Major and given command of the squadron.

By October of 1918 his record of victories was exceeded by only two other pilots then at the front, W.G. Barker and R. Collishaw (both Hall of Fame 1974). Just two weeks before the Armistice he had his last enemy engagement, bringing his total score of victories to forty-eight aircraft and six balloons. He was awarded the Distinguished Service Order (D.S.O.). France awarded him the Croix de Guerre and made him a Chevalier of the Legion of Honour.

At war's end in 1918, he assisted with the formation of the non-permanent Canadian Air Force that came into being in 1920 under the administration of the Canadian Air Board. In the spring of 1921 he was back in Vancouver, and in 1924 he bought a Curtiss JN-4 and formed Pacific Airways Limited at Vancouver, in 1925, carrying out fishery patrols and aerial surveys for the Canadian government. He served as Executive Officer and Chief Pilot of the far-ranging fleet until 1928, when his company merged with Western Canada Airways Limited.

When MacLaren became Superintendent of the Pacific Coast Division of Western Canada Airways, with headquarters at Vancouver, he expanded the air operations into the Yukon using the latest available aircraft, on which he became qualified. Pilots under his command in the sub-Arctic, the Yukon and throughout British Columbia included N.G. Forester and S.R. McMillan (both Hall of Fame 1974). In 1929 he and H. Hollick-Kenyon (Hall of Fame 1974) flew the experimental airmail service between Regina and Moose Jaw, Saskatchewan, and Medicine Hat, Lethbridge and Calgary, Alberta.

Western Canada Airways was absorbed by Canadian Airways Limited in 1930. MacLaren was named Assistant General Manager for British Columbia and the Yukon, a position he held until 1937.

In 1937 MacLaren was hired by Trans-Canada Airlines (TCA, Hall of Fame 1974) as its first employee, Assistant to the Vice-President. He was appointed Vice-President of Operations in Ottawa, and selected airline pilots for this new airline from among the best of Canada's well known bush pilots. Within three years he was appointed Superintendent of Stations and Director of Passenger Services. In 1945 he was named Executive Assistant to the President, Pacific Area. He retired from TCA in 1958.

The Air Cadet movement was one of MacLaren's long-time interests. In 1941 he formed the first Air Cadet Squadron in Winnipeg, Manitoba. He rose from Provincial Chairman to the Presidency of the Air Cadet League of Canada (Belt of Orion 1989). Air Canada designed the D.R. MacLaren Trophy in his honour. It is presented annually to the most proficient Royal Canadian Air Cadet Squadron in British Columbia.

MacLaren died in Vancouver on July 4, 1989, at the age of 96.

Donald Roderick MacLaren was inducted as a Member of Canada's Aviation Hall of Fame in 1977.

Merlin William (Mac) MacLeod
(1892 – 1959)

NATIONAL ARCHIVES OF CANADA C-84254

M.W. 'Mac' MacLeod holds the cowl flap which he designed to regulate engine temperatures.

Merlin William (Mac) MacLeod was born in Olympia, Washington, U.S.A., on February 1, 1892. He attended school there and at Tacoma, Washington, until 1910 when he moved to Vancouver, British Columbia.

MacLeod's inventive genius led to many aircraft-related technical advances. His inventions resulted in lower maintenance costs, as well as safer and more efficient operations. While his accomplishments were recognized by his peers, much of what he did has gone unnoticed by the Canadian public.

MacLeod joined Canadian Airways Limited at Winnipeg, Manitoba, in 1929 as a flight mechanic and worked with bush pilots in Canada's north. On one occasion, after his aircraft crash-landed in an uninhabited area and splintered the propeller, he hand carved another which worked well enough to enable the pilot to fly the aircraft to civilization. In 1933 he was severely injured in an aircraft crash near Lac du Bonnet, near the southern tip of Lake Winnipeg, Manitoba. Although unable to walk, he was credited with saving the life of his pilot through emergency first aid.

In 1937 MacLeod was employed by Trans-Canada Airlines (TCA, Hall of Fame 1974) in Winnipeg as an air engineer, before moving to Dorval, Quebec, as Superintendent of production overhaul. He became, successively, Superintendent of job methods and development, and Development Engineer.

MacLeod's inventive genius led to many aircraft-related technical advances. He invented the brake disc slotting system which provided more efficient cooling of the discs, thus reducing warping of aircraft brake discs. This application is used world-wide. He developed a cowl flap which was designed to regulate engine temperatures. It greatly increased the time required between engine over-hauls, and was an immediate success. Not only did it benefit Canadian air transport operations, it is used internationally. In 1949 he was responsible for inventing the cross-over exhaust system which greatly reduced noise in the cabins of North Star aircraft.

A classic in aeronautical design was his ball and socket principle for exhaust systems, which added to the safety and economy of aircraft engine exhaust systems in Canada, the United States and Great Britain. Numerous other inventions and improvements in the aircraft industry are credited to him, such as pneumatic deicers, emergency fuel systems and hydraulic and lubrication systems.

Perhaps less tangible, but with equal impact on the aviation industry generally, were the methods he used to instruct those under his command in job handling and personnel training.

He was named an Associate Fellow of the Canadian Aeronautics and Space Institute and was honoured with the McCurdy Award in 1954 for his sustained contributions in the field of aviation. The citation stressed his consistent display of ingenuity, and his abilities to pass on to others his experiences and ways of accomplishing certain tasks.

MacLeod retired from TCA in 1959, and died at Pointe Claire, Quebec, on December 12, 1959.

Merlin William (Mac) MacLeod was inducted as a Member of Canada's Aviation Hall of Fame in 1977.

Wilfrid Reid (Wop) May
(1896 – 1952)

Wilfrid Reid (Wop) May, O.B.E., D.F.C., was born in Carberry, Manitoba, on March 20, 1896. He moved with his family to Edmonton, Alberta, in 1902, and attended school in Edmonton and Calgary. In 1916 he enlisted with the 202nd City of Edmonton Sportsman's Battalion, and gained the rank of Sergeant Gunner. He qualified for his wings at the Royal Flying Corps (RFC) School of Instruction at Acton, England, and took higher instruction with 94 Squadron, RFC. With only 54 1/2 hours flying time logged, Lieutenant May was posted to the RFC 209th (9th Naval) Squadron in France on April 9th, 1918, as a fighter pilot.

On April 20, 1918, during an aerial engagement over enemy territory, he shot down one aircraft before he was attacked by the 'Red Baron', Manfred von Richthofen. With his guns jammed, he retreated towards home with the German 'Ace' on his tail. The Red Baron was shot down by Squadron Leader A. Roy Brown of the 209th Squadron. By the end of World War I, Captain May had destroyed 13 enemy aircraft, and was awarded the Distinguished Flying Cross (D.F.C.).

In 1919 May returned to Edmonton and formed May Airplanes Limited, the first air service at Edmonton. He made the first commercial flight from May Field in Edmonton on June 2, 1919. The company engaged in barnstorming activities and

Many people have asked where the nickname 'Wop' came from. It has been said that it originated with a young cousin who couldn't pronounce 'Wilfrid,' and May's brother, Court, made the mispronunciation stick.

operated a flying school in Edmonton. In 1920 he received Commercial Pilot's Licence No. 7 and in 1921 he earned his Air Mechanic's Licence. In 1921 he was granted a commission in the Canadian Air Force and completed a refresher course in navigation at Camp Borden, Ontario.

May persuaded Imperial Oil Limited to use freighter aircraft for their Northwest Territories oil operations at Fort Norman. Imperial Oil hired him and George Gorman to ferry two Junkers JL-6 monoplanes from New York to Edmonton in January 1921. These aircraft became known as 'Vic' and 'René', and were flown by Gorman and E.G. Fullerton (Hall of Fame 1974) for Imperial Oil on an oil exploration trip deep into the Northwest Territories.

May continued to fly commercially, and his unshakeable faith in Edmonton's air future encouraged him to establish Canada's first commercial airport at Blatchford Field in 1927. The same year he founded the Edmonton and Northern Alberta Aero Club, and was named its first President. With partners Cy Becker and Vic Horner, he founded Commercial Airways at Edmonton and became their Chief Pilot. The company was awarded the Mackenzie River district airmail contract and he led a group of five aircraft on the first air mail flight to the Arctic. He was pilot of one of the three aircraft that went on to Aklavik. This 1,600 mile (2,575 km) flight was the first winter air voyage to the Arctic. May was awarded the Trans-Canada (McKee) Trophy in 1929 in recognition of his work in organizing air services to outlying districts.

On January 3, 1929, May and co-pilot Vic Horner flew a mercy mission in a two-seater open cockpit Avro Avian aircraft from Edmonton to Fort Vermilion, Alberta, a distance of some 600 miles (965 km). For the most part, their route was over sparsely inhabited country. They encountered many snow storms and temperatures down to –30°F (–33°C). The purpose of the flight was to carry diphtheria anti-toxin to combat a diphtheria epidemic at the isolated post of Little Red River. Urgent action was necessary and no other means of transport would have met the need. The serum was wrapped and placed beside a charcoal warmer to keep it from freezing. Their flight was successful, and the serum did the job. This aerial drama captured the attention of the world press and gave further stature to Canadian 'Bush Pilots'. May's heroism was rewarded with civic and provincial honours.

May's company, Commercial Airways, was absorbed by Canadian Airways in 1931, and May and his wife Vi were transferred to Fort McMurray, Alberta. He served as a pilot for their northern services, and carried mail to communities in Northern Alberta. In January 1932, the Royal Canadian Mounted Police (RCMP) commissioned him to work with them in the search for the man known as the 'Mad Trapper' (Albert Johnson), who had terrorized local trappers and killed an RCMP officer. Flying a ski-equipped Bellanca, May's 16-day aerial quest took him to Aklavik and through the Mackenzie Mountains ferrying passengers,

and food and gear to the searchers. He spotted the elusive 'Mad Trapper' on the Porcupine River, 175 miles (280 km) from the Alaska border, from the air on February 16th and informed the RCMP posse. He and his air mechanic, Jack Bowen, watched the final shoot-out on the following day. On February 18 he flew a wounded RCMP officer, the RCMP Inspector, and the body of the 'Mad Trapper' back to Aklavik.

In 1935 he was named Officer of the Order of the British Empire (O.B.E.) for his numerous contributions to Canadian aviation. The following year he was named Superintendent of the Mackenzie River District of Canadian Airways and was transferred back to Edmonton.

Early in World War II he was appointed Supervisor of the British Commonwealth Air Training Plan (BCATP) schools in Western Canada, operated by CPA, which took over Canadian Airways at that time. He served as General Manager of No. 2 Air Observer School at Edmonton from 1942 to 1946. During this time he conceived the idea of aerial rescue crews to assist ferry pilots and other fliers who went down in northern British Columbia and the Yukon en route to Siberia. He recruited and trained a team of paramedics who

volunteered their services to parachute into crash sites, saving the lives of many airmen. For this action, he was awarded the Medal of Freedom with Bronze Palm by the United States Government in 1947.

In 1947 May was appointed Director of Northern Development by Canadian Pacific Airlines (CPA), with the task of opening air bases in Northwest Territories, Yukon, Alaska, and northern British Columbia. In 1949 he was transferred to Vancouver as Director of Development for CPA and for two years worked to open bases in the Far East and the South Pacific.

In 1951 he was transferred to Calgary as Manager of CPA (Repairs) Ltd., and undertook the task of forming the company, recruiting employees and building the operation at RCAF Station Lincoln Park into a viable operation. The task was to retrieve, repair and test operational aircraft that had crashed.

On June 21, 1952, while hiking with his son, Denny, to Timpanagos Cave National Monument near Provo, Utah, May died of a heart attack at age 56.

Wilfrid Reid (Wop) May was inducted as a Member of Canada's Aviation Hall of Fame in 1974.

Captain W.R. 'Wop' May, Royal Flying Corps, England. 1918.

William Sidney May

(1909 – 1981)

William Sidney May was born in Madawaska, Ontario, on December 24, 1909. He was educated in Melville, Saskatchewan, and Winnipeg, Manitoba, where he worked as an apprentice for Canadian National Railways. In 1928 he had his first airplane ride in an Avro Avian and was determined to learn to fly. In 1930 he began flight training at the Northwest Aero Marine and earned his Commercial Pilot's Licence that year. He was hired by that company, and in 1933 attended the Instructor's course given by the Royal Canadian Air Force (RCAF) at Camp Borden, Ontario. On his return to Winnipeg, he became Manager and Instructor for Northwest Aero Marine until it was taken over by Wings Limited of Winnipeg.

After several years of instructing, barnstorming and charter flying, in 1935 he went to England and was hired as a pilot by Imperial Airways Limited. In 1936 he was assigned as First Officer aboard the airline's new Short Brothers flying boats and two years later received his own

In 1966 William May was recognized for his pioneering of the North Atlantic route, his high level of qualifications, and his exceptional record, when he was awarded the Master Air Pilot Certificate of the British Guild of Air Pilots and Navigators. The presentation was made by the Grand Master of the Guild, Prince Philip. In 1980 he was made an Honorary Member of Canadian Air Line Pilots Association (CALPA, Belt of Orion 1988).

"With superlative mastery of all aspects of aircraft flight, he has displayed the highest order of professionalism over four decades, with results that have been of outstanding benefit to Canadian aviation." —Induction citation, 1979

William May took delivery of BOAC's first Boeing Stratocruiser. c. 1950.

command. In this, the largest aircraft of its type in world service, he flew established routes from England to Palestine, the Persian Gulf, South Africa, Singapore, and Karachi. On the eastern route he was called upon to land on the Sea of Galilee, then fly across five hundred miles of desert. His southward route carried him up the Nile River to Mozambique, and to Durban in South Africa.

British Overseas Airways Corporation (BOAC) absorbed Imperial Airways in 1939 and May was placed in charge of pilot training for the new company. During this period he had flown all of the company's routes as Captain-in-Command and had earned Licences for Navigation, Engineering and Wireless Operation.

In 1940, when Britain was at war with Germany, many of the routes usually used to the East were cut off, and May was asked to find an alternate route. He flew the first flying boat from Lisbon, Portugal, down the west coast of Africa to Nigeria and into the Belgian Congo to connect with an established overland route.

The following year, May was assigned to the Return Service Ferry Command at Montreal, Quebec, an organization operated by BOAC personnel, and administered by the Royal Air Force (RAF). His job was to pilot high priority

passengers and cargo to Britain across the North Atlantic Ocean, and return with pilots who had previously ferried operational aircraft to the United Kingdom. By the end of World War II he had completed 280 flights across the Atlantic in modified B-24 Liberator bombers. His foresight and planning resulted in the selection of Reykjavik, Iceland, as a refueling point for westbound flights, which was required because of strong headwinds encountered during most of the year. He then commanded the first Liberator flight to that airport.

During the latter stages of the war, he captained a Consolidated Liberator over the 2,200 mile (3,540 km) route from Newfoundland to Great Britain in six hours and 20 minutes, a speed record that lasted until the introduction of jet aircraft on that route. In 1949 he completed flight training on the Stratocruiser at Boeing Commercial Airplane Company in Seattle, Washington. He then took delivery of BOAC's first Stratocruiser and ferried it to England, where he trained 35 crews on the aircraft as well as flying the line himself.

A desire to return to Canada along with the possibility of taking early retirement from BOAC prompted May to retire in 1951. He returned to Calgary, Alberta, and accepted a new position with Canadian Pacific Airlines at their repair depot there. In this role he test flew a number of different aircraft types following repairs. The following year he accepted a position with Queen Charlotte Airways to establish new routes along the coast of British Columbia.

With the amalgamation of Queen Charlotte Airways and several other small airways, Pacific Western Airlines (PWA) was formed under the management of R.F. Baker (Hall of Fame 1975). May's vast experience was put to good use with PWA, flying many types of aircraft. In early 1969 May was qualified as Captain on the Boeing 737. He retired from active flying shortly thereafter, with 41 years of experience and 29,000 flying hours. He remained with PWA to take charge of their flight simulator training program at Vancouver, British Columbia. He retired permanently in 1975, and died in Vancouver on July 29, 1981.

William Sidney May was inducted as a Member of Canada's Aviation Hall of Fame in 1979.

Fred Robert Gordon McCall

(1895 – 1949)

Fred Robert Gordon McCall, D.S.O., M.C.*, D.F.C., was born in Vernon, British Columbia, on December 4, 1895. His family moved to Calgary, Alberta, in 1906, and he completed his education there. He joined the 175th Battalion of the Canadian Expeditionary Force in 1916. He arrived in England as a Sergeant, was commissioned and transferred to the Royal Flying Corps (RFC) as a Lieutenant pilot trainee in June 1917. By year's end he was brevetted a pilot and assigned to 13 Squadron, RFC, in France, flying reconnaissance and photographic missions.

Within a month McCall had scored his first aerial victory and the excellence of his artillery patrols brought his first decoration, the Military Cross (M.C.), in March 1918. The following week he downed three more enemy machines and by April 15 had raised his score to six confirmed during a major German

Barnstorming activities after World War I and in the early 1920's were exciting and risky, and drew large numbers of spectators, many of whom had never seen an aircraft before. Stunt-flying took place during many country fairs, and accidents did happen. One spectacular accident occurred during the 1919 Calgary Exhibition when Fred McCall was piloting a Curtiss JN-4 with two young passengers. The engine quit on take-off and McCall chose to land it atop a merry-go-round instead of on the crowded midway. No injuries were suffered as a result.

offensive. He was awarded a Bar to his Military Cross.

A transfer to 41 Squadron followed where he was given a single-seater SE 5a fighter aircraft to fly. In May he destroyed four enemy aircraft and was awarded the Distinguished Flying Cross (D.F.C.). During the following five weeks of flying, after promotion to the rank of Captain, he brought down nine more enemy machines, raising his total victories to 24. For these actions he was awarded a fourth decoration for gallantry, the Distinguished Service Order (D.S.O.) with the following citation:

> "A brilliant and gallant officer he has accounted for fourteen enemy machines (since his last decoration). On a recent date he destroyed four during a morning patrol and another in the evening, in each case closing to point-blank range with his opponent. His courage and offensive spirit have inspired all who serve with him."

On August 17, 1918, he was engaged in the deadliest aerial duel of his career when he and W.G. Claxton were attacked behind enemy lines by a German squadron numbering 40 aircraft. By skillful manoeuvering and aggressive action both he and Claxton shot down three enemy machines. Claxton's aircraft was disabled and he landed in enemy territory, to be captured. McCall landed safely at his own aerodrome. Within days he was taken ill and invalided back to England, with 30 ½ German machines to his credit. His fifth citation for bravery came with a Mention in Despatches of his aerial action by Sir Douglas Haig in November 1918.

At war's end he established McCall Aero Company Limited at Calgary and together with W.R. 'Wop' May (Hall of Fame 1974) as an additional pilot, they flew commercial freight and passengers throughout the prairie provinces and barnstormed the prairie fairs circuit for three years. In 1928 McCall organized Great Western Airways Limited at Calgary, to operate commercial flights. Always

Fortunately, no injuries were suffered in this unusual accident which occurred during the Calgary Exhibition. 1919.

ready to accept new aviation undertakings, he contracted in February, 1929 to transport by air, for the first time in Canada, 200 quarts (227 L) of nitroglycerin from Shelby, Montana, to Calgary in his newly-acquired Stinson Detroiter. This extremely sensitive explosive was ordered by an oil-well drilling company for blasting purposes at one of its well sites at Turner Valley in southwestern Alberta.

In subsequent years he worked with M.A. Seymour (Hall of Fame 1974) to encourage the formation of a system of Canadian Flying Clubs. Shortly after the outbreak of World War II he was recalled to service with the Royal Canadian Air Force (RCAF) as an Administrative Officer. Promoted to the rank of Squadron Leader, he served The British Commonwealth Air Training Plan (BCATP) at several western Canadian bases, commanding both the No. 7 Initial Training School at Saskatoon, Saskatchewan, and the Administrative Unit, North West Air Command, Edmonton, Alberta. He died in Calgary on January 22, 1949.

When the City of Calgary opened its new airport in 1956, it was named McCall Field to honour his pioneering achievements and his outstanding military accomplishments.

Fred Robert Gordon McCall was inducted as a Member of Canada's Aviation Hall of Fame in 1978.

George William Grant McConachie

(1909 – 1965)

George William Grant McConachie was born in Hamilton, Ontario, on April 24, 1909, and grew up in the Calder area of Edmonton, Alberta, where he was educated. He worked at part-time jobs with Canadian National Railways, and left the University of Alberta in his freshman year to take flying lessons from M. 'Moss' Burbidge (Hall of Fame 1974). He qualified for his Private Pilot's Licence in 1929, a Commercial Pilot's Licence in 1930, and acquired a used aircraft the following year.

His first contract was to fly fish from northern lakes during the winter months. He barnstormed prairie communities during the remainder of that year, for a total of 650 flying hours. Despite financial setbacks and physical hazards, including a bankruptcy and a near-fatal crash, he co-founded Independent Airways at Edmonton. A pattern of air services began to emerge throughout northern British Columbia and into the Yukon Territory with his founding of United Air Transport in 1933.

When the name was later changed to Yukon Southern Air Transport, McConachie took command and pioneered the first scheduled airmail and passenger service

Grant McConachie championed flights over polar routes as the shortest and most economical way to go. The most spectacular of these ventures was CPA's great-circle route over the Arctic Ocean from Amsterdam to Vancouver, non-stop. The inaugural east-west flight was captained by R.C. 'Bob' Randall (Hall of Fame 1974).

Grant McConachie in his Toronto office showing models of new jets acquired by CP Air. 1962.

between Edmonton and Whitehorse, Yukon, in 1939. This achievement, which he forged into a dependable service despite the near insurmountable obstacles of weather, inhospitable terrain and mechanical difficulties, earned him the Trans-Canada (McKee) Trophy for 1945. McConachie, like many of the bush pilots of the north, completed numerous emergency flights which resulted in the saving of lives.

When government officials began planning the Northwest Staging Route, they looked for the shortest, safest route to follow. McConachie was using a route surveyed in 1935 by A.D. 'Dan' McLean (Hall of Fame 1974) from Edmonton to the Alaska border. The route, which began in Edmonton and went on to Whitehorse, Yukon, through Grande Prairie, Fort St. John, Fort Nelson, and Watson Lake, was found to be the best way to reach Alaska. By using information from McLean's surveys, both the Alaska Highway and the Canol Pipeline Project were brought to an earlier, successful conclusion than otherwise would have been possible. From the late 1930's through World War II, McConachie's home airport, the Edmonton Industrial Airport, became the busiest airport in North America as American aircraft flew from there north to Alaska.

Canadian Pacific Railways (CPR) bought a number of small airlines in 1941, including Mackenzie Air Service, owned by L. Brintnell (Hall of Fame 1976), and McConachie's Yukon Southern Transport. McConachie was named Assistant to the President of the CPR at that time. When Canadian Pacific Airlines (CPA) was formed in 1942 he was appointed General Manager of the Western Lines. In 1942 C.H. 'Punch' Dickins (Hall of Fame 1974) was hired as Vice-President and General Manager of CPA, with the responsibility of amalgamating the eleven small scattered airlines into one cohesive air transportation network serving western Canada.

In 1947 McConachie, at the age of 38, was named President of CPA, and his daring initiatives resulted in the uniting of Canada and Asia by long-range aircraft. By 1949 he had inaugurated scheduled air passenger service from Vancouver, British Columbia, over the 8,400 mile (13,500 km) route to Sydney, Australia, and the 6,500 miles (10,460 km) from Vancouver to Tokyo, Japan, and Hong Kong. This was a multi-million dollar gamble on the future of air transportation, and it achieved his goal of a successful Canadian great-circle route by air to the Orient.

McConachie was a dynamic, persuasive and effective executive, and by the end of 1957 he had directed the launching of seven more international routes, including the capital cities of Mexico, Peru, Argentina, Chile, Holland, Portugal, and Spain.

Still unsatisfied with Canada's role in international air service, he pressed for competitive air operations on the nation's flyways, and a more equitable deal for Canada on the trans-border routes to the United States. The result of his concerted drive was a major overhaul of the air pact existing between the two countries, to this nation's benefit. As well, the government altered its National Air Policy to allow a measure of competition within Canada. In recognition of his great crusade for private enterprise on air routes, he was honoured by Sales Executives International in 1963, as Canadian Businessman of the Year. He died in Long Beach, California, on June 29, 1965.

George William Grant McConachie was inducted as a Member of Canada's Aviation Hall of Fame in 1974.

John Alexander Douglas McCurdy

(1886 – 1961)

John Alexander Douglas McCurdy, M.B.E., M.E., D.Eng., D.Cn.L. (Hon), LL.D. (Hon), was born in Baddeck, Nova Scotia, on August 12, 1886. He was educated at Baddeck Academy and at the University of Toronto, from which he graduated with a Masters Degree in Mechanical Engineering (M.E.) in 1907.

That summer McCurdy invited a fellow engineering graduate, F.W. 'Casey' Baldwin (Hall of Fame 1974), to visit his home at Baddeck. They spent time with Alexander Graham Bell (Hall of Fame 1974), who invited them to become his partners in the Aerial Experiment Association (AEA) at Baddeck, to test the feasibility of powered flight. Also included in the AEA was Glenn H. Curtiss, a well-known engine builder from Hammondsport, New York, and Lieutenant Thomas Selfridge of the U.S. Army. They continued Bell's experiments with kites at Baddeck, on Cape Breton Island, and when they decided to begin working on powered flight, they moved their base of operations to Hammondsport to be able to use Curtiss' machine shop.

"The dedication of his engineering talents to the development of manned flight was a prime factor in the birth of North America's aviation industry and has proven to be of outstanding benefit to Canada."

—Induction citation, 1974

J.A.D. McCurdy flies the Silver Dart over Bras D'Or Lake at Baddeck, Nova Scotia. The triangular-shaped ailerons are visible at the tips of the wings. 1909.

McCurdy and Baldwin worked on the design and construction of their first aircraft, the Red Wing, conceived by Bell and flown on March 12, 1908, by Baldwin. This flight made Baldwin the first British subject to pilot a heavier-than-air machine. Then followed the construction and test flights of other aircraft designed by the group, the White Wing, the June Bug and the Silver Dart.

While at Hammondsport, McCurdy was gaining valuable flying experience. He made over 200 short flights in the AEA's experimental aircraft, and on August 28, 1908, he flew the June Bug for more than two miles.

McCurdy was the chief designer of the Silver Dart. On this aircraft, control devices were much improved over the three previous designs. The ailerons, triangular sections hinged to the tips of the wings, were operated by a control yoke tailored to the pilot's back and shoulders. The pilot lowered or raised a wing by leaning in the appropriate direction; that is, he raised a down-going wing by leaning away from it. The control wheel moved the rudder and elevator, and provided nose wheel steering. On December 6, 1908, he test flew the Silver Dart at Hammondsport. He flew it successfully many more times that month, the longest flight being about one mile.

The Silver Dart was shipped by rail to Baddeck in January of 1909. On February 23, 1909, McCurdy lifted off from the ice-covered surface of Bras d'Or Lake, for a half-mile flight at heights between 10 and 30 feet (3 to 9 m), reaching a speed of 40 miles (60 km) per hour. Thus he made the first heavier-than-air machine flight in Canada. It was also the first controlled flight of an aircraft by a British subject flown anywhere in the British Empire. Up to now, flight occurred mostly on a straight path, but the

While in Florida, McCurdy's plans included a trans-ocean flight. On January 30, 1911, he set out from Key West, Florida in an attempt to fly across the 90 mile wide (145 km) Florida Strait to Havana, Cuba, in a Curtiss biplane. The U.S. Navy had four destroyers stationed along his course to provide escort and assistance if needed. All went well until engine trouble forced him to glide to a gentle landing on the water only one mile from Cuba. He was picked up almost immediately by a boat from one of the warships. Although he did not reach his goal, he had made the longest over-water flight at the time. He was given a hero's welcome in Havana, but at the state dinner afterwards, the envelope he was presented contained only torn pieces of newspaper. He did not receive the $10,000 prize money he was promised!

addition of control surfaces, such as the aileron and rudder, allowed the pilot to turn the aircraft. On March 20, 1909, McCurdy piloted the Silver Dart on a circular course of more than 20 miles. The objective of manned, powered flight had been achieved by the AEA, and the Association was disbanded on March 31, 1909.

At this time, McCurdy and Baldwin formed the Canadian Aerodrome Company at Baddeck, Canada's first aircraft manufacturing company. They constructed two biplanes, Baddeck I, completed July 1909, and Baddeck II, completed September 1909, both patterned after the successful Silver Dart, and a monoplane, completed in March 1910. Their goal was to interest the public in the possibilities of flight and to attract buyers.

McCurdy demonstrated the Silver Dart at the military base at Camp Petawawa, Ontario, on August 2, 1909, in an attempt to interest the military in the use of aircraft. Four successful flights were made there, but a crash on the fifth flight destroyed the Silver Dart on the soft sand landing area he had to use. McCurdy was the only person to fly the Silver Dart.

McCurdy and Baldwin were still keen to demonstrate their aircraft to Department of Defence officials. Baddeck I was shipped to Petawawa where successful demonstration flights were made on August 11 and 12, 1909. However, while McCurdy was demonstrating it on August 13th, it stalled and crashed. This was a great disappointment to them, but the aircraft was repaired and flown again later. Baddeck II was flown by both McCurdy and Baldwin in the fall and winter of 1909 – 10, some flights covering more than ten miles (16 km). Their attempts

to gain the interest and support of the government failed, and the work of the Canadian Aerodrome Company ceased about a year after it began.

From July 1910, to June 1911, McCurdy did extensive exhibition flying in the U.S. He made history on August 27, 1910, by transmitting the first wireless messages from an aircraft to a ground receiver while flying out of Long Island, New York. He was the fifth person to obtain a pilot's licence in the U.S., issued in October 1910.

When World War I broke out in 1914, McCurdy tried again to interest the military in establishing a flying corps, but was again rebuffed. By 1915 he was managing the Curtiss Aviation School at Toronto, Ontario, which trained 600 young Canadians for the Royal Naval Air Service. During World War I he also managed Curtiss Airplane and Motors Ltd. in Toronto, which produced the famous Curtiss JN-4, or a version of the 'Jenny' known as the 'Canuck'. After the war, he was involved in the founding of the Royal Canadian Air Force (RCAF) in April 1924, along with W.G. Barker and W.A. Bishop (both Hall of Fame 1974).

McCurdy formed the Reid Aircraft Company at Montreal, Quebec, in 1928. The following year he arranged a merger, resulting in the Curtiss-Reid Aircraft Company Limited of which he became President.

At the outbreak of World War II McCurdy was named Assistant Director of Aircraft Production for the Government of Canada, a post he held until 1947. He was named a Member of the Order of the British Empire (M.B.E., Civil). His career reached its peak in 1948 when he was appointed Lieutenant Governor of Nova Scotia, an office he held until 1952. He was made a Knight of the Order of St. John of Jerusalem (K.St.J.).

McCurdy received many honours for his achievements in aviation. He was awarded several Honorary Doctorates and Fellowships. His name is perpetuated by the Canadian Aeronautics and Space Institute's annual McCurdy Award. He retired to private life in 1952. In 1959, on the fiftieth anniversary of his first flight of the Silver Dart in Canada, he was awarded the Trans-Canada (McKee) Trophy. He died in Montreal, Quebec, on June 25, 1961.

John Alexander Douglas McCurdy was inducted as a Member of Canada's Aviation Hall of Fame in 1974.

McCurdy with a model of the Silver Dart.

NATIONAL ARCHIVES OF CANADA PA-089944

Gordon Roy McGregor

(1901 – 1971)

Gordon Roy McGregor, C.C., O.B.E., D.F.C., B.Sc., LL.D. (Hon), was born in Montreal, Quebec, on September 26, 1901. He was educated there and at St. Andrew's College, Toronto, Ontario. He graduated from McGill University in Montreal, in 1923 with a B.Sc. degree in engineering. He then joined Bell Telephone Company in Montreal, and after serving several years in the engineering department, he became Division Engineer at Ottawa, Ontario, in 1929. He was promoted to District Manager at Kingston, Ontario, in 1932, and moved back to Montreal in 1938 as Central District Manager.

McGregor's flying career began at Kingston in 1932 and the following year he obtained his Pilot's Licence at Ottawa. He entered piloting competitions, and won the Webster Trophy in 1935, 1936 and again in 1938, as the best amateur pilot in Canada. He then joined 115 Auxiliary Squadron of the Royal Canadian Air Force (RCAF) as a Flying Officer and in 1939 he proceeded overseas with 1 RCAF Fighter Squadron.

He served as a fighter pilot during the Battle of Britain and was awarded the Distinguished Flying Cross (D.F.C.) for his actions against enemy aircraft. In 1941 he

The DC-8 was the first jet aircraft in use by an airline in Canada, put into service by Trans-Canada Airlines in 1960. This jet cruised at 550 mph (885 kph) on domestic routes. When TCA was formed in 1937, one of its transport airplanes was the Lockheed 10A, which had a cruising speed of 150 mph (240 kph).

> *"His dedication to the linking together of this nation's far-flung communities by a national air service has been of outstanding benefit to Canadian aviation."*
>
> —*Induction citation, 1974*

Alexander Daniel (Dan) McLean

(1896 – 1969)

> *"The total commitment of his aeronautical expertise to improving this nation's airways and airports, has resulted in outstanding benefit to Canadian aviation."*
>
> —*Induction citation, 1974*

Gordon McGregor with a model of a Douglas DC-9. c. 1966.

was promoted to Squadron Leader and commanded both the 1st and 2nd Canadian Fighter Squadrons in England. He returned to Canada in 1942 to assist in the development of fighter operations in Western Air Command. As Commanding Officer of X Wing he was appointed to head the force sent to Alaska, and served as the point of contact between the Alaska Defence Command and the RCAF. McGregor subsequently headed 14 Fighter Squadron in the Aleutians before commanding the RCAF Station at Patricia Bay, British Columbia, with the rank of Group Captain.

In 1944 McGregor was named an Officer of the Order of the British Empire (O.B.E.), and for his exceptional services as a wartime leader and administrator in the European theater of operations, was decorated with the Netherlands' Order of Orange Nassau with Swords, France's Croix de Guerre with Silver Star, and Czechoslovakia's War Cross.

When the war ended in 1945, McGregor was hired by Trans-Canada Airlines (TCA, Hall of Fame 1974) at Montreal as General Traffic Manager. In 1948 he was named President of the airline, taking over from TCA's second President, H.J. Symington. McGregor was the principal figure in guiding that airline through its difficult years of expansion, with the result that Air Canada, as it was renamed in 1965, became one of the world's leading carriers. He oversaw the move of TCA's head office from Winnipeg to Montreal in 1949, and the addition of several new, more comfortable passenger aircraft, including Lockheed Super Constellations in 1954, turboprop-powered Vickers Viscounts in 1955, Vanguards in 1960, Douglas DC-8 jet aircraft in 1960, and Douglas DC-9's in 1966. McGregor retired in 1968 after twenty years as President.

McGregor was active in community service and aviation-related organizations. He was named to the board of management of the Montreal General Hospital, the advisory council of the Royal Canadian Air Force Association, and the national council of Boy Scouts of Canada. After serving on the traffic committee of the International Air Transport Association (IATA), he was elected to the executive committee in 1949, and in 1953 was elected President of that organization.

McGregor's many honours included being named an Honorary Fellow in both the Canadian Aeronautics and Space Institute (CASI) and the Royal Aeronautical Society. He was named a Commander Brother of the Order of St. John of Jerusalem (C.St.J.) and was awarded an Honorary Doctor of Laws degree by McGill University. During Canada's centennial year, he was presented with CASI's 1967 C.D. Howe Award for his services to the nation. In 1968 he was created a Companion of the Order of Canada (C.C.), and awarded the Pioneer Aviation Medal of the United States. He was appointed to a one year term as Grand President of the Royal Canadian Flying Clubs Association. He died at Montreal, Quebec, on March 3, 1971.

Gordon Roy McGregor was inducted as a Member of Canada's Aviation Hall of Fame in 1974.

Alexander Daniel (Dan) McLean, O.B.E., was born on January 31, 1896, in Maxville, Ontario, where he began his schooling. In 1907 his family moved to Innisfail, Alberta, where he completed his education. He then attended Normal School in Calgary, Alberta, and became a teacher. He taught school in that province for a short time, and in 1917 he enlisted in the Royal Flying Corps (RFC). After ground training at the School of Military Aeronautics at the University of Toronto in Ontario, he was ordered to England where he graduated as a commissioned

The survey flight initiated by McLean in 1935 from Edmonton to the Alaska border showed the natural airway from Edmonton through the Yukon to Alaska, and on to the Orient. The route he chose as a shortcut to the Orient was the 'Great Circle' route through Fort St. John and Fort Nelson, British Columbia, and Whitehorse, Yukon. This route shortened the flight distance between Chicago, Illinois, U.S.A., and Shanghai, China, by 4,000 miles (6,440 km).

pilot. He served as a flying instructor until the war ended in 1918.

While attending the University of Alberta in Edmonton during 1919-20, McLean joined the Canadian Air Force Reserve, attended a refresher course at Camp Borden, Ontario, in 1921 and obtained his Civil Commercial Pilot's Licence. Instead of remaining in aviation, he joined his father in business at Innisfail until the Royal Canadian Air Force (RCAF) called him back into service in 1927. After completing several airmanship courses, he spent two years on aerial photographic missions in Ontario, Quebec, and the Maritimes. On January 28, 1929, he piloted the inaugural airmail flight from Ottawa, Ontario, to St. John, New Brunswick. Two days later he completed the inaugural return flight. Then, for a short period, he was pilot of an experimental airmail service between Halifax, Nova Scotia and St. John, New Brunswick.

The Government of Canada's Department of National Defence hired him in April 1929, as Inspector of Western Airways, with headquarters at Regina, Saskatchewan, under the Controller of Civil Aviation, J.A. Wilson (Hall of Fame 1974). While stationed there he organized construction of the first airways system on the prairies, from Winnipeg, Manitoba to Calgary, and from Regina to Edmonton, Alberta. This operation saw the construction of a chain of airports between these centres, complete with night-lighting and weather and radio services. He then completed an aerial survey of a southern Rocky Mountain flyway to Vancouver, British Columbia, from Alberta, and selected the route through the Crow's Nest Pass. In 1931 he was transferred to Ottawa to replace J.H. Tudhope (Hall of Fame 1974) as Acting Superintendent of Airways and Airports. In this position he directed construction of all new flightways, from Winnipeg throughout eastern Canada.

During July 1935, McLean was in charge of a 7,000 mile (11,300 km) survey flight in the Mackenzie River, Great Bear Lake, Yukon and Northern British Columbia areas. Leaving the South Cooking Lake float base near Edmonton, the party stopped at Fort McMurray, then at all points down the the Mackenzie River to Aklavik, and back through Yukon and northern British Columbia to Prince Rupert, for the purpose of checking landing and other facilities connected with air traffic. The pilot on this historic flight was C.H. 'Punch' Dickins (Hall of Fame 1974), flying a Canadian Airways' Fairchild.

A move to rejoin the RCAF in his rank of Squadron Leader at the outbreak of World War Two was prevented by a government order freezing him in his civil position. For the duration of the conflict, he was made responsible for the selection, surveying and development of all airports provided for the British Commonwealth Air Training Plan (BCATP). For his work in establishing Canada's airport system, he was awarded the Trans-Canada (McKee) Trophy for 1941. McLean was appointed Director of Civil Aviation in 1941, and assumed the additional responsibility for the civil administration and maintenance of the country's principal airports. For his wartime service he was named an Officer of the Order of the British Empire (O.B.E., Military).

McLean was appointed to the Air Transport Board in 1950, a position he held until 1962. In 1954 he headed a government negotiating team for air agreements in Australia, and later that year, he was sent to Japan to negotiate bi-lateral air transport agreements. In 1958 he attended air agreement talks in Switzerland. He retired in 1962 and died in Ottawa on May 16, 1969.

Alexander Daniel (Dan) McLean was inducted as a Member of Canada's Aviation Hall of Fame in 1974.

Alexander Daniel 'Dan' McLean in training with the Royal Flying Corps, England. c. 1917.

NATIONAL ARCHIVES OF CANADA PA-9930

Alan Arnett McLeod

(1899 – 1918)

Alan Arnett McLeod, V.C., was born in Stonewall, Manitoba, on April 20, 1899. He received his education there and enlisted in the Royal Flying Corps (RFC), which had established training bases in Canada. In August 1917, having completed his Canadian training, he sailed for England where he underwent his operational training and joined 51 Squadron, RFC, as a Lieutenant on home defence duties. In November 1917, he was assigned to 2 Squadron, RFC, on the Western Front as pilot of a two-seater bomber on photographic, spotting and bombing missions.

He was honoured with a Mention in Despatches for a daring operation on January 14, 1918, when he and his observer, Lieutenant Reginald Key, attacked and brought down a heavily-defended observation balloon. They were set upon by three German fighters. However, Lieutenant McLeod, by skillful flying, placed his machine in a position to permit his observer full range of his gun to send one of the enemy aircraft down.

The action for which Lieutenant McLeod was awarded the Victoria Cross came on March 27, 1918, shortly after the opening

Alan Arnett McLeod was the youngest of three Canadian fliers to receive the Victoria Cross during WW I—he was not yet 19 years of age—and while most of the aerial V.C.'s of World War I were awarded to pilots flying single-seater aircraft, Lieutenant McLeod earned his decoration while piloting a bomber.

"His winning of the Victoria Cross in aerial combat must be regarded as one of the most outstanding contributions possible to the military aspect of Canadian aviation." —Induction citation, 1974

A/V/M K.M. Guthrie, Air Officer Commanding No. 2 Air Command, presenting a portrait of the late Lieutenant Alan A. McLeod, V.C., RAF, to the principal of the school bearing his name. Winnipeg, Manitoba. 1945.

of the greatest German offensive that threatened to break the Allied lines. With six other planes from 2 Squadron, Lieutenant McLeod, flying an Armstrong-Whitworth FK reconnaissance aircraft, and his observer, Lieutenant A. W. Hammond, M.C., took off from their aerodrome in the morning for a bombing and strafing attack on German troop concentrations at Bray-sur-Somme, near Albert, France. Bad weather forced them near the ground where their aircraft was damaged by concentrated ground fire. Lieutenant McLeod returned across Allied lines, landed at 43 Squadron's field for repairs and took off again, reaching the target area shortly thereafter.

The London Gazette of May 1, 1918, announced the award of the Victoria Cross (V.C.) to Lieutenant McLeod with the following citation:

> "While flying with his observer, Lieutenant A.W. Hammond, M.C., attacking hostile formations by bombs and machine gun fire, he was assailed by eight enemy triplanes which dived at him from all directions, firing from their front guns. By skillful manoeuvering, he enabled his observer to fire bursts at each machine in turn, shooting three of them down, out of control. By this time Lieutenant McLeod had received five wounds and while continuing the engagement a bullet penetrated his petrol tank and set the machine on fire. He then climbed onto the left bottom plane (lower wing),

controlling the machine from the side of the fuselage, and by sideslipping steeply kept the flames to one side, thus enabling the observer to continue firing until the ground was reached.

> "The observer had been wounded six times when the machine crashed in 'No Man's Land', and Lieutenant McLeod, notwithstanding his own wounds, dragged him away from the burning wreckage at great personal risk under heavy machine gun fire from enemy lines. This very gallant pilot was again wounded by a bomb while engaged in this act of rescue, but he persevered until he had placed Lieutenant Hammond in comparative safety, before falling himself from exhaustion and loss of blood."

Lieutenant Hammond received a Bar to his M.C. for his part in the action.

Lieutenant McLeod spent many months in hospital. His father, Dr. A.N. McLeod, went to England to be at his son's side during his convalescence, and accompanied him to Buckingham Palace when he received his Victoria Cross from King George V. In September 1918, father and son returned to Canada. In late October, his lungs weakened by smoke and flames, young McLeod contracted influenza and died in Winnipeg, Manitoba, on November 6, 1918.

Alan Arnett McLeod was inducted as a Member of Canada's Aviation Hall of Fame in 1974.

Stanley Ransom (Stan) McMillan

(1904 – 1991)

Stanley Ransom (Stan) McMillan was born in Dryden, Ontario, on October 3, 1904, and moved to Edmonton, Alberta, where he learned to fly with the Royal Canadian Air Force (RCAF) Reserve in 1925. He left a university engineering course to join the RCAF in 1927 and flew on northern Canadian operations for two years, until he was granted leave from the service to join Dominion Explorers Limited (Domex) as a pilot, exploring the unmapped Arctic and sub-Arctic regions.

In March and April of 1929 he shared with another pilot, Charles Sutton, the distinction of being the first airmen to penetrate the vastness of the Barren Lands, in a 4,000 mile (6,400 km) trip from Winnipeg, Manitoba, to north of the Arctic Circle in winter. Col. MacAlpine, Domex President and mining engineer, contracted the trip, the purpose of which was to check on supplies and fuel caches at Domex bases. They stopped at Tavani, about 250 miles (400 km) north of Fort Churchill, and beyond Baker Lake, but any hoped-for explorations were curtailed by winter storms, and the group returned to Winnipeg.

Following this significant accomplishment, Col MacAlpine planned an autumn

Stan McMillan regarded the Inuit's skills and ability to survive in Arctic conditions with awe. His memories of their totally unselfish and happy nature throughout the difficult days of encampment on the Arctic coast are mixed with the knowledge that without them, the MacAlpine party would surely have perished.

expedition to inspect company activities. McMillan, flying Fairchild CF-AAO, and Tommy Thompson, flying a Fokker Super Universal, G-CASK, on charter from Western Canada Airways, piloted this two-plane expedition carrying their air engineers and a four-man geological team. The party left Winnipeg on August 24, 1929, with plans to investigate mineral deposits across the Barren Lands and along the Arctic coast. They were beset by mechanical difficulties and unusually bad weather from the beginning. They were last seen at Baker Lake on September 8th, when they headed towards the Arctic coast. Bad weather and low fuel supplies forced a decision to land when they saw the first signs of habitation. The three Eskimos (Inuit) could not speak English, but with the arrival of other Inuit, the party knew that they could survive until they reached the nearest outpost, Cambridge Bay on Victoria Island, about 80 miles (130 km) across the Dease Strait. Without fuel, the aircraft were abandoned. With no means of communication, the party was lost to civilization for six weeks. They lived on the tundra, sheltered and fed by the Inuit, and waited until the ocean waters froze sufficiently to carry their weight.

When conditions were right, they followed their Inuit friends as they began the trek across the channel to Cambridge Bay and reached the safety of that isolated outpost two days later, on November 3rd, fifty-six days after they had last been seen. It took another month for rescuers to be able to bring them out to Winnipeg. Their desperate plight had captured the headlines of the international press for three months, and triggered the largest aerial search in Canadian history.

In 1931 McMillan was employed by Commercial Airways, a company formed by W.R. 'Wop' May (Hall of Fame 1974), which was soon absorbed by Canadian Airways Limited. His assignment took him throughout northern Alberta and British Columbia, as well as the Yukon and

Stan McMillan standing beside a Bellanca Pacemaker which he flew for Mackenzie Air Service. c. 1935.

Northwest Territories, flying mail, passengers and freight. One outstanding three week aerial operation resulted in the salvage of the crashed aircraft used by the ill-fated Burke expedition into the mountains of northern British Columbia. The following year he was based at Carcross, Yukon, and flew the first airmail from there to Atlin, British Columbia.

Leigh Brintnell (Hall of Fame 1976) hired McMillan in 1932 to fly for his company, Mackenzie Air Service, at Edmonton, Alberta. For the next seven years McMillan completed a number of exceptionally difficult flights. In 1933 he delivered eight prospectors and their summer supplies, in relay flights, 1,000 miles (1,600 km) north of Edmonton to the headwaters of the upper Liard River, over unmapped territory, and during winter storms. As Chief Pilot in 1935 he made the first commercial link with Alaskan Airlines by flying over the mountains to Whitehorse, Yukon.

NATIONAL ARCHIVES OF CANADA C-17761

"He has made outstanding contributions to Canadian aviation by the unselfish application of his exceptional skills as a pilot and navigator, despite adversity, and was instrumental in designing new operational procedures in northern Canada that have benefited this nation's growth."

—Induction citation, 1974

During his flying career, he had flown on numerous searches for lost companions and completed a number of mercy flights. In 1936 he piloted a relief flight to Letty Harbour on the Arctic Ocean in mid-winter, without radio or navigational aids, to rescue three seaman who had been marooned for eight months. In the fall of 1936 he devoted six weeks to flying the Barren Lands with other bush pilots on a search for two missing RCAF aircrew, F/L Coleman and L/A Fortey, who were eventually found by Matt Berry (Hall of Fame 1974).

McMillan's leave from the RCAF ended in September 1939, when he was recalled for service as a Flight Lieutenant. He was able to use his exceptional long range navigational skills as an operational pilot and commander on anti-submarine patrols out of Newfoundland and Nova Scotia, and ferrying flying boats from Bermuda to the United Kingdom. He also served on operational duties in Ceylon and Northern Ireland, leading three squadrons from 1943 until war's end, with the rank of Wing Commander. For exceptional services he was honoured with a Mention in Despatches.

For two years after the war he flew aerial photographic surveys for Arctic Airlines, then formed Air Surveys Limited with a partner and continued survey flights for the Government of Canada until 1952. Four years later he joined Pacific Western Airlines (PWA) as Chief Pilot, Operations Manager, and then was named Co-Divisional Manager. His years of experience in cold weather aircraft operations were considered essential to PWA's safe flying procedures during the construction of the Distant Early Warning (DEW) Line radar bases along the rim of the Arctic Ocean in the mid-1950's.

When PWA sold their bush flying operations to Northward Aviation in 1966, he was named General Manager of the new company. In 1970 he formed Wraymac Sales at Edmonton, becoming an aircraft broker and parts supplier to the industry.

McMillan served as President of the International Northwest Aviation Council in 1963. He was named to their Aviation Roll of Honour in 1976. He died in Edmonton on March 4, 1991.

Stanley Ransom (Stan) McMillan was inducted as a Member of Canada's Aviation Hall of Fame in 1974.

"His quest for perfection as an Arctic airman, despite adversity, helped make the term 'bush pilot' synonymous with 'resourcefulness' and has been of outstanding benefit to Canadian aviation." —Induction citation, 1974

Archibald Major (Archie) McMullen

(1906 – 1983)

Archibald Major (Archie) McMullen was born on July 29, 1906, in Gilbert Plains, Manitoba. He moved to Nanton, Alberta, as a child and was educated in Alberta. He worked as a mechanic in Calgary, Alberta, until 1927, when he joined World War I 'ace', F.R. McCall (Hall of Fame 1978) as a mechanic. This move resulted in the formation of Great Western Airways at Calgary in June 1928, involving himself, McCall, J.E. Palmer (Hall of Fame 1988) and two other aviators. They started operations with one Stinson Detroiter.

The firm acquired the distributorship for de Havilland aircraft, and several DH Moths were shipped from Toronto, assembled in Calgary and sold. The company then formed a flying school, and after obtaining an Air Engineer's Licence, McMullen earned both his Private and Commercial Pilot's Licences by March of 1929. During that summer, he barnstormed extensively throughout western Canada.

In September 1929, he joined W.R. 'Wop' May (Hall of Fame 1974) as a pilot for the newly formed company, Commercial Airways, at Edmonton, Alberta, which had a government contract to carry mail to northern communities. On December 9, 1929, McMullen, along with May and air engineer A.G. Sims (Hall of Fame 1974), and three others, left Fort McMurray with the first mail to be flown down the Mackenzie River. He was credited with the portion of the inaugural airmail flight to Fort Chipewyan, Alberta. The following year he flew the first airmail between Fort Providence and Fort Simpson in the Northwest Territories. Due to the large accumulation of mail, all company aircraft were carrying mail and cargo to all the posts and settlements along the Mackenzie River as far as Aklavik.

Commercial Airways was absorbed by Canadian Airways Limited in 1930. McMullen made his first trip to Echo Bay on Great Bear Lake in August 1931. The mining rush into that area was going on. During the next three years he completed a number of additional inaugural airmail

It was early November, and ice was forming rapidly along the snye that joins the Athabasca and Clearwater rivers at Fort McMurray. McMullen's plane had been hoisted onto blocks for between-season overhaul when an urgent message came through by radio from Fort Smith on the border of the Northwest Territories about 300 miles (483 km) north. A trapper had trudged day and night for 72 hours to reach Fort Smith with word that a boy had been shot through the foot with a high calibre bullet. He needed immediate medical attention. Mechanics worked all night to prepare the plane for flight on floats. Then they blasted a path through the ice for the plane to get to open water. Finally, McMullen took off through the thick cakes of ice. He made the flight successfully, carried the patient to Fort Smith hospital, then returned to Fort McMurray, landing his plane in a narrow ribbon of open water that remained. Four hours later, this water froze over and it was winter in the north.

Archie McMullen, right, and his crew have just put their float-equipped Bellanca into the river at Fort McMurray. c. 1937.

flights. After flying the last seasonal mail down the Mackenzie River to Aklavik on floats in 1933, skis were put on his plane and he completed a difficult mercy flight to Shingle Point on the Arctic coast, where the Mission had burned and four patients had to be brought to hospital. He carried out several more emergency flights into the north that winter.

In 1937 he joined Mackenzie Air Service, and in the fall of that year was called upon to assist in an extensive search for Russian aviator Sigismund Levanevsky and his crew, missing on a flight over the Arctic Ocean to Alaska. McMullen took over from H. Hollick-Kenyon (Hall of Fame 1974) as pilot for searchmaster, Sir Hubert Wilkins. They made several intensive search flights between Aklavik and Edmonton, but the Russian crew was never found.

Through the next few years, McMullen flew what he called routine trips, flying mail, freight, passengers, and emergency flights, throughout northern Canada, aiding new areas of development and habitation.

In December 1940, McMullen began to work with the Department of Munitions and Supply as a test pilot for repaired aircraft used by the British Commonwealth Air Training Plan (BCATP). He was then assigned to Consolidated Aircraft Company at San Diego, California, to test fly several types of aircraft, among them the four-engined B-24 Liberator bomber and twin-engined PBY flying boats. When he returned to Edmonton, he was test pilot on rebuilt military aircraft.

In 1945 he joined Canadian Pacific Airlines (CPA), which had acquired Canadian Airways Limited. He served as a check pilot for CPA, supervising all of the company's pilots in the Edmonton district, as well as those on air operations during the construction of the Distant Early Warning (DEW) Line radar bases along the Arctic Ocean, until 1956. He retired from aviation in 1963, following a 30-year career during which he logged 22,000 hours as pilot-in-command on 38 types of aircraft. McMullen died on June 13, 1983.

Archibald Major (Archie) McMullen was inducted as a Member of Canada's Aviation Hall of Fame in 1974.

Robert Wendell (Buck) McNair

(1919 – 1971)

Robert Wendell (Buck) McNair, D.S.O., D.F.C.**, C.D.*, was born in Springhill, Nova Scotia, on May 15, 1919, and grew up in North Battleford, Saskatchewan. During the summers of 1937 to 1940 he worked for Canadian Airways Ltd. as a ground wireless operator, relaying weather and other information necessary for the safety of bush pilots operating in the north.

He joined the Royal Canadian Air Force (RCAF) in June 1940, and graduated as a Sergeant-pilot in March 1941. He was transferred to 411 Squadron in England in June 1941. His first victories came while flying a Spitfire in September and October, when he downed a Messerschmitt Me 109 and damaged two other enemy aircraft.

McNair was transferred to 249 Squadron in Malta in March 1942, a posting which included a flight from the deck of aircraft carrier HMS Eagle delivering new pilots and aircraft into Malta. This was a difficult

In 1953 McNair won the Queen's Commendation for Brave Conduct for his actions during a crash landing of a North Star Transport at RCAF Sea Island, Vancouver, British Columbia. He was a passenger, but as Senior Officer, he conducted the evacuation of the aircraft. Although injured and his clothing soaked with gasoline, he returned to the wreckage until all of the passengers and crew were accounted for.

exercise since the Eagle was not a large carrier, and the Spitfire was not designed for this type of operation. Also, the distance was beyond the Spitfire's normal range, and each aircraft had to carry a supply of parts. The addition of a belly fuel tank extended its range. Increased lift for take-off was accomplished by inserting small wooden wedges between the flaps and the underside of the wings. When the aircraft was taking off, the wedges held the flaps in a slightly open position to provide additional lift. When the flaps were retracted, the wedges were released.

The delivery of aircraft to Malta was successful and during the balance of his four-month tour McNair destroyed five enemy aircraft and damaged eight others. He was awarded the Distinguished Flying Cross (D.F.C.) and promoted to Flight Lieutenant. He rejoined 411 Fighter Squadron in the U.K. in July of 1942 and damaged several more enemy aircraft during a fierce air battle over Dieppe, France, on August 19, 1942.

In September of 1942 McNair, now a Flight Commander, was sent on a six-month coast-to-coast promotion of Canada War Bonds. He returned to England in early 1943 and became Squadron Leader, first of 416 and then 421 Squadrons. In a short period, he added eight more victories and received two Bars to his D.F.C.

On July 20, 1943, as he was leading a patrol along the Dutch coast, his Spitfire's engine began to lose power. He left the squadron and turned for home accompanied by his wing man. Twelve miles from the French coast his engine burst into flames and his aircraft dived out of control. At 5,000 feet (1,520 m) he struggled free, and with his face badly burned, bailed out of the aircraft. The parachute was partially burned, but he freed himself from the jammed harness and landed in the water, supported only by his Mae West life preserver. He was rescued within a few hours, and was flying again within three weeks.

In October of 1943 he became Wing Commander of 126 RCAF Wing, the leading Fighter Wing in the Second Tactical Air Force. In April 1944, he was awarded the Distinguished Service Order (D.S.O.) with the citation noting that:

> "Throughout, Wing Commander McNair has set a magnificent example by his fine fighting spirit, courage and devotion to duty both in the air and on the ground. He has inspired his pilots with confidence and enthusiasm."

When his combat days were over, he had destroyed at least sixteen enemy aircraft and damaged many others. He became the RCAF's second-ranking ace of World War II and one of its most successful wing leaders.

McNair served as Commander of No. 17 Sector in 1944. He attended the first post-war course at Royal Air Force (RAF) Staff College, and on completion of the Empire Central Flying School course in April 1946, he was sent to Fakenham, Norfolk, to fly the first British operational jet aircraft, the Gloster Meteor. In 1947 he was awarded the French Croix de Guerre with Palm Leaf and the Chevalier of the Legion of Honour.

In the post war years, Colonel McNair served in staff positions at Washington, DC, U.S.A., Quebec, and finally, in Tokyo during the Korean conflict. He was frequently called upon to fly and evaluate the latest jet aircraft.

In January 1956, he was promoted to Group Captain and commanded No. 4 Fighter Wing in Baden-Soellingen and in 1961 was assigned to North American Air Defence (NORAD) Region Headquarters at St. Hubert, Quebec. He was appointed Deputy Commander of NORAD's Duluth sector in 1964 and in 1968 became Senior Air Liaison with the Canadian Joint Staff in London. He died there on January 15, 1971.

Robert Wendell (Buck) McNair was inducted as a Member of Canada's Aviation Hall of Fame in 1990.

The airstrip at Normandy, France, being strafed by enemy attack. June 15, 1944.

Bert William Mead

(b. 1923)

Bert William Mead, C.D.*, was born on May 21, 1923, in Vermilion, Alberta. He attended school there and at the University of Alberta until 1942 when he joined the United States Public Roads Administration as an engineer's assistant on the surveying of the Alaska Highway route. The following year he enlisted in the Royal Canadian Air Force (RCAF), trained at several bases, graduated as a commissioned pilot in 1944 and was posted to instructional duties in Canada.

Mead wanted to serve in combat, so he resigned from the RCAF in 1945 and enrolled in the Royal Navy as a pilot with the rank of Sub-Lieutenant. The war in Europe ended shortly after he completed operational training, so he transferred to the Royal Canadian Navy (RCN). During the next two years he completed several advanced training courses. He returned to 883 Squadron, RCN, at Dartmouth, Nova Scotia, and served at sea for a year aboard the aircraft carrier HMCS Magnificent as Deck Landing Control Officer.

In 1949 he was posted to HMCS Shearwater as maintenance test pilot and then to the RCAF's Winter Experimental Establishment at Edmonton, Alberta. There he was instrumental in developing

The Air Cushion Vehicle, or hovercraft, has the ability to operate over water, land, snow, ice, and swamp. It has been used in rescue missions which could not have been performed by ships or helicopters. Of particular significance, it inflicts minimal, if any, damage to the tundra during summer operations.

"His record can be matched only by those airmen of high endeavor and professional calling, who have devoted their lives and skills to the benefit of the free world despite adversity, and whose contributions have substantially benefited Canadian aviation."

—Induction citation, 1974

new techniques for sophisticated aircraft, flying as many as six types in a single day. In 1953 he was sent to England to attend the Empire Test Pilot's Course, following which he was promoted to Lieutenant Commander.

Because of his extensive experience in all aspects of heavier-than-air flight, Mead was appointed to VX-10 Squadron, RCN, in 1954 as a special projects officer. His prime responsibility was flight testing one of the world's first successful automatic take-off and landing systems for aircraft. The project was designed to permit military aircraft to depart from or land on an aircraft carrier in any weather, in any type of sea. His skills as a pilot contributed to the perfection of the system and modified versions were put to use on modern passenger jet and military aircraft. Mead spent eight years with VX-10, accepting command of the unit from J.C. Sloan (Hall of Fame 1974) in 1959.

In 1962 Mead was moved to Naval Headquarters in Ottawa. Three years later he was named to head a group of military experts as Flying Evaluator in the testing and reporting on the selection of aircraft for all Canadian Forces. A recurring medical problem caused by an earlier crash resulted in his early retirement from the service in 1967.

In 1967 he helped found Hoverwork Canada Limited to bring into Canada the first commercial Air Cushion Vehicle (ACV), or hovercraft, and undertook an extensive course of instruction in England. The hovercraft had been invented by Sir Christopher Cockerell, whose original concept arose from an attempt to improve a boat's performance by reducing hydrodynamic drag.

During the winter of 1967-68, Mead directed cold weather trials of the hovercraft over Hudson Bay, out of Port Churchill, Manitoba. He then worked with

the Ministry of Transport (MOT) to develop an ACV Search and Rescue Unit at Vancouver, British Columbia, selecting and training all personnel to hovercraft standards, and devising the operating procedures. He commanded this unit, which conducted over 230 rescue missions at sea. He was then transferred to Ottawa and named senior ACV captain, assigned to test and develop new vehicles and assist in the writing of regulations governing their operations.

In 1972 Mead joined Northern Transportation Limited at Edmonton to take command of their ACV test program of the Canadian-made Voyageur. As the most punishing test he could devise, it was flown, under his command, the full length of the Mackenzie River in mid-winter.

From 1973 to 1977 he was Director of ACV Operations for Northern Transportation. The ACV's were used to transport personnel to offshore rigs on artificial islands on the Beaufort Sea, supporting the oil drilling programs of several companies. After these operations ceased, Mead negotiated the sale of the ACV's to the Coast Guard for use in Search and Rescue work on the west coast of Canada. He retired from Northern Transportation Co. Ltd. in 1979.

As a military test pilot for almost two decades, he flew more than 100 types, from trainers through super-sonic jet fighters and four-engine bombers. As the nation's first certified ACV pilot, he logged some 1,500 hours on ten types, all of which were designated as airplanes by the MOT.

Bert William Mead was inducted as a Member of Canada's Aviation Hall of Fame in 1974.

Bert Mead beside an ACV during trials at Churchill, Manitoba. 1967 – 68.

Almer Leonard (Al) Michaud

(1914 – 1998)

Almer Leonard (Al) Michaud was born on March 19, 1914, in New Westminster, British Columbia, and was educated in the Langley area. His brother Lloyd, a partner in Gilbert's Flying Service, taught him how to fly prior to World War II. He joined the Royal Canadian Air Force (RCAF) in 1941 and served as staff pilot at No. 2 Air Observers School (AOS) in Edmonton, Alberta, and No. 5 AOS in Winnipeg, Manitoba.

In 1942 Al Michaud and his brother Lloyd bought the remaining shares in Gilbert's Flying Service, but wartime restrictions suspended all operations of the company. In 1945 the Michaud brothers returned from wartime flying duties and resumed operations as a new company, Vancouver U Fly, with Al Michaud holding the position of President and Chief Executive Officer. Their company developed into one of the most successful flying schools ever formed in western Canada.

They became distributors of Cessna aircraft in 1946 and also received an Air Transport Board licence to operate land and sea air charter services from their base in Vancouver. British Columbia's rugged

Al Michaud recalled the days when public interest in aviation was growing rapidly and the airport was one of the places to go for a Sunday drive. Visitors were not content to sit and watch, but would line up enthusiastically to buy a fifteen minute ride over the city. For many at that time, the first ride in an airplane was in a small aircraft, which is not true for most people today.

Al Michaud beside a twin-engine aircraft used for training and charter purposes.

coastline and costs of building roads caused companies engaged in lumbering, mining and fishing to rely to a large extent on air travel, which made up the bulk of the charter business. The charter service was such a success that by 1955 the company's name was changed to West Coast Air Services, which seemed to describe the scope of operations more appropriately.

After the federal government took over the Vancouver Airport from its former owner, the City of Vancouver, plans for future use and development of the airport began to emerge. By 1964 operational restrictions imposed at Vancouver International Airport limited its use to licenced pilots only, and therefore, ab initio flight training was moved to a nearby airport, Pitt Meadows. The one aspect of West Coast Air Services business most affected by the new ruling was their flying school. They decided to phase out pre-licence pilot training and concentrate on the senior phases of training, such as commercial, instructor and instrument ratings.

Al Michaud served as a Director of the British Columbia Aviation Council from 1947 to 1967, when he became President of the Council. He also served as Chairman of the Air Transport Association of Canada (ATAC) at this time. During his tenure as Chairman, he directed the

preparation of the draft of the Regional Air Carrier Policy for the Minister of Transport, the Honourable J.W. Pickersgill. This policy continues to provide the main frame-work for air transport in Canada.

In 1967 West Coast Air Services Ltd. purchased the Class 4B charter service of Pacific Western Airlines at Vancouver, Kamloops, and Nelson, which included contract work for the British Columbia Department of Lands and Forests for patrols and fire suppression. In that year, Al Michaud was awarded the Canadian Centennial Medal.

From 1981 to 1982 Michaud was appointed a member of the Justice Dubin Commission and Advisory to the Minister of Transport on Air Safety and other related matters. From 1984 to 1991 he served as Chairman of Time Air Inc., which was formed in Lethbridge, Alberta. He was one of the principal shareholders in this company. In 1986 he was honoured by the International Northwest Aviation Council (INAC) by being named to their Honour Roll for his promotion of the field of aviation. He died in Vancouver on October 20, 1998.

Almer Leonard (Al) Michaud was inducted as a Member of Canada's Aviation Hall of Fame in 1993.

Robert Bruce Middleton

(1912 – 1970)

Robert Bruce Middleton, A.F.C., was born on May 5, 1912, in Fort Francis, Ontario. The family moved to Australia in 1920 but returned to Canada two years later, to live in Winnipeg, Manitoba. He obtained his Private Pilot's Licence in October of 1932, and shortly after, his Commercial Licence. Unable to find a flying job in Canada, he boarded a cattle boat to England with the intention of joining the Royal Air Force (RAF). Upon arrival he was informed that they could not take applications for six months, so he returned to Canada, penniless.

Unable to find work, he lived with his family, and among other things, did some barnstorming. In December he returned to London, England, by the now familiar cattle boat and was accepted by the RAF, but was told he was not needed immediately. He returned home once more. In March 1934, he finally received word of his commission and crossed the Atlantic for a fifth time to commence flying training in Scotland. He received his RAF pilot wings in August.

During a period of leave in 1935, Middleton returned home to Canada and was married. After a short period in Scotland, he was

R. Bruce Middleton was one of three brothers from Dauphin, Manitoba, to serve in the RAF. Bruce, Douglas and Donald all earned their wings in England. The Middletons were the only Canadian family with three sons in the RAF, and they were the only brother trio to have taken aerial bombing courses in the RAF.

posted to Malta with 22 Flying Boat Squadron which was protecting British interests there during the period of tension when Italy invaded Ethiopia.

In 1936 Middleton applied in London to fly for Imperial Airways, and in 1937, with a newly acquired Civil Air Navigator's Licence, he began flying for them on the London-Paris route. In March he returned to Canada, and began flying for Canadian Airways Limited in northern Manitoba, Ontario and Quebec.

In October 1937, he went to work for the fledgling Trans-Canada Airlines (TCA, Hall of Fame 1974) and was on the first test run of the twin engine Lockheed Electra from Winnipeg to Vancouver, British Columbia. In December he became one of the founding members of the Canadian Air Line Pilot's Association (CALPA, Belt of Orion 1988). In 1938 he captained the first TCA airmail flight from Vancouver to Winnipeg and a year later, the inaugural passenger flight on that route.

In May of 1939, he returned to Imperial Airways and flew the London-Frankfurt-Budapest route. He landed in Frankfurt, Germany on September 3rd, 1939, the day that World War II was declared, and after some difficulty, was allowed to continue his flight back to London. Middleton completed 45 passenger flights over Europe before returning to Canada.

Middleton returned to the RCAF, which he had joined as a Reserve Officer while he flew for TCA, and was posted to Bermuda. From there he made five aircraft deliveries across the Atlantic for Ferry Command. In July 1941, he was posted to 116 Bomber Squadron at Dartmouth, Nova Scotia, and flew one of the Lockheed Hudson aircraft taking the Duke of Kent on a tour of the British Commonwealth Air Training Plan (BCATP) facilities. In October he was test-flying a Bell Aircobra fighter and was severely injured when it crashed in the Gatineau Hills in Quebec.

Imperial Oil's first executive aircraft, a Douglas DC-3, 'CF-ESO', which was delivered in May 1947.

On January 1, 1943 he was promoted to Wing Commander and awarded the Air Force Cross (A.F.C.). That same month he was posted to 164 Squadron in Moncton, New Brunswick. This group, under the direction of Group Captain Z.L. Leigh (Hall of Fame 1974), was organized to speed delivery of materials and personnel for the construction of the Goose Bay, Labrador, airport, which was used as a fuel stop in the Atlantic Ferry operation.

In October 1943, Middleton was placed in command of 168 (Mail) Squadron, responsible for carrying mail overseas, and in December he piloted the first flight of airmail to the United Kingdom and the Middle East. In March of 1944, he was placed in charge of the Overseas Wing of RCAF Transport Command.

After demobilization in 1945, Middleton flew for Argentine Airlines from Buenos Aires to New York and London. He returned to Canada a year later and was persuaded by T.M. 'Pat' Reid (Hall of Fame 1974) to join Imperial Oil Limited. In 1946 he began flying for Imperial Oil as Chief Pilot, and became Manager of Flight Operations, a position he held for 21 years. Under his management, the air transport arm of Imperial Oil grew from one to eight aircraft, becoming one of the largest corporate fleets in Canada. During this period he was also a Director of the Toronto Flying Club, and a member of the advisory board of the Canadian Business Aircraft Association. He retired in 1968 with 15,000 hours of air time logged. He died in Mexico on March 24, 1970.

Robert Bruce Middleton was inducted as a Member of Canada's Aviation Hall of Fame in 1989.

Jack Moar

(1905 – 1977)

Jack Moar, B.Sc., B.Eng. (Mech.), was born in Maniwaki, Quebec, on August 13, 1905, and attended school at Semans and Moose Jaw, Saskatchewan. He learned to fly with the Royal Canadian Air Force (RCAF) in 1924 while attending the University of Saskatchewan, from where he graduated with a B.Sc. in 1926. The RCAF offered him a permanent commission, and he was given leave to study at McGill University in Montreal, Quebec, where he obtained his degree in mechanical engineering in 1929.

Moar flew forestry patrols for the RCAF in northern Saskatchewan and Manitoba. The engineering disciplines he had acquired led him to press for the establishment of sub-bases and fuel caches in the wilderness areas of these provinces. In 1929, after a tour of duty as test pilot, Moar resigned from the RCAF to join H.A. 'Doc' Oaks (Hall of Fame 1974) as a pilot for Western Canada Airways. Based at Cranberry Portage, Manitoba, he learned the secrets of sub-zero flight and aircraft maintenance.

In 1930, with N.G. Forester (Hall of Fame 1974), Moar was assigned to spray Stanley Park, Vancouver, British Columbia, to destroy a caterpillar infestation. That summer, he flew across Canada's unmapped north to deliver a spare aircraft

In 1970 Jack Moar proposed that a large number of emergency landing strips be built in the Northwest Territories, equipped with cabins and emergency supplies. He felt that these could have been built for what is spent each year for search and rescue missions.

"His contributions as an airman in converting wilderness areas into habitable communities, and his pioneering night airmail flights to improve the nation's communications system, despite adversity, have been of outstanding benefit to Canadian aviation." —Induction citation, 1974

engine to W.E. Gilbert (Hall of Fame 1974), who was pilot for the Major L.T. Burwash expedition. Gilbert was waiting at Coppermine for the repairs to Fokker Super Universal G-CASK, which had been left on the Arctic coast the previous year when the MacAlpine party had to abandon their aircraft due to lack of fuel.

When Western Canada Airways instituted the night airmail service across the prairie provinces, Moar piloted the inaugural eastbound flight through Lethbridge, Alberta, and remained with the operation until it was cancelled by the government in 1932. Gold was then revalued and a major mining boom in Canada's north strained the facilities of Western Canada Airways, which through a merger, became Canadian Airways. He was appointed Flying Traffic Manager of this new company.

In 1934 Moar and F. Roy Brown (Hall of Fame 1974) and two fellow pilots formed Wings Limited, an air-freighting company with headquarters at Winnipeg, Manitoba. By freeze-up, they had ten aircraft at work. One of the first junior pilots he hired was H.W. Seagrim (Hall of Fame 1974). To put the Berens River gold mines into production, they flew the components for an entire sawmill, mining plant and hydro-electric plant across 200 miles (320 km) of wilderness, about half way up the east side of Lake Winnipeg. In 1936 he and air engineer J. McGinnis flew to the Barren Lands, and set up operations at Eskimo Point, 500 miles (805 km) from the nearest supporting aircraft and beyond radio range. From ports on the west coast of Hudson Bay, Moar transported freight and passengers to inland Hudson's Bay Company posts and other settlements, and brought out furs, for two successful seasons.

In 1937, with several other pilots, he formed Skylines Express Limited, and hired

H. Hollick-Kenyon and T.F. Williams (both Hall of Fame 1974) as pilots. The company scheduled air service between Toronto, Ontario, and Winnipeg, to service mining communities, but the Canadian government removed their operating licence to pave the way for Trans-Canada Air Lines.

Moar went to Edmonton, Alberta, in 1938 when he was hired as Operations Manager of Yukon Southern Air Transport by G.W. Grant McConachie (Hall of Fame 1974). That summer he helped the Department of Transport select landing fields between Fort St. John, British Columbia, and Whitehorse, Yukon. These sites would later become the Northwest Staging Route, so valuable to the Allies during WW II.

Moar flew many mercy flights in the north. A particularly difficult one was when a critically-ill patient at Cameron Bay, on Great Bear Lake, required immediate hospitalization during the spring break-up. It was not safe to fly aircraft on skis or floats, but the mining crew blasted a channel through the ice with dynamite and Moar flew the man to Yellowknife, Northwest Territories, safely.

During World War II, Moar joined Aircraft Repair Limited at Edmonton, working with H.W. Hayter (Hall of Fame 1974) to maintain Canada's military aircraft. In 1942, when Northwest Airlines designed their Edmonton to Fairbanks, Alaska route, it was Moar's aeronautical skills they sought to guide the inaugural flight.

At war's end he returned to flying the Mackenzie River route until 1949, when he retired after logging over 10,000 hours in the cruelest of geographic areas. Moar died in Victoria, British Columbia, on April 26, 1977.

Jack Moar was inducted as a Member of Canada's Aviation Hall of Fame in 1974.

Jack Moar receives his Order of Icarus Medal from Chairman C.H. 'Punch' Dickins. 1973.

Angus Curran Morrison

(b. 1919)

"His dedication to the betterment of the Air Transport Industry has been of outstanding benefit to Canadian aviation." —Induction citation, 1989

Angus Curran Morrison was born in Toronto on April 22, 1919, and educated at Upper Canada and Bishop's Colleges. He served in the Royal Canadian Armoured Corps in the United Kingdom, North Africa, and Italy, and became a pilot before demobilization. He founded and operated his own firm, Atlas Aviation Ltd., in 1947 in Ottawa, Ontario, with bases extending as far as the Quebec North Shore. He was appointed Executive Secretary of the Air Industries and Transport Association of Canada (AITA) in 1951.

In 1962 AITA experienced a change in its organizational structure, with the operators forming their own organization, the Air Transport Association of Canada (ATAC), which at that time represented 95 percent of Canadian air carriers, fixed base operators and helicopter operators. Morrison was appointed Executive Director, and later President and Chief Executive Officer of ATAC. He thus became a full-time officer associated with all undertakings of ATAC.

As Past President of ATAC, he is recognized for his contribution to the development of the aviation industry. Many examples of the results of his efforts could be cited regarding lasting improvements for all members, enhancing all aspects of Canadian air transportation. For

The Air Transport Association of Canada is charged with the responsibility to provide the basic ground-work upon which the Canadian government can establish a sound aviation policy, a policy which is essential to long term planning by carriers.

Angus Morrison during a visit to NASA, with Space Orbiter perched atop a 747.

A.C. MORRISON COLLECTION

government, he championed integrity and air safety within member air operators, service organizations and manufacturers. For the industry, he lobbied for more liberal government regulations. His endeavors over the years resulted in duty-free treatment of aircraft, engines, and parts when a type or size was not made in Canada, saving the commercial operators very large sums of money. He worked hard for an agreement with the Department of Labour to allow operators to average hours of work over a 52-week period, thereby making it possible to comply with the standard labour code. Aviation training was enhanced due to his influence in the establishment of Instructor Refresher Courses which were jointly developed by the Royal Canadian Flying Clubs Association (RCFCA) and ATAC.

In 1977 ATAC received the Diploma of Honour from the Fédération Aéronautique Internationale (FAI) in Paris for the Association's contribution to the air transport industry under Morrison's leadership. He personally was awarded the Fédération's Paul Tissandier Diploma, "Pour son importante contribution depuis 1947 à la promotion et à l'accroissement des activités aeriennes."

Morrison retired from the Air Transport Association of Canada in 1985 and was made an honorary life member at that time. In 1986 he was awarded the C.D. Howe Award by the Canadian Aeronautics and Space Institute (CASI), "For achievement in the field of planning, policy-making and leadership in aeronautics and space."

In 1987, at an Aviation in Transition Recognition Dinner held in Winnipeg, Manitoba, the Aero Space Museum Association presented him with a trophy which read: "To Angus Morrison, an aviation pioneer whose contribution to the industry has added immeasurably to its development." He became an Associate Fellow of the Canadian Aeronautics and Space Institute in July 1987.

Angus Curran Morrison was inducted as a Member of Canada's Aviation Hall of Fame in 1989.

136 MEMBERS OF CANADA'S AVIATION HALL OF FAME

A souvenir program: "Edmonton's Salute to her Bush Pilots on the Occasion of Canada's Golden Anniversary of Flight."
The dinner, sponsored by Edmonton's Chamber of Commerce, had an impressive guest list of pioneer pilots, most of whom
would later become Members of Canada's Aviation Hall of Fame.

Headlines in the Vancouver News Herald, July 31, 1937,
announcing the 'Dawn to Dusk' flight in which Hon.
C.D. Howe's plane made a "Record Run From Montreal."
The plane is shown as it touched down at Vancouver's
civic airport. The lower photo, taken a few minutes later,
shows Mayor George C. Miller welcoming Mr. Howe to
the city.

Inaugural airmail envelopes used on northern mail routes. They were often signed by the crew of the aircraft.

Leigh Brintnell set up his Mackenzie Air Service office in this building in Yellowknife, N.W.T. 1932.

A DC-3 of Maritime Central Airways operated by Carl Burke stands in front of the airport terminal at Charlottetown, P.E.I. 1942.

Above: H.A. 'Doc' Oaks took this photo of J.A. McDougall, treasurer of Western Canada Airways, standing in the doorway of WCA's first office at Hudson, Ontario. December 1926.

Right: W.R. 'Wop' May's Commercial Airways staffhouse at Fort McMurray. c. 1928.

A team of horses is oblivious to a Trans-Canada Airlines Lockheed 14 at Winnipeg, 1943.

At Vancouver International Airport, April 1971. A Fleet 2 is dwarfed by Air Canada's Boeing 747.

Captain Rosella Bjornson and her husband, Bill Pratt, First Officer, on their first assignment together in a Boeing 737 of Canadian Airlines. She had just been promoted to Captain and her fourth stripe had not yet been added to her sleeve.

Members of West and East Canada Sections of Ninety-Nines, following the ceremony at which they were awarded the Belt of Orion. Alberta's Lieutenant-Governor, the Hon. Gordon Towers and Mrs. Towers, centre front, joined the group of women pilots for this picture. Back row: Yvonne Coates, Joy Parker-Blackwood, Elaine Tanton, Mary Lee Burns. Front row: Lou Milhausen, Mary Oswald, Rosella Bjornson, Joan Lynum. Government House in Edmonton, 1995.

Clockwise, from top:

A large diorama on display at the Hall of Fame shows the Eldorado mine at Port Radium on Great Bear Lake in the Northwest Territories. It was designed from photographs taken in the early 1930's. The development of this mine, supplied almost entirely by air, would affect the outcome of World War II when uranium processed from the pitchblende made the atomic bomb possible.

Robert Bradford at work on a painting of Bellanca CF-AWR shown in the diorama above. The dark green and yellow airplane was a familiar sight on bush operations in the north.

The 'Rusty' Blakey Commemorative Sculpture was unveiled in 1988 on the shore of Ramsey Lake, Ontario. Blakey died in 1986 after a long flying career with Austin Airways from the Ramsey Lake base.

Jan Zurakowski beside a model of the Avro CF-105 'Arrow', and Jack Woodman in a replica of the Silver Dart. The display at the 1958 Canadian National Exhibition, Toronto, celebrated the up-coming 50th Anniversary of powered flight in Canada.

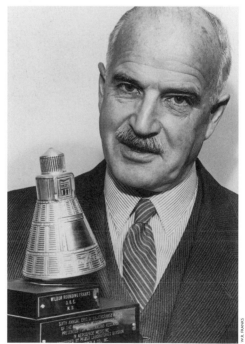

Dr. Wilbur R. Franks was presented the Eric Liljencrantz Award of the Aerospace Medical Association for his outstanding research in Aerospace Medicine. Two of his better-known inventions are the G-suit and human centrifuge. April 1962.

Pratt & Whitney President, Elvie Smith, with the 20,000th turbine engine built by the Pratt & Whitney company, 1981.

Austin Airways began operating at Toronto Air Harbour in 1934. During the winter they moved to the Toronto Flying Club field.

The rescue mission to Letty Harbour on the Arctic coast near Paulatuk, east of Aklavik, to bring out Bishop Falaize and his group of two adults and four children, was extremely difficult, but successful. Shown are Matt Berry's passengers beside his Junkers at Letty Harbour Mission. December 1936.

Jan Zurakowski, right, receives the first James C. Floyd Award for Lifetime Achievement, March 1990.
Left, Jim Floyd, Patron, and centre, David Onley, President of the Aerospace Heritage Foundation of Canada.

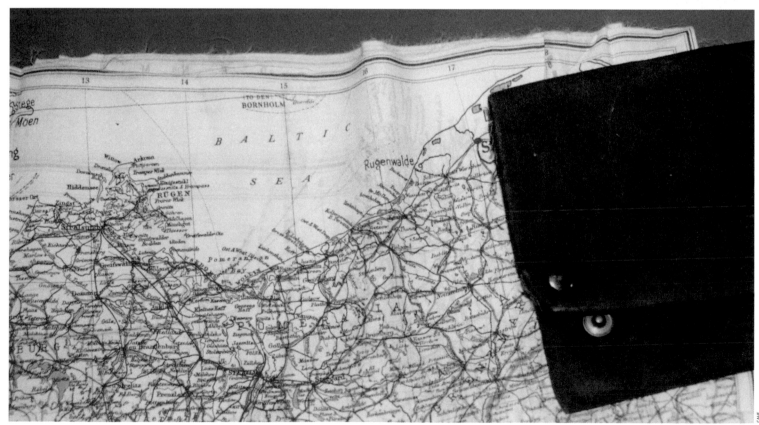

The RAF escape map carried by Jan Zurakowski during his sorties over northern Europe in World War II.
Poland, on the right-hand portion of the map, borders Germany on the Baltic Sea.

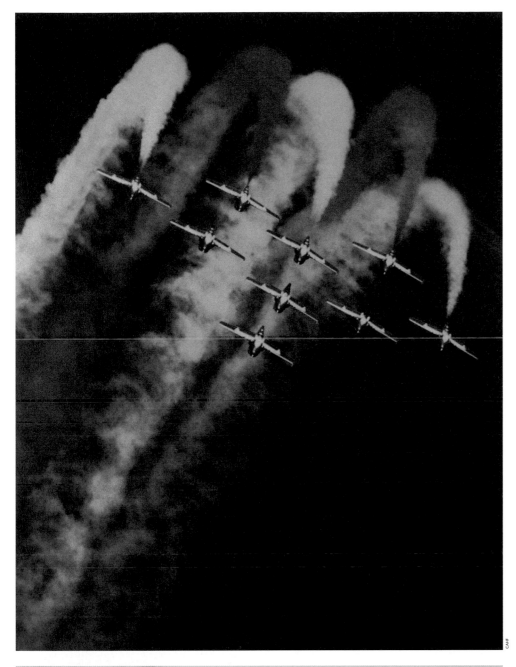

Clockwise, from left:

With grace and precision, and seeming effortlessness, the Snowbirds entertain many thousands of spectators at airshows across Canada every year.

A certificate presented to W.F. Sheldon Luck to record his meritorious services to the war effort as Captain of Aircraft between June 1942 and June 1945. In September 1940, the Air Services Department of the CPR was formed in Montreal to ferry bombers urgently required in Great Britain. In 1941, this organization was taken over by the Royal Air Force Ferry Command and disbanded when victory in Europe was won.

Stan Reynolds holds the M.F. 'Molly' Reilly Memorial Trophy which was awarded to him by the Alberta Aviation Council in 1987 in recognition of his 40 years of outstanding contribution to aviation in Alberta.

Curtiss HS-2L flying boat, La Vigilance, of Laurentide Air Service Ltd., restored and now on display at the National Aviation Museum at Ottawa.

Ken Saunders took his flying training on a Wright Biplane at the Wright Brothers School in Dayton, Ohio, in 1915. Below is his licence, dated October 27, 1915, and recognized by the Federation Aeronautique Internationale. On the following page is the training agreement made between Ken Saunders and the Wright Company on September 10, 1915.

TRAINING AGREEMENT

Date Sept. 0, 1915

The Wright Company agrees to give _____

_____ Ken. F. Saunders. _____

lessons in flying under the following conditions :

First:—The signing of the release of responsibility appended hereto.

Two hundred and fifty dollars ($250.00)

Second:—The payment of $25.00 (Twenty-five dollars) per lesson, terms cash in advance unless otherwise arranged with our representative. which entitles the pupil to a total of four (4) hours of training flights.

Third:—A lesson shall consist of one flight of fifteen minutes or more duration at the option of the instructor. The company does not agree to train a pupil to fly in any definite number of flights, nor does it assume any responsibility beyond the breakage of the machine during the training. The pupil, therefore, can take as many lessons as he may in his own judgment deem necessary.

Fourth:—A record shall be kept of each lesson furnished with the pupil's acknowledgment.

THE WRIGHT COMPANY,

Witness: Mabel Beck

Per Orville Wright

Acceptance:—I hereby accept the above conditions for taking lessons to fly the Wright aeroplane.

In taking these lessons with _____ the appointed _____ Operator I do so of my own volition and hereby assume whatever risk of personal injury there may be connected with it. I agree for myself and my heirs not to hold _____ the appointed _____ Operator, or The Wright Company, either individually or collectively, liable for any injury which I may sustain from these flights.

K F Saunders

Witness: Mabel Beck.

Canadair's CL-215 Water Bomber. Harry Halton was Program Manager at Canadair, responsible for the production of this aircraft, from the design stage through to development and certification.

Julien Audette in his 1958 Schweizer 1-23G glider CF-ZDO over the Livingstone Range of the Rocky Mountains, near Cowley, Alberta. He purchased this glider in 1961 and reached over 30,000 feet in it near Pincher Creek, Alberta, in April of that year.

Left: A trio of Beavers of West Coast Air Services operated by Al and Lloyd Michaud. They are docked on the Fraser River near Vancouver, British Columbia. c. early 1960's.

Right: A badge showing the logo used by Leigh Brintnell's Edmonton-based company, Mackenzie Air Service. c. 1932.

Below: Wardair purchased Airbus A-310's in the 1980's. This one was named "S.R. 'Stan' McMillan".

Fairchild 71, CF-AOP, being refuelled by hand-pump on the ice of Lake St. John, Roberval, Quebec. 1941.

Fokker Universal, G-CAGD, in front of Western Canada Airways first office at Pine Ridge, Ontario. January 1927.

The first of the 'heating hoods' on a Fokker Universal at Hudson, Ontario, January 1927.
The air engineer used a plumber's fire-pot to keep the engine warm and to heat his working area.

A Pacific Western DC-4 is met by dog teams to haul mail and supplies back to their communities. c. 1960's.

Before the era of large freight haulers such as the DC-4 above, northern regions were served by smaller aircraft such as the one shown here. c. 1930's.

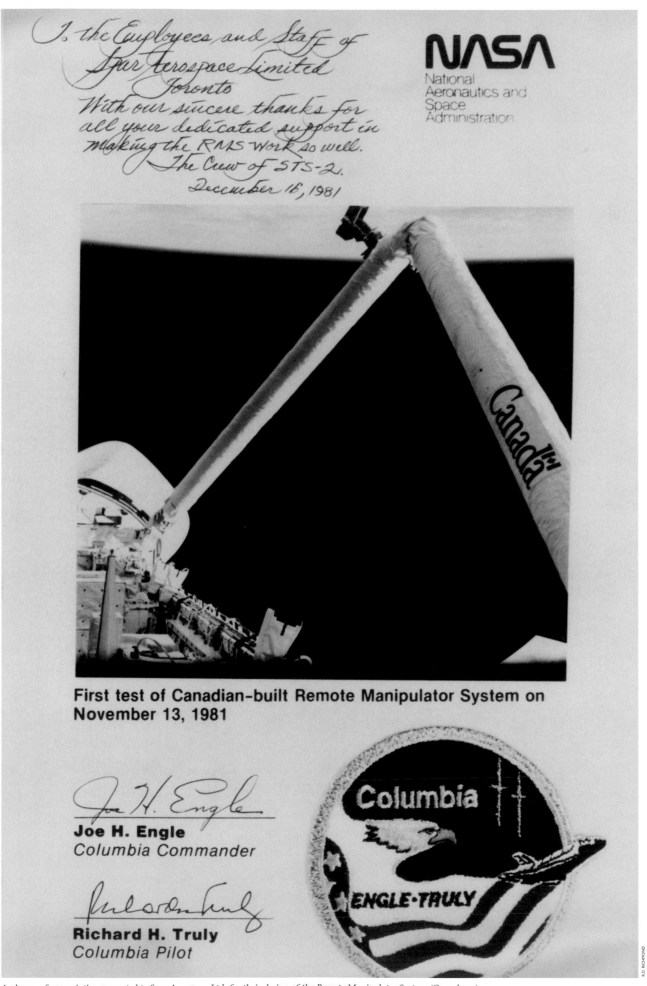

To the Employees and Staff of Spar Aerospace Limited Toronto

With our sincere thanks for all your dedicated support in making the RMS work so well.

The Crew of STS-2.

December 16, 1981

NASA

National
Aeronautics and
Space
Administration

First test of Canadian-built Remote Manipulator System on November 13, 1981

Joe H. Engle
Joe H. Engle
Columbia Commander

Richard H. Truly
Richard H. Truly
Columbia Pilot

A plaque of appreciation presented to Spar Aerospace Ltd. for their design of the Remote Manipulator System (Canadarm) which performed so successfully during the flight of the space shuttle 'Columbia' commanded by Joe Engle and piloted by Richard Truly. November 1981.

Raymond Alan Munro

(1921 – 1994)

Raymond Alan Munro, C.M., was born in Montreal, Quebec, on July 14, 1921, and was educated in Canada and the United States. He commenced flying at Toronto, Ontario, in 1937 and joined the Royal Canadian Air Force (RCAF) in 1940. He was posted to 145 Squadron of the Royal Air Force (RAF) under Squadron Leader P.S. Turner (Hall of Fame 1974), and became a Spitfire pilot. He survived three major crashes and was returned to Canada and medically discharged in March of 1942. He then became adjutant of the RCAF's Repatriation Depot at Ottawa, Ontario.

Munro was hired as a cub reporter by the Toronto *Daily Star* in 1942, and thus began a 17-year career in journalism. He learned court reporting, story-writing, and the art of news photography, and soon became a senior reporter, available wherever news was breaking. He spent a few months as a pilot and crime reporter for the *Globe and Mail*, then moved to Vancouver, British Columbia, and began working for the *Vancouver Sun* as a pilot, photographer, and investigative reporter.

He left the *Sun* and was offered a job at the *Vancouver Province* in 1948 after his aerial photo reports of the Fraser River flood were published. He received a provincial government commendation for his air

Ray Munro was one of the founding members of Canada's Aviation Hall of Fame. When the idea of an Aviation Hall of Fame presented itself, Munro single-handedly enlisted the support necessary to open it in a year, and he served the critical first four years as Managing Director.

"He has consistently displayed a dogged persistence in overcoming every aeronautical challenge facing him, and despite adversity has made outstanding contributions to Canadian aviation in several areas of flight."

—Induction citation, 1974

delivery of strategic supplies, and the rescue of marooned persons. He had piloted an aircraft from dawn to dusk for 14 consecutive days, often in unfavourable weather.

In 1949, after a week-long patrol of the weather-shrouded Rocky Mountains, Munro located two fliers who had crashed in a spring snow storm. Then, despite deteriorating weather, he led an RCAF aircraft back to the isolated location from which they were eventually rescued by military parachutists. The following year, during a severe storm, he flew a shipment of vitally-needed blood and plasma to an isolated coastal community. For this mission, which resulted in the saving of human life, he was awarded a Canadian Red Cross Society commendation for heroism, matching another he had received earlier for the winter rescue of a drowning victim.

While with the *Province*, Munro exposed the corruption within the Vancouver Police Department, then left to try charter flying into the northern areas of British Columbia, Yukon and Alaska. In 1956 he moved back to Ontario and worked as a reporter for the *Chatham News*, soon becoming Editor-in-Chief. In 1957 he took a leave to cover the Arab-Israeli war, and reported on activities there.

In 1958 he ended his newspaper career to follow flying adventures and take up parachuting. In 1962 he taught parachuting to the U.S. military. He made hundreds of descents, becoming one of Canada's most avid parachutists.

Selected as Canada's Expo '67 Polar Ambassador, he and geophysicist Ivan Christopher flew a specially designed single-engine aircraft, a Cessna 180, on a 26-day goodwill flight over Canada's far north. They travelled over 8,500 miles (13,680 km) in mid-winter through the high Arctic to honour Canada's pioneer bush pilots and prospectors who helped open the north.

In early 1969 he arranged to make his final parachute jump, his 528th, onto the Polar ice cap. He contracted with W. 'Weldy' Phipps (Hall of Fame 1974) to fly him over the North Pole area for the jump, which he made from 10,000 feet (3,048 m), onto a small ice floe, where Phipps landed to take him back to his Arctic base at Resolute Bay.

Munro's interests turned to ballooning in 1969. He ordered three balloons from the Raven Balloon Works and began to research aerostatics, the science related to piloting a balloon. On November 24, 1969, he lifted 'Canada 1' to an altitude of 17,943.86 feet (5,469.29 m) from Russell, Ontario. On December 17, 1969, he reached a height of 25,407 feet (7,743.69 m), which gave Canada an official world altitude record, recognized by the Fédération Aéronautique Internationale (FAI). In 1971, using 'Canada 2,' he became the first person to pilot a balloon across the Irish Sea from southern Ireland to northern England.

Munro was appointed a Member of the Order of Canada (C.M.) in December of 1974. In 1978 he worked for several months as Chief Administrator of the Halton Regional Police Force, in Halton, Ontario. He wrote a book about his life's experiences, titled *The Sky's No Limit*, published in 1985.

He has been honoured by governments, societies and groups with honorary citizenships, citations, and achievement medals, in addition to his many photo-journalism awards. Munro died on May 29, 1994.

Raymond Alan Munro was inducted as a Member of Canada's Aviation Hall of Fame in 1974.

Ray Munro beside 'Canada 1'. 1969.

Andrew Charles (Andy) Mynarski

(1916 – 1944)

Andrew Charles (Andy) Mynarski, V.C., was born in Winnipeg, Manitoba, on October 14, 1916. He attended King Edward and Isaac Newton Schools, and St. John's Technical School. He was employed as a leather worker. He enlisted in the Winnipeg Rifles in 1940 and transferred to the Royal Canadian Air Force (RCAF) the following year. In 1942 he graduated from training as an air gunner and was sent to active duty in England.

On completion of operational training he was posted to 9 Squadron, Royal Air Force (RAF), and in 1944 joined 419 Squadron, RCAF, where he completed 12 operational flights and was promoted to Pilot Officer on June 11. The following night Mynarski took his position as mid-upper gunner of an Avro Lancaster bomber. The aircraft never returned to base.

When the war ended and the prisoners of war were liberated, some outstanding acts of bravery previously unknown were revealed. Among them was one which brought a posthumous Victoria Cross to

In 1984 the Canadian Warplane Heritage Museum honoured the memory of Pilot Officer Andrew Mynarski, V.C., by restoring a Lancaster MKX to full flying condition. It was dedicated to his memory at a ceremony held at Hamilton Civic Airport, Mount Hope, Ontario. The surviving crew members of the fateful June 12, 1944, mission were present for the dedication ceremony.

Andrew C. Mynarski, RCAF. c. 1942.

Pilot Officer Andrew Charles Mynarski. The six survivors of Mynarski's crew who were liberated from German prisoner-of-war camps told the story of the events of that night. The citation accompanying the honour tells the complete story:

> "Pilot Officer Mynarski was mid-upper gunner of a Lancaster bomber, detailed to attack a target at Cambrai in France on the night of June 12, 1944. The aircraft was attacked from below and astern by an enemy fighter and ultimately came down in flames. As an immediate result of the attack, both port engines failed. Fire broke out between the mid-upper turret and the rear turret, as well as in the port wing. The flames soon became too fierce and the captain ordered the crew to abandon the aircraft.

> Pilot Officer Mynarski left his turret and went towards the escape hatch. He then saw that the rear gunner was still in the turret and apparently unable to leave it. The turret was, in fact, immovable, since the hydraulic gear had been put out of action when the

port engines failed, and the manual gear had been broken by the gunner in his attempt to escape.

> Without hesitation Pilot Officer Mynarski made his way through the flames in an endeavor to reach the rear turret and release the gunner. Whilst doing so, his parachute and his clothing, up to his waist, were set afire. All his efforts to move the turret and free the gunner were in vain. Eventually the rear gunner clearly indicated to him that there was nothing more that he could do and that he should try and save his own life. Pilot Officer Mynarski reluctantly went back through the flames to the escape hatch. There, as a last gesture to the trapped gunner, he stood to attention in his flaming clothing and saluted, before he jumped out of the aircraft. Pilot Officer Mynarski's descent was seen by French people on the ground. Both his parachute and his clothes were on fire. He was found eventually by the French, but so severely burned that he died from his injuries.

> The rear gunner had a miraculous escape when the aircraft crashed. He subsequently testified that had Pilot Officer Mynarski not attempted to save his comrade's life, he could have left the aircraft in safety and would, doubtless, have escaped death.

> Pilot Officer Mynarski must have been fully aware that in trying to free the rear gunner he was almost certain to lose his life. Despite this, with outstanding courage and complete disregard for his own safety, he went to the rescue. Willingly accepting the danger, Pilot Officer Mynarski lost his life by a most conspicuous act of heroism which called for valour of the highest order."

Andrew Charles (Andy) Mynarski was inducted as a Member of Canada's Aviation Hall of Fame in 1974.

George Arthur Neal

(b. 1918)

George Arthur Neal was born in Downsview, Ontario, on November 21, 1918. He learned to fly at the Toronto Flying Club in 1935 and earned his Private Pilot's Licence in 1936. From 1937 to 1941 he was employed at de Havilland Aircraft Canada (DHC). In 1941 he enlisted in the Royal Canadian Air Force (RCAF) and was posted on leave to No. 10 Air Observers School in Chatham, New Brunswick, where he became a Flight Commander, Chief Test Pilot and Assistant Maintenance Superintendent.

In 1946 he rejoined DHC where he would be employed for the next 37 years. His first job was in the engine shop, and in 1947 he was transferred to the flying staff as a full time pilot and took over the development testing of the new DHC-1 Chipmunk. He became Chief Test Pilot in 1948 and was involved in several flight test programs which were unique for that time. One was the testing of a twin-engine de Havilland Dove as a float plane. In addition to learning that the floats did not enhance the lateral/directional characteristics of the Dove, it was shown

George Neal has long been interested in vintage aircraft. During the 1950's he procured a copy of the original drawings for the Sopwith Pup and built an award-winning replica. He won the Keith Hopkinson Award from the Canadian Owners and Pilots Association (COPA, Belt of Orion 1993) for the best home-built aircraft in 1967. This aircraft is now on display at the National Aviation Museum in Ottawa.

"His contribution to the testing, development and promotion of Canadian-designed and built STOL aircraft has gained world wide recognition and respect for the Canadian aviation industry and all Canadians." —Induction citation, 1995

George Neal preparing for a flight in the British-designed Vampire Jet. c. 1948.

that the aircraft had no positive climb performance on one engine.

In 1948, with the introduction of the British de Havilland Vampire jet into service in the RCAF, Neal became one of the first civilian pilots in Canada to become jet qualified. He did a considerable amount of demonstration and development testing of this aircraft. Once, while testing an emergency engine relight system, the engine failed to re-start. Neal was well north of Toronto at the time, but was able to glide the Vampire back to the airport at Downsview for a successful deadstick landing.

The flight testing of the Beaver, first flown by Russ Bannock (Hall of Fame 1974), was completed by Neal in 1948. This included the civilian flight certification required to obtain a Civil Type Rating. His convincing demonstration of the short take-off and landing (STOL) features of the Beaver led to sales throughout the world where it has become one of the most famous of Canadian aircraft.

On December 12, 1951, he piloted the first flight of the DHC-3 Otter. Over the next two years he succeeded in obtaining certification of this aircraft at increased gross weights in the original land-plane configuration, and later in the float and ski-plane versions. The Otter and the Beaver

were both acquired by the U.S. Army. The Otter was used widely by the U.S. Army in Viet Nam, the U.S. Navy in the Antarctic, and throughout the world by the RCAF. The Otter was the only light transport to satisfy the low speed flying qualities required by the International Civil Aviation Organization (ICAO) Category C Standards.

The first flight of the prototype Caribou was flown by Neal on July 30, 1958. His demonstration flights left no doubt as to its STOL capabilities. The Caribou was the first multi-engine aircraft designed and built by DHC, and was the first Civil Aviation Regulation '4b' Transport Category aircraft to be certified by the Department of Transport.

Toward the end of the Caribou program, during high speed trials, a modified version developed flutter. After the loss of part of the tail surface, it became unmanageable, and Neal and the accompanying Department of Transport test pilot were forced to abandon the aircraft. Neal's attention to detail before he bailed out prevented fire following the crash, and enabled a clear study of the cause of the flutter. He was made a member of the Caterpillar Club. (This club was sponsored by the Irvin Parachute Company. Only those who have used a parachute to survive an unserviceable aircraft can become a member.) The Caribou was purchased in quantity by the RCAF, the U.S. Army and many other foreign military services.

In all of the DHC designs mentioned above, Neal was a valued ambassador in demonstrating and promoting these aircraft. Much of their success in the world markets was due to the first hand impressions that he was able to convey to customers.

During the development period of the new DHC aircraft, Neal took part in the testing of many aircraft in repair, overhaul, and modification programs. These included the Canso flying boat, Avro Lancaster, Harvard trainer, Canadair Northstar, the Alvis Leonides-powered Beaver, and the DH-built twin engine Grumman Tracker, 100 of which were built for the Canadian Navy. He was involved in the development testing of Twin Otters, Buffalos and Dash-7's. Two experimental programs involved one heavily modified 'Batwing' Otter, which was used to study flap downwash, and another, 'Silent Otter' study for the U.S. Army.

In 1975 Neal was made Director of Flight Operations of de Havilland Canada, where he became responsible for the flight standards and flying discipline. He was also responsible for production testing, flight instruction, flight demonstrations, and aircraft deliveries throughout the world. He retired in 1983 but was called back to assist in the production testing of the Dash-7 and Dash-8.

Neal was Chief Pilot for the National Aviation Museum until 1991, when the program of flying their vintage aircraft ended. He flew the Sopwith Pup, Avro 504K, and Nieuport 17, which are in the museum's collection. He has also rebuilt a Hawker Hind for the museum. He presently owns and flies a DH Hornet Moth and Chipmunk, and a Piper Arrow. He has accumulated over 14,700 hours on over 100 different aircraft.

In 1989 Neal won Canada's most prestigious aviation award, the Trans-Canada (McKee) Trophy. The citation reads, in part, " ...Perhaps no other pilot in Canada has had such a varied and complete career in aviation." On October 18, 1997, Neal was inducted into the de Havilland Aircraft of Canada's Hall of Fame.

George Arthur Neal was inducted as a Member of Canada's Aviation Hall of Fame in 1995.

William Francis Montgomery (Bill) Newson
(1917 – 1988)

William Francis Montgomery (Bill) Newson, D.S.O., D.F.C.*, C.D.**, B. Eng., was born in Calgary, Alberta, on July 19, 1917. He graduated from Edmonton's Garneau High School in 1935, after having received his primary and early secondary education in British Columbia and Ontario. He attended Royal Military College in Kingston, Ontario, where he graduated in Civil Engineering in June 1939, and immediately joined the Royal Canadian Air Force (RCAF). He learned to fly at Camp Borden and Trenton, Ontario, and upon graduation was awarded the Sword of Honour. He was posted to 11 Bomber Reconnaissance Squadron at Dartmouth, Nova Scotia, where he flew with Z.L. Leigh (Hall of Fame 1974) as a pilot on coastal operations, escorting convoys on Atlantic crossings, often under very difficult weather conditions.

In July 1942, after a tour of instruction at Patricia Bay, British Columbia, Newson was transferred to the United Kingdom, flying an aircraft for Royal Air Force (RAF) Ferry Command en route. On arrival in England, he joined RCAF 408 Squadron.

Bill Newson envisioned Canada's Aviation Hall of Fame as a unique institution which held a collection of historical and educational displays, highlighting the role of aviation in Canada's history through the stories of its Members. It would focus on preserving and presenting the human aspects of Canadian aviation for the benefit of the nation.

"His lifetime dedication to aviation in both war and peace, particularly his outstanding effort to preserve and present the human aspects of aviation for the purpose of increasing public knowledge and appreciation for Canada's aviation heritage has been of considerable benefit to Canadian aviation and to the nation."

—Induction citation, 1984

Bill Newson in full flight gear, including inflatable life jacket. n.d.

During operations with this squadron his aircraft sustained serious damage on two occasions. For outstanding courage and leadership he was awarded the Distinguished Flying Cross (D.F.C.). In June of 1943 he was posted as Squadron Commander to 431 Squadron. Again he demonstrated outstanding courage and leadership in the completion of very long range bomber sorties, for which he was awarded a Bar to his D.F.C.

In October 1944, Group Captain Newson was appointed Commanding Officer of 405 Pathfinder Squadron, where he remained to the end of hostilities in Europe. The London Gazette of September 21, 1945, recorded the citation for Group Captain Newson's Distinguished Service Order (D.S.O.) as follows:

"This officer has a long and varied career of operational duty. After completing a tour of duty with Coastal Command in Canada, he was appointed to command a squadron in this country. He has taken part in many sorties since the award of the D.F.C., many of them in a most important role. The success of a number of sorties against such heavily defended objectives as Chemnitz and Zweibrucken has been due in no small measure to his work as Master Bomber. Group Captain Newson is an outstanding officer who, by his keenness and efficiency, has set a fine example."

Following World War II, General Newson held a number of senior staff and command appointments in Canada and overseas. These included Commandant of RCAF Staff College in Toronto, Ontario, and Commander of No. 36 North American Air Defence Division (NORAD) in Maine, U.S.A. In this latter position he was responsible for the air defence of the northeastern approaches to North America. From 1968 to 1971 he was Assistant Chief of Air Operations, Central Europe.

General Newson retired from the Armed Forces on July 19, 1972, and had accumulated nearly 6,000 flying hours. Throughout his career he was an enthusiastic and dedicated airman flying at every opportunity. He qualified on 25 types of aircraft.

In 1977 Newson was approached to take on the task of Executive Vice-President of Canada's Aviation Hall of Fame from R.A. Munro (Hall of Fame 1974). He took over control of the Hall when it was still in its embryonic stage in the Edmonton Law Courts building. From 1977 to 1983 he negotiated with Edmonton City Council, architects and designers in order to implement a move to the Edmonton Convention Centre, where the Hall was located until June 1992, when it was moved to its present location at Wetaskiwin, Alberta.

Newson served as President of the Sir Winston Churchill Society in Edmonton in 1984, President of the Wartime Aircrew Association in Edmonton from 1981 to 1983, as a member of the Senate of the University of Alberta for six years, and as Vice-Chairman of the Salvation Army Advisory Board. He died in Edmonton on March 24, 1988.

William Francis Montgomery (Bill) Newson was inducted as a Member of Canada's Aviation Hall of Fame in 1984.

Harold Anthony (Doc) Oaks
(1896 – 1968)

Harold Anthony (Doc) Oaks, D.F.C., B.A.Sc., was born in Hespeler, Ontario, on November 12, 1896. He was educated there and at Galt, Ontario. Oaks joined the Canadian Army in 1915 and served overseas until 1917 when he transferred to the Royal Flying Corps in England. He earned his pilot's wings and a promotion to Captain, served in France as a fighter pilot with 2 and 48 Squadrons, Royal Air Force (RAF), and was awarded the Distinguished Flying Cross (D.F.C.) for gallantry. He attended the University of Toronto where he graduated as a mining engineer in 1922. During the summer months he worked as an assistant geologist for Mackenzie River Oil Company.

He worked for the Canadian Geological Survey in the field for a year, then joined Hollinger Gold Mine, prospecting for minerals in northern Ontario and Quebec. In 1924 he was hired by the Ontario Provincial Air Service (Belt of Orion 1991) after receiving his Commercial Pilot's Licence, and flew forestry patrols out of Red Lake, Ontario. Following a year of prospecting for minerals in the same area, he organized and managed Patricia Airways and Exploration Company at Sioux Lookout, Ontario, in 1926, with air mechanic S.A. (Sammy) Tomlinson (Hall

'Doc' Oaks was a leader in pioneering air transport in Canada in the 1920's. He introduced the use of aircraft to fly men and equipment to outlying areas for mining and development work, at the same time helping two industries, aviation and mining, to thrive by working together.

'Doc' Oaks with his first 'nose-hangar' which was built on skids so that it could be positioned over an aircraft more easily. Hudson, Ontario. January, 1927.

of Fame 1974). Their main service lines were to the gold mining regions of Red Lake and Woman Lake north of Dryden, Ontario.

Oaks envisioned the saving of time and money with low cost air transport of people and equipment over vast distances. He persuaded financier James A. Richardson, (Hall of Fame 1976), who had a similar vision, to form a new air line. In December 1926, Western Canada Airways was incorporated at Winnipeg, Manitoba. Oaks became general manager and sole pilot, flying a Fokker Universal from its base at Hudson, near Sioux Lookout. This company expanded rapidly, and became the first of Canada's major airline services.

Under Oaks' command, Western Canada Airways fulfilled a Canadian government contract in March of 1927 to airlift men and equipment from Cache Lake, Manitoba, to Fort Churchill, on Hudson Bay. Two pilots were hired for this difficult undertaking, the first of its kind ever attempted. Bernt Balchen (Hall of Fame 1974) and F.J. Stevenson flew in open cockpit aircraft through sub-zero temperatures and over alien ground, to make possible the creation of a new open port for Canada. In a month's time, they made twenty-seven round trips, transporting thirty tons (27,200 kg) of material and equipment and a crew of fourteen government engineers.

Marion Alice Powell Orr
(1918 – 1995)

Marion Alice Powell Orr, C.M., was born in Toronto, Ontario, on June 25, 1918. Having lost her parents at a young age, she joined the work force after completing grade eight to earn the money necessary to meet her earliest ambition—learning to fly. She commenced her flying lessons at Barker Field, Toronto, and qualified for her Private Pilot's Licence in December of 1939. During the next two years she was employed by de Havilland Aircraft of Canada Limited as an aircraft inspector. She earned a Commercial Pilot's Licence in December 1941, and seven months later passed the required flight tests at Royal Canadian Air Force Station, Trenton, Ontario, for a Flying Instructor's Rating, one of only six women to do so.

In August 1942, Orr was hired as Manager and Chief Flying Instructor (CFI) by the St. Catharines Flying Club in Ontario, thus becoming the first woman in Canada to operate a flying club. She was hired by No. 12 Elementary Flying School of the British Commonwealth Air Training Plan (BCATP), at Goderich, Ontario. Here she became the second woman licenced as a control tower operator of Canada.

Marion Orr claimed she was born to fly—she never wanted to do anything else. During a career of over forty years, she logged more than 24,000 hours of which over 17,000 were as an instructor on single and twin-engine aircraft equipped with wheels, skis and floats, and in helicopters, a total of 100 different types. She taught thousands of pilots.

On-site repairs of broken struts and skis were made with materials on hand. This shows the undercarriage repairs of Fokker Universal GC-AFU. Hudson, Ontario. c. 1927.

It was at this time that Oaks and his air engineer, Al Cheesman, designed and built the first portable nose-hangar to enable mechanics to work on an aircraft's engine without freezing in the bitter cold. The small three-sided frame structure was equipped with a heater and a canvas flap which allowed the aircraft's nose to be inserted inside and kept relatively warm. Oaks was the first person to be awarded the Trans-Canada (McKee) Trophy. This was for the year 1927 in recognition of his work in organizing and operating air transport in northern Ontario, Manitoba and Saskatchewan.

When Northern Aerial Mineral Exploration Limited (N.A.M.E.) was formed in 1928 to search for potential mining properties in areas far removed from civilization, Oaks accepted the post of General Manager and Director of Air Operations. During this period he was involved in a number of emergency flights. One of the most notable was in the company of T.M. 'Pat' Reid (Hall of Fame 1974), when they flew 1,600 miles (2,575 km) along the sub-Arctic shores of Hudson Bay through inclement weather to locate a party of 13 stranded prospectors and return them to base. It was the first mid-winter flight into the area by a private company.

As one of the earliest known pilot/geologists, Oaks foresaw immense financial potential locked in the far reaches of the Canadian Shield, accessible only by canoe through twisting waterways. In 1928 he based his operation at Fort McMurray, Alberta, and flew engineers and prospectors, with their supplies, into promising wilderness locations. His pioneer flights into unmapped territory spurred other aviators to penetrate still further into the Northwest Territories. He remained with this company until 1930, when he formed his own aviation concern, Oaks Airways Limited, operating from Sioux Lookout until 1935, and from Port Arthur, Ontario, until 1943. During this time he earned his Air Engineer's Licence.

In 1943 Oaks was associated with the Clark Ruse Aircraft Company at Halifax, Nova Scotia, and Central Aircraft Manufacturers at London, Ontario, as Manager of Flight Operations. From 1945 to 1953 he continued his work as a mining engineer at Port Arthur. In 1953 he became an aviation consultant to James A. Richardson and Company in Toronto. He died in Toronto on July 21, 1968.

Harold Anthony (Doc) Oaks was inducted as a Member of Canada's Aviation Hall of Fame in 1974.

In the meantime her application to join the Air Transport Auxiliary (ATA) in the United Kingdom was accepted and in December 1942, she was hired by British Overseas Airways Limited as a pilot with the ATA. She flew the remainder of the war years ferrying 40 different types of single and twin-engine military aircraft, including Harvards, Hurricanes, Spitfires, Ansons, Swordfish and Tiger Moths from factories in the British Isles to the front line bases, returning with damaged machines to repair depots.

On her return to Canada at the end of the war, Orr was employed as a flight instructor with Gillies Flying Service, Buttonville Airport, Ontario. In 1947 she assumed the responsibilities of Manager and CFI of Aero Activities Limited at Barker Field, Toronto, and two years later purchased the company. Within two years she had trebled its flying hours and turned losses into profits. The sale of Barker Field for development purposes required that a new location be found for her company. In the spring of 1954 work commenced at a new site at Maple, a small town about 20 miles (32 km) north of Toronto, but only after she persuaded the residents that the airfield would be a valued addition to their town. The airfield was officially opened in September 1954, and she became the first woman licenced to operate an airport in Canada.

Marion Orr, Manager of Aero Activities Ltd., with DHC Chipmunk. Maple, Ontario. May, 1956.

In 1957 Aero Activities Limited was sold and Orr returned to the flight line with Gillies Flying Service as an instructor. She also spent some time with the Sudbury Flying School where she was one of the first women to become involved in bush flying. In 1958 she left aviation for a year and returned in 1959 as the CFI of her former company, Aero Activities. In 1960 she joined Markham Toronto Airways with whom she remained for a year.

During 1961 she became interested in helicopter flying and on May 16 she was licenced to fly helicopters, the first woman in Canada to do so. Two months later she earned her Instructor's Rating, also a first for a woman in Canada, and was appointed CFI by Vendair, the helicopter school from which she received her training. In September 1961, while on an instructional flight in a Brantley B-2, the engine failed, and in the emergency landing she suffered a broken back. In June 1962, while recuperating in Florida, she received permission from the Federal Aviation Administration of the United States to instruct there on helicopters.

In July 1962, she returned to Canada to instruct at Donway Flying Service, Buttonville Airport, on light aircraft. However, her back would not tolerate the long hours of sitting in a cockpit, and in July 1963, she decided to give up her life's work. However, she kept in practice when possible by recreational flying. Twelve years later she renewed her Instructor's Rating and returned to flying as an instructor with Toronto Airways Limited.

In 1976 her outstanding achievements in aviation were recognized by the International Organization of Women Pilots, The Ninety-Nines, which awarded her one of its highest honours, the Amelia Earhart Medallion. She was named a Member of the Order of Canada (C.M.) in 1987. Orr died in a car accident in Ontario on April 4, 1995.

Marion Alice Powell Orr was inducted as a Member of Canada's Aviation Hall of Fame in 1982.

John Ender (Jock) Palmer
(1896 – 1964)

"His pioneering work in the use of air to ground wireless, his piloting the first international mail run and his continued dedication to instructing others to fly have been of outstanding benefit to Canadian aviation."

—Induction citation, 1988

John Ender (Jock) Palmer, A.F.C., D.C.M., was born in Cambridge, England, on December 28, 1896. The family moved to Canada and settled in Lethbridge, Alberta, in 1901. He joined the 10th Battalion as a Private on September 1, 1914, and embarked for England with the first contingent on October 3, 1914. He was posted to France on February 15, 1915, promoted to Lance Corporal in March and

'Jock' Palmer described the many hazards of flying the delicate airplanes of the 1920's. Two incidents involved inadequate landing fields: the first was landing in a field with gopher and badger holes which caught the undercarriage of his aircraft, damaging it beyond repair. Another incident involved an automobile which drove in front of his aircraft just as he was coming in for a landing. He had to swerve to avoid the car, resulting in a groundloop which tore off the undercarriage and damaged the wing. He was not injured in either incident.

to Corporal in June. He was awarded the Distinguished Conduct Medal (D.C.M.) in July of 1915 and in November was promoted to Sergeant. He was transferred to the 2nd Brigade, Machine Gun Company on February 3, 1916, commissioned as a Lieutenant in May and transferred back to the 10th Battalion where he was wounded in June and invalided back to England.

Palmer was eventually transferred to the Royal Flying Corps where he learned to fly. He was promoted to Captain on April 1, 1918, and at the end of the war was credited with nine victories. He was seconded to the Canadian Air Force in July of 1919, and attended ground school for radiophone communications. While with Technical Services Squadron in Kent, he assisted in the design of air to ground wireless communication. He returned to Canada in November of 1919.

On return to civilian life in Lethbridge in 1920, he flew with flight examiner Basil Hobbs (Hall of Fame 1987) and received Commercial Pilot's Licence #64. That same year, Palmer formed the Lethbridge Aircraft Company, where he served as pilot.

Throughout Alberta, he was involved in barnstorming, stunt flying, and wing walking adventures. He flew passengers, did aerial advertising and aerial photography. His attempt to fly the first international mail between Canada and the United States in June 1922, ended in a crash in Minot, North Dakota, when he sacrificed his plane to avoid hitting a carload of people on the landing field.

In 1923 Palmer built radio station CJOC in Lethbridge, choosing call letters C for Canada, and JOC for 'Jock'. He operated this broadcasting station until it was sold in 1928.

He maintained his interest in flying during these years, and in 1927 he obtained his Air Engineer's Licence and Night Flying Endorsement. He formed Lethbridge Commercial Airways with financial aid from C.B. Elliott and E. (Emil) Sick, owner of the Lethbridge Brewing Company. At one time, the wings of Palmer's aircraft carried an advertisement for the Brewing Company. It is believed that the biplane on today's Lethbridge Pilsner Beer is Palmer's Curtiss Jenny. In 1927 Palmer owned and flew the only civilian-owned aircraft in Alberta.

Palmer moved to Calgary in 1928 when Sick purchased a Stinson Detroiter, which was flown from Detroit to Calgary in April by Palmer and Fred McCall (Hall of Fame 1978). It became known as 'Purple Label', the aircraft which was used for transporting Brewery executives and charter flying. The business was so successful that Palmer and McCall formed Great Western Airways in June of 1928. Palmer was Chief Pilot and instructor, while McCall was appointed Managing Director of the company. The business included flying explosives to oilfields in Alberta, air exhibitions, and flight instruction. They took delivery of two new DH-60 Moths for instruction purposes.

The depression period of the early 1930's created hardship for the company, and it was forced to close, as were other air services in Calgary. From 1932 to 1936 Palmer operated his own flying school and aircraft repair service in Calgary. In 1937 he moved this operation to the Windermere Valley, south of Radium, British Columbia, and also flew Forest Service patrols.

In 1940 Palmer returned to Calgary and became an instructor for the Aero Club which operated #5 Elementary Flying Training School in Lethbridge and later in High River, Alberta, for the British Commonwealth Air Training Plan (BCATP). He became Chief Flying Instructor, Radio Communications Officer and finally, Officer Commanding. For his contribution to the BCATP, he was awarded the Air Force Cross (A.F.C.). Palmer retired from flying in 1955 with over 18,000 hours. He died in Calgary on November 19, 1964.

John Ender (Jock) Palmer was inducted as a Member of Canada's Aviation Hall of Fame in 1988.

'Jock' Palmer with one of the de Havilland DH-60's flown by Great Western Airways. c. 1930.

Ronald Peel

(b. 1922)

Ronald Peel, D.F.C., B.Sc., was born in Leeds, England, on March 10, 1922. His family immigrated to Canada two years later to settle in Toronto, Ontario. After graduating from high school he joined the Royal Canadian Air Force (RCAF) as an Observer. He graduated in 1941 at the top of his class and was posted to England. While serving as a navigator/bomb aimer, he was burned in a near fatal crash on December 6, 1941. Following his recovery, he completed a tour of 30 operations and was awarded the Distinguished Flying Cross (D.F.C.). He was Mentioned in Despatches for distinguished service to the Royal Air Force (RAF) Transport Command.

In 1943 he was seconded to Trans-Canada Airlines (TCA, Hall of Fame 1974) to assist in the operation of the Canadian Government Trans Atlantic Air Service (CGTAS). Following his discharge from the RCAF he became TCA's first Chief Navigator,

Throughout his career, Ronald Peel maintained his competency in navigation. Since his retirement from aviation, Peel has devoted considerable time and energy to improving the quality of Canadian Power and Sail Squadron courses as Navigator Course Director. He revised and updated that organization's most advanced celestial navigation course, and used his aviation knowledge and experience in the preparation of a comprehensive electronic marine navigation course. He retired from those endeavors in 1997.

"His superb navigational and organizational skills and ability to develop comprehensive training methods and operating procedures are an asset to Canadian and world aviation." —Induction citation, 1991

a position he held for eight years. During this time his aviation innovations included the use of Long Range Aerial Navigation (LORAN), periscopic sextants and the Lambert Conformal Plotting Charts. He developed techniques for the selection of optimum routes, flight altitudes and cruise control for long range flights. His contributions to the development of Pressure Pattern Navigation were published in 1953 in the Journal of the Institute of Navigation in England. He also assisted Canadian Pacific Airlines (CPA) in setting up its overseas department and was a founding officer and president of the Canadian Institute of Navigation.

In 1953 Peel became Supervisor of Flight Operations Ground Training for TCA. He also participated, until 1969, in International Air Transport Association (IATA) activities related to improving flight crew training standards and overcoming problems in making the transition to the jet age. He presented a paper to the Airline Pilot's Association (APA) in Chicago to help the aviation industry meet this challenge. He also checked out as a First Officer with a Class I Instrument Rating and flew the Douglas DC-3 and later Viscount aircraft to ensure his ground training program met all requirements. In 1959 Peel set up a computer system for maintenance inventory, and introduced courses for the Vanguard, DC-8 and DC-9 aircraft.

While working full time at TCA, which became Air Canada in 1965, Peel attended Sir George Williams University and graduated with a Bachelor of Science degree (with Distinction) after eight years of evening studies. He was appointed Manager of Flight Operations Training Administration and enrolled in an evening program at McGill University for courses in finance and business statistics. Peel contributed to the development of Canada's first community college pilot education program. He also participated in the study

Ronald Peel at an operational site in Great Britain during World War II. c. 1941.

group that established the feasibility of a computerized flight planning system for Air Canada, and of a no-reservation service between Toronto and Montreal.

Between 1969 and 1971, Peel held a number of operational positions, culminating as Flight Operations Special Project Director, the latter post until 1978. He presented recommendations to the Air Canada board of directors which resulted in the use of Inertial Navigation Systems (INS) and redeployment of navigators. He developed and implemented policies during the Organization of Petroleum Exporting Countries (OPEC) energy crisis as well as assisting IATA to reduce airline costs over north Atlantic routes. In 1979 he was appointed Chairman of the IATA North Atlantic/North American Technical Panel where, for a 20 year period, he made recommendations concerning world wide navigation, communications, and Air Traffic Control systems.

Peel was seconded to the International Civil Aviation Organization (ICAO) in 1981 to prepare its course (M1) on the training of Flight Dispatchers and Operations Officers. As an aviation consultant, he prepared a "Manual of Guidance for Member States on the Preparation of Operations Manuals" for ICAO, and developed the IATA M10 course "Flight Operations and Management". He was also responsible for the script and development of visual aids when Air Canada obtained a contract for the de Havilland Dash-8 audio-visual training program. Using IATA's Program for Developing Nations, he assisted the management of airlines from twenty countries to improve the safety and efficiency of their flying operations. He retired in 1989.

Ronald Peel was inducted as a Member of Canada's Aviation Hall of Fame in 1991.

George Hector Reid Phillips
(1893 – 1977)

George Hector Reid Phillips was born near Orangeville, Ontario, on August 17, 1893. As a youth he worked in Moose Jaw, Saskatchewan, and Iroquois Falls, Ontario, until he enlisted in the Second Canadian Pioneer Battalion in 1915 at Timmins, Ontario. He served in France as a machine gunner until 1917, when he was commissioned as a First Lieutenant, was wounded and Mentioned in Despatches for heroism under fire. Shortly before war's end he transferred to the Royal Air Force (RAF) as an Observer and served again briefly in France with the Independent Air Force. In 1921 he joined the Canadian Air Force as an Observer, but resigned shortly after.

Phillips was hired in 1921 by the Forestry Service of the Province of Ontario as a tower observer. In 1924 the Ontario Provincial Air Service (OPAS, Belt of Orion 1991) was formed. It urgently needed pilots, air engineers and suitable aircraft for its work. In 1927 the Department assigned him to a flight course with the Royal Canadian Air Force (RCAF) at Camp

To be successful in fighting forest fires, speed and the ability to fly fire-fighters and their equipment safely into and out of small lakes meant the difference between a small fire or one that would soon spread out of control, destroying valuable timber and endangering human settlements before it could be checked or put out by nature. George Phillips knew how to get into the small lakes for this kind of work.

S/L John H. Phillips with his father, George Phillips, seated in the cockpit of a CF-100. April 9, 1953.

Borden, Ontario. He graduated in 1928 with his Commercial Pilot's Licence and became one of the first pilots hired by the Forestry Service, flying Curtiss HS-2L flying boats out of Sioux Lookout, Ontario. Several de Havilland Moths and other float and seaplanes were added to the fleet at that time. In 1929 he also served as instructor for the OPAS, teaching pilots the kind of flying required for forestry work.

In 1931 Phillips was appointed Superintendent of the Eastern Flying Operations for the OPAS, with his headquarters at Sault Ste. Marie, Ontario, a position he held until 1940. During his early command of this wilderness area, he carried out a number of hazardous forestry and fire patrol flights. Mercy flights were also commonplace. One difficult flight involved bringing a doctor to a patient after dark, landing along the rocky shoreline of Lake Superior. The provincial police services also called upon him on a number of occasions for emergency flights.

During 1931 he flew 770 hours, largely in an area where fire hazard was high and the work particularly strenuous. In July of that year he logged 202 hours and did not miss one day of flying during the entire month. In recognition of his work for the Provincial Forestry Branch during that year, he was awarded the Trans-Canada (McKee) Trophy.

In these years of intense air activity he was involved in designing and perfecting new methods of forestry control and fire-fighting techniques. At Camp Borden he completed another specialized RCAF course of instruction from Elmer Fullerton (Hall of Fame 1974). When the Ontario government offered air support for the rescue of the men trapped by a rock slide in the depths of Nova Scotia's Moose River mine in April 1936, his was the first aircraft to reach the scene, bringing emergency rescue equipment and supplies.

At the outbreak of World War II he volunteered for service with the RCAF, was accepted in 1940 and assigned to instructional duties at Camp Borden. His extensive flight knowledge was then directed towards ferrying aircraft across the South Atlantic Ocean. He was captured by the Vichy French at Dahomey, Africa, and held for ten weeks, until Allied forces took Casablanca in December 1942. On his return to Canada he was promoted to Squadron Leader and given command of the RCAF base at Edenvale, Ontario. Prior to his retirement from the RCAF in 1944 he was named Commander of a British unit at Natal, Brazil.

Early in 1945 Phillips returned to the Department of Lands and Forests, and became Superintendent of Ontario's Algonquin Park. New aircraft, especially designed for work in the northern bush regions were purchased by the OPAS, such as the Noorduyn Norseman, and the de Havilland Beaver and Otter. He remained in the position of Superintendent for 15 years before retiring to his farm near Orangeville in the fall of 1959. He had flown 14,000 hours in command of numerous aircraft types. He died on July 20, 1977.

George Hector Reid Phillips was inducted as a Member of Canada's Aviation Hall of Fame in 1974.

Welland Wilfred (Weldy) Phipps

(1922 – 1996)

Welland Wilfred (Weldy) Phipps, C.M., was born in Ottawa, Ontario, on July 23, 1922. He attended school there until 1940 when he joined the Royal Canadian Air Force (RCAF) as an aero-engine mechanic. The following year he was posted to 409 Squadron, RCAF, in England, and a short time later transferred to night-bombing duties as an aircrew Sergeant with 405 Squadron. On the night of April 1, 1943, while on his 28th operational flight, bombing a target in Germany, his aircraft was shot down. He was forced to parachute and landed safely, but was captured and held as prisoner-of-war for the next two years. In 1945 he returned to Canada for his discharge as a Warrant Officer First Class.

'Weldy' Phipps brought his family, Fran and most of their eight children, to live in Resolute year round. Those of their children who had completed grade six had to continue their education 'on the outside'. Fran became the first woman to land on the North Pole. On April 5, 1971, she accompanied 'Weldy' and co-pilot, Jack Austin (Hall of Fame 1974), when they flew there in a Twin Otter to prepare for an up-coming publicity flight with Commissioner Stuart Hodgson of the Northwest Territories and a Vancouver reporter, Pat Carney. Ms Carney was very disappointed when she learned that she would not be the first woman at the Pole.

'Weldy' Phipps compares the standard Super Cub tire with his balloon tire that made it possible to land light aircraft on the Arctic tundra.

Phipps joined Atlas Aviation, a charter company in Ottawa, and was encouraged to earn both his pilot and engineer licences. He became a partner in the company, along with Angus Morrison (Hall of Fame 1989), and remained there for two years. In 1947 he joined Rimouski Airlines of Quebec, where he flew as staff pilot for two years. He became associated with Spartan Air Services at Ottawa and during the next eight years he rose to Chief Pilot, Operations Manager, and finally Assistant General Manager. His main task with Spartan Air Services was to develop their high altitude photographic operations. He introduced the use of the Lockheed P-38 Lightning which he personally modified and flew as a two-place machine capable of 35,000-foot (10,668 m) altitude photo survey work. This was especially important for the preliminary work in establishing the Distant Early Warning (DEW) Line which would be built in the early 1950's.

While on Arctic research operations he conceived the idea of using lightweight, super-size balloon tires, allowing his small aircraft to operate on tundra, snow, and rock-strewn ground. In 1958 he joined Bradley Air Services at Ottawa as Vice-President and Operations Manager. He worked to perfect the balloon tire type wheels: his design consisted of greatly oversized balloon tires—25 inches (64 cm) on a four-inch (10 cm) hub—using seven pounds air pressure per square inch. The big wheels cushioned the aircraft and prevented jarring shocks from boulders, and prevented the plane from sinking into boggy ground. He soon enlarged the company's fleet to ten aircraft. During the summer of 1958, he took a PA-18 Piper Super Cub into the Arctic for the use of two geologists, who were able to cover 30,000 square miles (78,000 km²) in 300 hours of flying over a period of three months. Prior to this, geologists used dog teams and canoes and were restricted mainly to the coastal areas.

In 1959 Phipps returned to the Arctic with five Super Cubs, using improved gear: tires were increased to 35 inches (89 cm) and pressure reduced to four pounds per square inch. As a result of survey work showing the presence of oil and minerals, land was beginning to be staked in the Arctic. For the 1961 season, Phipps extended his development to two de Havilland Otters, using larger tires. These flew on Polar Shelf expeditions very effectively, and enabled geologists to work extensively on oil explorations in the Arctic.

For his development of the super-balloon tires and his research into their various arctic uses, he was awarded the Trans-Canada (McKee) Trophy for 1961. Being able to land where other aircraft could not, Phipps was called upon to use his aircraft to fly rescue missions. He once flew a doctor into Grise Fiord on Ellesmere Island, a community 3,100 miles (5,000 km) north of Ottawa, to deal with a deadly whooping cough outbreak.

In 1962 he formed his own company, Atlas Aviation, based at Resolute Bay on Cornwallis Island in the Northwest Territories. He bought a Twin Otter in 1967 and persuaded the Department of Transport officials to allow his initials as a special registration for the aircraft. They assigned call-letters CF-WWP, and the airplane became known as 'Whiskey Whiskey Papa'. While his company's operations were confined mainly to transporting passengers, fuel and supplies through the Queen Elizabeth Islands and north Greenland, he did make several extended flights to the North Pole for scientific purposes and in support of expeditions.

He ended his flying career in 1971 with the sale of his company to Kenting Aviation Limited at Toronto. He bought a sailboat he named 'Whiskey Papa', which became the Phipps' home for parts of each year.

Phipps was named a Member of the Order of Canada (C.M.) in 1976 for his contributions to Arctic aviation, particularly in developing techniques to allow landing on rough terrain. He died in Ottawa on October 29, 1996.

Welland Wilfred (Weldy) Phipps was inducted as a Member of Canada's Aviation Hall of Fame in 1974.

John Lawrence Plant
(b. 1910)

John Lawrence Plant, C.B.E., A.F.C., C.D.*, B.A.Sc., LL.D. (Hon), was born in Swansea, Wales, U.K., on August 20, 1910. He immigrated with his family to British Columbia in 1919. He graduated with a Bachelor of Science degree (with Honours) in Mechanical Engineering from the University of British Columbia in 1931. Plant began flying as a Provisional Pilot Officer with the Royal Canadian Air Force (RCAF) in 1929, received his wings and was granted a permanent commission in 1931.

Plant enrolled in a flying instructors course at Camp Borden, Ontario, in 1936, and was posted to 20 Auxiliary Bomber Squadron at Regina. He organized and operated a squadron pilot training program with both ground and air instruction to convert the flying qualifications of young officers to squadron standards.

Early in 1941 Plant piloted a Catalina flying boat on a trans-Atlantic ferry trip from Bermuda to Greenock, Scotland in 20 hours, a speed record that stood for quite

While serving as Air Member Personnel, John Plant considered that pay scales were inadequate and that the restriction on flying pay for active aircrew had removed an important incentive for staff officers to maintain their flying proficiency. He was the only Air Vice-Marshal holding a valid instrument rating at that time. By example and amendments to the pay regulations, he brought about a great increase of active flying throughout the RCAF.

John Plant, on right, with pilot C. McLaurin, in a Curtiss HS-2L, at Alert Bay, British Columbia. 1920.

some time. On May 7, 1941, he was posted as Wing Commander to the RCAF Station at Patricia Bay, British Columbia. He placed the station on full alert after the Japanese bombed Pearl Harbor on December 7, 1941.

On March 3, 1942, Plant was posted to the command of 413 Squadron which proceeded to Ceylon (now Sri Lanka). He flew many patrols from Ceylon, one of which was a cover operation for the British landings on the island of Madagascar.

In January of 1943 he was posted to England as Commanding Officer of RCAF Station Dishforth, Yorkshire, home base for 425 and 426 Squadrons. He was later posted to RCAF station Leeming, Yorkshire, which housed 408, 427 and 429 Bomber Squadrons, remaining at this post until November 23, 1943. During this extremely difficult time for bombers, his squadrons operated against occupied Europe and Germany. He flew as crew on flights to such places as Wilhelmshaven, Mannheim and Kassel.

After returning to Canada in December of 1943, Plant attended Army and Navy College in the United States. In May 1944, he was posted to Air Force Headquarters in Ottawa as Deputy Air Member, Air Staff. He was named Commander of the Order of the British Empire (C.B.E., Military).

On May 1, 1945, with the rank of Air Commodore, Plant was appointed Air Officer Commanding, No. 9 (Transport) Group. He immediately became qualified on all types of the Group's aircraft, including the Consolidated B-24 Liberator and Boeing B-17 Fortress. He made flights to all units in the Group, both in Canada and overseas. In November 1945, he flew as Captain of a B-17 from Canada to Warsaw, Poland, carrying penicillin donated by the Canadian Red Cross to the people of that shattered country. The flight was very risky at the time because of the developing 'Cold War', and for his efforts he was awarded the Air Force Cross (A.F.C.).

On February 16, 1946, Plant was appointed Air Officer Commanding, Western Air Command, and again qualified on all of the types of aircraft used in the command. On December 1, 1947, he was posted to Air Force Headquarters as Air Member for Personnel. In 1950, when the European Air Division was being established, he obtained approval for dependents to accompany RCAF members on North Atlantic Treaty Organization (NATO) postings. This had a profound effect on overall morale of the Air Division and was one of the factors that helped make it the most efficient of the NATO air elements. In August 1951, he saw these effects first-hand while serving at the headquarters of Allied Air Forces, Central Europe. His overall contribution to the NATO alliance was recognized by his appointment in 1953 as Chief of Staff and his promotion to Air Marshal.

In 1954, on returning to Canada, he reverted to his permanent rank of Air Vice-Marshal on appointment to the post of Air Member, Mechanical Services. His major concern during this period was the technical supervision of the design and procurement teams for the Canadair Argus, a long-range patrol aircraft, and the CF-105 Avro Arrow. In 1956, while serving as Air Officer Commanding, Air Material Command, he resigned his commission in order to open up promotion to others, in keeping with the policies he had advocated as Air Member for Personnel.

Plant was appointed Executive Vice-President of Collins Radio of Canada until 1958, and then was appointed President and General Manager of Avro Aircraft Ltd. He resigned from Avro six months after the cancellation of the Arrow project and returned to Collins Radio. He retired in 1970.

Plant was honoured in 1945 with an Honorary Doctor of Laws degree from his alma mater, the University of British Columbia.

John Lawrence Plant was inducted as a Member of Canada's Aviation Hall of Fame in 1985.

Peter Geoffrey Powell

(b. 1917)

Peter Geoffrey Powell, D.S.O., D.F.C., was born in Rosedale Abby, Yorkshire, England, on April 19, 1917, but grew up in Sorrento, British Columbia. He returned to England to complete his education and for Merchant Marine Officer's Training. In his five years at sea he rose from an apprentice to a licenced ship's mate.

He joined the Royal Canadian Air Force (RCAF) aircrew in the summer of 1940 and because of his experience he was selected as a navigator. He received his commission and was sent overseas in 1941. His first operational trip was as bomb-aimer/navigator on the one-thousand bomber raid on Cologne in 1942. He was awarded the Distinguished Flying Cross (D.F.C.).

His ability as a navigator resulted in a promotion to Flight Lieutenant. When he was sent to 405 (Pathfinder) Squadron, he was promoted to Squadron Leader. He served as navigator for the Squadron Commander, Group Captain J.E. Fauquier

The bomber raid on Peenemunde on the Baltic Coast on August 17, 1943, was meant to destroy the German V-2 rocket research centre, which was under the direction of Werner Von Braun, who later became director of the United States National Aeronautics and Space Administration. Peter Powell's skills in navigation were so accurate that wave after wave of bombers were led over the target. Destruction of the rocket development centre delayed the use of V-2 rockets by a full year.

Peter Powell using a sextant as third mate of S.S. Nerissa, prior to his aviation career. c. 1937.

(Hall of Fame 1974), and as navigational leader for the squadron.

After making seventeen passes over the target during the raid on Peenemunde in August of 1943, and following a similar mission over Berlin a few nights later, he was awarded the Distinguished Service Order (D.S.O.), with the citation stating:

> "In addition to his operational tasks Squadron Leader Powell has rendered yeoman service in the training of other navigators and his excellent work has been reflected in their numerous successes."

After sixty-three operational trips with Bomber Command, he was promoted to Wing Commander and attached to No. 6 Group Headquarters as Navigational Inspector for the Canadian bomber force in England. His duties were largely instructional and his efforts to improve the standard of navigation in all squadrons were so noteworthy that he was Mentioned in Despatches in the London Gazette on January 1, 1945.

Shortly after Victory-in-Europe Day (V-E Day), Wing Commander Powell was sent to Halifax, Nova Scotia, to prepare for operations in the Pacific, but when the war ended in August of 1945 he took his discharge from the RCAF.

On January 3, 1946, Powell joined Trans-Canada Airlines (TCA, Hall of Fame 1974) as Assistant Chief Navigator. Although the work was mainly in administration, he still flew a few line flights across the North Atlantic. He took a leave of absence during the winter of 1950-51 to serve as navigator for California Eastern, transporting troops from Oakland to Tokyo for the Korean War. When he returned to TCA, which became Air Canada in 1965, he soon became Chief Navigator and later Superintendent of Navigation, a position he held until his retirement from Air Canada in 1977.

During his years with Air Canada, Powell had built a very strong department. When the International Civil Aviation Organization (ICAO) examined the navigational performance of airlines flying the Atlantic, the Air Canada group was among the best. He became an Air Canada representative to the International Air Transport Association (IATA), and was chosen to represent them at ICAO meetings. One year before his retirement, ICAO requested his services. Initially on loan to ICAO, he stayed with them another five years after retiring from Air Canada. During this time he was involved in the financial agreements between Denmark and Iceland and the countries whose airlines used their North Atlantic navigation services.

His greatest contributions to Air Canada were the navigation procedures he developed and the navigators he recruited, trained and supervised. The high degree of accuracy and competence these men displayed have contributed to the excellent operating reputation of TCA/Air Canada. Another important contribution was the development of pressure pattern flying from a haphazard procedure into one of considerable accuracy, in which the aircraft takes advantage of the winds. Similar procedures are still used daily to establish tracks to be followed by all aircraft flying long oceanic routes.

Peter Geoffrey Powell was inducted as a Member of Canada's Aviation Hall of Fame in 1990.

Robert Cheetham (Bob) Randall

(b. 1908)

Robert Cheetham (Bob) Randall was born in Saskatoon, Saskatchewan, on November 2, 1908, where he was educated. He learned to fly with the Saskatoon Aero Club in 1928, and the following year obtained licences in both the Private and Commercial Pilot categories. He was hired by Cherry Red Airlines operating out of Prince Albert, Saskatchewan, to the Lac La Ronge area. He worked for Bilby Air Service at Saskatoon. Duncan Motors at Regina acquired his services a year later for barnstorming activities in the Saskatoon area.

In 1931 he joined Brooks Airways at Prince Albert as a bush pilot, and in 1932 was given leave to complete a Royal Canadian Air Force (RCAF) instrument flight course where he distinguished himself by receiving top honours. A flying assignment in 1934 to the Yukon Territory resulted in employment with Northern Airways, based at Carcross, on Lake Bennett. Here, Randall pioneered the mail run between Atlin and Telegraph Creek.

The National Geographic Society hired him in 1935 to make photographic and supply

The Randalls are a flying family. Mrs. Randall was flying her own aircraft as early as 1929. At the time of his retirement, three of Robert Randall's sons were flying for CPA. Twins, Bob, Jr., and Ted were hired in 1952, and in 1968 were serving as Captains on CP Air jets, and John, who joined CPA in 1965 was serving as First Officer on DC-8 aircraft on overseas routes.

"His pioneer flights over unmapped mountains, and his dedication to purpose during the 1937 aerial search for six Russian fliers, despite adversity, have been of outstanding benefit to Canadian aviation."

—Induction citation, 1974

The 'Flying Randalls': Captain Robert Randall with son Ted on his right, and Bob, Jr. and John in the foreground, in a CP Air DC-8. June 1965.

flights over the unmapped territory of the St. Elias range for their Yukon Expedition led by explorer Bradford Washburn. Mountain peaks in this range, which straddles the Yukon-Alaska border, average 12,000 feet (3,657 m), topped by Mount St. Elias at 18,000 feet (5,486 m) and Mount Logan, Canada's highest mountain at 19,850 feet (6,050 m). He completed these high altitude flights in a Fairchild 71 with no supplemental oxygen supply. He made the first landing of an aircraft on a Canadian glacier. In recognition of his valuable assistance, he was named a member of the National Geographic Society that year.

In 1937 Randall began to fly for Mackenzie Air Service, operated out of Edmonton, Alberta, by Leigh Brintnell (Hall of Fame 1976). He was assigned to fly a route that took him through the mining areas of Goldpines, Saskatchewan, and Yellowknife, Northwest Territories, to the Eldorado radium mine on Great Bear Lake, and down the Mackenzie River to the Arctic coast.

During the late summer and fall of 1937 he was involved in what was to become one of aviation's longest aerial searches, covering the western Arctic from Siberia through Alaska and the Northwest Territories. The Russian pilot, Sigismund Levanevsky and his five companions, missing on a trans-polar flight from Moscow, U.S.S.R., to Fairbanks, Alaska, were never found. During the months-long search Randall covered thousands of flight miles, contributing immeasurably to Canada's knowledge of the Arctic coast. He gained the distinction of being second only to Charles Lindberg in making the dangerous flight between Aklavik in the Northwest Territories, and Point Barrow, Alaska. For his contribution to the search, he was named a Member of the Explorers Club.

In 1940 he was promoted to Operations Manager of Mackenzie Air Service and continued in that capacity when the company was merged with Canadian Airways to form United Air Services. Canadian Pacific Airlines (CPA) absorbed this company in 1942 and Randall was loaned to Bechtel, Price & Callahan, an American contracting firm engaged in building the Canol pipeline from Norman Wells, Northwest Territories, to Whitehorse, Yukon. He was responsible for organizing and managing the flying operations until the job was completed one year later.

He returned to CPA, and for the next ten years, he flew as captain on domestic routes out of Edmonton, Alberta. In 1952 he was transferred to Vancouver, British Columbia, to fly overseas routes. In 1955 he captained the first scheduled airline flight over the north polar route, from Amsterdam, Holland, direct to Vancouver. In 1968 CPA officially changed its name to CP Air. Randall retired in 1968, after forty years of professional flying. He had flown in excess of 30,000 hours as Captain-in-Command of 44 types of aircraft, ranging from the smallest trainer to the largest jet, representing more than 10,000,000 miles (16,100,000 km) of flight distance.

Robert Cheetham (Bob) Randall was inducted as a Member of Canada's Aviation Hall of Fame in 1974.

Bernard Anderson (Barney) Rawson

(1907 – 1996)

Bernard Anderson (Barney) Rawson was born in Fort William, Ontario, on October 27, 1907, and educated in that province at Coldwater and Toronto. He graduated with a Commercial Pilot's Licence from the Dungan School of Aviation at Cleveland, Ohio in 1928. Until 1934 he was employed as Chief Pilot for three American companies. For two years he flew open-cockpit biplanes for the U.S. Weather Bureau taking daily upper air readings at 18,000 feet (5,486 m). These flights were the beginning of mass air analysis, permitting present-day long-range weather forecasting.

Rawson was employed as a pilot with American Airlines on continental routes until 1938, when he joined Trans-Canada Airlines (TCA) as a line captain. He was appointed flight instructor, and in 1940 he was named an officer of the company in charge of eastern operations. In 1942 he was named Director of Operations for TCA's entire system, which included Canada, the United States, the Caribbean, South America, the North Atlantic and Europe. In this position he was responsible for the selection and training of air crew, flight dispatchers and the development of

'Barney' Rawson was the first non-military pilot to fly a jet aircraft in Canada when he flew the British Gloster Meteor Fighter at Edmonton, Alberta. A side light in his career is that he, along with Frank I. Young (Hall of Fame 1974) originated the National Air Show in 1953, which is held annually at the Canadian National Exhibition in Toronto.

"The application of his aeronautical talents towards designing the Great Lakes Airway and his airborne work to improve runway lighting systems, have substantially benefited Canadian aviation." —Induction citation, 1974

'Barney' Rawson in Gloster Meteor at Edmonton. 1947.

flight technical manuals. In 1946 he was named Director of Flight Development, a position he held until 1953.

During this period, he convinced the Department of Transport (DOT) that a straight line airway between Toronto and Winnipeg over the Great Lakes was feasible and practical. The airway would allow Sault Ste. Marie and the Canadian Lakehead to become part of TCA's network and save substantial operating costs. During the one year construction period of the Great Lakes Airway, he was involved with and assisted the DOT in the selection of airports and navigational aid positions. Rawson was awarded the Trans-Canada (McKee) Trophy for 1947 for meritorious service in the advancement of aviation in Canada. In 1949 Rawson moved to Montreal with TCA when they moved their main offices from Winnipeg.

In April 1953, Rawson joined Canadian Pacific Airlines (CPA) in Vancouver as Director of Flight Operations, and under his supervision the company expanded to serve five continents. He implemented the dream of Grant McConachie (Hall of Fame 1974) to link Vancouver, British Columbia, with Amsterdam, Holland, by non-stop flights across the Arctic region. To provide crews with modern training facilities, he outfitted CPA with electronic flight simulators, selected and trained personnel

"His mapping of this nation's northern frontier during pioneer air expeditions, and the dedication of his skills to seeking lost airmen, have been of outstanding benefit to Canadian aviation." —Induction citation, 1974

and evaluated new aircraft and operational equipment.

During his years of service with TCA and CPA, he served as technical representative for the Government of Canada at International Civil Aviation Organization (ICAO) conferences, and as a delegate to the International Air Transport Association (IATA). As a technical representative to IATA, he served as Chairman of the Lighting Committee which was organized to develop standards of lighting for approach and landing during poor visibility. A group of airline pilot representatives made zero-zero weather approaches at Arcata, California, to test lighting configurations that were selected and installed for testing purposes.

Rawson joined Radio Corporation of America (RCA) in December 1958, as Director of Custom Aviation Products in Camden, New Jersey. In 1960 he was named their Government Service Division Administrator. In this capacity he dealt with the U.S. Weather Bureau, Coast and Geodetic Survey, and the National Aeronautics and Space Administration. As a Director of Airline Marketing for Fairchild Hiller Corporation from 1962 until 1968, he conducted marketing research for regional air line type aircraft for acceptable design parameters. The sales success of de Havilland Aircraft of Canada's Twin Otter in the U.S. was due in part to his excellent marketing strategies as an executive of the Miami Aviation Corporation, their American distributors. In 1973 he was named Aviation Director of Flood and Associates, consulting engineers at Jacksonville, Florida.

During a 45 year career as a professional pilot, he captained more than 100 aircraft types, logging more than 20,000 hours. Rawson died in Alabama on July 4, 1996.

Bernard Anderson (Barney) Rawson was inducted as a Member of Canada's Aviation Hall of Fame in 1974.

Thomas Mayne (Pat) Reid
(1895 – 1954)

Thomas Mayne (Pat) Reid, D.F.M., was born in Ballyroney, County Down, Northern Ireland, on August 22, 1895, where he was educated. As a youth he served a term as mechanic's apprentice with the Ferguson Automotive Company at Belfast. In 1915 he enlisted in the Royal Naval Air Service in England as an air engineer. He was posted to Dunkirk, France, in 1917, as a crew member on twin-engine flying boats with the Royal Flying Corps (RFC) on anti-submarine duties. On one sortie he repaired their damaged flying boat after a forced landing in the North Sea caused by gunfire from a surfaced German submarine. They took off again in the repaired aircraft and returned to sink that submarine. In 1918 Reid was awarded the Distinguished Flying Medal (D.F.M.) for heroism under fire.

In 1919 Reid was employed by the Handley-Page Transport Company in various capacities and in 1924 became Manager of their operations in Switzerland. Later that year he immigrated to Canada and joined the Ontario Provincial Air Service (OPAS, Belt of Orion 1991) as an air observer based in Sudbury, Ontario. After two years on forestry patrol duties, he attended the Ontario Air Service school of instruction, followed by a course at Camp Borden, Ontario. He graduated in 1926 with a Commercial Pilot's Licence.

After another year with the OPAS, flying de Havilland Moths and Curtiss HS-2L

'Pat' Reid and 'Phil' Garratt (Hall of Fame 1974) have the distinction of being the only two people to be honoured with the Trans-Canada (McKee) Trophy twice, Reid for the years 1942 and 1943, and Garratt for the years 1951 and 1966.

NATIONAL ARCHIVES OF CANADA PA-089764

'Pat' Reid with Fairchild 71, CF-AJK, during the Eielsen Search, winter of 1929-30. In background is the whaling ship 'Nanuk' stranded in the ice in the Bering Strait between Alaska and Siberia.

flying boats from northwestern Ontario bases, Reid was hired by H.A. 'Doc' Oaks (Hall of Fame 1974), to carry out remote explorations for the Northern Aerial Mineral Exploration (N.A.M.E.) Company. In the spring of 1928, in company with two other pilots, including Matt Berry (Hall of Fame 1974), in separate aircraft, he flew a prospecting party from Winnipeg, Manitoba, north through Fort Churchill, to Baker Lake, where they left the prospectors. He continued his exploration flight to Coppermine on the Arctic Ocean, then followed the Mackenzie River to Edmonton, Alberta. The expedition ended in Winnipeg six months after it began, and crossed 25,000 miles (40,232 km) of wilderness, without the benefit of navigational aids or weather services. They provided early Canadian map makers with some of their earliest knowledge of the uncharted northland.

One of the numerous mercy flights he undertook was with Oaks in January 1929, when they flew 1,600 miles (2,575 km) along the eastern sub-Arctic coast of Hudson Bay through inclement weather to locate a party of 13 stranded prospectors and return them to their base. In the fall of 1929 Reid played a leading role in the search for the MacAlpine party which was missing in the Arctic. One of his responsibilities was to fly material and supplies for the use of the large search party.

Reid joined a search mission as Chief Pilot during the winter of 1929-30 to locate the famed American pilot Carl Eielson, lost with a companion in an aircraft off the coast of Siberia, where he was flying relief supplies to a stranded schooner. The Aviation Corporation of Delaware hired Reid to lead a three plane expedition from a base of operations at Fairbanks, Alaska. Enroute from there to Nome, he himself was forced down in a blizzard in a mountain pass and severely damaged a wing. He and his air mechanic waited out the storm for a week, repaired the aircraft and proceeded to their destination. From Nome he made a number of flights across the Bering Strait and along the coast of the Chukchi Sea. Some 450 miles (724 km) from base, and 200 miles (322 km) north of the Arctic Circle, he located the wrecked aircraft and subsequently flew the bodies of the two airmen back to Alaska.

In 1931 Reid became Western Aviation Manager of Imperial Oil Limited and that summer he flew the Company's Puss Moth, CF-IOL, as leader of the Trans-Canada Air Pageant. The tour was a two-way transcontinental flight, visiting every city in Canada where landing was practical. It was a showcase for the fledgling Canadian aviation industry and displayed the latest in civil and military aircraft. The following year he was named Aviation Representative of Imperial Oil, with headquarters in Toronto, Ontario.

Reid was awarded the Trans Canada (McKee) Trophy for 1942 for his efforts in the advancement of flying in Canada, and his logistical organization of aviation fuel supplies for the war effort needs of the British Commonwealth Air Training Plan (BCATP) and Ferry Command. The award of the Trophy was extended to him through 1943, and he became the first person to receive this honour for two years. Reid and his wife were killed in an airline crash at Moose Jaw, Saskatchewan, on April 8, 1954.

Thomas Mayne (Pat) Reid was inducted as a Member of Canada's Aviation Hall of Fame in 1974.

John Hardisty (Jack) Reilly
(b. 1921)

John Hardisty (Jack) Reilly was born in Edmonton, Alberta, on March 1, 1921, and was educated there. He became an 'airport kid' who ran errands and refueled aircraft for many of the airmen who have since been named to Canada's Aviation Hall of Fame.

Reilly began flying in Edmonton in 1938, then joined the Royal Canadian Air Force (RCAF) in June 1940, and completed his flying training at No. 6 Service Flying Training School (SFTS) Dunneville, Ontario. He completed the flying instructor's course, and served as a flying instructor and flight commander at No. 9 SFTS Summerside, Prince Edward Island, and Centralia, Ontario. In September 1943, he was posted back to Summerside for the General Reconnaissance Course where he received his Navigator's Certificate. He was assigned pilot duties on Canso and Catalina flying boats on operational patrols on Canada's west coast and Alaska. Prior to being posted overseas, he carried out instructional duties at No. 3 Operational Training Unit (OTU) at Patricia Bay, British Columbia. Until the end of World War II, he captained Coastal Command Sunderland flying boats on anti-submarine patrols from bases in northern Scotland and Ireland.

His exceptional flying abilities led to a posting with RCAF 426 Transport Squadron at Bedfordshire, England as captain of a

'Captain Jack', as he is known to his friends, applied his skills as an aviation manager and pilot for a period of 59 years, and at age 78 still maintains an Airline Transport Pilot Certificate with a Class 1 Instrument Rating.

Jack Reilly, with Stan Reynolds' personal Tiger Moth, CF-DAL. Jack led the fly-past of antique aircraft on opening day of Reynolds-Alberta Museum and Canada's Aviation Hall of Fame in this aircraft on September 12, 1992.

modified B-24 Liberator Bomber on VIP flights to India. Before retiring from the service as a Flight Lieutenant in 1946, he had completed the most advanced military flight instructor's course available, the senior administration course, and earned the most senior military pilot's licence.

Until 1949 he was associated with Leavens Brothers Air Service at Toronto, Ontario, as Chief Pilot of the largest flying school in Canada at that time, and as Chief Pilot and administrator of their provincial forest spraying contract.

In 1949 he joined Kenting Aviation of Toronto, which recognized his broad vision of aerial management. They accepted his ideas for high altitude photographic surveys using World War II aircraft and operating at stratospheric heights. He was named Chief Pilot in 1951, and personally flew these demanding flights, using modified Mosquito fighters, a Sea Hornet and Boeing B-17's. His duties carried him to many countries and he was required to remain qualified on several types of heavy twin and four-engine aircraft at the same time.

In 1956 he joined Canadian Aircraft Renters Ltd. at Toronto and their subsidiary, Southern Provincial Airlines, as Superintendent of Operations over their Toronto, New York, Washington, D.C., and Chicago charter routes, as well as their services in the Arctic.

Reilly was hired in 1959 as Chief Pilot for Peter Bawden Drilling of Calgary, Alberta. He was widely recognized for his extensive knowledge of aircraft operations over unmapped and inhospitable terrain under punishing weather conditions, and for extended periods of time. He was joined by his wife, 'Molly' Reilly (Hall of Fame 1974) as co-captain of a Douglas DC-3. They flew to most of the major oil fields in western and northern Canada, and throughout the United States. During his 14 years of service, he and his pilots flew 1,800,000 accident free miles from the Gulf of Mexico to Canada's northernmost islands. Aircraft under his control blazed new frontiers in the north, often without benefit of radio communication or navigational aids and during extended periods of darkness.

From 1973 to 1981, Reilly was engaged in various corporate aviation operations. In 1981 he joined Transport Canada as a Civil Aviation Inspector, and for assistance he provided to 431 Air Demonstration Squadron he was made an Honorary Snowbird. He has flown more than 30,000 hours as captain-in-command of 70 different types of aircraft, without a fatality in any operation under his command. Since retiring in 1989, he has devoted himself to the Reynolds-Alberta Museum in Wetaskiwin, Alberta, which is the home of Canada's Aviation Hall of Fame.

John Hardisty (Jack) Reilly was inducted as a Member of Canada's Aviation Hall of Fame in 1974.

Moretta Fenton Beall (Molly) Reilly
(1922 – 1980)

Moretta Fenton Beall (Molly) Reilly was born in Lindsay, Ontario, on February 25, 1922 and educated there. She joined the Royal Canadian Air Force, Women's Division, in 1942 as a photographer and served in Canada as a Non-commissioned Officer until 1946.

She undertook flying instruction in Toronto, Ontario in 1944, and graduated with her Commercial Licence two years later. She used her military re-establishment credit to gain an instructor's rating in 1948. During her training she won the runner-up award in the national Webster Trophy competition against a formidable field of male pilots. Leavens Brothers Air Services in Toronto hired her as an instructor and charter pilot in 1948, then granted her leave to complete an advanced instrument flying course at Spartan School of Aeronautics at Tulsa, Oklahoma, U.S.A. After graduation she qualified for her Canadian Public Transport Pilot Licence.

Even pregnancy did not stop Molly Reilly. Jack remembers, "In those days there was no paid maternity leave, and the guys would look askance at a pregnant crew member. I don't think there was anything written, but we kept the first one a secret." Molly and Jack Reilly flew many trips together. According to Jack, "Each recognized the other's ability. We had no trouble flying together, and when we got home we closed the hangar doors."

"Her dedication to flight, her self set demands for perfection, the outstanding abilities she has developed despite adversity, have made her a guiding light in aviation circles for others of her sex to follow and have been of outstanding benefit to Canadian aviation."

—Induction citation, 1974

Molly Reilly in the cockpit of the Beechcraft Duke. 1976.

Within three years Reilly had earned her twin-engine aircraft rating, completed a float-plane flying course at Port Alberni Airways School in BC, then went to England to earn a British Commercial Pilot's Licence. In 1954 she became Chief Flying Instructor and charter pilot with Canadian Aircraft Renters at Toronto. During the next three years she upgraded her skills to earn a Class 1 Instrument Rating and Airline Transport Pilot Licence. She is believed to be the first woman in Canada to hold these qualifications. She won a promotion to Captain against professional male competition in the Company's subsidiary, Southern Provincial Airlines, and became qualified to fly Douglas DC-3's, Lockheed Lodestars and twin Beech aircraft. She then assisted in the development and operation of their highly regarded air ambulance service throughout Eastern Canada.

In 1959 she was hired by Peter Bawden Drilling Services of Calgary, Alberta. Here she joined her husband, 'Jack' Reilly (Hall of Fame 1974), as co-captain of a Douglas DC-3 flying to most of the major oil fields in western and northern Canada, and throughout the United States. She remained in this position for five years. During this period of intense air activity in the Arctic regions, she piloted company aircraft on runs to Frobisher (Iqaluit) and Resolute Bay and other northern centres, through extended periods of darkness and extreme weather conditions, often without radio communication or navigational aides.

In 1965 Reilly joined Canadian Coachways of Edmonton, Alberta, and when Canadian Utilities absorbed that company several years later, she was named Chief Pilot. She was now qualified to fly a Beechcraft Duke, a sophisticated, pressurized, radar-equipped, all-weather twin-engine aircraft throughout North America. She had modifications made as necessary to improve the Duke for use in the Arctic, and received a personal commendation from Beechcraft Chairman, Mrs. Olive A. Beech.

'Molly' Reilly completed over 10,000 hours as pilot-in-command, all accident free. She died in Edmonton on November 24, 1980.

Moretta Fenton Beall 'Molly' Reilly was inducted as a Member of Canada's Aviation Hall of Fame in 1974.

Molly and Jack Reilly following the Induction Ceremony in 1974. They are the only couple to be inducted as Members of Canada's Aviation Hall of Fame.

James Armstrong Richardson
(1885 – 1939)

James Armstrong Richardson, B.A., LL.D. (Hon), was born in Kingston, Ontario, on August 25, 1885, where he attended Hillcrest Academy and Queen's University, graduating in 1906 with a Bachelor of Arts degree. He then entered the family business of James A. Richardson & Sons Limited, based in Winnipeg, Manitoba. He gave personal direction to the company's affairs during its greatest era of expansion in Canada's grain industry and its entry into the field of investment securities. He served as company President from 1918 until 1939.

Richardson's initial interest in aviation was inspired by a desire to develop the mineral wealth of northern Ontario. To accomplish this, he formed Western Canada Airways Limited in 1926, contending that with suitable aircraft, able pilots and good business management, an air transport company could bring in untapped mineral resources at least twenty years sooner than would ordinarily have been the case. H.A. 'Doc' Oaks (Hall of Fame 1974) became the first manager and pilot for the new company at its base in Hudson, Ontario.

The following year, Western Canada Airways expedited the opening of a port at

In 1994, in order to commemorate its 50th anniversary, the International Civil Aviation Organization (ICAO) struck a medal to be awarded based on outstanding contribution to civil aviation in a member state. Canada's nominee was James A. Richardson, who was ICAO's choice over all to receive this medal.

Fort Churchill, Manitoba, when it carried out the Churchill airlift during March 1927. Using two open-cockpit aircraft, without radio communications or weather sciences, fourteen men and thirty tons of supplies and equipment were transported from Cache Lake, Manitoba, to Fort Churchill during a thirty day period, under severe winter conditions. The successful completion of this country's first major airlift was to bring a rare signal to Western Canada Airways from the Department of National Defence at Ottawa, "...there has been no more brilliant operation in the history of commercial flying."

Western Canada Airways under Richardson's Presidency had, in a few years, opened air routes from the mines of northern Ontario to the islands off the Pacific coast and to the shores of the Arctic Ocean. The records and accomplishments of the company in the transport of bulk freight, airmail service and night flying were so laudable as to attract the attention of other nations. In 1926 Richardson had been named Director of Fairchild Aerial Surveys and the following year, Director of Canadian Vickers Ltd. In 1928 he began supporting the newly formed Aerial League of Canada, designed to foster the development of aviation.

To further investigate the Canadian Shield's mineral potential, Richardson became a director and majority shareholder of Northern Aerial Mineral Explorations Limited (N.A.M.E.). In 1929 he became a Director of the Aviation Corporation of Delaware, U.S.A., a corporation which in turn controlled a number of other aircraft companies.

While Western Canada Airways was successfully establishing the long prairie link of a future trans-Canada airway, a number of eastern companies were experiencing financial and management difficulties, leading to less than satisfactory performance in mail delivery. Since a distinct threat existed that control of some of their business ventures might fall into

Natives with dog team meet Canadian Airways Junkers aircraft at Fort Chipewyan, Alberta, to take passengers and express to the village. Two canoes strapped to the wings are part of the cargo. c. 1937.

Inhabitants of a lonely outpost meet the Canadian Airways Fairchild 71 that has just landed on their lake. c. 1930's.

the hands of American companies, Richardson helped to develop the Aviation Corporation of Canada. This step was then carried to its logical conclusion by forming one single operating company by the merger of Western Canada Airways with a group of smaller air operators across Canada. His goal was to provide coast-to-coast air transportation and mail delivery under Canadian control.

The new company, Canadian Airways Limited, came into operation in 1930, with Richardson appointed President. During the period of rapid change of the 1930's and the Depression that affected the entire country, Richardson's company kept civil aviation alive in Canada. There had been discussions in Ottawa for several years about the formation of an air service which would connect Canada from east to west, and Richardson believed that his airline would be involved in providing this service.

In 1936 the Department of Transport was formed, with its first Minister, C.D. Howe (Hall of Fame 1976) in control. Howe formed Trans-Canada Airlines (TCA) in 1937, assuring a monopoly for TCA in flying passengers and mail across Canada. His plans did not include Richardson's company and its established air routes.

In the early 1940's, Canadian Pacific Railways acquired Canadian Airways Limited, along with several small air operations, and began to operate Canadian Pacific Airlines (CPA) in 1942. In 1957 the prairie service of CPA was taken over by Pacific Western Airlines, operated by R.F. Baker (Hall of Fame 1974), which would later purchase CPA and form Canadian Airlines International.

Several pilots and air engineers employed by Canadian Airways would in the future be inducted as Members of Canada's Aviation Hall of Fame. Those who served in 1934 as pilots/managers of Canadian Airways bases from Moncton to Vancouver: W.W. Fowler, J.P.R. Vachon, H. Hollick-Kenyon, C.H. Dickins, T.W. Siers (all Hall of Fame 1974) and D.R. MacLaren (Hall of Fame 1977).

Richardson was awarded an Honorary Doctor of Laws from Queen's University in 1929. This honour coincided with his appointment as Chancellor of that University, a position he held until his death. He died in Winnipeg, Manitoba, on June 26, 1939, at the age of 53.

James Armstrong Richardson was inducted as a Member of Canada's Aviation Hall of Fame in 1976.

Robert Dick Richmond

(b. 1919)

Robert Dick Richmond, B.Sc., D. Eng. (Hon.), was born on January 13, 1919, in Winnipeg, Manitoba, and moved with his family to Toronto in 1933. He enrolled at the University of Michigan, obtaining a Bachelor degree in Aeronautical Engineering in 1942. While at the University he learned to fly, and soloed in a Piper Cub J-3F airplane. He worked at National Steel Car Co., Malton, Ontario, for two summers on the production of Westland Lysander leading-edge wing slats, and elevators.

Richmond joined Fairchild Aircraft Ltd., at Longueuil, Quebec, where he was responsible for the design and development of a target-towing version of the Bristol Bolingbroke, and skis for winter rescue of downed aircraft. He was Chief of Aerodynamics for a utility bush aircraft, the Fairchild Husky, from its inception through certification in 1946.

In early 1947, following closure of Fairchild Aircraft Ltd., Richmond was hired by Canadair Ltd., of Montreal, for a position in a newly-formed Preliminary Design department. In 1948 he became Section Chief of Aerodynamics, where his initial assignment was the development and certification of the North Star aircraft, a derivative of the Douglas DC-4.

By 1951 Richmond was assigned to Aerodynamics and Flight Test Engineering,

Before leaving Spar in 1980, Dick Richmond directed the integration into Spar Aerospace of the space activities of RCA Canada and Northern Telecom, which enabled the company to become a prime contractor in the manufacture of satellites.

a position which included performance development of the Canadian-built F-86 Sabre Mk 5 and 6. He also led design studies to define a maritime patrol aircraft for the RCAF. These studies culminated in a contract being awarded in May 1954, for the Argus, a long-range patrol aircraft. He was appointed Chief Development Engineer in February 1954, responsible for Canadair's entry into missile development.

During that period, Richmond and Canadair Test Pilot Al Lilly (Hall of Fame 1984) tried to interest the RCAF in a small jet trainer to replace the World War II Harvard, but received an official negative response. In early 1954 Richmond drafted preliminary specifications for a trainer which featured side by side seating and the then questionable items of pressurization and ejection seats. The result was the Canadair CL-41, the Tutor jet trainer.

In mid 1957 he was named Chief Engineer of Special Weapons, to manage a unit established for missile development, but the Sparrow missile program was cancelled as a result of the demise of the Avro Arrow. He redirected the division to pursue a new field: surveillance systems. By the time he left Canadair in 1960, development was beginning on what would later become Canadair's successful CL-89 surveillance system.

In April 1960, Richmond joined Pratt and Whitney of Canada (P&WC) as Vice-President of Operations, and in December, 1963 was appointed to the Board of Directors, then Deputy to the President. He directed the production of the first 3,500 PT-6 engines. Simultaneously, the manufacturing capacity was increased to absorb total production for all P&WC piston-engine parts. He also established, in 1963, a division to partially manufacture

and assemble the Sea King Helicopter for the Department of National Defence (DND), and supply components to Sikorsky for U.S. production.

In 1970 he joined McDonnell Douglas of Canada as President, and was named a Vice-President of the parent corporation. Here he directed the manufacture of DC-9 and DC-10 wings at Malton.

In 1974 Richmond become President, Chief Operating Officer and a Director of Spar Aerospace. Richmond guided this company in the development and marketing of specialized systems and subsystems. The most notable program was the Canadarm, for which he established the organization, and oversaw its development. He negotiated with the National Aeronautics and Space Administration (NASA) for procurement of follow-on units.

Richmond returned to Canadair in January 1981, to become the Executive Vice-President and Chief Operating Officer. He is credited with turning the Challenger business jet into a strong international competitor by directing the completion

of certification and delivery of CL-600 and CL-601 aircraft. These have been sold to corporations and governments in over 30 countries.

Following retirement in December 1987, Richmond continued as a senior advisor on the Canadair Regional Jet program during its definition phase.

Richmond is a Fellow, founding Member and Past President of the Canadian Aeronautics and Space Institute, and a recipient of their C.D. Howe award for leadership in Aerospace. He is an Associate Fellow of the American Institute of Aerospace Sciences, a Member of the Professional Engineers of Ontario, a Past President of the Canadian Delegation to NATO Industrial Advisory Group, and a Past Chairman and Honorary Life Member of the Aerospace Industries Association of Canada. He was awarded an Honorary Doctorate in Engineering from Carleton University in Ottawa in 1998.

Robert Dick Richmond was inducted as a Member of Canada's Aviation Hall of Fame in 1995.

Dick Richmond in the first Fairchild Husky after certification on floats. 1946.

Donald Howard Rogers

(b. 1916)

Donald Howard Rogers was born in Hamilton, Ontario, on November 26, 1916, and received his early education in Dundas, Ontario. He earned his Pilot's Licence in 1936 at the Hamilton Aero Club in 1935, followed by a Commercial Licence in 1938, and an Instructor's Rating in April 1939. He attended the Royal Canadian Air Force (RCAF) instructor course at Camp Borden Military Base, Ontario, in September 1939.

Rogers instructed RCAF Provisional Pilot Officers and civilian students at the Hamilton Aero Club until October 1940. From that date until December 1941, he was Assistant Chief Flying Instructor at No. 10 Elementary Flying Training School (EFTS) at Mt. Hope, Ontario. In 1941 he was transferred to the aircraft division of the National Steel Car Co. plant at Malton Airport, Toronto, Ontario, serving as a test pilot for their Westland Lysanders and Avro Ansons until April 1943.

Rogers obtained a posting with the Royal Air Force Ferry Command (RAFFC) flight test section at Dorval, Quebec, flying Lockheed Hudsons and Venturas, North

Rogers' career in aviation, like so many fellow Members of Canada's Aviation Hall of Fame, has been interesting and varied. He began flying in the mid-thirties, and went on to become chief test pilot at Avro Canada, reaching speeds of more than 500 miles per hour in the Jetliner in the mid-fifties. In the sixties and seventies he test-flew and demonstrated the slow-flying STOL aircraft at de Havilland Canada.

Avro Canada test pilots with the CF-100. Donald Rogers is at centre, with Mike Cooper-Slipper, Chris Pike, Peter Cope and Jan Zurakowski. 1950.

American B-25 Mitchell and Consolidated B-24 Liberator bombers from May through August 1943. He delivered a Hudson and a B-24 to the United Kingdom (U.K.) and during one trip spent five days at the A.V. Roe test flight center at Woodford, test flying Lancasters.

He became a test pilot for Victory Aircraft Ltd. at Malton Airport, test flying their Canadian-built Mk 10 Lancasters from September 1943, until the war's end in August of 1945. In December 1945, Avro Canada Ltd. was formed, and took over the Victory Aircraft Ltd. facilities.

In December 1945, he joined the newly formed Avro Canada Ltd. as Chief Test Pilot flying Venturas, B-25's, C-47's, and Lancasters following overhaul and modifications for the RCAF, as well as the Hawker Sea Fury for the Royal Canadian Navy (RCN). At this time Avro Canada was planning to build a 30-seat turbine-powered airliner for Trans Canada Airlines. James C. Floyd (Hall of Fame 1993) arrived from Avro (U.K.) to be Chief Technical Officer on the airliner project. The Avro C-102 Jetliner made its first flight on August 10, 1949, at Malton Airport, the first flight of a turbo-jet airliner in North America. Rogers was the co-pilot on this flight, with Avro (U.K.) Chief Pilot Jim Orell, and Bill Baker as Flight Engineer. Rogers was pilot-in-command on April 18, 1950, when the

C-102 carried the world's first jet-transported air mail from Toronto to New York.

Rogers did most of the test and demonstration flying of the C-102 Jetliner. In addition to the many local flights in which he tested handling, performance, fuel consumption, and de-icing, numerous demonstration flights were made with senior airline pilots in New York, Miami, Chicago, and Winnipeg, as well as military pilots at the Wright-Patterson Airforce Base at Dayton, Ohio, U.S.A. He also spent a period of six months in California flying the Jetliner with Howard Hughes of Trans World Airlines.

Rogers logged a total of 340 hours on the Jetliner. However, it was considered economically impractical and no orders were received. The C-102 Jetliner was scrapped in 1956.

During Rogers' employment with Avro, the Lancaster was being used as a 'flying test bed' for the new jet engine, the Orenda. He was the pilot on the first flight, and further development flights, of the Lancaster which had its two outboard Merlin engines replaced with Orenda engines.

He made the first flight of the Orenda-powered Avro CF 100 Mk 2, and eventually accumulated hundreds of hours test flying all marks of this all-weather interceptor. In 1958 he was appointed Flight Operations manager for the test-flying program of the Avro Arrow.

Following cancellation of the Arrow and the final shut down of Avro Canada, Rogers moved to the flight operations department of de Havilland Aircraft of Canada at Downsview Airport, Toronto, as a test, demonstration, and training pilot on all of their short take-off and landing (STOL) aircraft including the Beaver, Otter, Turbo Beaver, Twin Otter, Caribou, Buffalo, and Dash 7.

In addition to the hundreds of local test flights and training of the customers' pilots in STOL procedures, Rogers carried out many demonstration tours, including flying a Turbo Beaver through Central and South America. He then flew a Caribou to Anchorage and Prudhoe Bay in Alaska, a Buffalo to Brazil and Argentina, a Twin Otter from Morocco through the Middle East and India to Kuala Lampur, and a Twin Otter from England through Scandinavia and return to Downsview via Iceland, Greenland, and Baffin Island. He also demonstrated a water-bomber version of the Twin Otter on floats across Canada.

Delivery flights were also his responsibility. They often involved remaining for a sufficient period of time to train and check out the customer's pilots in the operation of STOL aircraft. Such deliveries included a Caribou to Kawajalen Island in the Pacific, a Buffalo to Togo in Africa, and Twin Otters to Puerta Mont, Chile, as well as to Panama, Switzerland, Iran, and Nepal. Rogers spent six months in Nepal training Royal Nepal Airline pilots, and wrote operational procedures for take-off and landing on their short strips in the Himalayan Mountains.

In 1980, at age 63, Rogers retired from the flight operations department at de Havilland but continued to do part-time flight training and ground school instructing of their customers' pilots for another seven years. Since 1987, with more than 12,000 flying hours on 30 aircraft types, he has been fully retired.

In recognition of his years of testing and demonstrating the Avro Jetliner and many other Canadian designed and built aircraft throughout the world, Rogers was awarded the Trans-Canada (McKee) Trophy for 1983. He was made an Associate Fellow of the Canadian Aeronautics and Space Institute (CASI) in February 1957, and promoted to Fellow in 1998.

Donald Howard Rogers was inducted as a Member of Canada's Aviation Hall of Fame in 1998.

Lindsay (Lindy) Rood

(b. 1911)

Lindsay (Lindy) Rood was born on March 17, 1911, in Berwick, Nova Scotia, and was educated there and at Dalhousie University in Halifax. He enrolled in an extension course with the Royal Canadian Air Force (RCAF) and began his long and eventful career in aviation. After earning his wings and a commission as a Pilot Officer in the RCAF Reserves, he entered commercial aviation as a flying instructor and barnstormer throughout Nova Scotia, and obtained an Engineer's Licence as well.

In 1933 Rood became a flight instructor with the Cape Breton Flying Club at Sydney, Nova Scotia, and two years later went to England to join British Airways as a pilot. From 1935 to 1937, he flew routes which included London, Copenhagen and Stockholm. At this time, he earned his British Navigator's Licence.

In 1937 he returned to Canada as one of the first pilots to be hired by the newly-formed Trans-Canada Airlines (TCA, Hall of Fame 1974), pioneering the Rocky Mountain route between Lethbridge, Alberta, and Vancouver, British Columbia. He became one of the founding members of the Canadian Air Line Pilots Association (CALPA, Belt of Orion 1988) when a group

Throughout Lindy Rood's years as head of the Flight Operations Branch, he was an advocate for the development and use of 'motion' systems to make aircraft simulators fly more realistically. He introduced the first of such systems in an early Air Canada simulator, a concept that has since been accepted throughout the aviation industry.

"His leadership, dedication to safety of flight operations and wide-ranging contributions to Canadian and international aviation have left an indelible mark on the airline industry and have been of significant benefit to Canada." —Induction citation, 1974

Lindy Rood in cockpit.

of TCA pilots met in Winnipeg, Manitoba, in December 1937, to form an association.

At the outbreak of World War II, Rood was declared essential to the public service and prohibited from joining the military. The Hon. C.D. Howe (Hall of Fame 1976), who was head of the Canadian Department of Munitions and Supply, seconded him in 1942 to the Return Ferry Service, Royal Air Force Transport Command, flying the north Atlantic Ocean between Montreal, Quebec, and Prestwick, Scotland. Pilots engaged in this war-time effort flew Liberator aircraft, converted to carry people rather than bombs, and brought ferry crews back to Canada after they had made their delivery of aircraft to the U.K. In 1943 he was assigned to 10 Bomber Reconnaissance Squadron at Gander, Newfoundland, and instructed on Liberator B-24 bombers.

Rood was asked to help in the formation of the Canadian Government Trans-Atlantic

Air Service (CGTAS), designed to deliver high ranking Allied officers, government officials, special cargo and mail between Canada and the U.K. with the greatest possible speed. He was named Chief Pilot of this service and remained in that post until war's end when the service was taken over by TCA.

During the years of expansion of TCA, Rood was highly regarded for his abilities in every area of flight operations. He was put in charge of all flying personnel selection and training, and played a major role in determining aircraft types used by the airline. He was named a senior member of many world aviation councils, representing TCA.

In 1944 Rood went on to become Chief Pilot of TCA's Atlantic Operation, and in 1947 he was named Superintendent of Flight Operations for TCA's trans-Atlantic service. One of his major contributions was his leadership in aircraft cockpit design and layout, which, with advanced electronics, resulted in two pilots being capable of flying even the largest aircraft safely and efficiently.

From 1950 to 1968, he was Director of Flight Operations for TCA, which was re-named Air Canada in 1965. He served as Vice-President of Flight Operations for Air Canada until his retirement in 1971, with nearly 20,000 hours as pilot-in-command.

Lindsay (Lindy) Rood was inducted as a Member of Canada's Aviation Hall of Fame in 1974.

Frank Walter Russell

(1909 – 1994)

Frank Walter Russell was born in Toronto, Ontario, on October 19, 1909. He began his career in aviation with de Havilland of Canada in 1929. While there he assembled the first Tiger Moth to be built in Canada. Later, this aircraft joined the Austin Airways fleet.

In 1934 Russell accepted a position with Capreol and Austin Airways as their first employee. Initially, he was responsible for the maintenance and servicing of two Waco aircraft at the company's waterfront location in Toronto. During the first winter, 1934-35, Austin Airways established a maintenance base at the airport in North Toronto. He received his Air Engineer's Licence in 1936.

He set up a new base for Austin Airways at Sudbury, Ontario, on the shore of Ramsey Lake. This enabled the company to serve the prospectors, mine operators, lumber camps, and people of northern Ontario more efficiently. In 1940 Russell was issued his Aircraft Maintenance Engineer's Licence, with Category A, B, & D endorsements, and became Superintendent of Maintenance for Austin Airways, a position he held for 35 years. The demand to transport goods and people by air in Canada's north prompted the growth of Austin Airways fleet, with the addition of seven Noorduyn Norseman aircraft, five

Frank Russell continued in aviation after retirement by doing Certificate of Airworthiness inspections on aircraft. He also spent ten years with the Canadian Warplane Heritage Museum in Hamilton, Ontario, supervising the work on the aircraft there until 1982.

"His ingenuity and dedication to the quality servicing and maintenance of aircraft over a span of 60 years has made him a respected player in the development of bush flying and has been of major benefit to Canadian aviation." —Induction citation, 1994

Air Engineer Frank Russell loading mail at Kenora, Ontario, for Red Lake. Austin Airways. c. 1940's.

de Havilland Beavers, three Cessna 180's, one Fairchild Husky, three Avro Ansons, two amphibious Cansos and two Douglas DC-3's. By the mid-1950's, Russell had 23 aircraft to keep airworthy.

Maintaining the company's aircraft in good repair was a dawn-to-dusk business for Russell. In good weather, pilots would be off at daybreak, and would fly back and forth between the base and wherever they were serving—a camp site, forest fire fighting, a mine, or chartering passengers. Each time a plane returned, Russell would help with loading and check any mechanical needs of the aircraft.

Russell's work in the winter of 1945 on a Fleet Freighter, CF-BJW, was recorded by a Canadian Aviation Historical researcher in the following manner:

> "The original engines with grease-lubricated rockers were replaced with later model L-6MB engines with pressure-lubricated rockers and constant speed props were installed. The oilrads and engine control system from a Cessna were installed. The original Fleet system of wire sliding in a fibre-

lined tube had a tendency to pick up moisture that could freeze, so these were all replaced. The old slow-acting tail plane trim system was redesigned to eliminate the need for excessive trim wheel spinning. The floats had been damaged and replaced the previous summer. BJW was re-covered and finished with the Austin Airways colors of black fuselage with silver trim and red wings. The Austin Airways crest was applied to sides of the forward fuselage." BJW was but one of the dozens of aircraft ingeniously modified by Frank Russell.

On one occasion, when an aircraft failed to arrive on schedule, a search was planned for the following morning. While the pilots slept, Russell and his crew worked and had the Fleet serviced and ready for take-off before daybreak. The downed plane was found before ten o'clock the next morning.

At one point he purchased a Norseman Mk V fuselage in order to facilitate the replacement of one on a Mk VI. The Mk VI was too busy to be taken out of service so Russell took the Mk V fuselage and some spare parts and built a Mk V Norseman, CF-IGG. Austin Airways Chief Pilot, Rusty Blakey (Hall of Fame 1992) declared CF-IGG to be the best performing Norseman in the fleet.

In 1955 a Canso ran aground on the Winisk River, which empties into Hudson Bay. Russell was among those called to plan the salvage. The Canso was partially submerged and it appeared to be a total loss. The river current was swift, approximately 25 mph (40 kph) and the plane was grounded just upstream from rapids. Russell's crew used quick-drying cement to plug the holes, and pumps to refloat it. The salvage operation was a success.

The tasks of the aviators serving the Arctic were made easier through Russell's efforts. Much of the credit given to Austin Airways for helping the native population and in the control and elimination of tuberculosis was due to the work of Frank Russell. After more than 41 years with Austin Airways, Russell retired in 1975. He died on December 15, 1994.

Frank Walter Russell was inducted as a Member of Canada's Aviation Hall of Fame in 1994.

William John (Jack) Sanderson

(1898 – 1984)

William John (Jack) Sanderson was born in Lakewood, Ohio, U.S.A., on November 24, 1898, and was raised on a farm near London, Ontario. At the outbreak of World War I, he joined the 9th Battalion, Canadian Railway Troops and went overseas in 1916. In mid-1917 he transferred to the Royal Flying Corps, and was posted to France. As a pilot with 110 Squadron, he flew de Havilland DH-9A's in high altitude bombing raids against Germany. At the end of the war, he returned to his father's farm in Ontario. In 1928 the London Flying Club was formed, and following completion of an instructor's course, he was hired as the Club's flight instructor.

A chance meeting with Major R.H. Fleet, President of Consolidated Aircraft Corporation in Buffalo, New York, resulted in a change of plans. Sanderson was hired as the Canadian representative for the company and began demonstrating Fleet 2 aircraft in Canada in October 1929. Fleet Aircraft of Canada Limited was incorporated in March 1930, and aircraft manufacturing began that year. As General Manager and Test Pilot, Sanderson divided his time between managing the company, testing each new aircraft and flying the Fleet demonstrator at flying club meets

Jack Sanderson was interested in the development of pilot training programs at Flying Clubs across Canada. He felt that the Flying Clubs Associations should train their own instructors, air engineers and maintenance mechanics in order to provide a broader service to Canadian aviation.

"As a pre-eminent aerobatic and test pilot and as a pioneer and leader in the Canadian light aircraft industry, he contributed substantially to the advancement of Canadian aviation."

—Induction citation, 1983

W. SANDERSON PHOTO

Jack Sanderson beside a de Havilland DH-60 of the London Flying Club, Ontario. c. 1928.

throughout Ontario. He took a Fleet 7 to Ottawa in October 1930, for extensive testing by the Royal Canadian Air Force (RCAF), following which the company received an order for twenty aircraft.

Sanderson was recognized as one of the best aerobatic pilots in Canada, and he participated in the Trans-Canada Air Pageant in 1931 in a Fleet 7. He sustained the company during the next two years when orders for new aircraft were virtually nonexistent, by performing aerobatics at airshows, and overhauling aircraft. In 1934 he secured the rights for the Waco line of aircraft. After modification for Canadian operating conditions, a number were sold and operated across the country.

By late 1934, orders for new Fleet aircraft were again being placed, and in 1937, the Fort Erie plant was expanded. The company was reorganized as a Canadian-owned company under the name Fleet Aircraft Limited, with Sanderson as President and General Manager. He concentrated part of his efforts on the development of a twin-engine freighter for bush flying and on February 22, 1938, he flew the prototype of the Fleet 50 Freighter.

During the late 1930's, under his direction, Fleet built more aircraft than any other Canadian firm.

Sanderson was appointed Director of the Commercial Air Transport and Manufacturers Association of Canada in November 1937. He met with British trade missions to discuss the establishment of a consortium of companies in Canada to manufacture British aircraft. These meetings led to the formation of Canadian Associated Aircraft Limited.

In October 1939, Sanderson was hired by the Defence Purchasing Board, and in April 1940, was appointed Director of Aircraft Supply, Department of Munitions and Supply. He was responsible for the ordering and production of the various aircraft required for the British Commonwealth Air Training Plan (BCATP). His own company's major war production program included the manufacture of the Fleet Finch and Hampden bomber fuselages, the Fairchild PT-23 and PT-26, Cornell, and the outer wings for the Lancaster Mk 10.

He returned to Fleet Aircraft in October 1940, to oversee the manufacture of the Fleet Fort advanced trainer until 1942. He spent the remainder of the war years in the United States engaged in the development and production of plastic material for use in aircraft.

At war's end, Sanderson established Central Aircraft in Toronto, Ontario, operating as a component sub-contractor to de Havilland Aircraft of Canada Limited, and Cessna distributor. In 1958, when a fire destroyed the property, he reorganized under the name Sanderson-Acfield Aircraft Limited, and continued as a Cessna sales agency. At age 65, he completed a season of amphibious flying in Newfoundland. He moved to British Columbia in 1967, where he took instruction and became qualified to fly helicopters. He died in Victoria, British Columbia, on January 22, 1984.

William John (Jack) Sanderson was inducted as a Member of Canada's Aviation Hall of Fame in 1983.

Kenneth Foster Saunders
(1893 – 1974)

Kenneth Foster Saunders, D.S.C., A.F.C., was born in Victoria, British Columbia, on February 6, 1893, and like so many others, found his education interrupted by the outbreak of World War I. His desire to join Britain's growing air service led him to the Wright Company's Flying School in Dayton, Ohio, U.S.A., where the required 350 minute flying course cost $1.00 per minute.

On October 15, 1915, Saunders received his Aviation Certificate No. 353, signed by Orville Wright, and sailed for England, all at his own expense. He completed the remainder of his service training at Eastchurch, England, graduating as Flight Sub-Lieutenant in the Royal Naval Air Service. He flew naval patrols, and used a Sopwith Pup in a series of experimental landings on an improvised carrier deck. He served with distinction and ended the war as a Captain with a Distinguished Service Cross (D.S.C.) and an Air Force Cross (A.F.C.).

In 1919 he was offered a two-year contract to promote the sale of British Avro 504 aircraft in Sweden. This barnstorming-type of operation gave him his first experience with ski-equipped aircraft. After returning to Victoria in 1922, he obtained his Commercial Pilot's Licence.

In August 1923, Saunders joined Fairchild Aerial Surveys of Canada Ltd., a new

In his role as Government Inspector, Ken Saunders had the reputation of a tough disciplinarian with a mixture of fatherly advice and humour. He always signed his correspondence in green ink and the stories of his tenure in office are legendary.

G.K. SAUNDERS PHOTO

Ken Saunders, Superintendent, Air Regulations, beside the Waco aircraft which he flew throughout the Edmonton Region on Department of Transport business.

company being organized in conjunction with the Laurentide Pulp and Paper Company to assist in mapping Quebec's forests. The Fairchild organization in New York was developing better cameras and improving techniques for aerial mapping. Saunders began the photography experiments out of Grand'Mère, Quebec, with a Curtiss Seagull flying boat, but the addition of a Standard J-1 on wheels and skis made the company the first to provide year-round bush services in Canada. The new company was the first to develop bush flying into a full-scale commercial operation in Canada.

Saunders' growing experience in aerial photography was sought by the U.S. Fairchild Company in building aircraft especially suited for photo mapping. He took part in the planning of the Fairchild FC (Fairchild cabin) series of monoplanes, tested the first FC-1, then took delivery of the first FC-2 on floats from the factory for Canadian operation. He demonstrated the seaplane version on both sides of the border, resulting in further sales of this highly successful type.

As the operation at Grand'Mère grew, it added charter flying to its activities. In 1927 Saunders flew a Curtiss HS-2L in the Quebec government-sponsored search flights for the missing French trans-Atlantic flyers Nungesser and Coli, without success. The biggest aviation news story of 1928 was the crossing of the Atlantic from east to west in April by a German aircrew flying a Junkers aircraft, the 'Bremen'. They were off course and landed on Greenly Island, in the Strait of Belle Isle, which separates Newfoundland from Labrador. Saunders flew newspapermen from Quebec to New York City, where a reception for the crew was held.

By the time the company joined Canadian Airways Ltd. in 1931, it was the largest bush operator in eastern Canada. Saunders' role included opening new routes along the entire lower St. Lawrence for passengers, mail and freight. Other routes served Great Whale, Senneterre, and Port Harrison (Inoucdjouac) on Hudson Bay.

In April 1936, Saunders, with 21 years of flying experience, joined the Government Air Regulations Branch as a Department of Transport (DOT) Inspector. After a short period at DOT headquarters in Ottawa, and six months in Vancouver, he was assigned to the Edmonton region. From this base, Saunders covered Saskatchewan, Alberta, and the Northwest Territories by plane, boat and train. Later the district was reorganized to include Alberta, the Northwest Territories and the Yukon. By 1939 he was Regional Superintendent of Air Regulations for the Edmonton district. He continued to fly the Department's aircraft until his retirement.

After 42 years in aviation, including 21 years of government service and 10,000 hours of flying, Saunders retired in 1958 to live in Victoria, where he died on July 1, 1974, at age 81.

Kenneth Foster Saunders was inducted as a Member of Canada's Aviation Hall of Fame in 1997.

Rayne Dennis (Joe) Schultz

(b. 1922)

Rayne Dennis (Joe) Schultz, D.F.C.*, O.M.M., C.D.**, was born in Bashaw, Alberta, on December 17, 1922. In early 1941, at age 18, he realized his boyhood dream when he was accepted for pilot training by the Royal Canadian Air Force (RCAF). His initial flight training was on Tiger Moths at Sea Island, Vancouver, and he earned his wings on Avro Ansons at Macleod, Alberta. He was posted overseas in early 1942.

In England, he took flight engineer training before attending a Night Fighter (NF) Operational Training Unit (OTU) on Bristol Blenheims and Beaufighters. In late 1942, he joined 410 NF Squadron just as it was converting to the NF version of the DH Mosquito. He was to fly this versatile aircraft until the war ended.

During his first tour with 410 Squadron he flew defensive patrols over England and night intruder missions into enemy territory. On the night of December 10/11, 1943, he and his Radio Observer (RO) F/L V.A. Williams, destroyed three Dornier bombers over the North Sea in less than fifteen minutes. Each received an immediate Distinguished Flying Cross (D.F.C.). By the end of their tour in June

Rayne D. 'Joe' Schultz made other tangible contributions to flight safety. These stemmed from his dynamic support of the development of such far-reaching programs as flight data recorders, crash position indicators, reduction of bird hazards to aircraft, and a means of reducing the vulnerability of helicopters to wire strikes.

"Over many years in cooperation with the military and civilian agencies associated with aviation, his vision, dedication and pursuit of excellence resulted in significant advancement in air operations generally and flight safety accident prevention programs in particular." —Induction citation, 1997

1944, they had destroyed five enemy bombers. In December 1944, he rejoined 410 Squadron for a second tour in France and Holland. With his new RO, F/O Jack Christie, three more enemy aircraft were destroyed over Germany, earning Schultz a Bar to his D.F.C.

Before returning to Canada in August 1945, he completed an advanced weapons course to prepare for transfer to the Pacific Theater. The war against Japan ended, and Schultz was transferred back to Canada. He spent the next several years performing test and ferry flying from St. Hubert, Quebec, Rockcliffe and Trenton, Ontario.

In 1948 the RCAF began to rebuild, with the de Havilland Vampire Jet heralding a new era. As an experienced fighter pilot, Schultz was selected for training at No. 1 Fighter OTU. This became the re-formed 410 Fighter Squadron in January 1949. A few months later Schultz and three others formed the first official RCAF jet aerobatics team, the Blue Devils.

In June 1950, he left 410 Squadron on an exchange posting with the Central Fighter Establishment in England. He returned to North Bay, Ontario, where the newly established No. 3 All Weather (AW) OTU was about to be equipped with the Canadian Avro-built CF-100 'Canuck'. His two-year tour there as the Chief Flying Instructor was followed by four years as Staff Officer, Operations, at Air Defence Command (ADC) Headquarters. One of his more important responsibilities in this capacity was as the ADC pilot representative on the Avro Arrow program.

When the CF-105 Avro Arrow was cancelled, Schultz was reassigned to Bagotville, Quebec, first as Squadron Commander of 413 AW Squadron, then as Chief Operations Officer and finally as Commander of 432 AW Squadron. In mid 1961, he was named to lead the air crew team to work with the United States Air

Force (USAF) for training on the CF-101 Voodoo which was to re-equip the All Weather squadrons in place of the Arrow. This group re-formed as 425 AW Squadron at Namao, Alberta, and was responsible for converting the other AW Squadrons to the Voodoo. As soon as this task was completed, Schultz was sent to 4 Fighter Wing in Germany as Chief Operations Officer, to prepare for the arrival of the CF-104 Starfighter which was assigned to a nuclear strike role with the North Atlantic Treaty Organization (NATO). Both of these high profile and demanding programs received international recognition, bringing credit to the RCAF and Canada.

A transfer in 1966 to the Directorate of Flight Safety in Ottawa, as Chief Accident Investigator, ended his operational flying but he maintained full flying status until retirement. With promotion to Group Captain in 1977, he became Director, Flight Safety. Over the next ten years he developed and managed one of the most highly regarded flight safety programs. In recognition of this and previous exceptional service he was appointed an Officer in the Order of Military Merit (O.M.M.) in 1974.

Group Captain Schultz was convinced that an aggressive accident prevention program would save lives and enhance operational effectiveness. He used his extensive experience, integrity and determination to convince much of the aviation community that a major change in philosophy was needed. Accordingly, he reduced the threat of 'blame and punishment' and wherever possible, give privileged status to flight safety reports. Almost immediately, a significant increase in accident reports showed that there was a new trust in the system and an acceptance of the principle that complete and candid reports were a key factor in prevention. Even a simple step, such as replacing the harsh, derogatory word 'ERROR', had an immediate and positive effect on attitudes.

Schultz's efforts in the field of accident prevention were recognized internationally in 1977 by a special award from the International Flight Safety Foundation in 1977 and honorary membership in the USAF Aerospace Safety Hall of Fame. He was awarded the Trans-Canada (McKee) Trophy for 1978 for his work in promoting flight safety. After more than thirty-six years of continuous service, he retired in 1977 as Group Captain.

Rayne Dennis (Joe) Schultz was inducted as a Member of Canada's Aviation Hall of Fame in 1997.

Eugene Howard (Gene) Schweitzer

(b. 1915)

Eugene Howard (Gene) Schweitzer was born on June 20th, 1915, in Kincardine, Ontario, where he was educated. He moved to Glendale, California, to study at the Curtiss-Wright Technical Institute. After graduating, he returned to Canada, earned his Aircraft Maintenance Engineer's Licence, and joined the fledgling Pratt & Whitney Aircraft of Canada Ltd. (P&WC) at Longueuil, Quebec, in July 1940. After becoming familiar with the company's engines and Hamilton Standard propellers, he was made responsible for field support across Canada.

World War II escalated quickly, and the need for aircraft for crew training and combat became critical. To speed up deliveries from North America, the Royal Air Force Ferry Command (RAFFC) was created to deliver the desperately needed airplanes overseas, at a time when trans-ocean flights were still newsworthy and pilots feared the often-stormy Atlantic.

Initially, ferry pilots returned to Canada by ship, but the pilot shortage demanded faster returns of the flight crews. In May 1941, under C.H. 'Punch' Dickins (Hall of Fame 1974) of Canadian Pacific Air Services, a two-way scheduled service on the North Atlantic route was started. Schweitzer became involved in the modification and flight testing of seven Consolidated B-24 Liberator aircraft at St.

Gene Schweitzer's career spanned over forty years at Pratt & Whitney Canada. He pioneered complete customer support for both commercial and military operators as new equipment and uses developed.

Group Captain 'Joe' Schultz beside a CF-100 on his way to the last rocket meet in Cold Lake, Alberta. 1960.

CANADIAN FORCES PHOTO

"Through the transition from piston to turbine power and from bush flying to airlines, business and commuter aviation, he applied his knowledge of aircraft engines, corporate management and public relations to the benefit of air transportation across Canada and around the world." —Induction citation, 1996

Gene Schweitzer following his induction as a Member of Canada's Aviation Hall of Fame, 1996. He is wearing the Medal of the Hall of Fame and the Order of Flight Medal presented by the City of Edmonton.

Hubert, Quebec. The Liberator became the first land plane used for trans-Atlantic year-round scheduled service.

Ferry Command depended heavily on his crew for engine maintenance and handling operating problems such as severe icing, and flying with extended use of high power settings. Schweitzer provided technical service and training for the introduction of PBY Canso aircraft on North Atlantic Patrol. Long hours were needed to maintain the rigorous delivery schedules. The technical staff, by their resourcefulness and diligence, contributed in large measure to the success of the ferry service.

At the end of WW II he became the Sales and Service Representative for P&WC serving major airlines, bush operators and regional carriers throughout Canada. With his experience and knowledge of the R-1830 engine, he advised airlines which had acquired surplus DC-3 aircraft on engine handling techniques, and greatly improved their success and safety record. He assured P&WC support for CPA when they acquired a fleet of DC-4's. As the airlines added DC-6 and Convair aircraft to their fleets in the 1950's and 1960's, Schweitzer's Operations Engineering and Services staff were key in the successful operation of the R-2800 engines.

Several new aircraft emerged soon after the war, all of them featuring P&WC engines. The Fairchild Husky and de Havilland Canada DHC-2 Beaver were both equipped with the Wasp Junior R-985 engine. Schweitzer worked closely with DHC's engineers to adapt the engine to the Beaver which, because of its short take-off and landing (STOL) features, caused unique cooling problems. In 1950 de Havilland

began production of the Otter aircraft, selecting the P&WC Wasp R-1340 engine based on the company's reputation for product support.

By the late 1950's, transition from piston to turbine power was proceeding rapidly, and the business sector was beginning to understand the utility of corporate aircraft. As owners faced new equipment, personnel and training needs, they demanded dedicated support from the manufacturers, and under Schweitzer's direction as P&WC Service Manager, their expectations were fully met. His responsibilities were for service and support for engines, propellers, Sikorsky helicopters and all technical services, including technical publications.

In 1966 Schweitzer was appointed Vice-President of Product Support. As the company's international business expanded with the design and production of the PT-6 and PW-100 turboprop engines,

he established a complete and comprehensive turbine engine training centre. With the rapid growth of the commuter airline market, he was selected in 1980 to lead P&WC's Commuter Airline Group as Vice-President. He coordinated the company's response to the needs of commuter airlines around the world.

He retired as Vice-President, Commuter Operations in 1981, but continued to serve as an airlines consultant until his full retirement in 1982. He has been a member of the Canadian Aeronautics and Space Institute since 1954. In post retirement he has volunteered with Canadian Executive Services Overseas in Central America, and provided assistance to aircraft companies. He continues to work on various historical projects.

Eugene Howard (Gene) Schweitzer was inducted as a Member of Canada's Aviation Hall of Fame in 1996.

Herbert Walter (Herb) Seagrim

(1912 – 1998)

Herbert Walter (Herb) Seagrim, C.M., was born in Winnipeg, Manitoba, on August 25, 1912, where he was educated. He learned to fly at the Winnipeg Flying Club in 1931, and the following year was employed there as a part-time mechanic. To increase his flying experience he worked extra jobs in exchange for air time, and barnstormed throughout the prairie provinces. In 1933 he earned an Air Engineer's Licence and joined Konnie Johannesson's Flying Service in Winnipeg as a mechanic and relief pilot. In partial payment for his services he accepted advanced instruction in aerobatics. The next year he was hired as a pilot by Wings Limited, operated by F. Roy Brown and Jack Moar (both Hall of Fame 1974) at their Lac du Bonnet, Manitoba, air base and until late 1937, flew bush aircraft throughout northern Ontario, Manitoba and Saskatchewan.

When Trans-Canada Airlines (TCA, Hall of Fame 1974) was formed in 1937, he and Lindy Rood (Hall of Fame 1974) joined the firm as pilots on the same day. All the newly hired pilots took extensive training in Lockheed 10A aircraft during which, for the first year before carrying passengers, all phases of flying were conducted 'under the hood', using instruments. This was practiced until instrument flight became second nature and visual reference to the ground a mere distraction.

Herb Seagrim was so determined to fly that he arranged a deal with the Winnipeg Flying Club to work a whole day as a mechanic's helper in return for 15 minutes of flying time.

Seagrim captained the inaugural westbound mail flight from Winnipeg to Regina, Saskatchewan, in 1938. With several other pilots he pioneered the Rocky Mountain route between Lethbridge, Alberta, and Vancouver, British Columbia. In 1942, in addition to operating his regularly scheduled TCA flights, he was engaged as a test pilot with the Boeing Commercial Airplane Company at their Vancouver overhaul plant.

In 1943, in recognition of his management abilities, coupled with his excellent piloting record, Seagrim was promoted to Chief Pilot of the Western Region. Based at Lethbridge, his job consisted mainly of flight instruction to meet the demands of the rapidly expanding airline. The following year he was returned to Winnipeg as Assistant Superintendent of Flight Operations, an assignment which included the duties of Chief Flying Instructor. That same year he was appointed Superintendent of Flight Operations, a title later changed to Director of Operations.

The airline had changed in seven years from a fledgling air service into a far-ranging, dependable national airline. To further improve the company's efficiency, and to maintain its superior safety record, Seagrim was assigned to write the basic flight and instructional procedures, many of which have remained in the manuals. As captain of a Canadair North Star aircraft in 1948, he flew the Vancouver, British Columbia, to Montreal, Quebec, route in six hours and fifty two minutes to establish a new speed record.

When TCA's headquarters were moved to Montreal in 1949, Seagrim was appointed General Manager of Operations in charge of flying, tele-communications, passenger service, maintenance, engineering and stations. His success in that position led to a promotion to Vice-President of Operations in 1956, and Senior Vice-President of Operations in 1962. During these years he was largely responsible for

Herb Seagrim, centre, as captain of the record flight in a North Star, Vancouver to Montreal, in just under seven hours. 1948.

TCA's selection of Douglas DC-8 and DC-9 jet aircraft. He underwent line pilot training on both of these aircraft and flew the first DC-8 transcontinental flight for TCA in 1960, and the first DC-9 transcontinental flight in 1966. In 1965 the company name was changed to Air Canada.

The responsibility for all the line departments was given him that year when he was promoted to Executive Vice-President for the airline. In 1969 he became First Vice-President. He took early retirement in 1970. He died in Toronto on November 13, 1998.

Seagrim was made a Member of the Order of Canada (C.M.) in 1987 for his contributions to building and administering Air Canada. He was a Fellow of the Canadian Aeronautics and Space Institute (CASI) and the Royal Aeronautical Society.

Herbert Walter (Herb) Seagrim was inducted as a Member of Canada's Aviation Hall of Fame in 1974.

Murton Adams Seymour

(1892 – 1976)

Murton Adams Seymour, O.B.E., B.A., K.C., was born in St. Catharines, Ontario, on July 6, 1892, and moved to Vancouver, British Columbia, the following year. He attended the University of Toronto, where he received his B.A. with Honours in Political Science in 1915, and Osgoode Hall Law School in Toronto. He returned to Vancouver and as a student of law he articled with the firm of Gwillim, Crisp and McKay in that city.

With several other aviation enthusiasts he purchased a Curtiss Pusher aircraft and formed what became known as the Aero Club of British Columbia. He learned to

Murton Seymour trained in 1915 in an OX-powered Curtiss pusher built about 1912. He gained his initial instruction by sitting on the leading edge of the lower wing and watching the actions of his instructor, William M. Stark, during demonstration flights. Then he practiced taxiing on the ground, with his instructor sitting on the wing beside him and shouting his instructions. Stark placed a block under the foot throttle to control the amount of power generated by the engine. As Seymour became more proficient at taxiing, his foot throttle block was shaved down progressively, until finally he had enough power to make short hops at anywhere up to three or four feet off the ground. After that accomplishment, he was on his own.

"His efforts in having the nation's private flying clubs designated as military pilot training schools during World War II has been of substantial benefit to Canadian aviation." —Induction citation, 1974

fly at the race track in Vancouver, on land now occupied by the International Airport. In 1916 the Royal Flying Corps (RFC) commissioned him in the Special Reserve to attend the School of Aeronautics at Oxford University in England, from which he graduated as a pilot.

A posting to 41 Squadron, RFC, followed and he flew fighter aircraft from an advanced base in Belgium. After several months he was medically restricted to low level flying because of an intolerance to oxygen-limited air. He was posted to administration duties and finally ordered to Camp Borden, Ontario, in 1917, to assist in setting up RFC flying training squadrons. As a Captain he was given the responsibility of designing pilot training facilities at Fort Worth, Texas for the RFC winter training programs. In 1918 he was promoted to Major and named to the headquarters staff of the RFC, which later became the Royal Air Force (RAF), in Canada. At war's end he was placed in charge of demobilizing Canadian officers serving with the RAF in Canada.

Prior to leaving the service, Seymour was admitted to the Bars of both Ontario and British Columbia as Barrister and Solicitor. He then joined the firm of Ingersoll and Kingstone at St. Catharines, Ontario. He started his own law practice in 1933, and in 1934 he became a King's Counsel (K.C.)

The Flying Clubs of Canada came into existence in 1927-28 under a subsidy policy established by the Civil Aviation Branch of the Department of National Defence. The objectives were to establish aerodromes throughout Canada, as at that time there were practically no airports, to create air consciousness among Canadians, and to create a reserve of partially trained pilots for defence of the country in the event of war. In 1928 Seymour incorporated the St. Catharines Flying Club, preparing its constitution and by-laws, and served as its first President until 1936. He was a founding member and Director of the Canadian Flying Clubs

Association (CFCA), serving as President from 1939 to 1944.

Early in 1939, Seymour discussed the situation concerning the defence of the country with the Civil Aviation Branch, and the possibility of flying clubs undertaking the elementary flying training instruction of a number of provisional pilot officers for the RCAF. By the fall of 1939 an agreement was in place, and this formed the basis for the civil Elementary Flying Training Schools of the British Commonwealth Air Training Plan (BCATP).

In recognition of his personal endeavors in negotiating an agreement between the flying clubs of Canada and the Department of National Defence for the training of military pilots during wartime, he was awarded the Trans-Canada (McKee) Trophy for 1939 and the Gold Medal of the CFCA. In 1943 he was named a Member of the Order of the British Empire (O.B.E.) for his contributions. In 1951 he was elected a Life Bencher of the Upper Canada Law Society, having been named a Bencher in 1936. He was appointed Honorary Counsel to the Royal Canadian Flying Clubs Association. Seymour died in St. Catharines on December 27, 1976.

Murton Adams Seymour was inducted as a Member of Canada's Aviation Hall of Fame in 1974.

Murton Seymour with a Curtiss biplane. c. 1914.

John Gavin (Jack) Showler
(1912 – 1989)

John Gavin (Jack) Showler, A.F.C., C.D.*, was born in Winnipeg, Manitoba, on June 15, 1912. He attended the University of Manitoba until 1935, when he joined the Hudson Bay Mining and Smelting Company at Flin Flon, Manitoba, as a chemist. In 1936 he began taking flying instruction at the Regina Flying Club in Saskatchewan, but was severely injured in an aircraft accident at Flin Flon, Manitoba. He resumed his pilot's course with the Winnipeg Flying Club in 1939, and enlisted in the Royal Canadian Air Force (RCAF) in 1940.

After training at Thunder Bay, Camp Borden and Trenton, in Ontario, Showler received his wings and a promotion to Pilot Officer. Until 1942 he instructed at Summerside, Prince Edward Island, and Trenton, where he was promoted to Flight Lieutenant. His exceptional skills were recognized by an assignment to tour all RCAF flying schools in Canada during 1943 to re-categorize flying instructors. A posting followed to 164 Heavy Transport

Geodetic survey is the basis of all other forms of survey. It provides a grid of known points from which measurements may be taken. By 1949 the coasts of the Arctic Islands and the Arctic coast of the mainland were sketched in, but there were large areas on the mainland and the interior of the islands that could not be mapped, even with the aerial photographs available, because of the lack of geodetic reference points. The SHORAN program provided this information.

Squadron, RCAF, at Moncton, New Brunswick, where he completed a transport captain's course in 1944. Promoted to Squadron Leader, he was named Detachment Commander of the squadron at Goose Bay, Labrador, on air operations to Greenland and Iceland, and was awarded the Air Force Cross (A.F.C.).

When the Canadian government launched a 3,000 mile (4,800 km) military trek through the western Arctic in 1946, code-named Operation Muskox, which involved the Canadian Army and the RCAF, Showler was promoted to Wing Commander and chosen Commander of the Air Element. The objective of this exercise during the winter and spring of 1946 was to test the possibilities of moving men and motorized equipment across the Canadian Arctic. He then served as Commanding Officer of the RCAF Station at Fort St. John, British Columbia, until 1948. He graduated from the Air University of the United States Air Force at Montgomery, Alabama, in 1950, and was transferred to RCAF Headquarters at Ottawa, Ontario. Showler was assigned to the RCAF Station at Goose Bay, Labrador, in 1952 as Chief Administrative Officer.

Two years later, he was appointed Commanding Officer of 408 Photo Squadron at Rockcliffe, Ontario. The main task of the squadron was the SHORAN (Short Range Aid to Navigation) survey and photography of Canada. SHORAN is basically an electronic distance-measuring device, consisting of both airborne and ground radar equipment. Through its use, unknown positions can be mapped accurately.

The SHORAN operation was unique in that completely self-contained stations, each weighing 8,000 pounds (3,600 kg), were airlifted to pre-selected sites, all of which Showler chose by on-the-spot checking. Each station contained three technicians from the squadron, their shelter, housekeeping equipment, fuel, navigation and radio equipment, generators and a 60-foot (18 m) antenna. Precise planning was

required to ensure that the thousands of items of equipment could be pre-positioned by sea or aircraft. During the 1957 program, more than 100,000 pounds (45,000 kg) of technical gear and more than 250 personnel were airlifted to Thule, Greenland, and Resolute Bay on Cornwallis Island.

Showler's personal drive and ability to accurately assess the capabilities of his men and equipment were largely responsible for the success of the 1957 Arctic SHORAN program and the completion of the Geodetic Survey of the whole of Canada, a survey program begun in 1949. For this achievement, he was awarded the Trans-Canada (McKee) Trophy for 1957.

Showler retired from the service in 1961 after a four year tenure as Director of Transport and Rescue Operations at Ottawa. He established a tourist business at Portland, Ontario, which he operated for several years. In 1973 he retired permanently to Brentwood Bay, British Columbia. He died on August 28, 1989.

John Gavin (Jack) Showler was inducted as a Member of Canada's Aviation Hall of Fame in 1974.

On the Greenland icecap, about 160 miles (260 km) north of Thule. W/C Showler is shown here ready to leave the SHORAN station, taking only the 3-man crew, SHORAN sets, radios and records. Shortly before take-off, a lone Greenland Inuit appeared, apparently to claim the materials left behind. Without spoken language, the handshake seals the deal.

"His role in aerially mapping this nation's Arctic frontier has been of outstanding benefit to Canadian aviation." —Induction citation, 1974

Thomas William (Tommy) Siers

(1896 – 1979)

Thomas William (Tommy) Siers was born in Dewsbury, Yorkshire, England, on May 13, 1896. He came to Canada in 1913 to live in Winnipeg, Manitoba. In 1917 he enlisted in the Lord Strathcona Horse Regiment of the Canadian Army, and served in England and France until war's end in 1918. After returning to Canada, he completed several technical school courses.

He began his career servicing aircraft engines and equipment with the Canadian Air Force in 1920, where he earned his Air Engineer Certificate. He went to work for the Canadian Air Board at Winnipeg and northern Manitoba, maintaining their flying boats. Two years later he joined Laurentide Air Services Limited as an air engineer, leaving the same year to work for Huff-Daland Aero Corporation in Ogdensburg, New York, on aircraft assembly and motors. In 1924 he joined the Ontario Provincial Air Service (OPAS, Belt of Orion 1991) at Sault Ste. Marie, Ontario.

In 1928 Siers joined Western Canada Airways at Winnipeg as Chief Mechanic. The following year he was promoted to Superintendent of Maintenance, in charge of overhauling and servicing engines, aircraft and related equipment. During his early years with the company, commercial air transportation in Canada emerged to become a vital factor in the country's

Tommy Siers has been recognized for other outstanding contributions to aircraft operations, including improvements to skis, ski pedestals, ski harness, cabin heaters, and methods of heating engines in extremely cold weather.

"His consummate skills with aircraft, painstakingly developed during almost four decades in the cruelest of geographic arenas and applied with invention and determination, have been of outstanding benefit to Canadian aviation."

—Induction citation, 1974

growth. However, most commercial aircraft in use in Canada were not designed specifically to meet the requirements of the Canadian climate, and had to be modified to overcome problems that arose.

While working for Western Canada Airways, Siers became known for his expertise in modifying parts of aircraft to adapt them to northern flying. His pioneering work on the development of the Worth principle of oil dilution for aircraft engines was, perhaps, the most valuable of his contributions to the aircraft industry and to the exploration of the Arctic by aircraft. Once the oil dilution system was perfected, pilots were able to thin the engine oil with gasoline to make cold weather starting easier.

In the fall of 1929, when the MacAlpine expedition of eight people was reported missing somewhere in the Arctic, a search party using several aircraft was organized. Siers was placed in charge of the mechanics responsible for maintaining these aircraft during the extensive search period. Members of the search teams were dogged by bad weather, breakdowns, and problems caused by seasonal change when landings were not safe using either skis or floats. Often they required rescuing themselves, and suffered from the extremely cold temperatures.

During this search, Siers' resourcefulness became legendary. He repaired punctured floats, broken skis and ski struts, often creating new parts from materials carried in the aircraft or found locally. When Fokker G-CASQ broke through the sea ice at Bathurst Inlet on the Arctic Ocean, it sank nose first, until the leading edge of the wing touched the ice. It was essential that this machine be removed from the salt water as quickly as possible and in as good condition as possible, for the only way to get it back to Winnipeg was by flying it there. Working without protection from the extreme cold, Siers and his crew salvaged 'SQ, completely overhauled the engine and had it operational ten days later.

Hall of Fame Chairman C.L. 'Punch' Dickins places a pin on Tommy Siers' lapel at his induction as a Member of Canada's Aviation Hall of Fame. 1974.

When Canadian Airways Limited absorbed Western Canada Airways in 1936, Siers remained with the new firm and had a diverse array of commercial aircraft under his supervision. He received the Trans-Canada (McKee) Trophy for the year 1940, in recognition of his adaptation of the Worth oil-dilution system to cold weather flying in Canada. The following year he was loaned to the Department of Munitions and Supply for one year to supervise aircraft overhaul. It was largely due to his efforts that an advanced course was offered at the University of Manitoba to improve the efficiency of air engineers.

In 1942, when Canadian Pacific Airlines (CPA) acquired Canadian Airways, Siers took on additional responsibilities with his appointment as General Supervisor of Repair Plants for CPA at Montreal. He was transferred to Vancouver and appointed Assistant to the Director of Maintenance and Engineering. He retired in 1961, and died in Vancouver on May 20, 1979.

Thomas William (Tommy) Siers was inducted as a Member of Canada's Aviation Hall of Fame in 1974.

Arthur George (Tim) Sims

(1907 – 1982)

Arthur George (Tim) Sims was born in London, England, on January 22, 1907. He was educated at University College School before coming to Canada in 1927. He spent the next four years working for Canadian Wright Limited and its associated company, British Aeroplane Engines Limited at Montreal, Quebec, in the assembly, overhaul and testing of their engines. He later became technical representative, visiting operators across Canada.

Because of his extensive knowledge of low-temperature engine operation, he was loaned to Commercial Airways of Edmonton for the inaugural airmail flight from Fort McMurray, Alberta, to Aklavik on the Arctic Ocean, in 1929. He flew as mechanic with W.R. 'Wop' May (Hall of Fame 1974) in a Wright-powered Bellanca on this 1,600 mile (2,575 km) trip down the Mackenzie River.

During this period Sims earned his Air Engineer's A & C Certificate, and qualified for a Commercial Pilot's Certificate in Montreal. He also completed a Royal Canadian Air Force navigation and night flying course at Camp Borden, Ontario. In 1931 he joined the Trans-Canada Air Pageant which toured Canada as a showcase for the latest in Canadian civil and military aircraft. Sims' role in the tour was as an expert on the highly respected Wright aircraft engine.

In 1932 he flew for Northern Skyways at Rouyn, Quebec, as a bush pilot, and earned

'Tim' Sims enjoyed aviation history and writing about aviation. During his retirement, he devoted much time to both. As well, he served on the National Aviation Museum Committee.

"The application of his exceptional skills as an aero-engine expert and his laudatory service as a wartime Ferry Command pilot, despite adversity, have been of outstanding benefit to Canadian aviation." —Induction citation, 1974

A.G. 'Tim' Sims at the freight door of a Fairchild 82 which he flew for Newfoundland Skyways. 1936.

the Air Engineer's D Certificate. The following year he was co-founder, with C.R. Troup, of Dominion Skyways, operating in northern Ontario, Quebec and Labrador. During 1936-37, while he was Chief Pilot and Manager of Newfoundland Skyways, an associated company, he organized and carried out the transportation of geologists and prospectors seeking gold in the interior of Labrador. No gold was found there, but large iron ore deposits were discovered on the Labrador-Quebec border at Knob Lake (now called Schefferville).

Until 1938 he flew the Canadian Shield area of eastern Canada on freighting and passenger contracts to mining operations. This seven-year, accident-free bush operation testified to the aerial competence of Sims and his crews. During this period, he completed an instrument-flying course at the Boeing School of Aeronautics at Burbank, California. He was hired as Vice-President for Aero Engines of Canada Limited at Montreal because of his extensive knowledge of aircraft engines. At the same time he flew as test pilot for Canadian Vickers Limited.

The Government of Canada seconded Sims in 1940 to the Department of Munitions and Supply at Ottawa as Director of Engine and Propeller Overhaul. He was appointed to the National Research Council Aero Engine Committee. During this period, he also test-flew military designated aircraft.

From 1942 until war's end in 1945 he flew military aircraft across the Atlantic and Pacific Oceans to the United Kingdom, Australia, Egypt, India and West Africa, for the Royal Air Force Ferry Command.

Sims then obtained his Transport Pilot's Licence and Instrument Rating. During 1946-47, he flew a Bristol Freighter on a 40,000 mile (64,000 km) demonstration flight throughout North and South America, followed by charter freight operations in Venezuela and Labrador.

From 1948 to 1964, he worked as sales representative for Canadair Limited at Montreal. For the first two years he led the North Star aircraft sales teams to the United Kingdom, South Africa and Italy. He was then appointed Service Manager and given responsibility of support programs for the Canadair-built F-86 Sabre and T-33 jet aircraft in Canada, United Kingdom, France, West Germany, Greece, Turkey and Colombia. He was appointed Director of the Air Industries and Transport Association.

Sims was promoted to Director of Military Aircraft Sales for Canadair in 1955, providing liaison with the RCAF, RAF, British Army, U.S. Air Force and U.S. Navy. He held this position until he retired in 1964. He died at Clearwater, Florida, on January 26, 1982.

Arthur George (Tim) Sims was inducted as a Member of Canada's Aviation Hall of Fame in 1974.

John Charles (Jaycee) Sloan

(1924 – 1983)

John Charles (Jaycee) Sloan, C.D.*, was born in Rockburn, Quebec, on April 11, 1924. He was educated there and at Ormstown, Quebec, from where he enlisted in the Royal Canadian Air Force (RCAF) in 1942. His outstanding abilities as a pilot earned him a promotion to Flying Officer and a posting to instructional duties. Hoping to see active service, he transferred to the Royal Navy (RN) early in 1945 and joined what was to become Canada's first naval fighter squadron. In September 1945, he transferred to the Royal Canadian Navy (RCN), and was promoted to Lieutenant in the permanent forces.

For two years Sloan served with 803 Squadron as an operational pilot from both shore bases and afloat until he was assigned to additional flight training with the Royal Navy in England. His outstanding flying abilities and grasp of modern operational flying concepts were recognized, and he was appointed to the staff of the Canadian Directorate of Naval Aircraft. In 1949 his completion of an instrument flying course at Centralia, Ontario, was followed by appointment to the Empire Test Pilot's course in England.

In 1951 the United States Navy (USN) requested Sloan's services as a test pilot and

J.C. Sloan's flying experience includes command time on 48 aircraft types, from single to four-engined aircraft and helicopters. He had more than 300 carrier deck landings to his credit, 80 of them at night. When he retired from the service, he commanded a most sophisticated and still-secret air experimental squadron.

"His record can be matched only by those airmen of high endeavor and professional calling, who have devoted their lives and skills to the benefit of the free world, despite adversity, and whose contributions have substantially benefited Canadian aviation." —Induction citation, 1974

liaison officer. For the next three years he experimented with the most sophisticated and fastest jet fighters known, at the USN Test Centre at Patuxent River, Maryland, U.S.A. He later carried out duties as executive officer of an all-weather, single-seat, night fighter squadron with the USN Sixth Fleet in the Mediterranean Sea, and was promoted to Lieutenant Commander. In 1952, while preparing to conduct tactical test evaluations of night refueling techniques with test leader, Alan B. Shepard, who later became an astronaut, his jet aircraft caught fire just ten miles (16 km) out and at 3,500 feet (1,070 m) above sea level. He ejected at low level over the water and and was able to swim ashore. After completing that tour of duty he returned to Canadian service in 1954 and was assigned duties as Communications Officer aboard a destroyer in Korean waters.

His next assignment, in 1955, was Air Staff Officer, Atlantic Command, at Halifax, Nova Scotia, in which he played an important part in formulating training and operational plans for submission to RCN Headquarters. During this period he was seriously injured when the engine of a fighter aircraft he was piloting failed on take-off. After a year's hospitalization and recuperation, he was back flying and in command of VX-10 Experimental Squadron, a post he held until 1959, when he again went to sea as Executive Officer of a frigate in North Atlantic waters. His squadron's performance during that period was officially commended by the Board of the Royal Canadian Navy and the United States Chief of Naval Operations.

In 1961 Sloan was promoted to the post of Naval Air Staff Officer in Ottawa, Ontario. His evaluations of command requirements and his initiative in tackling the formulation of new defence weapons and their deployment, resulted in another appointment in 1964, as Special Weapons Co-ordinator at National Defence Headquarters in Ottawa. There he prepared studies concerning the relative

J.C. Sloan climbing into a Tactical test McDonnell 'Banshee' at United States Navy Test Centre at Patuxent River, Maryland, U.S.A. 1952.

effectiveness of various weapons in both air and sea environments. He worked directly with several government departments and travelled extensively to effect liaison with U.S. and other North Atlantic Treaty Organization (NATO) governments and military agencies.

Sloan retired from the RCN in 1968 with the rank of Lieutenant Commander, after twenty five years of military flying. For a time he became a demonstration pilot and aviation consultant. He died on December 26, 1983.

John Charles (Jaycee) Sloan was inducted as a Member of Canada's Aviation Hall of Fame in 1974.

Elvie Lawrence Smith

(b. 1926)

Elvie Lawrence Smith, C.M., B.Sc., M.Sc., D.Eng. (Hon), LL.D. (Hon), D.Sc. (Hon), was born in Eatonia, Saskatchewan, on January 8, 1926. He graduated from the University of Saskatchewan with a Bachelor of Science in Mechanical Engineering (with Great Distinction) in 1947. He earned his Master of Science degree at Purdue University in Indiana. While at Purdue he pursued his other interest, flying, and qualified for his Private Pilot's Licence.

Smith spent five years at the National Research Council (NRC) as Research Engineer in its engine laboratory. He worked on projects dealing with gas turbine anti-icing and thrust boosting, as well as research on after-burning. He was the principal engineer involved in the development of a unique system where the after-burner fuel was sprayed directly into the turbine blades to reduce their temperature, and then burned in the after-burner downstream of the turbine. During his last two years with the NRC, he was seconded to the Flight Research Section where he was the Project Manager carrying out the testing of these after-burners on a Gloster Meteor and a Canadair F-86 Sabre.

He joined Pratt & Whitney Aircraft of Canada (P&WC) in January 1957, as an Analytical Engineer and a key member

Elvie Smith maintains his love for flying. He holds a multi-engine Instrument Flight Rules (IFR) rating, a float endorsement as well as glider instructor rating. He is the fourth Canadian to hold the Gold C badge in gliding. He also flies regular aerobatic routines in a Yak 55M.

"His vision, dedication and leadership in the design, development, and manufacture of gas turbine engines, from both the technical and managerial aspects, has been of lasting benefit to Canadian aviation."

—Induction citation, 1993

Col. (Ret.) James Young, founding President of Pratt & Whitney Company, being briefed about the PT6 gas turbine engine by Elvie Smith, Engineering Manager. 1964.

of a team assembled to initiate the design, development and manufacture of gas turbine engines. Initially, he examined engines in the 1,500 to 2,000 shaft horse-power (shp) category and then the team began work on the development of an engine for the new, light Canadair CL-41 Jet Trainer, the Tutor. The JT-12 engine, although rejected for the CL-41, was further developed by Pratt & Whitney at Hartford, U.S.A., and proved successful.

In 1958 Smith toured a number of airframe companies with other members of the P&WC team, promoting a small turbine engine. At Beech Aircraft it was learned that a cabin class aircraft had just flown and that Beech was interested in gas turbine engines. The team returned to Montreal and redesigned the engine from its initial rating of 350 shp rating to 450 shp to meet Beech's requirements. That engine was the PT6, and today it is the most successful and highest-production gas turbine engine in commercial aviation history. The latest models produce nearly 2,000 shp.

By 1961, Smith was responsible for all gas turbine development and activity at

P&WC. In 1962, as Engineering Manager, his responsibility covered all engineering activities. In 1966 he was named Vice-President, Engineering, and in 1970, Vice-President, Operations. During the next eight years he oversaw the growth of engineering and manufacturing activity, and the continued development of a number of P&WC gas turbine engines. These engines set world standards for design excellence and dependability in all types of environments. In 1978 he was appointed P&WC's Executive Vice-President, Operations, and in March 1980, President and Chief Executive Officer. Smith's interest in engineering education and research promoted cooperation between P&WC and advanced educational institutions. He also increased the company's budget for Research and Development.

During the following years, markets were enlarged and production reached 3,300 gas turbine engines per year, making P&WC the world's largest producer of small aircraft gas turbine engines. These engines are now used in more than 150 countries and power more than 140 types of aircraft. In 1984 Smith was made Chairman of the Board and Chief Executive Officer. He retired from active management in 1987, but remained Chairman of the Board until 1994.

He was awarded several Honorary Doctorates in recognition of his leadership in the field of engineering. These included: Doctor of Laws (Concordia, 1983), Doctor of Engineering (Carleton, 1984), Doctor of Engineering (Purdue, 1987), and Doctor of Science (Saskatchewan, 1997).

Smith is a Fellow of the Canadian Aeronautics and Space Institute (CASI) from which he received the McCurdy and C.D. Howe Awards in 1973 and 1983 respectively. Other awards for his work include: the Thomas W. Eadie Medal of the Royal Society of Canada, the Gold Medal of the Polish Peoples Republic, the American Society of Mechanical Engineers R. Tom Sawyer Award (all awarded in 1985). In 1992 he was appointed a Member of the Order of Canada (C.M.). In 1994 he was awarded the Society of Automotive Engineers (SAE) Aerospace Engineering Leadership Award.

Elvie Lawrence Smith was inducted as a Member of Canada's Aviation Hall of Fame in 1993.

Franklin Ernest William (Frank) Smith

(1913 – 1996)

Franklin Ernest William (Frank) Smith, D.F.C., A.F.C., was born in Calgary, Alberta, on April 22, 1913. His family moved to Vancouver, British Columbia, in 1922. He entered the University of British Columbia in 1929 to take advantage of the Provisional Pilot Officer course with the Royal Canadian Air Force (RCAF) that was offered to selected undergraduates in Applied Science. He trained on the Cirrus Moth in the summer of 1931 at Camp Borden, Ontario. However, the course was discontinued in 1932 and he was not involved with aviation again until World War II.

Smith joined the RCAF in August of 1940 and graduated with a Pilot Officer commission in May of 1941, through the British Commonwealth Air Training Plan (BCATP). He became an instructor following training at Patricia Bay on Vancouver Island, British Columbia. In 1942 he was posted to 12 Communications Squadron, Rockcliffe, Ontario, as the full

Smith was an accomplished writer. An early work, titled "A Lexicon for Airline Pilots", sought to define and outline a pilot's profession. He wrote The First Thirty Years—a History of CALPA, published in 1970. He was a regular contributor to Canadian aviation publications. He was also a well known public speaker, and in 1977 he was retained by Air Canada to help publicize their 40th Anniversary, and in that capacity appeared in major cities across Canada.

"His pioneering efforts with IFR flying with the RCAF, his service to Air Canada and to the Canadian Air Line Pilots Association combined with his abilities to preserve aviation history in written form have all been of outstanding benefit to Canadian aviation." —Induction citation, 1998

Frank Smith being congratulated after receiving his Air Force Cross from Viscount Alexander. 1945.

time instructor of Instrument Flight Rules (IFR) in the RCAF, being himself trained by Z.L. Leigh (Hall of Fame 1974) and M. Kennedy (Hall of Fame 1979). Smith subsequently trained most of the original pilots for 164 and 165 Transport Squadrons.

In 1943 Smith was named Commander of 165 Squadron's detachment in Edmonton, Alberta. This detachment supplied the RCAF units along the North West Staging Route and elsewhere in the north. The Staging Route roughly followed the route of the Alaska Highway, and was used primarily to ferry warplanes to Alaska and Russia in defence of the North in the early 1940's. Smith organized a daily scheduled service from Edmonton to Whitehorse and operated supply charters to the Staging Posts, including Aishihik and Snag in the Yukon, and down the Mackenzie River to Fort Simpson and Norman Wells, Northwest Territories.

This unit flew IFR and developed a good reputation for all-weather operations. At that time, there were no route or approach charts for those northern areas. Smith drew up his own, which he had photoprinted for his pilots. As they were the best and most accurate of any in the area, the detachment was soon selling them to other pilots working in the north. This business prospered until the first Canada Air Pilot charts were published by the Ministry of Transport in 1944. He was awarded the Air Force Cross (A.F.C.) and promoted to Squadron Leader for his leadership and organization, and for the hazardous airdrops he made to mountain troops training on the north flank of Mount Edith Cavell near Jasper, Alberta.

Late in 1944, Smith became Flight Commander of 436 Operational Transport Squadron in India and Burma. This Squadron was based first at the Kangla strip in the Imphal Valley, India, then at Akyab, and finally Ramree Island—the wettest place on the Arakan Coast, on the Bay of Bengal. He was the only IFR qualified pilot in the squadron and convinced the Commanding Officer that it was much safer to fly using instruments through the monsoon clouds than to fly the valleys visually. This enabled the unit to fly 1,000 hours a month more than any other squadron in the Combat Cargo Task Force, and without the heavy losses the others were experiencing. It was through his inspiration that a weather reporting aircraft, code named 'Watchbird', flown by himself and the Commanding Officer, would guide the squadron's aircraft through the heavy weather and promote confidence in instrument flight. During this tour of duty, Smith was awarded the Distinguished Flying Cross (D.F.C.).

Smith returned to Canada in September 1945, and resigned from the RCAF. He then joined Trans-Canada Airlines (TCA, Hall of Fame 1974) in 1946 at Winnipeg, Manitoba, and after his initial training, was assigned to Vancouver. He accumulated nearly 19,000 hours in the service of TCA, which was renamed Air Canada (AC) in 1965.

He retired from AC in 1973 at age 60, and flew for Air Jamaica until mid-1976, accumulating another 2,200 hours. While with Air Jamaica he assisted management and published their flight operations periodical.

Throughout his career, Smith was active in the Canadian Air Line Pilots Association (CALPA, Belt of Orion 1988), holding executive offices continually from 1950 to 1963. For three years he edited and published the Association's quarterly magazine, The Pilot. In 1976 he was awarded CALPA's Ken Wright Trophy for outstanding leadership and professionalism, and was made a Life Member of that organization in 1978. He organized and became the founding president of CALPA for Retired Air Line Pilots in 1976.

He was active in a number of other organizations, including the British Columbia Aviation Council, the Quarter Century in Aviation Club, the Vancouver Air Force Officer's Association and the Burma Star Association. In September 1977, he was awarded the Air Canada Award of Merit for his outstanding contributions to aviation and to that airline. He died at Delta, British Columbia, on March 26, 1996.

Franklin Ernest William Smith was inducted as a Member of Canada's Aviation Hall of Fame in 1998.

Ernest Walter Stedman

(1888 – 1957)

Ernest Walter Stedman, C.B., O.B.E., was born in Malling, Kent, England, on July 23, 1888. He attended boarding school in Kent, followed by four years of practical training at H.M. Dockyard Sheerness Apprentice School. He was accepted at the Royal College of Science, London, as a Whitworth Scholar, and completed his formal education in 1911.

For the next two years Stedman was employed as a draftsman on marine engines and taught evening classes in engineering subjects at Hartley University. As a result of a general interest in aviation and a visit to the National Physical Laboratories at Teddington where he saw experimental work being done in a wind tunnel, he applied for a position. He was hired as a Junior Scientific Assistant in 1913 and spent a year engaged in pioneer work in aerodynamics.

With the advent of World War I, he began work in the Design Branch of the Air Department of the Admiralty, attached to the Royal Naval Air Service (RNAS). His engineering abilities were soon recognized and he held a number of appointments related to aircraft design during the war. In 1918 he transferred to the Royal Air Force (RAF) and assumed command of an

In 1919 E.W. Stedman came to Harbour Grace, Newfoundland, as the engineer in charge of the Handley-Page bomber that was competing for the Daily Mail prize of $10,000 for the first non-stop Trans-Atlantic flight—a prize which was won by Alcock and Brown in a Vickers Vimy bomber on June 14.

A twin-engined Handley Page V/1500 aircraft 'Atlantic' during trials before being shipped to Newfoundland to compete in the race for the first successful trans-Atlantic flight. Cricklewood, England, April, 1919.

CREDIT: NATIONAL ARCHIVES OF CANADA PA-121815

Aircraft Repair Depot in France. Later, he worked on applied design in the Air Ministry, where he remained until 1919. For his dedication and contributions to the technical development of the aeroplane, Lieutenant-Colonel Stedman was appointed an Officer of the Order of the British Empire (O.B.E., Military).

He immigrated to Canada in 1920 and was appointed to the Technical Branch of Canada's Air Board for the control of aeronautics. In 1922 he established the Aircraft Inspection Department at Camp Borden, Ontario which was responsible for the airworthiness of all aircraft in Canada. He transferred to the Canadian Air Force in May 1922, where he, as Wing Commander, provided direction to the research and development of better and safer aircraft and the regulations which govern their design. He prepared a critical report for the RAF that compared aircraft and engines of various countries. It recognized the need to develop an advantageous speed differential for British aircraft, recommendations which had far reaching effects. The Supermarine Company developed racers which won the seaplane race for the Schneider Cup. The new, streamlined design for this aircraft was the basis for the development of the Spitfire.

With the reorganization of Canada's Department of National Defence in 1927, an Aeronautical Engineering Division headed by Stedman was formed to serve the RCAF, the Civil Air Operations Branch, and the Controller of Civil Aviation. For thirteen years in this capacity he contributed to the advancement of aeronautical research and aircraft maintenance.

From 1939 Stedman was actively involved in the rapid expansion of the RCAF to meet its operational wartime commitments, as well as the varied technical requirements of the British Commonwealth Air Training Plan (BCATP). He rose through the Officer ranks and was promoted to Air Vice-Marshal in 1940. He is credited with the foresight to recommend the purchase of helicopters for search and rescue, radar aids for pilots and the entry of Canada into the field of jet propulsion. He was at the centre of every major technical development in which the RCAF was involved, including the development of Canada's first jet engine by Orenda, a subsidiary of Avro Canada Ltd.

His contributions to Canadian aviation have been recognized by numerous honours. In 1939 he received the Julian C. Smith Memorial Medal from the Engineering Institute of Canada; in 1944 he was appointed a Companion of the Most Honourable Order of the Bath (C.B.), and in 1945 he received the Legion of Merit of the United States in the Degree of Commander. He was awarded the prestigious Daniel Guggenheim Medal for excellence in the field of engineering and science.

Following his retirement from the service in 1946, Stedman was appointed Assistant Professor in the Engineering Department of Carleton College, Ottawa. His well-rounded career has been thoroughly described in his memoirs, "From Boxkite to Jet", which were completed shortly before his death in Ottawa on March 27, 1957.

Ernest Walter Stedman was inducted as a Member of Canada's Aviation Hall of Fame in 1982.

Alexander Mackay (Mickey) Sutherland

(1910 – 1993)

Alexander Mackay (Mickey) Sutherland was born in Edmonton, Alberta, on December 30, 1910, and educated there. In the fall of 1927 he joined the Edmonton and Northern Alberta Aero Club and received flight instruction from W.R. 'Wop' May and M. 'Moss' Burbidge (both Hall of Fame 1974). He obtained his Private Pilot's Licence in December of 1929 and his Air Engineer's Licence in 1931.

He was employed by Spence McDonough Air Transport as an Air Engineer in the summer of 1931, operating from their base at Fort McMurray, Alberta, into the Northwest Territories, northern Manitoba and Ontario. He participated in many flights north, as far as Coppermine on the Arctic Ocean, and Great Bear Lake, delivering prospectors and supplies.

During one of these trips in 1933, Sutherland and pilot Bill Spence were landing their Fairchild CF-AAO at a camp on the Camsell River in a heavy overcast. They spotted the so-called run-way marked on both sides with spruce boughs, but in the whiteness they could not see snow

Air Engineers in the north were famous for their ingenuity in repairing broken aircraft. Sometimes repairs were made from materials found on shore or at a prospector's camp. Occasionally materials would be found among the supplies being flown to a customer, as on the trip when Sutherland used a mining company's forge and some steel runners to repair a badly damaged landing gear.

"His adventurous spirit, innovative mind and ability to function under the most severe conditions while opening the Canadian north were of benefit to Canadian aviation."

—Induction citation, 1991

Air Engineer A.M. 'Mickey' Sutherland loading furs onto Canadian Airways plane at McMurray, Alberta. The bale he is holding is destined for London, England. c. 1934.

piled in 3 – 4 foot (1 m) drifts. On impact, the undercarriage broke off and the propeller was badly damaged. They managed to jack up the aircraft, and with great ingenuity, Sutherland rebuilt the undercarriage, and repaired the propeller by sawing six inches off one tip to make it match the damaged one, all in –50°F (–46°C) weather.

Early in 1934 Sutherland joined Canadian Airways Limited in Winnipeg, Manitoba, where he worked as air mechanic for pilot Z. Lewis Leigh (Hall of Fame 1974), operating out of their Fort McMurray base and north as far as Great Bear Lake. Together they made particularly difficult trips to Windy Lake in the Northwest Territories with prospectors, followed by many loads of supplies. They were then sent to Great Bear Lake to operate their aircraft on skis until they could fly out on floats in June. On one occasion, Sutherland made a difficult change-over from skis to floats on a stony beach.

Sutherland teamed up with many well-known bush pilots who operated out of Fort McMurray, including 'Wop' May,

Archie McMullen, C.H. 'Punch' Dickins (all Hall of Fame 1974) and Rudy Huess. While on one flight with May, he noticed movement in one of the upper cylinders of the engine. An emergency landing was made and Sutherland carried out a cylinder change, including studs, which allowed them to return to base.

Canadian Airways' Chief Pilot Walter Gilbert (Hall of Fame 1974) asked him to move to their Prince Albert, Saskatchewan, base, as Chief Mechanic. On one occasion in 1936, in what was planned to be the last trip before freeze-up, Sutherland was in a float-equipped Fairchild with pilot Bill Windrum when they ran into a blinding snowstorm on their way to Goldfields, Saskatchewan. They landed on a lake near Lake Athabasca, but when they awoke in the morning, they found about six inches (15 cm) of slush on the surface of the lake, the heavy snowfall continuing, and the temperature dropping rapidly to –30°F (–33°C). The floats were beginning to freeze into the ice on shore. They managed to free the floats, and took off from the ice as quickly as possible.

On another occasion the oleo-leg to fuselage fitting on a Lockheed Vega was seriously damaged by a snow-covered rock during a ski equipped take-off from Lac la Ronge. He managed to make a good repair using a welding outfit and some metal straps that were flown in from the base.

Sutherland's bush-flying career ended in the fall of 1937 when he began a long career with Trans-Canada Airlines (TCA, Hall of Fame 1974). He was involved in establishing sub-bases and line stations, and assisted in the design of hangars and shops. He became Director of Maintenance and Overhaul, and from 1940 to 1945, he assisted in the maintenance and overhaul of aircraft and components for Air Training Command.

In February 1953, Sutherland joined Slick Airways, a freight airline, in Burbank, California, as Director of Engineering and Maintenance. He was hired by Douglas Aircraft where his responsibility was to help design the DC-9 for low maintenance requirements. He traveled around the world in connection with the DC-9 and DC-10. He retired from Douglas Aircraft in 1975, after forty eight years in aviation. He died on February 28, 1993.

Alexander Mackay (Mickey) Sutherland was inducted as a Member of Canada's Aviation Hall of Fame in 1991.

Claude Ivan Taylor
(b. 1925)

Claude Ivan Taylor, O.C., D.C.L. (Hon), LL.D. (Hon), was born in Salisbury, New Brunswick, on May 20, 1925, where he obtained his early education. He attended McGill University's Extension Department, graduating as a Registered Industrial Accountant in 1953.

Taylor joined Trans-Canada Airlines (TCA, Hall of Fame 1974) as a reservations agent in Moncton in 1949. At that time, the airline had just added Canadian-built North Stars to its fleet of DC-3's and moved its headquarters from Winnipeg to Montreal. He moved to Montreal, Quebec, as a Clerk for the airline in 1951. A number of promotions followed, placing him in various administrative positions. On January 1, 1965, the airline had a new look and a new name: Air Canada. By 1973 Taylor was named Vice-President, Public Affairs.

In February 1976, Taylor was appointed President and Chief Executive Officer and Director. He became Chairman of the Board in June 1984. In August of 1990 he assumed the additional duties of President

One of Claude Taylor's goals when he became President of Air Canada was to cut the large deficit the airline had accumulated. He oversaw the reorganization of the airline following the passing of the Air Canada Act in 1977, which made it a Crown Corporation, with greater freedom to conduct its operations. Under the terms of the Act, the federal Government allowed Air Canada to write down a large portion of its long-term debt.

"The unselfish dedication of his great leadership and administrative abilities in the service of his nation and of his company have been of outstanding benefit to Canadian aviation."

—Induction citation, 1985.

Claude Taylor, right, receives a framed certificate as an Honorary Director of Canada's Aviation Hall of Fame from Chairman Elvie Smith at the 1998 Induction in Montreal.

and Chief Executive Officer. In February 1992, he reverted to his former position of Chairman of the Board.

Long an advocate of the privatization of Air Canada he was successful in persuading the Government of Canada to privatize the airline in two stages—49% in 1987, followed by 100% privatization in 1988.

Taylor served on the Executive Committee of the International Air Transport

Association (IATA) and was President of IATA for the 1979-80 term. He was presented with the First Industry Service Award for his work in 1978 in developing the new IATA membership structure. He was the Founding Chairman of the International Aviation Management Training Institute and is today its Honorary Chairman. He continues to serve on a number of Boards and is Governor Emeritus of Concordia University. He was made an Officer of the Order of Canada (O.C.) in 1986, and is a Commander in the Order of St. John of Jerusalem (C.St.J.). He holds an Honorary Doctorate of Civil Law from the University of New Brunswick and an Honorary Doctorate of Laws from McMaster University.

Taylor has received numerous awards; among them the Royal Canadian Air Force Gordon R. McGregor Trophy in 1980, the Human Relations Award from the Canadian Council of Christians and Jews, the B'nai Brith Canada Award of Merit, the Silver Wolf Award for Services of the Most Exceptional Character to Scouting and the C.D. Howe Award for Leadership in Aeronautics and Space. In 1993 he was awarded the Salvation Army Order of Distinguished Service Cross. In 1996 the Western Canada Aviation Museum recognized him as a Pioneer in Canadian Aviation.

In 1993 he was named Chairman Emeritus of Air Canada and continues to be a member of the Board, the Corporate Governance and Nominating Committee, and the Pension Investment Policy Committee.

Claude Ivan Taylor was inducted as a Member of Canada's Aviation Hall of Fame in 1985.

Harold (Rex) Terpening

(b. 1913)

Harold (Rex) Terpening was born on July 23, 1913, in Wainwright, Alberta, and moved to the Fort McMurray area of northern Alberta at an early age. The educational facilities at that frontier village were meager but fortunately a school program was soon offered.

Fort McMurray became the base for several early aviation companies and there were many opportunities to learn the skills required of a maintenance engineer. By working without pay, Terpening obtained ample experience on every type of maintenance and repair procedure that could be carried out in the field. Only part-time jobs existed and these he augmented by trapping, cordwood cutting, and working on the river boats. Thus he survived until he could qualify for his Air Engineer's Licence and obtain permanent employment with Canadian Airways Limited in 1935.

For the next several years Terpening flew as air engineer with many well known pilots throughout the Canadian Arctic. These were the beginning years for aviation in the north, with the equipment untried, the facilities primitive, and the terrain unmapped and largely uninhabited—a time of hardship and hazard for all.

Following retirement, Terpening has endeavored to preserve, with text and photographs, some record of the early aviation history of the north during the bush flying days of the 1930's. Several of these stories have been published in Canada's leading aviation historical magazines.

"With innovative ability, resolution and courage, in the most arduous situations, he kept the early aircraft flying. His skills as an air engineer, and later as a manager, span the history of aviation from the earliest bush operations to the modern jet era, and are of significant benefit to transport aviation in Canada."

—Induction citation, 1997

Rex Terpening as a young air engineer. c. 1934.

In November of 1934, Terpening and Canadian Airways pilot Rudy Huess broke through the ice with a fully loaded aircraft. Extricating the passenger who was trapped between the load and the roof, Terpening forced open the cabin door and they made their escape.

In 1936, on a trip with Matt Berry (Hall of Fame 1974), their aircraft was severely damaged during a desperate landing in fog and darkness at Fort Good Hope. Poor visibility caused them to collide with a pile of gas drums, breaking one ski, twisting the ski pedestal, bending the propeller and tearing out fuselage cross-members. Temporary repairs in order to ferry the plane to Fort McMurray required a week. Temperatures were below –60°F (–51°C).

Also in 1936, Terpening and Berry flew a Junkers to isolated Paulatuk, 400 miles east of Aklavik, to bring out Bishop Falaize and his party, marooned when their schooner was caught in early ice between Coppermine and Letty Harbour. To make matters worse for the small group, most of their food supply was lost to pillaging polar bears. After their arrival at Paulatuk, Terpening and Berry were storm-bound for ten days and were becoming increasingly short of fuel, food—and daylight! An attempt to leave Paulatuk on December 14 failed due to white-out conditions. Airborne once again on December 19, they survived a violent landing during another white-out, and the group of six adults and four children spent a bitterly cold night on the Barrens, huddled together in a make-shift shelter under the aircraft. They arrived at Aklavik the following day, December 20, with their fuel exhausted. Years later, Berry called this Paulatuk trip the most hazardous and difficult he had ever experienced.

In November of 1937, Terpening and Huess flew from Edmonton to Aklavik with a load of radio equipment urgently needed in the search for Russian trans-polar pilot Levanevsky and his crew. With the southern rivers still not frozen over, they loaded gasoline into the aircraft cabin, transferring this to the wing tanks in flight. With this added range they were able to reach a safe landing area, after 500 miles of poor visibility and icing conditions.

In 1938 Terpening, assisted by engineer Ted Bowles, was assigned to salvage a Noorduyn Norseman, CF-BAU, damaged near Yellowknife. They lived for five weeks in a tent which was set up to cover the front end of the aircraft, providing shelter while they carried out repairs in temperatures down to –50°F (–46°C).

Following a propeller inflicted injury in 1938, Terpening was transferred by Canadian Airways to Brandon, Manitoba, where he worked with Albert Hutt (Hall of Fame 1992) on developing the first Oil Dilution System. This involved injecting gasoline into the engine oil at shutdown, preventing it from congealing in the cold and making draining unnecessary. It allowed the engine to be re-started without the laborious and risky process of preheating both oil and engine. The system was installed in Junkers CF-AQW, which was then moved to Stevenson Field at Winnipeg, Manitoba, where Terpening carried out the cold weather starting procedures with Tom Siers (Hall of Fame 1974). Numerous equipment modifications followed, but success was finally achieved on February 21, 1939, with the first successful start of a diluted, cold-soaked engine. The system allowed the engine to start at temperatures down to –44°F (–42°C).

In early winter of 1939, Terpening was engineer on a rescue mission to Repulse Bay, located inside the Arctic Circle, 700 miles (1,126 km) north of Churchill, Manitoba. A young priest was suffering with severely frost-bitten hands after falling through thin ice on a hunting trip, and by the time a request for help was received, gangrene was beginning to destroy his right hand. Pilots W.A. Catton and A.J. Hollingsworth left Winnipeg on November 27 in a wheel-equipped Junkers, flying through low and ice-laden clouds to God's Lake, where they changed to skis. They pushed on to Churchill, Eskimo Point, Chesterfield, and finally, to Repulse Bay. Poor visibility and endless blizzards caused agonizing delays. They finally returned to Winnipeg on December 20, after completing the longest emergency flight in the history of the company.

With the start-up of the British Commonwealth Air Training Plan (BCATP) in 1940, Terpening was transferred to No. 2 AOS (Air Observers School) at Edmonton and was tasked with sorting out numerous initial problems of untrained personnel, unfamiliar aircraft and lack of spare parts. In 1941 he became Maintenance Superintendent of the newly-opened No. 7 AOS at Portage la Prairie, Manitoba, and soon developed his department to an award-winning level of efficiency. After one year, Terpening was recalled to airline activities with Canadian Airways at Edmonton. At this time, several small companies, including Canadian Airways, were brought together to form Canadian Pacific Air Lines (CPA), with maintenance under the direction of Albert Hutt.

During the early 1940's, Terpening was assigned to do aerial survey work for the Canol Pipeline Project being developed to bring crude oil from Norman Wells to Whitehorse. The United States Air Force used a twin-engined Douglas C-47 for this work, which proved to be an arduous task, as Terpening's camera position was unheated, there was little shelter from the slipstream and air temperatures were in the –20°F (–6°C) range.

From 1946 to 1950, he was stationed at Regina, Saskatchewan, as District Chief Mechanic, maintaining CPA's Lockheed Lodestar and Douglas DC-3 aircraft. He was later moved to a similar position in Vancouver, British Columbia, in charge of maintenance in the B.C. and Yukon districts, working on aircraft such as the Convair 240 and DC-4, the DC-6B and the Boeing 737.

This was a time of dramatic change for CPA, including a change in name: in 1968 CPA became known as CP Air. The airline dealt with rapid expansion, developing new routes, setting up new field stations, and hiring and training new personnel. There were added responsibilities for Terpening, and he became Manager, Line Maintenance, for the airline.

At the time of his retirement in 1978 he was responsible for maintenance activities for CP Air in western Canada, and for all of its international bases in Europe, Central and South America, the Pacific and the Orient.

Harold (Rex) Terpening was inducted as a Member of Canada's Aviation Hall of Fame in 1997.

Making repairs in the middle of nowhere, with tools laid out on the wind-driven snow. c. 1936.

Samuel Anthony (Sammy) Tomlinson

(1900 – 1973)

Samuel Anthony (Sammy) Tomlinson was born on September 26, 1900, in Willenhall, England, and was educated at Birmingham. At the outbreak of World War I, at age 14, he was apprenticed to the Birmingham Mint as a machinist. Two years later he enlisted in the Royal Flying Corps (RFC) as a Boy Airman and was posted to the RFC station at South Farnborough, where he received his initial air engineer's training and his early flight experience.

In 1917 he was ordered to front line service in France to assemble and repair fighter aircraft and to assist in test-flying evaluations. At war's end he transferred to the Royal Naval Air Station, Martlesham Heath, to work as an engineer on the latest experimental aircraft and there he flew with the foremost British test pilots.

Tomlinson was discharged in 1922 and became associated as an engine expert with boat designer Gar Wood at Grosse Isle, Michigan. He came to Canada in 1924, and joined the Ontario Provincial Air

'Sammy' Tomlinson and a fellow air engineer completed the first Canadian major overhaul of an aircraft engine outside of a repair depot, on the ice at Wilke Lake, Ontario, in 1929. He was recognized as a master of his craft, no matter what the situation. Once, he spent fourteen hours with only a saw-file, hand cutting a new timing gear to successfully repair the disabled aircraft of C.H. 'Punch' Dickins (Hall of Fame 1974), who had been forced down on a northern lake.

"His consummate skills with aircraft, learned from childhood and applied with invention and determination, despite adversity, have been of outstanding benefit to Canadian aviation." —Induction citation, 1974

S.A. 'Sammy' Tomlinson, air engineer, beside a Curtiss Lark flown by H.A. 'Doc' Oaks of Patricia Airways and Exploration Company, Ontario. c. 1926.

Service (OPAS, Belt of Orion 1991) at Sudbury, Ontario, as an Air Engineer on flying boats. He then became a founding partner of Patricia Airways and Exploration Company, with H.A. 'Doc' Oaks (Hall of Fame 1974), serving the Woman Lake and Red Lake areas, carrying supplies, passengers and mail.

When James A. Richardson (Hall of Fame 1976) founded Western Canada Airways in 1926 at Hudson, Ontario, Tomlinson was hired as Chief Mechanic, first at Hudson and then at Sioux Lookout, Ontario, until 1929, when he assumed the same position with the company's prairie air mail division. He served at Winnipeg, Moose Jaw, Edmonton, and Fort McMurray, and three years later was transferred to Lac du Bonnet, Manitoba.

At the outbreak of World War II, Tomlinson joined the Royal Canadian Air Force (RCAF) and served during the Battle of Britain with 2 Canadian Fighter Squadron in England. In 1943 his expertise was requested by No. 8 Repair Depot, RCAF, Winnipeg, where he

commanded the engine test bench and served on the crash investigation board. He was discharged in 1945 with the rank of Warrant Officer First Class.

During his wartime service, Canadian Pacific Airlines (CPA) had absorbed his former company and he was named Chief Mechanic of the new line at Lac du Bonnet, but left two years later to take charge of mechanics for Lamb Airways at Kenora, Ontario. In 1951 he returned to CPA as Chief Mechanic of their Lincoln Park maintenance depot at Calgary, Alberta. He resigned in 1964 to join Austin Airways at Sudbury, Ontario, and two years later retired from aviation.

During a dedicated career that spanned a half-century, Tomlinson maintained the engines and aircraft for many of Canada's early bush pilots, flying with them on many historic flights. He died on October 14, 1973, in Calgary, Alberta.

Samuel Anthony (Sammy) Tomlinson was inducted as a Member of Canada's Aviation Hall of Fame in 1974.

"*The individual roles played by the Company's maintenance personnel and pilots during its formative year, provided an increased safety factor for its passengers, resulting in outstanding benefit to Canadian aviation.*" —Induction citation, 1974

Trans-Canada Airlines

(April 10, 1937)

Trans-Canada Air Lines (TCA) was created on April 10, 1937, by a special Act of Parliament as a wholly-owned subsidiary of the Canadian National Railway Company (CNR), to provide air transportation, freight and mail service to all regions of the country.

From that start, with three small aircraft and fewer than 100 employees, TCA went on to become one of the largest air carriers in the world and a major force within the Canadian economy. With a fleet of two 10-seat Lockheed 10A Electras, the inaugural flight was made between Vancouver, British Columbia, and Seattle, Washington, on September 1, 1937. A Stearman bi-plane was used primarily to survey new routes for the line.

For many years there had been discussion of a trans-continental airline in Canada. It had been anticipated that when the airline was formed, both the Canadian Pacific Railway (CPR) and CNR would be involved. However, when CPR negotiators were unable to agree to the management plan for this airline, they withdrew, leaving the way clear for TCA to be organized as a subsidiary of the CNR. The President of the CNR, S.J. Hungerford, thereby became the first President of TCA, while maintaining the Presidency of the CNR.

The Hon. C.D. Howe (Hall of Fame 1975), who at the time was the Minister of

Among the original group of TCA pilots in early 1938, the following became Members of Canada's Aviation Hall of Fame: W.W. Fowler, H. M. Kennedy, Z. L. Leigh, G.B. Lothian, R.B. Middleton, L. Rood, H.W. Seagrim, and F.I. Young.

The Douglas DC-3 airliner, first purchased by Trans-Canada Airlines in 1945. Between 1945 and 1963, thirty of these aircraft were operated by TCA.

Transport, proved to be the driving force behind the organization of TCA. He set about obtaining the services of several Americans, whom he considered to be highly qualified from their previous backgrounds with U.S. airlines, to serve as technical advisors.

A very significant trans-Canada flight was made on July 30, 1937. It was dubbed the 'dawn-to-dusk' flight and its purpose was to show that the airway was serviceable. It originated in St. Hubert, near Montreal, Quebec, and terminated in Vancouver, taking 17 1/2 hours. The captain was J.H. 'Tuddy' Tudhope (Hall of Fame 1973), with Jack Hunter and Lew Parmenter as additional crew members. The passengers were C.D. Howe, C.P. Edwards, Deputy Minister of Transport, and H.J. Symington, a director of TCA, who later served as President of TCA from 1941-47.

Within a few short years, TCA began to develop a reputation for technical and mechanical excellence. This fact was recognized in 1938 when TCA was awarded the Trans-Canada (McKee) Trophy for the exemplary service provided by the line through the outstanding application of the talents of its engineers and pilots.

Passenger service between Vancouver and Montreal began on April 1, 1939. Two years later, TCA operated the Canadian Government Trans-Atlantic Air Service (CGTAS), providing scheduled flights across the Atlantic Ocean, primarily to assist government services during World War II.

The company's Winnipeg, Manitoba, base continued to play a major role, both in the airline's operation and in the war effort itself. TCA operated an engine and propeller overhaul shop for the Department of Munitions and Supply, where military aircraft components were maintained.

By 1947 the line had grown to be a truly Canadian carrier, linking all of the major centres of the country. New routes through United States' gateways were opened and the basis laid for an international network of flight paths.

Under G.R. McGregor (Hall of Fame 1974), who succeeded to the Presidency in 1948, TCA began to grow rapidly. Service was begun to Bermuda, the Caribbean Islands and Tampa, Florida and trans-Atlantic travel increased as Shannon, London, Paris, and Dusseldorf were added. The line ushered in the era of long-range travel in the 1950's with Lockheed Super Constellation aircraft. It ran the first all-gas-turbine fleet in North America with the purchase of Vickers Viscounts and Vanguards, followed by the acquisition of Douglas DC-8 and DC-9 jet equipment.

In that same decade additional services were undertaken. Polar flights to Europe from western Canada were introduced and the airline also became the first in North America to have a direct service to Moscow, Russia. Other major routes were opened from Canada to Miami and Los Angeles, and to Brussels, Zurich, Copenhagen, Vienna, and Frankfurt.

Throughout this era of dramatic change and growth from piston power to gas turbine power, maintenance continued to play a dominant role. In 1960, a multi-million dollar maintenance base was opened at Dorval, Quebec. In view of the increasingly large role played by TCA in the arena of international competition, the name of the airline was changed to Air Canada in 1965.

Trans-Canada Air Lines was inducted as a Member of Canada's Aviation Hall of Fame in 1974.

Leonard John (Len) Tripp

(1896 – 1985)

Leonard John (Len) Tripp was born in St. Keverne, Cornwall, England, on May 21, 1896, where he was educated. At the outbreak of World War I, he enlisted in the Duke of Cornwall's Light Infantry Regiment, and was ordered to combat in France in 1915. The following year he was granted a commission for services in the field. He was wounded in 1916 and sent to hospital in England, where, on recovery he transferred to the Royal Flying Corps (RFC) for pilot training.

Tripp learned to fly at Hounslow, England, flying an Avro 504K. He was posted back to France after graduation, as an RE-8 pilot with 6 Squadron. He transferred to 48 Squadron where he flew Bristol fighters with H.A. 'Doc' Oaks (Hall of Fame 1974). Tripp was shot down and crashed in what was known as 'No Man's Land'. He escaped to the Allied lines after two days and was hospitalized. On recovery he was assigned to flight instruction duties at Hounslow, England, until the war ended in 1918. He accepted a short term

In 1927 'Len' Tripp did some barnstorming and stunt flying from May to November. He described one episode: a gentleman contracted to have Tripp fly out over a lake with an inner tube tied to the undercarriage. The passenger climbed out of the cockpit, hooked his legs through the inner tube and hung, head down. But the weight of his body stretched the tube and he began to swing far out, making it difficult to control the aircraft. Tripp cut that stunt short.

"The application of his superlative skills as a flight instructor to two generations of Canadians for nearly a half century, despite adversity, has been of outstanding benefit to Canadian aviation." —Induction citation, 1974

L.J. 'Len' Tripp with de Havilland 60 'Moth' at the St. Catharines Flying Club, Ontario. 1929.

NATIONAL ARCHIVES OF CANADA C-61750

commission with the Royal Air Force (RAF) as an instructor. In 1923 he left the service and immigrated to Canada.

In 1924 Tripp was employed by the Ontario government's Forest Air Service at Sudbury and Sioux Lookout piloting Curtiss HS-2L flying boats. In 1926 he left to help found the Jack V. Elliot Flying School at Hamilton, Ontario. He remained there as Chief Instructor until 1929, when he moved to St. Catharines to found that city's flying club.

Tripp's outstanding skills as a flight instructor were recognized by Leavens Brothers Air Services, which hired him in 1936 as instructor at Barker Field, Toronto, Ontario. At the outbreak of World War II, he became Chief Instructor and General Manager. He administered that firm's contract to train pilots for the Elementary Flying Training School, a program for the

British Commonwealth Air Training Plan (BCATP). At this time he had instructed more students to licence standards than any other pilot in Canada.

During 1944 he opened his own flying training school at Barker Field at Toronto and remained the dean of Canadian flight instructors until his retirement from active flying in 1962. He then joined Legatt Aircraft at Buttonville, Ontario, in sales and service until he retired in 1968. He died in Newcastle, Ontario, on February 28, 1985.

Leonard John (Len) Tripp was inducted as a Member of Canada's Aviation Hall of Fame in 1974.

John Henry (Tuddy) Tudhope

(1891 – 1956)

John Henry (Tuddy) Tudhope, M.C.*, was born in Johannesburg, South Africa, on April 17, 1891. He was educated there at St. John's College, and at Tonbridge, Kent, England, where he completed his schooling before returning to South Africa as an engineer in the family-run diamond mine and to oversee the family farm.

At the outbreak of World War I, Tudhope enlisted in the British Army as a trooper to serve in German South West Africa. In 1917 he transferred to the Royal Flying Corps (RFC), and earned his pilot's wings. He flew as a fighter pilot with 40 Squadron, RFC, and was awarded the Military Cross (M.C.) and Bar for destroying 15 enemy aircraft in combat. At war's end he retired from the Royal Air Force (RAF) with the rank of Major and immigrated to Canada to farm at Lumby, near Vernon, British Columbia.

In 1920 Tudhope joined the Canadian Air Force (CAF) and served as a flying instructor at Camp Borden, Ontario.

"His pioneer flights to establish an airmail service to and from trans-Atlantic Ocean liners and his aerial survey work in designing initial flight routes for Trans-Canada Air Lines, have been of outstanding benefit to Canadian aviation."

—Induction citation, 1974

J.H. 'Tuddy' Tudhope in a DH-9A cockpit. World War I.

In 1923, he was promoted to Squadron Leader and given command of the Dartmouth, Nova Scotia Air Station, followed by command of the Vancouver, British Columbia Air Station when the Royal Canadian Air Force (RCAF) was formed in 1924.

At Air Headquarters at Ottawa, Ontario, in 1927, he became Superintendent of Airways with the Department of National Defence. One of his first tasks was to make preliminary flights for the development of an airmail service. One plan was to speed the delivery of mail coming from, or going to, Europe by having aircraft connect with trans-Atlantic Ocean liners docking at Rimouski, Quebec, to transfer mail to and from inland areas of Canada. Tudhope made the first experimental flight in September 1927, using a Vickers Vanessa seaplane, and although a storm damaged his aircraft on this trip, he went on to make many flights to meet incoming and outgoing steamships.

In 1928 plans were made under the Controller of Civil Aviation, J.A. Wilson (Hall of Fame 1974), for the survey and construction of airports across Canada for a trans-Canada airway. Many of the larger centres across Canada already had landing strips, developed when the government decided to assist the flying clubs in 1927. Landing strips were needed between these

The Vancouver Air Station, established in 1920, was known for its training of homing pigeons. Squadron Leader J.H. Tudhope supported the use of these birds to carry S.O.S. messages back to base. Many pigeons were carried by pilots of flying boats along the British Columbia coast. In the event the aircraft was forced down, the pilot attached a message to the bird's leg and released it to find its way home. They had been used in World War I and were credited with saving many lives. F/L R. Leckie (Hall of Fame 1988) used pigeons when he put his H-12 flying boat down in the North Sea in 1917 in order to save the crew of a DH-4. One bird reached its base and Leckie's message led to the rescue of the fliers. In 1923, S/L A.E. Godfrey (Hall of Fame 1978), who took over command of the Air Station a year previously, proved the pigeon's worth when he was forced down at sea. He was picked up by a station motor boat a short time after dispatching a pigeon.

airports. Selection of sites for western Canada was done by A.D. 'Dan' McLean (Hall of Fame 1974), while selection of sites from Winnipeg to Halifax was done by Tudhope and others. To accomplish the task of charting the most suitable routes, they travelled by air, rail and on foot. The Trans-Canada (McKee) Trophy for 1930 was awarded to Tudhope for conducting the early, experimental airmail flights from Rimouski, Quebec, and for his supervision of the prairie airmail service in 1930.

In October 1931, Tudhope became Inspector of Airways, and continued the task of selecting sites for aerodromes. He was seconded from the RCAF in November, 1936 to continue serving civil aviation under the newly formed Department of Transport (DOT). In 1937 he was in charge of the calibration of radio ranges from Winnipeg to Vancouver in preparation for the trans-Canada air services.

Tudhope piloted the DOT's Lockheed 12A Electra in which government officials, including the Rt. Hon. C.D. Howe (Hall of Fame 1976), made the first pre-inaugural inspection flight over the route Trans-Canada Airlines (TCA, Hall of Fame 1974) would use from Montreal to Vancouver. This flight, on July 30, 1937, was known as the "Dawn to Dusk" flight.

He retired from the RCAF in 1938, and became Vice-President of Canadian Aviation Insurance Managers Limited. In 1943 he became General Manager of Operations for TCA. Five years later he was appointed the first Civil Air and Communications Attaché to the High Commissioner at London, England. Tudhope died there on October 12, 1956, and his ashes were scattered over the Rocky Mountains from the same aircraft he had commanded in 1937 on the TCA inspection flight. The ceremony was conducted jointly by the RCAF and the Department of Transport.

John Henry (Tuddy) Tudhope was inducted as a Member of Canada's Aviation Hall of Fame in 1974.

Wallace Rupert Turnbull

(1870 – 1954)

Wallace Rupert Turnbull, M.E., D.Sc. (Hon), was born in Saint John, New Brunswick, on October 16, 1870. After graduating with a degree in mechanical engineering (M.E.) from Cornell University, Ithaca, New York, in 1893, he undertook post graduate work in physics at the University of Berlin and Heidelberg, Germany. After a short period with General Electric Company, New Jersey, he returned to his home at Rothesay, New Brunswick. There he established his own research laboratory and set up his own company as a consulting engineer.

Turnbull became interested in problems related to heavier-than-air flight, and in 1902 constructed Canada's first wind tunnel to investigate the properties of airfoils. During the next decade he continued researching the longitudinal stability of aircraft and investigated several

Wallace Turnbull was characterized as a quiet, shy person, but determined to prove his theories. His wife tolerated his experiments, but in 1902, there were very few people who believed that a machine could get off the ground. She admonished him: "Don't, for pity's sake, let anybody know what you're doing, or you'll be put down as a flying machine crank!" He must have followed her advice, for few of his countrymen know of his aeronautical contributions—a Canadian who never piloted a plane but who invented the controllable-pitch propeller in his own backyard.

F/L E.L. Capreol and Turnbull, right, with his electrically controlled variable-pitch propeller installed on an Avro 504K at Camp Borden. 1927.

forms and curvatures of airfoils with respect to lift and drag. His findings, which proved to be of high scientific value, were published in aeronautical journals in the United States and Great Britain.

Turnbull found that only meager scientific data was available on the efficiency of the propeller. After extensive experimentation with propeller diameter and pitch coefficient he published an important paper titled "The Efficiency of Aerial Propellers" in the Scientific American Supplement, April 3, 1909. He realized that to operate efficiently under different conditions of flight—take-off, climb, cruise, etc.,—the characteristics of the propeller must be varied, and that the only characteristic which could be adjusted during flight was the pitch.

During World War I, he went to England to offer assistance to aircraft manufacturers, and designed propellers for Sage seaplanes, and a Short 184 seaplane, which attained an altitude record of 13,000 feet (3,960 m) on June 9, 1917. At this time he began to work on a mechanism which would allow the pilot to control the pitch during flight, like changing gears on a car, so that the pitch could be set at different angles for take-off and landing, and for level flight.

At war's end, Turnbull returned to Rothesay and continued work on the design of a variable pitch propeller for which he gained a patent in 1922. The propeller itself was made by Canadian Vickers Limited and fitted to a 130 hp Clerget engine on an Avro 504K. The Royal Canadian Air Force (RCAF) conducted the first test flights at Camp Borden and the Turnbull variable pitch propeller proved highly successful. However, the Canadian government refused to provide assistance beyond the testing stage because the project would then be classified as commercial. The patent rights were sold two years later and Turner's design became the Curtiss-Wright electric propeller, of which many thousands were manufactured during and beyond World War II.

Turnbull was elected a member of the research committee of the National Research Council of Canada (NRC). His interests extended into many fields, such as hydroplanes, a torpedo screen, bomb sights, and harnessing tidal power, but his systematic approach to aeronautical research was regarded by many as his greatest and most significant contribution. In recognition of his endeavors, the University of New Brunswick conferred upon him an Honorary Doctor of Science degree in 1942.

To add to his already formidable reputation as a designer-inventor, he was awarded the bronze medal of the Aeronautical Society of Great Britain along with an Associate Fellowship, and he was named a Fellow in both the Royal Aeronautical and the Royal Meteorological Societies. The Canadian Aeronautical Institute named him an Honorary Fellow in 1942 and in 1955 the annual W. Rupert Turnbull Lectures were established. The St. John airport, Turnbull Field, is named in his honour. The original propeller is displayed at the National Aviation Museum at Rockcliffe, Ottawa. He died in Saint John, New Brunswick, on November 26, 1954.

Wallace Rupert Turnbull was inducted as a Member of Canada's Aviation Hall of Fame in 1977.

Percival Stanley (Stan) Turner
(1916 – 1985)

Percival Stanley (Stan) Turner, D.S.O., D.F.C.*, C.D.*, was born in Devon, England, on September 3, 1916. His family immigrated to Collingwood, Ontario. He was educated there and at the University of Toronto. He joined the Royal Canadian Air Force (RCAF) Auxiliary Squadron in 1936, and two years later went to England to join the Royal Air Force (RAF), where he received his wings as a commissioned fighter pilot.

At the outbreak of World War II in 1939, Turner was posted to 219 Squadron, flying Bristol Blenheim fighter-bombers on night operations, and Hawker Hurricane fighters on night U-boat patrols over the Irish Sea. In 1940 he served with 242 All-Canadian Squadron, then volunteered for duty in France with 616 Squadron until that country's capitulation to German forces in 1940. As part of 616 Squadron he covered all phases of the Dunkirk operation as a fighter pilot, including the withdrawal of Allied troops. His squadron returned to England and came under the command and inspiration of Douglas Bader, the RAF's legendary legless pilot. Turner

At war's end Wing Commander Stan Turner was credited with destroying 14 hostile aircraft in combat and probably destroying six others, plus aircraft and equipment on the ground. He had fought on every front in Europe, North Africa and Malta, and was awarded the Distinguished Service Order (D.S.O.), Distinguished Flying Cross (D.F.C.) and Bar, Czechoslovakian Medal of Honour and the Czechoslovakian Medal of Valour.

"His record can only be matched by those airmen of high endeavor and professional calling, who have devoted their lives and skills to the benefit of the free world, despite adversity, and whose contributions have substantially benefited Canadian aviation."

—Induction citation, 1974

S/L Stan Turner, centre, with 417 Squadron in Malta prior to the invasion of Sicily. 1943.

distinguished himself during the Battle of Britain.

Turner was promoted to Squadron Leader and given command of 145 Squadron at Tangmere in 1941. This unit was equipped with cannon-armed Spitfires for high-altitude bomber escort missions and fighter sweeps into France. R.A. Munro (Hall of Fame 1974) served under him there and later, when the squadron moved to Yorkshire as fighter protection for North Sea convoys. He became Senior Training Officer of No. 82 Group, in Northern Ireland, followed by appointment in 1941 to lead 411 Squadron.

Turner was then given command of 249 Squadron on the Island of Malta, and when that Allied stronghold came under enemy siege, he was named leader in 1942 of the Malta fighter wing. He was shot down in combat in 1942 but continued to command Malta's air operations during his convalescence. He initiated night bombing attacks with Hawker Hurricane fighters on enemy targets in Sicily.

When the siege was lifted, he was transferred to Egypt and the Desert Air Force which Raymond Collishaw (Hall of Fame 1974) had originated. From there he was posted to sea duty aboard the aircraft carrier, HMS Arethusa, and led his sea-borne fighters on the ill-fated attack on Tobruk in June 1942. HMS Arethusa was sunk during this operation and he was ordered to HMS Orion on convoy duty into Malta. When he took command of 134 Squadron in the Western Desert, he led anti-tank Hurricane fighters against enemy armour, during which operations he survived a major crash. He was ordered to 417 Squadron in 1943 for the invasion of Italy and Sicily, and promoted to Wing Commander and leader of No. 244 Wing of the Desert Air Force in Italy. He continued to show outstanding leadership abilities, resulting in destruction of enemy aircraft and ground equipment. When Italy surrendered in 1943, he took command of No. 127 Wing, RCAF, in Europe, where he led 2,000 personnel and 72 fighter aircraft through France and Germany.

In 1946 Turner transferred to the RCAF and returned to Canada. After a tour of duty at the Royal Military College, he was appointed to command No. 20 Tactical Wing at Rivers, Manitoba. Postings followed as Command Senior Organization Staff Officer of the Northwest Air Command, and head of the Joint Air Training School. In 1951, while serving in Chatham, New Brunswick, he was named aide-de-camp to the Lieutenant-Governor of New Brunswick.

Turner was appointed to the Canadian Embassy in Russia in 1954 as Senior Military Air Attaché with the rank of Group Captain. Three years later he returned to command the RCAF station at Lachine, Quebec. Following a systems management course in the United States in 1960, he was transferred to Air Defence Command as Administrative Project Chief for the construction of a new radar chain, which was completed in 1963. He also served as a Canadian officer with the United States Air Force Electronics Division during the period of construction of the ballistic missile warning system.

In 1963 he retired from the service to become a sales manager for a Montreal investment firm. He served as a senior executive of Expo '67 and 'Man and His World' at Montreal, Quebec, for four years. Turner died on July 23, 1985.

Percival Stanley (Stan) Turner was inducted as a Member of Canada's Aviation Hall of Fame in 1974.

Joseph Pierre Roméo Vachon

(1898 – 1954)

Joseph Pierre Roméo Vachon was born on June 29, 1898, in Sainte Marie de la Beauce, Quebec, where he was educated. During World War I he served with the Royal Navy as an engineer until his discharge. In 1920 he enlisted in the Canadian Air Force and the following year was granted leave to join the air service of Laurentide Pulp and Paper Company at their Lac à la Tortue (Grand'Mère) base in Quebec as an engineer. In January 1921, he qualified for his Air Engineer's Certificate, and began to learn to fly on company aircraft. He completed his flying training at the General Motors School of Aviation in Dayton, Ohio. On gaining his Commercial Pilot's Licence in 1923 he became one of Canada's earliest bush pilots, flying Curtiss HS-2L flying boats on fire patrol and photographic work.

He joined the Ontario Provincial Air Service (OPAS, Belt of Orion 1991) when it was formed in the spring of 1924, flying forestry patrol. In 1928 Canadian Trans-continental Airways organized an air service to transport mail under government contract along the north

The Roméo Vachon Award was established in 1968 by the Canadian Aeronautics and Space Institute (CASI) in memory of one of Canada's outstanding bush pilots. It is presented "for outstanding display of initiative, ingenuity and practical skills in the solution of a particular physical problem relating to the art, science, and engineering of aeronautics, space, associated technologies or their application in Canada."

Roméo Vachon, centre, with Fairchild 71, CF-AAT, of Canadian Trans-continental Airways Ltd. in which he inaugurated airmail service between Montreal, Quebec, and St. John, New Brunswick. December 1929.

shore of the St. Lawrence River. Vachon was hired as pilot because of his familiarity with that area. He went to New York to ferry a new ski-equipped Fairchild monoplane back to Murray Bay, Quebec, and on the return trip, parachuted a sack of mail onto the Quebec City airport. It was the first time mail had been delivered in that fashion in Canada, a method the 'flying postmaster' would use almost routinely on his north shore rounds.

Vachon was assigned to fly the mail between the Quebec mainland and Anticosti Island in the Gulf of St. Lawrence, inaugurating the first airmail from La Malbaie to Port Menier on February 2, 1928. That same year he inaugurated the airmail to Rimouski, Quebec. During 11 consecutive winters, despite adverse weather conditions, he flew the mail from Quebec City to La Malbaie and Rimouski along the north shore of the St. Lawrence, to Anticosti Island, and to the Isles de la Madeleine, serving 31 communities. His early dream of uniting a string of isolated communities along the shores of the St. Lawrence River through airmail service became a reality.

When the German aircraft 'Bremen' completed the first non-stop, east-to-west crossing of the Atlantic Ocean in April 1928, and crashed on Greenly Island off the south-east coast of Labrador, Vachon flew from the base at Lac Ste. Agnès to the area with two representatives of the press, and brought back two members of the crew and the first photos and story of this event.

That same year he designed a new aerial service for the forwarding of mail to and from Europe, including the preparation of landing strips and the recruitment of pilots. The route included Toronto and Ottawa, Ontario, and Montreal and Rimouski, Quebec, based on a schedule that coincided with the arrival and departure of ocean-going ships at Point-au-Père, Quebec. In 1930, when Canadian Transcontinental Airways was taken over by Canadian Airways Limited, he joined the newly-formed company, and became District Superintendent for Quebec and eastern Ontario.

In 1931 a Trans-Canada Air Pageant was organized to demonstrate to Canadians how aviation was progressing in Canada, and to stimulate public interest. Vachon was chosen to pilot a large twin-engined amphibian flying boat, a Saro Cloud, built by Saunders-Roe Company of England. The pageant began in Hamilton, Ontario, on July 1, stopping at every major city across Canada in a round-trip which ended in mid-September.

Vachon was awarded the Trans-Canada (McKee) Trophy for 1937 to recognize his lengthy pioneering efforts in establishing airmail service in eastern Quebec and for providing radio and weather reporting stations in the same area to improve the safety of all air transport operations.

He left Canadian Airways in 1938 to become Assistant Superintendent of the Eastern Division of Trans-Canada Airlines (TCA, Hall of Fame 1974). During World War II he was loaned to the Department of Munitions and Supply to organize the overhaul of aircraft for the British Commonwealth Air Training Plan (BCATP).

He was a Member of the Air Transport Board in Ottawa from the time it was formed in 1944 until his death in Quebec City on December 17, 1954.

Joseph Pierre Roméo Vachon was inducted as a Member of Canada's Aviation Hall of Fame in 1974.

Achille (Archie) Vanhee

(b. 1909)

Achille (Archie) Vanhee was born in Jabbeke, Belgium, on September 15, 1909. He immigrated to Canada in 1925 and continued his education at College St. Laurent near Montreal, Quebec. In 1928 Vanhee began flying training with the Montreal Flying Club, and was later hired as a helper/mechanic. In 1929 he joined Continental Aero Corporation as an engineer and continued flying training. He obtained his Air Engineer's Certificate and Commercial Pilot's Licence in 1930, then joined the Societée d'Aviation du Quebec as pilot-engineer and flying instructor.

Central Airways at Amos, Quebec, hired Vanhee as pilot-engineer in 1935. Early in 1937 he joined Mackenzie Air Service where he flew the first official airmail between Yellowknife and Fort Resolution, Northwest Territories. During the same year, he flew with Stan McMillan (Hall of Fame 1974) on the Snyder Nahanni Survey Expedition.

In 1939 Vanhee obtained his Public Transport Licence and joined the Royal Canadian Air Force (RCAF). He was commissioned as a Flying Officer, and attended the Flying Instructor's School at

While on one of his northern mail runs, Vanhee rescued Louis Bisson and his passengers who had been missing for several days after engine problems with his Waco biplane. Bisson himself was on a mercy flight to the Fort Smith Mission Hospital with several Inuit children and a trapper who were suffering from serious frostbite.

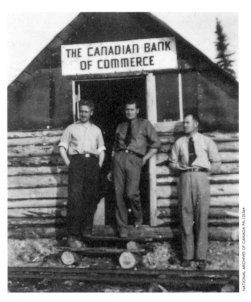

At the entrance to the newly constructed bank at Yellowknife, N.W.T., in 1938. Left to right: Archie Vanhee, bank manager, and Harry Hayter (Hall of Fame 1974).

Camp Borden, Ontario. After graduation he was posted to seaplane training at the RCAF station at Jericho Beach, British Columbia. In 1940 Vanhee moved to No. 13 Operational Training Unit (OTU) and instructed on several seaplane types.

In mid-1941 Vanhee was appointed to command 'C' Flight for instrument flying training. In 1942 he was transferred to Halifax, Nova Scotia, to take command of the Lockheed Hudson Training Unit, specializing in instrument flying training.

A year later Vanhee was appointed Commanding Officer of 160 Squadron at Yarmouth, Nova Scotia. In 1944 he joined No. 45 Atlantic Transport Group to ferry flying boats from North America to the United Kingdom. After returning to Halifax, he became Director of Instrument Flying Training and in October 1945, he was demobilized with the rank of Squadron Leader.

That same year he joined Canadian Pacific Airlines (CPA), which had taken over Mackenzie Air Service. He now flew as Captain on the Lockheed Lodestar and

Douglas DC-3. CPA, while still operating bush lines in northern areas, now ran scheduled air services. Vanhee flew CPA's Mackenzie District on schedules which included Edmonton, Fort McMurray, Yellowknife, Norman Wells, Fort Smith, and Fort Resolution.

In January 1949, he moved to Vancouver to fly for CPA Overseas Lines where he became one of the captains on several 'firsts for Canadian-registered aircraft': first flight to Tokyo, Shanghai and Hong Kong, using Canadair C-4M's (North Stars); familiarization flight to Honolulu, Fiji, Sydney and Auckland; and the inaugural flight by CPA to Honolulu, Fiji and Australia carrying the first paying passengers and air mail to the South Pacific. Later that same year he was captain of the first direct Vancouver-Honolulu flight by a Canadian aircraft.

During the period from 1952 to 1960, Vanhee completed a ground school course on the new British de Havilland Comet jet passenger aircraft, qualified as captain on the DC-6B, and captained CPA's inaugural flight between Lima, Peru and Mexico. He qualified as captain on the Vancouver-Amsterdam route, and on special invitation from Boeing Aircraft in Seattle, piloted the four-jet-engine 707 prototype. In April of 1958 he became captain on the Bristol Britannia turboprop.

In 1960 Vanhee left CPA, and for the next twelve years, returned to flight instruction in British Columbia and Ontario. During this period he also worked for several airways in Ontario. In 1967 he was awarded the Back and Bevington Air Safety Trophy by the British Columbia Aviation Council.

From 1973 to 1983 Vanhee flew for White River Air Service. He was allowed regular leaves of absence to work for the Canadian International Development Agency's Civil Aviation Project in several countries in Africa, where he was involved with pilot training on the DHC-6 Twin Otter. When Vanhee retired in 1983, at the age of 74, he had 56 years of unbroken active service in aviation and 25,000 flying hours.

Achille (Archie) Vanhee was inducted as a Member of Canada's Aviation Hall of Fame in 1987.

Maxwell William (Max) Ward

(b. 1921)

Maxwell William (Max) Ward, O.C., LL.D. (Hon), was born November 22, 1921, in Edmonton, Alberta, where he was educated. He joined the Royal Canadian Air Force (RCAF) in 1940, received his pilot's wings and served as a commissioned flight instructor at various Canadian bases until 1945. He received his Commercial Pilot's Licence in 1945 and began his flying career when he was hired by Jack Moar (Hall of Fame 1974) as a bush pilot for Northern Flights Limited, operating from Peace River, Alberta, to Yellowknife, Northwest Territories.

In 1946 he organized his own air operation, Polaris Charter Company Limited, based in Yellowknife, with one single-engine aircraft, a de Havilland Fox Moth, hauling prospectors and supplies into the mining exploration camps.

In 1947 the Air Transport Board (ATB) made it necessary for every air carrier operating in Canada to obtain an ATB charter licence. Since he did not have a licence, Ward was advised by a Member of the ATB, J.P. Roméo Vachon (Hall of Fame 1974), to form a partnership with a veteran bush pilot who already possessed a charter licence. In 1948 he and George Pigeon formed Yellowknife Airways on a 50-50 basis, each contributing one aircraft. Pigeon sold his portion of the company in

Max Ward's personal dedication, leadership and hard work were largely responsible for the success of Wardair. Through his enthusiasm and ability to inspire others, he created a team dedicated to the pursuit of excellence in every facet of the company's operations.

Max Ward starting up in the North—his Polaris Charter Company Ltd. began with this Fox Moth. At the Snare River, 90 miles (145 km) west of Yellowknife. 1947.

1949, forcing Ward to liquidate his share. In the fall of 1949 he left aviation to enter the home construction business in Lethbridge, Alberta.

Four years later Ward returned to Yellowknife with a newly-acquired de Havilland Otter and and a newly-formed company, Wardair Limited, with a licence to operate a domestic charter service from that location. He bought a DH Beaver in 1954, and a second Otter in 1955, gradually expanding his operation by adding a new aircraft each year. In 1957 he purchased the company's first heavy aircraft, a Bristol Freighter. Using oversized tires, he and his pilots pioneered the air transport of heavy equipment into the far Arctic, and in May 1967, made the first landing of an aircraft on wheels at the geographic North Pole.

In 1962 he introduced four-engined Douglas DC-6A freighter aircraft to high latitude operations, carrying heavy loads into semi-prepared landing strips. Ward received an ATB licence to operate international air charters, changed the corporate name to Wardair Canada Ltd., and opened an office in Edmonton. Despite numerous financial setbacks and governmental delays, he expanded his northern operation and commenced the first international overseas charter flight agency serving western Canada.

His airline became the third major Canadian carrier to operate pure jet aircraft in 1966, with the purchase of a Boeing 727, which he named 'Cy Becker'. Two years later he added a Boeing 707 and christened it 'Punch Dickins'. In 1969 he acquired another Boeing 707, named 'Wop May', and in 1973, a 452-passenger Boeing 747, and named it 'Phil Garratt'. By 1973 his company was serving destinations in England, Europe, the Mediterranean countries, the Caribbean and Mexico, the United States, Hawaii, the Orient and the South Pacific Ocean islands, and had developed into Canada's largest international air charter carrier.

Wardair Canada established a reputation second to none anywhere in the world for efficient operations and top-rated service to the travelling public. But the 'Open Skies' concept came too late for Wardair Canada to continue. Years of delays in governmental decision-making and bureaucratic obstacles, which prevented the company from developing to its full potential, caused Ward to consider his company's position. Rising costs and the prospect of deeper debt led to his decision to sell, and on May 2, 1989, the company was sold to the Pacific Western Airlines (PWA) Corporation, ending a brilliant chapter in the history of Canadian aviation.

Ward's outstanding achievements brought him recognition and honours. He was presented with the Billy Mitchell Award by the International Northwest Aviation Council (INAC) in 1971, and the Trans-Canada (McKee) Trophy for 1973 for his contributions to this nation's air transport services. In 1975 he was made an Officer of the Order of Canada (O.C.) for his outstanding contribution to aviation and to the development of Canada's north. He received several Honorary Doctor of Laws degrees. The Gordon R. McGregor Trophy was awarded him in 1979, and the C.D. Howe Award in 1991.

Maxwell William (Max) Ward was inducted as a Member of Canada's Aviation Hall of Fame in 1974.

Donald Netterville (Don) Watson
(b. 1921)

The beginnings of Saskatchewan Air Ambulance Service. The patient is transferred from a sleigh and hurried to Norseman, CF-SAH, waiting in a field.

Donald Netterville (Don) Watson was born on September 21, 1921, in Winnipeg, Manitoba, and was educated there. He worked after school hours as an apprentice to Konnie Johannesson's Flying Service. By 1938 he had soloed in an Avro Avion but since he was only 17, and the minimum age for licencing was 19, he could only build up flying time in the ensuing period. He earned an Air Engineer's Licence at that time.

Watson joined Canadian Airways the same year as an air engineer and remained there until 1940, when the Canadian government requested his assistance with

While he was President of PWA, Don Watson assisted people in many countries by sending company aircraft on emergency food and relief missions to Africa and other destinations.

the technical, administrative and flying functions of the newly formed British Commonwealth Air Training Plan (BCATP). He served that organization with distinction, assisting with the formation of No. 5 Air Observer's School. In 1945 he served the Alaskan Wing of the United States Army Air Force Transport Command as a Flight Engineer. At the end of World War II, he joined Canadian Pacific Airlines (CPA).

In 1946 he used his organizational skills to co-originate, with the Saskatchewan government, the first systematic air ambulance service on the North American continent. The world-respected Saskatchewan Government Air Ambulance Service operated with one specially-equipped Noorduyn Norseman, which he served as air engineer. J.J. Audette (Hall of Fame 1989) was also a pilot for this service. During Watson's tenure the service transported more than 6,000 patients in all types of flying weather, some from isolated and nearly inaccessible locations, to medical treatment centres, possibly saving hundreds of lives.

He joined Ontario Central Airlines at Kenora, Ontario, in 1949 and became Managing Director.

In 1958 Watson joined the executive staff of Pacific Western Airlines (PWA), which was incorporated in 1953 by R.F. Baker (Hall of Fame 1975). He was appointed Assistant to the Vice-President and General Manager. In 1964 Watson became Vice-President, management and technical services. PWA, Canada's largest independent airline, maintained scheduled flights in western Canada with charter flights to Europe, Hawaii and Mexico. During the expansion years of the late 1960's and early 1970's, the airline set up the triangle service between Vancouver, Victoria and Seattle, Washington; the Calgary-Edmonton, Alberta, air-bus service; and the northern service to Yellowknife and Inuvik. Watson rose to become President and Chief Executive Officer, an office he held from 1970 to 1976, when the airline was taken over by the Alberta government. He retired from PWA in 1976.

Watson was elected Chairman of the Air Transport Association of Canada (ATAC) for the 1964 and 1974 terms in recognition of his understanding of global air transport problems and their solutions, and his contributions to Canadian aviation. He succeeded C.L. 'Punch' Dickins (Hall of Fame 1974) as Chairman of the Board of Canada's Aviation Hall of Fame in 1975.

In 1976 he was appointed Chairman of Canadian Cellulose Company, and in 1978, President and Chief Executive Officer. In 1982 he was named Chairman of B.C. Resources Investment Corporation.

Watson was made an Honorary Life Member of ATAC in 1976. He was recognized by the International Northwest Aviation Council by being named to its Roll of Honour in 1986. In 1984 he was awarded a Lifetime Achievement in Aviation Award from the British Columbia Aviation Council, and was given a Pioneer Award from the Western Canada Aviation Museum in 1995.

Donald Netterville (Don) Watson was inducted as a Member of Canada's Aviation Hall of Fame in 1974.

Roland Burgess (Rollie) West

(b. 1919)

Roland Burgess (Rollie) West, D.F.C., A.F.C., C.D.*, was born in Medford, Nova Scotia, on January 25, 1919. He was educated there and at Kentville, Nova Scotia, before taking employment as a boat pilot on the Bay of Fundy. In 1941 he enlisted in the Royal Canadian Air Force (RCAF), trained in eastern Canada and was awarded his pilot's wings the following year. After operational training at Nassau, British West Indies, he was promoted to Flying Officer and posted to 116 Squadron, operating out of the Maritimes, Newfoundland and Labrador. For his service on anti-submarine patrols over the North Atlantic Ocean, he was awarded the Distinguished Flying Cross (D.F.C.) in 1945.

West attended the Staff Course at Toronto, Ontario in 1946, and was transferred to 103 Search and Rescue Squadron at Greenwood, Nova Scotia. As a captain, during the next two years he flew approximately 2,000 hours on search and rescue operations for missing aircraft, ships at sea, and transporting critically ill patients to hospital.

In 1947 West was awarded the Air Force Cross (A.F.C.) for two consecutive mercy flights which resulted in the saving of

In June 1948, 'Rollie' West was chosen to perform the first large-scale Rain-Making Operation in Canada, which successfully produced large quantities of rain north of Sault Ste. Marie, Ontario, where forest fires burned out of control. He used a Lancaster aircraft with heavy loads of dry ice to 'seed' the tops of clouds at a high altitude.

F/O Roland West, right, receives the Trans-Canada (McKee) Trophy from Hon. Brooke Claxton, Minister of National Defence. Rockcliffe, Ontario. 1949.

human life. The first was made from Halifax, Nova Scotia, to Harrington Harbour, on the north shore of the St. Lawrence River, through difficult winter flying conditions, to evacuate a 15 year-old pneumonia patient to hospital at Goose Bay, Labrador. On the heels of this successful mission he was ordered to Mutton Bay, Labrador, through equally difficult weather, to fly out a seriously ill expectant mother. This flight was accomplished despite damage to the flying boat by rough seas. Prior to these particular rescue missions, he had completed a number of other rescue missions in different coastal areas.

The Trans-Canada (McKee) Trophy for 1948 was awarded to West in recognition of his outstanding contribution to advancement in the field of aviation search and rescue operations during the year. During the Fraser River floods in British Columbia in 1948, West flew many hours carrying sandbags and other essential materials. Sandbags were dropped from the air to ground crews who formed dykes to hold back the flooding waters. The flying done during this mission was under the leadership of Group Captain Z.L. Leigh (Hall of Fame 1974).

A promotion to Flight Lieutenant and appointment as recruiting officer at Brandon, Manitoba, in 1949 was followed by a tour of duty at Centralia, Ontario. In 1952 West was ordered to Summerside, Prince Edward Island, to eventually command the flying activities of the Air Navigation School, where he was promoted to Squadron Leader. A three-year posting to Goose Bay in 1953 was followed by a twelve-month jet pilot's course in 1956, at Portage La Prairie, Manitoba, and Cold Lake, Alberta. He was transferred to 416 Squadron at St. Hubert, Quebec, the following year, and was named Base Commander in 1959.

The Canadian Research and Development Establishment (CARDE) hired West in 1960 to work on infra-red research at Cartierville, Quebec. Here he flew Beech C-45's, de Havilland Otters, and Avro CF-100's. With this background he was sent to Patrick Air Force Base, Cape Canaveral, Florida, U.S.A., where he commanded the Canadian Task Force, known as Operation Lookout. This was a joint RCAF-CARDE operation on missile lift off and re-entry. He remained there for three years, flying CF-100's for research data.

In 1964 West returned to Rockcliffe, Ontario, and was named a senior officer of the Air Material Command. His responsibility was for all aircraft ferry operations throughout the RCAF, all aspects of flight safety and accident assessments, plus nuclear defence and emergency plans for all members of the unit. He retired from the service in 1966 to manage a branch of Merriam Graves Corporation in the state of Vermont.

Roland Burgess (Rollie) West was inducted as a Member of Canada's Aviation Hall of Fame in 1974.

Robert Allan (Bud) White

(b. 1928)

Robert Allan (Bud) White, O.M.M., C.D.**, B.A.Sc., M.B.A., was born on December 11, 1928, in Sudbury, Ontario, and educated at Kirkland Lake. He learned to fly in 1946 at Larder Lake, Ontario, and obtained his Private Pilot's Licence at Toronto, Ontario, while attending Upper Canada College. For two summers he was employed by Imperial Oil Ltd. as an engine-room seaman, initially on the Great Lakes, and in 1948 aboard oil tankers to South American ports.

His desire to become a military pilot resulted in acceptance into the Royal Military College (RMC) at Kingston, Ontario, in 1948 under a Royal Canadian Air Force (RCAF) Benevolent Fund Scholarship. During the summer of 1951 he obtained his pilot's wings at Centralia, Ontario, and the following year he graduated from RMC as a Flying Officer in the RCAF regular force. He then attended the University of Toronto during 1952-53 and graduated with a Bachelor of Applied Science degree in Mechanical Engineering.

After completing the fighter operational training course (OTU) at Chatham, New Brunswick, White was transferred overseas to 427 Fighter Squadron at Zweibrucken, Germany, where he flew F-86 Sabres for 3 1/2 years during the peak of the Cold War. He returned to Canada in 1957 for brief tours of duty as resident staff officer at the University of New Brunswick in

Wing Commander R.A. 'Bud' White set a Canadian altitude record of 100,100 feet (30,500 m) at RCAF Uplands, Ontario, on December 14, 1967. He borrowed a Gemini astronaut space suit for his attempts at setting a new altitude record.

Fredericton, and on the staff of Central Flying School, Trenton, Ontario. He then returned to England in 1959 as a Flight Lieutenant to attend the year-long course at the Empire Test Pilot's School at Farnborough.

White returned to engineering test-flying duties in Canada in 1960 with the Central Experimental and Proving Establishment (CEPE) at Edmonton, Alberta. There he served with the Climatic Detachment at Namao, and as the Detachment Commander and resident test pilot at Northwest Industries Ltd., conducting acceptance trials on Canadair T-33 and Fairchild C-119 aircraft for the RCAF. During this period, he received a commendation for saving his crew and a C-119 Boxcar aircraft during an engineering test flight. He also completed the Air Transport Command 'Captains' OTU course at Trenton, and the RCAF Staff School course at Toronto.

In 1962 White was one of four Canadians loaned to the United States Air Force (USAF) Space Systems Division at Los Angeles, California, for service with the National Aeronautics and Space Administration (NASA) space programs. He spent the first year with the Mercury manned program, then returned to the Gemini Launch Vehicle Directorate as an operations project officer with the rank of Squadron Leader. There he was responsible for propellants, loading and engine systems, and for the acceptance and pilot safety programs. During his 3 1/2 years with the USAF and NASA, working out of Los Angeles, Sacramento, Baltimore and Cape Kennedy (Canaveral), he served with distinction in the acceptance and launch programs for the last two Mercury and the first four Gemini manned NASA space flights, as well as some twenty other associated military launch programs.

He returned to Canada in 1965 to attend the last RCAF Staff College course before

W/C R.A. 'Bud' White climbs into the CF-104 'Starfighter' aircraft 12700X of the Aerospace Engineering Test Establishment for the 42nd and final mission.

being assigned to the Aerospace Engineering Test Establishment (AETA) as Officer Commanding flying operations. In 1967 he was promoted to Wing Commander and named Vice-Commander and Senior Test Pilot of AETA which at the time numbered over 3,700 personnel.

During 1967 he led the Canadian Centennial Team, composed of military, government and civilian personnel, in challenging the Russian-held World Altitude record for aircraft. They focused the highest level of Canadian technology on special instrumentation and modifications to a CF-104 Starfighter aircraft. Arrangements for tracking were made with the Defence Research Board and Telecommunications Establishment in Ottawa. After 42 flights, 12 of them above 96,000 feet (29,260 m), Wing Commander White terminated the program. He had piloted the aircraft to the new Fédération Aéronautique Internationale (FAI) Canadian record of 100,100 feet (30,510 m). He was awarded the 1968 Trans-Canada (McKee) Trophy for his leadership and flying skills in this undertaking. His unique CF-104 is still on display in the National Aeronautical collection in Ottawa.

The following year, White was appointed Director of Cadets and Military Training at the RMC. In this capacity he was responsible for implementing sweeping social and structural changes which greatly strengthened the ethos and ethics of officer education at the military colleges. In 1972 – 73 he attended the USAF Air War College at Montgomery, Alabama, graduating with distinction, while at the same time obtaining a Master of Business Administration degree from Auburn University. After his return to Canada in

1973, he was promoted to Colonel and took over the Directorate of Policy Coordination and Review, which eventually provided the secretariat and inner staffing for the Chief and Vice-Chief in the Defence Staff and the Deputy Minister at National Defence Headquarters (NDHQ), Ottawa.

In 1976 he was appointed Base Commander of CFB North Bay, Ontario, a North American Air Defence Command base and home of the 22nd NORAD region, with one of the largest underground military facilities in the western world. Originally sent to oversee the closure of the base, Colonel White convinced Air Command and NDHQ not only to retain the base, but to upgrade and modernize the underground facility.

In 1979, after 31 years of distinguished service and with 52 aircraft types to his credit, he took early retirement from the Canadian Armed Forces to accept an offer from Noranda Mines Ltd. to become Vice-President of their Special Metals Division manufacturing facility at Arnprior, Ontario.

For his engineering test flying and service with the USAF and NASA, and particularly for his leadership of the Centennial team, Colonel White was made an Officer of the Order of Military Merit (O.M.M.) by the Governor General of Canada in 1974.

White and his wife Lee live in New Zealand where he still holds a private pilot's licence. He is active in downhill skiing and races in the Masters in North America and New Zealand.

Robert Allan (Bud) White was inducted as a Member of Canada's Aviation Hall of Fame in 1974.

Thomas Frederic (Tommy) Williams
(1885 – 1985)

"His exemplary conduct in aerial combat and his half-century of dedication to the science of aeronautics, despite adversity, have inspired young and old alike, and his total involvement in flight has been of outstanding benefit to Canadian aviation." —Induction citation, 1974

Thomas Frederic (Tommy) Williams, M.C., was born on October 12, 1885, in Ingersoll, Ontario, where he was educated. At the outbreak of World War I he joined the Legion of Frontiersmen at Calgary, Alberta. He resigned from their ranks almost immediately to enlist with the Corps of Guides, then transferred again to the Provost Corps of the First Canadian Division. He arrived in France in February 1915. He served with distinction in the lines until recommended for a commission in the Royal Flying Corps (RFC) by Major General Sir Arthur Currie.

Following operational training in Scotland and England, Williams was awarded his wings and a promotion to Lieutenant. He was posted to 45 Squadron, RFC, in France as a fighter pilot, flying a Sopwith Camel

On October 12, 1971, the day he sold his Fleet 21M, 'Tommy' Williams flew it for 30 minutes, with loops, rolls and a spin, considering that this would be his final solo flying exhibition. It was. He had just started his eighty-seventh year of life that day!

from the front lines against Baron von Richthofen's 'Flying Circus'. During this period he destroyed four German aircraft in combat. The squadron was posted to Italy in December 1917. Within three months of fighting in the Alps, he had raised his score of enemy aircraft destroyed to ten, and was awarded the Military Cross (M.C.) for consistent gallantry and devotion to duty. The Italian government also decorated him with the Valore Militare Medal.

This string of victories led to his promotion as Flight Commander of 28 Squadron, RFC, with the rank of Captain. In 1918, when his aircraft was disabled by enemy anti-aircraft fire, Williams glided a long distance through mountain passes to a safe landing at an Allied base. A new wing and tank were fitted in the field and both Williams and his Camel returned to duty before dark that day. He outfought one hostile aircraft in the air and forced him to crash-land.

He ended his combat career with victories over 14 enemy aircraft. He was ordered to England in August 1918, for medical reasons and rest. Heart problems often became evident in pilots who flew at high altitudes for long periods of time without an auxiliary supply of oxygen. After being posted to the School of Air Fighting at Beamsville, Ontario, as an examining officer, he returned to England in 1919 to resign his commission.

Back in Canada, Williams took a refresher flying course in 1920 at Camp Borden, Ontario, during which time he earned his Commercial Pilot's Licence with night endorsement, and his Air Engineer's Certificate. He bought his father's farm at Sweaburg, Ontario, then leased an adjoining estate, purchased an airplane and turned the operation into an airport.

From 1927 to 1931, Williams owned a commercial air service in southwestern Ontario and later became flying instructor at the Kitchener-Waterloo Flying Club. In 1934 he was named Chief Flying Instructor at the London Flying Club in Ontario and earned his Instrument Flight Rating. Jack Moar (Hall of Fame 1974) hired him in 1937 as a pilot for Skylines Express out of Winnipeg, Manitoba, flying a daily service into the mining areas of northern Ontario. When the company ceased operations a year later, Williams became a charter pilot and instructor for a flying concern at Rouyn, Quebec.

When Canada declared war against Germany in 1939, Williams joined Fleet Aircraft Company at Fort Erie, Ontario, as Chief Pilot, a position he held for eight years. On retirement in 1947, he purchased the Fleet 21M that he had been using at Fleet Aircraft to test-drop parachutes, and flew it for pleasure. Before selling it in 1971, he performed one last solo aerobatic flight, in his 87th year, when he was officially recognized as the world's oldest active pilot. After 56 years as an aviator, he allowed his licence to lapse.

Williams died at Woodstock, Ontario, on July 25, 1985, less than three months short of his 100th birthday .

Thomas Frederic (Tommy) Williams was inducted as a Member of Canada's Aviation Hall of Fame in 1974.

'Tommy' Williams stands beside his Fleet 21M which gave him many years of flying pleasure.

Arthur Haliburton Wilson
(1899 – 1983)

Arthur Haliburton Wilson was born in Kendal, England, on July 27, 1899. He received his education at the Old College, Windemere, and Dover College, Kent, then joined the Royal Navy Air Service (RNAS) as a provisional officer in March 1918. After graduating from the Royal Naval College at Greenwich, he earned his pilot wings at No. 7 Training Depot Squadron, Feltwell, in October 1918. On completion of an instructor's course, his superior instructional abilities resulted in his return to Feltwell as a training officer, where he served until being demobilized in early 1919.

In 1923 Wilson immigrated to Canada to live in Victoria, British Columbia. Four years later he enrolled in a Royal Canadian Air Force (RCAF) refresher course which he completed at Camp Borden, Ontario. He joined British Columbia Airways Limited in 1929 to begin the first inter-city landplane service between Victoria and Vancouver in British Columbia, and Seattle, Washington, U.S.A., flying a Ford Tri-Motor aircraft. In this capacity he became the first captain of a multi-engined aircraft on the west coast. Following severe damage to this aircraft by

Inaugural flights always created excitement. On the first flight of B.C. Airways from Victoria to Vancouver, the Mayor of Vancouver rushed forward to greet the civic dignitary from Victoria and received a crack over the head from one of the propellers of the Ford Tri-Motor. This, it was felt, was of historical note, inasmuch as Mayor L.D. Taylor became one of the few persons who have survived this type of accident.

"The dedication of his superior instructional abilities in airmanship to several generations of embryonic pilots, and his general up-grading of aeronautical facilities, have been of substantial benefit to Canadian aviation."

—Induction citation, 1979

A.H. Wilson at Royal Naval College, Greenwich, as a probationary flight officer, age 18, in the Royal Naval Air Service. 1918.

another pilot, Wilson completed a seaplane course with the RCAF at Jericho Beach, Vancouver, in the spring of 1929. In the fall of that year, he joined Alaska-Washington Airways, flying a Fairchild 71 seaplane between Vancouver and Victoria, until this aircraft, too, was put out of service when it was crashed by another pilot.

Wilson joined the Aero Club of British Columbia at Vancouver in 1930 as Chief Flying Instructor. He earned a distinct reputation as a Club instructor, becoming the central figure in the drive for high standards of flying techniques so evident on the West Coast during his tenure. He was granted a Class 1 Instructor's Rating, the first issued in Western Canada by the Ministry of Transport. In 1936, when instruction in instrument flying was becoming a requirement of the Flying Clubs in Canada, he was chosen to take an instrument flying course at Camp Borden. He then became the instructor to which all other Club instructors in western Canada

came for training. As well, he was a proficient aerobatics instructor, and the first pilot in his area to fly a towed glider.

While he was with the Aero Club, Wilson became active in the RCAF's 111 Auxiliary Squadron at Vancouver during the late 1930's. In the opening stages of World War II he completed further flying courses with the RCAF at Camp Borden. His first assignment was to open Patricia Bay Air Station on Vancouver Island. He was then given Command of the Jericho Beach Air Station at Vancouver. In 1941 he was the first Commander of No. 10 Service Flying Training School (SFTS) at Dauphin, Manitoba. From there he was transferred to command No. 4 SFTS at Saskatoon, Saskatchewan.

Wilson retired from the service in 1944 with the rank of Group Captain, and joined the Airways Division of the Department of Transport. He later became Regional Superintendent of Airways in British Columbia. In this position he personally flew over all areas of the province to update existing airports and establish new flying fields. His innovations in many aeronautical fields brought new standards of flight safety to the province, including the installation of markers on cables which stretched across many of British Columbia's valleys.

In 1965 Wilson retired from aviation. He was honoured in 1979 by the International Northwest Aviation Council (INAC) for his accomplishments in instructing by having his name placed on the Honour Roll. He had qualified as a pilot on 68 aircraft types during a career which spanned almost half a century. He died on December 30, 1983.

Arthur Haliburton Wilson was inducted as a Member of Canada's Aviation Hall of Fame in 1979.

John Armistead Wilson
(1879 – 1954)

"The application of his engineering and management abilities to the problems facing the nation's emergence into the air age has been of outstanding benefit to Canadian aviation."

—Induction citation, 1974

John Armistead Wilson, C.B.E., was born in Broughty Ferry, Scotland, on November 2, 1879, and was educated there. At the age of sixteen he became apprenticed to an engineering firm in Scotland, and qualified as an engineer in 1901 at Leeds, England. He worked in Calcutta, India, as an engineer for four years, and in 1905 chose to settle in Canada. Until 1909 he worked as an engineer on the construction of Canada Cement Company plants at Exshaw, Alberta, and Hull, Quebec.

In 1910, because of his keen interest in early aviation, he joined the newly-formed Department of Naval Service as Director of Stores and Contracts. In 1918 he was promoted to Assistant Deputy Minister of

A.J. Wilson was passionately committed to the growth and well-being of civil aviation in Canada. He argued for the need to separate the control, administration and financing of military and civil aviation in order for civil aviation to develop and progress more rapidly. He felt that if civil aviation in Canada were strong, the military aspect would also be strong, for the civil branch could provide the basic training of personnel.

the Naval Service, responsible for organizing the Royal Canadian Naval Air Service (RCNAS) and the construction of naval air bases at Dartmouth and Sydney, Nova Scotia, for anti-submarine patrols. He was a member of the Governor-General's Foot Guards regiment from 1912 to 1920, and attained the rank of Captain.

Wilson was asked to draft the Air Board Act, later superceded by the Aeronautics Act. He became Secretary of the Canadian Air Board in 1920, and participated in drafting the first air regulations for Canada. The Air Board served three main purposes: to regulate civil aviation, conduct civil government operations, and organize and administer the aerial defence of Canada. A non-permanent Canadian Air Force (CAF) was formed in 1920.

The Department of National Defence (DND) was created in 1923, and all functions of the Air Board were assumed by the DND, in spite of the fact that most of the Air Board's dealings were purely civil. In 1924 the CAF was re-organized into a permanent force called the Royal Canadian Air Force (RCAF). Wilson was appointed Assistant Director and Secretary of the RCAF, responsible for civil aviation functions. The Air Board then ceased to exist.

During the summer of 1924, Wilson made a 10,000 mile (16,100 km) aerial survey trip across Canada in a flying boat, noting how aerial mapping could be done and the richness of the country's resources.

The rapid growth of aviation in Canada prompted the re-organization of the DND in 1927 into four directorates: the RCAF, Civil Air Operations, Control of Civil Aviation, and Aeronautical Engineering. Wilson was

appointed Controller of Civil Aviation and during 1927 – 28, promoted the growth of flying clubs to train pilots and develop public interest in aviation. Twenty flying clubs were organized at major centres with DND financial assistance and instructor-training at RCAF Camp Borden. Airmail routes were established between these cities.

In 1929 the government directed Wilson to arrange for the survey and construction of a trans-Canada air route from Halifax, Nova Scotia, to Vancouver, British Columbia, stretching some 3,100 miles (4,990 km). His branch would be responsible for surveying and selecting sites, constructing the airports, providing lighting, radio and weather services. In 1932 economic constraints forced the discontinuation of inter-city mail service, but the airway development continued, and provided employment during the worst years of the Depression.

During the summer of 1934 Wilson made a 15,000 mile (24,000 km) trip from coast-to-coast, and north to the Arctic Circle, using aircraft, train and automobile, to see the progress being made on construction of the trans-Canada airway. He and Inspector Bob Dodds flew a landplane over the new route between Ottawa and Winnipeg in 1935, and in July 1936, he accompanied Inspector J.H. 'Tuddy' Tudhope (Hall of Fame 1974) when he flew the Rt. Hon. C.D. Howe (Hall of Fame 1976) on a brief inspection tour of this route.

The Department of Transport was created in November 1936, with C.D. Howe as Minister, and all federal transportation and communication services, including Civil Aviation, were placed under this department. Wilson continued as Controller of Civil Aviation, and construction of the trans-Canada airways system continued without

interruption. On April 10, 1937, legislation created Trans-Canada Airlines (TCA, Hall of Fame 1974), and Wilson was appointed one of the government directors of the company.

When World War II was declared on September 3, 1939, civil aviation quickly became a military function. The Department of Transport took over almost all of the larger municipal airports so that their operation could be co-ordinated for both civil and military use. Wilson's responsibilities increased when the government decided to provide training for personnel for the war effort in Europe. The British Commonwealth Air Training Plan (BCATP), formed by agreement between Canada, Great Britain, Australia and New Zealand in 1940, was designed to train pilots, navigators, air gunners, bombers and wireless operators. Wilson's exceptional organizing abilities and broad knowledge of all phases of civil aviation throughout Canada helped him to accomplish the gigantic task of providing the necessary facilities and personnel.

In 1942 Wilson assisted in arranging the Canadian Government Trans-Atlantic Air Service (CGTAS), which was later organized and operated by TCA. The first flight took place on July 22, 1943, using a modified Lancaster aircraft, carrying official passengers, goods and mail between Canada and the United Kingdom.

Wilson, who drafted many of Canada's early civil air regulations, received many honours in recognition of his achievements. He was awarded the Julian C. Smith Memorial Medal of the Engineering Institute of Canada in 1944 for his achievement in the development of air transport in Canada. He was chosen to receive the Trans-Canada (McKee) Trophy for the year 1944 in recognition of his outstanding contribution to Canadian aviation and for his whole-hearted efforts in the development of civil aviation in Canada. In 1945 was appointed a Commander of the Order of British Empire (C.B.E.). He was presented with the Norwegian Medal of Liberation in 1948. He was named Honorary President of the Royal Canadian Flying Clubs Association.

Wilson retired from the position of Director of Air Services in 1945 after a 35-year career in aviation. He died in Ottawa on October 10, 1954.

John Armistead Wilson was inducted as a Member of Canada's Aviation Hall of Fame in 1974.

Trans-continental 'dawn to dusk' flight from Montreal to Vancouver, in the Department of Transport's Lockheed 12A. L to R: D.W. Saunders, L. Parmenter, F.I. Banghart, W.H. Hobbs, H.J. Symington, C.D. Howe, J.H. Tudhope, Cdr. C.P. Edwards, J.D. Hunter, J.A. Wilson, G. Wakeman, D.R. MacLaren. July 30, 1937.

Jack Fraser Woodman

(1925 – 1987)

Jack Fraser Woodman, C.D., was born in Saskatoon, Saskatchewan on May 14, 1925. In 1943, after graduating from high school, he joined the Royal Canadian Air Force (RCAF) at age 18. He was selected as an Air Gunner and sent overseas upon completion of gunnery school.

He arrived in England in June 1944, and was assigned to 433 Squadron, Bomber Command (RCAF Group 6). The crew completed 23 operational missions flying Handley Page Halifax and Avro Lancaster bombers before the war in Europe ended. He volunteered for duty in the Pacific, and was en route when V-J Day was declared.

He was discharged in 1945 as a Flight Sergeant and returned to Saskatoon where he enrolled in the University of Saskatchewan's School of Engineering. He rejoined the RCAF in 1948 and was sent to No. 1 Flying School in Centralia, Ontario, for pilot training. He received his pilot's wings in 1949 and was sent to 111 Communications and Rescue Flight, Winnipeg, Manitoba, where he flew Douglas Dakotas, Beech Expeditors and Noorduyn Norseman aircraft, gaining experience on wheels, floats and skis.

Two missions were of particular note during this period. During Operation Denholme, in June of 1951, Woodman was captain of the plane that made the sighting and completed the rescue of a lost

The NF-104A, with a rocket booster of 6,000 lb thrust supplementing its turbojet, was a highly supersonic aircraft. Jack Woodman made several flights at more than twice the speed of sound, and on August 21, 1963, he achieved Mach 2.6.

Jack Woodman in pressure suit, with the Lockheed NF-104A Aerospace Trainer. 1963.

Saskatchewan Airways aircraft. Also in June, in Operation Bishop, he flew a jet-assisted-take-off (JATO) equipped Dakota on a mercy flight to bring out an ailing Department of Transport (DOT) radio operator at Mould Bay, Prince Patrick Island, approximately 76 degrees north latitude, in the Arctic Ocean. At that time this mission covered the longest distance ever undertaken by the RCAF at 4,600 miles (7,400 km).

In late 1951, Woodman was appointed as Canada's representative to the Empire Test Pilots' School, Farnborough, England, a 10-month finishing school for test pilots, to which Commonwealth air forces were invited to send their single most outstanding flier. After graduating from Farnborough, he was assigned to the Central Experimental and Proving Establishment at Rockcliffe Air Base, Ontario, and then posted to the A.V. Roe aircraft company (Avro) in Toronto, Ontario, as an RCAF acceptance pilot, flying 17-ton Avro CF-100 all-weather jet interceptors. At the same time he was the acceptance pilot for the de Havilland Aircraft Company, flying Lancasters, Vampires, Otters and Chipmunks.

In June of 1955 Woodman demonstrated the CF-100 at the Paris Air Show for Avro

Canada, flying magnificent aerobatics, including the only spin of the whole show.

To prepare for the Avro CF-105 Arrow program, and to gain experience in supersonic flying, particularly in delta-winged aircraft, Woodman spent a year at Eglin Air Force Base (AFB) in Florida as part of the United States Air Force (USAF) team evaluating the F-102A. He also attended the USAF Fighter-Interceptor School at Tyndall AFB, Florida.

In early 1957, Woodman was again assigned to Avro Canada, this time as RCAF Project Pilot for the CF-105 Arrow program. Chief Experimental Test Pilot Jan Zurakowski (Hall of Fame 1974) made the first flight of the Arrow on March 25, 1958. Woodman flew the eighth flight of the Arrow on April 22, 1958, and made five more flights on subsequent models of the Arrow. When the program was cancelled in 1959, he was the only military pilot to have flown the aircraft.

With the cancellation of the Arrow program, he participated in the evaluation of several other aircraft for the RCAF. The Lockheed F-104 Starfighter was selected to fill the fighter-bomber role for No. 1 Air Division in Europe, and in January of 1960 he was transferred to Palmdale, California, as Project Pilot to work with Lockheed in the development of this new model. When the CF-104 went into squadron service in Canada, he was offered a position with the Lockheed Company in California. He was discharged from the RCAF in August 1962, as a Squadron Leader.

It is interesting that, unknown to him, Woodman was at the top of an unofficial list of three or four RCAF pilots who were possible candidates for the U.S. space program as astronauts. However, the Canadian government of the day did not commit the funding necessary to be a partner in the program.

Woodman was Project Pilot at Lockheed for the NF-104A Aerospace Trainer, an

F-104 with rocket assist, intended to train future test pilots on the intricacies of high altitude flying, weightlessness, full pressure suits, rocket engine handling, and flying with reaction controls. On one flight, he set an unofficial world altitude record for jets of 118,400 feet (36,088 m). But a control malfunction caused the aircraft to pitch up, enter a spin, and only after an 85,000 ft. (25,908 m) fall was he able to level the airplane off and land safely.

Lockheed began development of the L-1011 TriStar passenger transport in the mid-1960's. Woodman did most of the simulator development of the flying qualities for this aircraft.

In December 1968, he was appointed Chief Engineering Test Pilot and was responsible for all flying activity associated with Engineering Flight Tests in both military and commercial programs including F-104, S3, P3 Orion, a long-range maritime reconnaissance aircraft, and the L-1011.

In late 1973, Woodman was appointed Division Manager in charge of Commercial Operations which included Engineering Flight Test, Production Flight Test and Customer Training for the L-1011 TriStar. He flew the L-1011 around the world twice, demonstrating it to almost every major airline in the world. Due to its reliability, the wide-bodied L-1011 became a favourite with pilots.

In 1976 he was promoted to Director of Flying, Commercial Programs and Customer Requirements for Lockheed. He retired in 1982.

Woodman flew over 60 types of aircraft, had over 10,000 hours of flight time and 37 continuous years of flying. He was a Member of the Canadian Aeronautics and Space Institute and a Fellow and President-Elect in 1985 of the Society of Experimental Test Pilots. He died in California on May 16, 1987.

Jack Fraser Woodman was inducted as a Member of Canada's Aviation Hall of Fame in 1995.

Jerauld George (Jerry) Wright
(b. 1917)

Jerauld George (Jerry) Wright, D.F.C., C.D., was born in Liverpool, Nova Scotia, on August 31, 1917, where he received his education. He was employed at Liverpool as a certified pharmaceutical clerk until 1940, when he joined the Royal Canadian Air Force (RCAF). After graduating as a navigator, he served on operations out of England and India with 240 Squadron, Royal Air Force (RAF) and was employed on coastal operations until 1944.

During two tours of duty comprising more than 1,200 operational hours on flying boats, Wright was involved in some of the earliest Arctic flying and some of the war's longest patrol flights. He participated in flights to Spitzbergen, off the coast of Norway, Russia, and across the Indian Ocean. He was commissioned as a Pilot Officer in early 1942 and for one 23-hour continuous flight to Spitzbergen during the winter of that year, he was awarded the Distinguished Flying Cross (D.F.C.). These Arctic operations required the devising of

The R-Theta Computer is an ingenious automatic navigation instrument designed for use in long-range, high-speed aircraft. The system performs automatically and continuously most of the numerical and plotting operations usually carried out by the navigator. It does not rely on radio transmissions from ground stations and is immune to 'jamming' or radio interference. The pilot no longer has to fly in a series of straight lines in order for the navigator to carry on with conventional navigation.

special techniques and adaptations of equipment. This brought about the first of a long line of inventions to solve special problems having to do with the allocation, development and use of navigational equipment in a wide variety of environments.

Special duties in the Mediterranean, India and Burma followed, during which he was promoted to Flight Lieutenant. The flights he made required the development of special techniques in celestial navigation for landing with precise timing at night in small bays along the Burmese coast. For this work he was Mentioned in Despatches.

In 1945 Wright was sent to the Empire Navigation School at Shawbury, England, where he was engaged in test and development work related to aerial navigation. While there he completed the advanced specialist navigational course and in 1946 was posted to the Test and Development Establishment of the RCAF at Rockcliffe Air Base, Ontario, to work on compass problems. He was then named Head of the Test and Development Section of the Air Navigation School at Summerside, Prince Edward Island, to develop new techniques and equipment for Arctic flying. It was there that he developed the prototype of the Synchronous Astro Compass which greatly improved heading accuracy at all latitudes, and which is used in all Canadian Forces long range aircraft.

Wright remained at Summerside until 1949, when he was promoted to Squadron Leader and posted to RCAF Headquarters in Ottawa to take charge of the Navigational Instrument Development Branch of the Air Member for Technical Services Division. It was there that his flair for inventions was seriously noted, when he designed what was to become a family of distance/bearing type computers of which the best known were the R Theta and the Position and Homing Indicator Mark 3. The R Theta was designed to fit into an aircraft instrument panel and was

W/C J.G. Wright with the R-Theta Computer unit which he invented in 1951.

capable of two major roles. At the flip of a switch it could tell the pilot how many miles he was from home base and what compass heading to fly to get back to base. It could also show the pilot how many miles to fly to reach a destination and what direction to fly. For this invention, the first major breakthrough in aerial navigation in decades, Wright was awarded the Trans-Canada (McKee) Trophy for 1953. He invented and patented some 30 navigational devices, many of which were accepted for use by military agencies of other nations.

Wright was promoted to Wing Commander in 1954. As an indication of the confidence engendered by his inventive potential, he was assigned to complete a guided missile course in 1954, attend the RCAF Staff College at Toronto, Ontario, in 1957-58, and the senior anti-submarine detection course at the Joint Services Staff College in the United Kingdom in 1961.

During this extended period at RCAF Headquarters, Wright was responsible for studies and analyses, and development and/or selection of such equipment as flight instruments, navigation systems, anti-submarine warfare technical systems and flight simulators.

At the Naval Research Establishment, Dartmouth, Nova Scotia, he was responsible for studies and analyses

concerning underwater radar detection devices, hydrofoil operational feasibility and sonar research programs. His final assignment at Canadian Forces Headquarters was responsibility for the selection and/or development of avionics flight equipment and anti-submarine warfare tactical systems for all Canadian Forces aircraft.

In the 1955-65 period, Wright invented the Air Navigation and Tactical Control (ANTAC) system for the RCAF Argus, components of which were also used by France, Australia and Japan.

Wright is a Fellow of the Royal Meteorological Society and a Fellow of Honour of the Canadian Aeronautics and Space Institute. He holds the coveted Inventor's Award from the Canadian Government's Patent and Development Corporation.

On retirement from the service in 1966, after receiving numerous honours and awards from professional societies and groups, and a number of governmental presentations for his pioneering work, he formed his own consulting firm in Ottawa, JGW Systems. He also authored more than 50 technical and scientific papers on a wide range of aviation subjects.

Jerauld George (Jerry) Wright was inducted as a Member of Canada's Aviation Hall of Fame in 1974.

Dennis Kestell Yorath
(1905 – 1981)

"His business management abilities, coupled with a far-sighted appreciation of the country's civil flying requirements, were a prime factor in establishing a national pilot training scheme that has substantially benefited Canadian aviation."

–Induction citation, 1974

Dennis Kestell Yorath, M.B.E., LL.D. (Hon), was born in London, England, on April 30, 1905. His family immigrated to Canada in 1913 and settled in Saskatoon, Saskatchewan. He continued his schooling there and in Victoria, British Columbia.

He spent two years with the Imperial Bank of Canada at Edmonton, Alberta, and in 1924 joined the Edmonton staff of Northwestern Utilities Ltd., then a subsidiary of the International Utilities Corporation. He moved to Calgary, Alberta, in 1925 and was employed by another subsidiary, the Canadian Western

While still president of RCFCA, Yorath donated a trophy, the Yorath Trophy, to stimulate active competition among the flying clubs in Canada at the management level. The award went to the instructor-manager of a club which had used its facilities to the best advantage. M.D. Fallow (Hall of Fame 1992) of the Edmonton Flying Club, was awarded this trophy eight times in the period from 1950 to 1958.

Dennis Yorath with his Trans-Canada (McKee) Trophy, awarded for the year 1949.

Natural Gas Company. He served in various management positions and became president of the two subsidiaries in 1956. In 1962 Yorath was named chairman of the two companies, a position he held until 1969. From 1961 to 1972 he served as Vice-President and Director of International Utilities Corporation, and Vice-Chairman from 1973-76. The corporation's name was changed to IU International Corporation in 1973.

Yorath began his involvement in aviation in 1928 when he became a charter member of the Calgary Flying Club. He earned his Private Pilot's Licence in 1929. He served as Director for several years and Vice-President of this flying club from 1929 to 1933, an office he held again from 1939 to 1944. He became President of the club in 1944.

When the British Commonwealth Air Training Plan (BCATP) was instituted after the outbreak of World War II, Yorath was named Managing Director of No. 5 Elementary Flying Training School at Lethbridge, Alberta. In 1941 the school moved to High River, Alberta, where he remained in command until the BCATP concluded its operations in May 1945.

It was largely due to Yorath's exceptional management abilities that the High River Flying Training School was named by the government as one of the most outstanding elementary flying training establishments in Canada. For his work in directing pilot training, he was named a Member of the Order of the British Empire (M.B.E.) in 1946.

The Royal Canadian Flying Clubs Association (RCFCA) elected him Alberta Zone Director in 1944, and in that capacity, Yorath closely observed and analyzed private flying trends in Canada, including costs and revenue. He noted a declining interest in training, as well as in sport and recreational flying. He decided that the situation had to change if a pool of young pilots were to be maintained for future requirements of defence and commercial aviation.

During his term in office as national president of RCFCA from 1947 to 1949, the association carried out several successful projects designed to enhance the development of aviation in Canada. Outstanding examples were the revival of the Webster Trophy competition in 1947 and the National Flying Club Week, which was an annual publicity project; organization of the Model Aeronautics Association of Canada in 1948; and reinstatement of the Safe Flying Campaign of the RCFCA member clubs in 1948, which had contributed to a lowering of accident rates. Yorath was also instrumental in gaining federal government aid for student pilots in 1949. For these contributions he was awarded the Trans-Canada (McKee) Trophy for 1949.

He was awarded an Honorary Degree of Doctor of Laws from the University of Alberta in 1974. Dennis Yorath died on May 8, 1981.

Dennis Kestell Yorath was inducted as a Member of Canada's Aviation Hall of Fame in 1974.

Franklin Inglee (Frank) Young
(1909 – 1973)

Franklin Inglee (Frank) Young was born on August 7, 1909, in Toronto, Ontario. He received his education there, and began his flying instruction with Elliot Air Service at Hamilton, Ontario at the age of 17. He received his Private Pilot Licence in 1927, and two years later, his Commercial Pilot's Licence.

In 1928 Young joined a barnstorming group on a trans-Canada tour giving public exhibitions. He flew for several years as a bush pilot delivering prospectors, settlers and supplies to remote northern outposts of Ontario and Quebec. Early in 1930, he began flying for Century Airways and National Air Transport at Barker Field in Toronto as a flying instructor, but he made his living mostly from barnstorming.

He was selected by the Royal Canadian Air Force (RCAF) in 1932 to join the first group to attend a course at Camp Borden, Ontario, specializing in instrument and night flying, and navigation. He then helped revive the Brant-Norfolk Aero Club at Brantford, Ontario, as Chief Instructor.

In 1933 he joined Dominion Skyways at Rouyn, Quebec as a bush pilot, operating in Ontario, Quebec and Labrador. In 1935-36 he flew the company's first scheduled air service linking the Quebec centres of Montreal, Val d'Or and Rouyn, using a Norseman aircraft. During this period he

Through an event such as the National Air Show, Young hoped to bring to the minds of Canadians, and others from around the world, the fact that "Canada is second to none when it comes to designing, developing and constructing aircraft, and flying them."

flew many charter flights for the Ontario Provincial Air Service (OPAS, Belt of Orion 1991), assisting during serious forest fire outbreaks.

In January 1938, Young joined Trans-Canada Airlines (TCA) as a pilot, later flying some of the first official flights of this new airline. These flights included the leg from Winnipeg to Vancouver on the trans-continental run in 1940, and the first Toronto-New York run in 1941. In 1941 he was named Chief Pilot.

During World War II, TCA provided assistance in operating the Trans-Atlantic Ferry Command, through which planes and pilots were ferried to Great Britain. In addition to his responsibilities as Chief Pilot for TCA, Young played a key role in this war effort, serving as a check-pilot for American airmen applying to fly with the Trans-Atlantic Ferry Command, and instructing military pilots in instrument flying procedures.

Promotions followed for Young: in 1943 he became Superintendent of Operations for TCA's eastern region, at Moncton, New Brunswick. Two years later he was appointed Operations Manager for the central region at Toronto.

In the early 1940's, TCA was flying DC-3 aircraft, and both the airline and government authorities recognized the need to reduce trans-continental flight times. A more direct airway would eliminate the circuitous course around the Great Lakes to the north and would allow aircraft to fly directly over the lakes. The preferred route would pass through Sault Ste. Marie, cross the U.S. border into the State of Michigan, and follow the south shore of Lake Superior to the Keweenaw Peninsula. From there the route would cross Lake Superior to the Lakehead and go on to Winnipeg.

In 1946 Young was assigned the task of negotiating with the Michigan authorities to allow TCA to fly across their state. To fly this shorter route would require

The Trans-Canada (McKee) Trophy being presented to Franklin Young by Air Marshal C. Roy Slemon, Chief of Air Staff, at the annual meeting of the Air Industries and Transport Association, November 9, 1954.

the construction of additional airports and installation of lighting and navigation aids. As his technical assistant, Young chose B.A. 'Barney' Rawson (Hall of Fame 1974), who made the first aerial survey of the alternative route in May 1946. Negotiations were successful, surveys and airports were completed, and TCA made its inaugural flight over the new Great Lakes Airway on July 1, 1947. This project was of major benefit to TCA: it greatly reduced the flight time between Toronto and Winnipeg, and the weather along the new route was much better.

In 1951 Young became closely associated with the Royal Canadian Flying Clubs Association and served as president of the Toronto Flying Club from 1951 to 1953. At this time he conceived the idea of organizing a national air show in conjunction with the Canadian National Exhibition at Toronto. In 1953 he successfully produced the first National Air Show for Canada. The flying display, held over the water front of Lake Ontario, included the Governor-General's Cup Race,

and a program of precision flight performed by the RCAF.

The air show concept served to raise awareness about aviation in Canada, and earned Young the Trans-Canada (McKee) Trophy for the year 1953. He was awarded Canada's Centennial Medal in 1967 "in recognition of valuable service to the Nation".

In 1967 Young was named General Manager of Air Canada, formerly TCA, a position he held until his retirement in 1970. He was then appointed a commissioner of the Toronto Transport Commission. In 1972 he was named Chairman of that authority, completing his term the following year. He died in Toronto on October 11, 1973.

Franklin Inglee (Frank) Young was inducted as a Member of Canada's Aviation Hall of Fame in 1974.

Janusz (Jan) Zurakowski

(b. 1914)

Janusz (Jan) Zurakowski was born on September 12, 1914, in Ryzawka, Russia, and moved to Poland seven years later where he was educated at Garwolin and Lubin. As a youth he was interested in aviation, and won a 1929 national competition for building model airplanes. The prize was a ride in a plane, Zurakowski's first flight. In 1932, while attending high school, he learned to fly gliders built by his older brother.

In 1934 he joined the Polish Air Force, and in 1937 was posted to 161 Fighter Squadron at Lwow, Poland. At the outbreak of World War II in September 1939, he was an instructor in a Polish fighter squadron.

When Poland was defeated by Germany in 1939, Zurakowski escaped to England. He flew for the British Royal Air Force (RAF), and during the Battle of Britain, while flying with 234 and 609 Squadrons, he was credited with destroying three enemy aircraft in combat. In April 1942, he was promoted to Flight Lieutenant and several

In 1951, while flying a Meteor fighter at the Farnborough Air Show in England, Jan Zurakowski demonstrated a new aerobatic manoeuver. With a fully loaded Meteor, including rockets and wing-tip fuel tanks, he climbed vertically until it was almost stationary in the vertical plane. Then, by cutting one engine, he made the aircraft cartwheel in the vertical plane, wing over wing, as it fell. This became known as the 'Zurabatic Cartwheel'.

S/L Jan Zurakowski in London after breaking the international speed record on the London-Copenhagen-London flight in a Gloster Meteor Mk 8, April 4, 1950.

months later took command of 316 Polish Fighter Squadron. The following year he was named Deputy Wing Leader of the Northolt Wing. For his wartime services he was awarded the Polish Virtuti Militari and Polish Cross of Valour, with two Bars. He was twice Mentioned in Despatches for his conduct during engagements with the enemy.

In 1944, after completing the Empire Test Pilot's Course, Zurakowski was posted to the RAF's Aircraft and Armament Experimental Establishment, test flying de Havilland's Hornet fighter. In 1947 he joined the Gloster Aircraft Company as an experimental test pilot. He test flew the later models of the Meteor fighter, which was first flown in 1943 and was Great Britain's first jet fighter. He also test flew the Javelin, a delta-wing model. On April 4, 1950, he established a new international air speed record between London-Copenhagen-London in a Meteor Mk 8.

Zurakowski immigrated to Canada in 1952 to join Avro Aircraft Limited at Toronto, Ontario, as Chief Development Test Pilot. For the next few years he worked as test pilot on the development of the CF-100 fighter aircraft which was being built at that time. He flew the CF-100 Mk 4 supersonically in 1952, the first Canadian-designed aircraft to reach that speed.

During this period, initial work on a new Canadian supersonic aircraft was in

progress, the Avro CF-105. The idea of a supersonic interceptor, known later as the Arrow, originated in 1951 when the Avro team in Canada under Jim Floyd (Hall of Fame 1993) submitted a brochure to the Royal Canadian Air Force (RCAF) containing proposals for supersonic fighters. In March 1952, an operational requirement was received from the RCAF for an all-weather interceptor. In June 1952, the company presented two proposals: a single and a twin-engine delta-wing interceptor with a two-man crew. In June 1953, the company presented the CF-105 proposal and obtained instructions to go ahead with the design study. This aircraft was meant to defend Canada's Arctic against possible Soviet attack, and was designed to meet specifications that hold up today, including flying at Mach 2, twice the speed of sound.

After six years at Avro, Zurakowski was chosen to be the first pilot to fly the Arrow. On March 25, 1958, he completed the first flight of the prototype, checking the response of controls, engines, undercarriage and air brakes, handling qualities at speeds of up to 400 knots, and low speed in a landing configuration. He flew Arrow models 1, 2, and 3 on a total of 21 test flights, climbing higher and flying faster. He flew it at Mach 1.89, another Avro test pilot, W. 'Spud' Potocki took it to Mach 1.98, but it was never tried at maximum speed. On February 20, 1959, production of the aircraft was halted by the Canadian government and the five existing planes and others in production were ordered to be destroyed, along with all blueprints, brochures, reports and photographs.

Zurakowski was awarded the Trans-Canada (McKee) Trophy for 1958 in recognition of this experimental work and two years later retired from aviation to engage in the tourist business at Barry's Bay, Ontario.

Janusz 'Jan' Zurakowski was inducted as a Member of Canada's Aviation Hall of Fame in 1974.

"The dedication of his aeronautical skills to the successful flight testing of Canada's first supersonic aircraft resulted in outstanding benefit to Canadian aviation."

—Induction citation, 1974

Belt of Orion
Awards
for Excellence

CANADA'S AVIATION HALL OF FAME

**Canada's Aviation
Hall of Fame**

1973 to 1998

Canadian Air Line Pilots Association (CALPA)

CALPA was formed on December 1, 1937, to consolidate airline pilots' views regarding aviation concerns, with the authority to voice them when necessary.

In 1943, on the initiative of CALPA, an agreement of affiliation was signed between the Canadian, British and American Air Line Pilots Associations to promote the orderly development of international civil aviation. This affiliation was the fore-runner of the International Federation of Air Line Pilots Association (IFALPA), co-founded by CALPA in 1948. At that time, IFALPA represented the pilots of 65 nations, with CALPA as its second largest member. The Federation's mandate is to consolidate the opinion of its members on a wide variety of topics that concern aviation technology and safety, and present these to the International Civil Aviation Organization (ICAO), the International Air Transport Association (IATA), Interpol, and governments.

In 1976 bilingual traffic control was instituted at some Canadian airports. Spirited opposition by CALPA arose from the fact that it was a political decision with little regard for safety due to a lack of clear understanding of communications by unilingual pilots. CALPA helped to ensure that the policy was not instituted until procedures were developed to safely govern it. The development process took most of two years and a CALPA member was continuously present.

A very important division of CALPA worked in the technical and air safety field. Several committees at the local and executive council levels dealt with safety concerns and accident investigation. In 1956 CALPA's Safety Chairman and a Trans-Canada Airlines engineer graduated from the Accident Investigation course at the University of Southern California. They became the first trained accident investigators in Canada.

In 1979 the Dubin Commission was formed to inquire into aviation safety in Canada. CALPA was represented throughout, and the inquiry required major effort from CALPA's Technical and Air Safety Division, which presented 22 witnesses and seven complete briefs during the 116 days of hearings. CALPA had great influence on the many benefits to aviation that resulted from the Dubin hearings, such as the creation of the Canadian Aviation Safety Board, the independent accident investigation agency whose establishment CALPA had long been promoting.

CALPA worked tirelessly for four years to persuade the Canadian government to ratify The Hague and Montreal Conventions against hijacking. Thus security was enhanced at Canadian airports.

CALPA's Aeromedical Committee worked for many years to obtain a more enlightened attitude by the airlines and the authorities toward pilot medical fitness. As a result of the work of this committee, many highly trained pilots have been retained and have been able to continue their chosen profession.

CALPA has influenced the development of air transportation in Canada in a number of other ways. It has had impact on development of procedures for fire fighting, rescue work, and airport disaster planning. It has been active in the study of bird strike hazards, has played a major role in formulating procedures for the handling of dangerous goods, produced a

booklet on the function of an aircraft commander as a peace officer, and has at all times worked for a safer and more efficient air transportation system.

Early in its history, the Association began publication of a quarterly magazine, The Pilot, a widely respected periodical.

CALPA became a respected voice in aviation and thus fulfilled the aims of its founders, which were to consolidate and present the professional views of the airline pilot on his/her occupation.

In 1996, Air Canada Pilots left CALPA and formed their own organization, ACPA. The remaining members of CALPA then arranged a merger with the Air Line Pilots Association (ALPA), which took effect on February 1, 1997. ALPA's head office is in Herndon, Virginia, U.S.A.

The Belt of Orion Award for Excellence was conferred on the Canadian Air Line Pilots Association (CALPA) in 1988.

Air Cadet League of Canada

The Air Cadet League of Canada is a non-profit, civilian organization composed of leading business and professional people from all parts of Canada. The League functions through a national board of governors, provincial and regional directors, and local sponsoring bodies supporting each squadron. The League is aimed at providing citizenship and aviation training for Canadian youths in high school.

In early 1937, as war clouds started forming in Europe, several prominent men, mostly World War I veterans from the air division of the Royal Canadian Navy (RCN) and Royal Air Force (RAF), across Canada independently conceived the idea of establishing Air Cadet Squadrons in their home cities as a means of interesting the young men of the day in the possibility of future service with the Royal Canadian Air Force.

In 1939 the Federal Air Advisory Council appointed S/L Nick Carter of Vancouver, British Columbia, to organize the youth of the country in an Air Cadet Organization. He personally traveled across Canada expounding on the merits of such a program, which ultimately led to Air

It is significant to note that in 1981, His Royal Highness Prince Phillip, Air-Commodore-in-Chief, Royal Canadian Air Cadets, congratulated the League on its 40th anniversary. He especially emphasized that the training provided by the Air Cadet League of Canada does much more than foster an interest in aviation; it is equally important as a preparation for responsible citizenship.

"The Air Cadet League of Canada program has developed the attributes of good citizenship and leadership in Canadian youth while stimulating their interests in aeronautics and assisting in their pursuits of careers to the betterment of Canadian aviation." —Belt of Orion Award citation, 1989

Minister Powers sponsoring Order-in-Council PC 6647, which passed on November 11, 1940, and authorized the formation of the Air Cadet League of Canada.

In April, 1941, the Air Cadet League of Canada was granted a Dominion Charter and many squadrons were formed across the country. Over 3,000 cadets graduated into the RCAF and their gallant record in all theaters of the allied war operations provided tangible proof of the value of Air Cadet training towards Canada's war efforts.

Following World War II, there was a natural lessening of interest in Cadet activities and the organization floundered somewhat. In 1946 the Canadian government implemented a plan of sponsoring 15,000 Air Cadets, and a peacetime program was adopted to combine citizenship training along with aviation instruction.

In addition, a scholarship program was established whereby all senior Cadets could compete annually for 250 positions to train for a Transport Canada Private Pilot Licence. Within this program, successful Cadets were provided with six weeks of powered flight instruction at various flying schools across the country during their summer holidays.

In 1968 the League lost its original partner, the RCAF, due to unification of the Canadian Armed Forces. The League adopted gliding instruction as part of their program in order to keep the "air" in Air Cadets and provide more flight instruction to the Cadet membership. More than 45,000 glider flights have been carried out each year since that time and over 320 Air Cadet glider pilots are licenced annually. Presently, the League owns more than 50 gliders and 27 tow planes which are operated by the Department of National Defence in support of the League's training program.

In 1975 membership was opened to include girls, thereby extending the Air

Cadet training influence to the total youth of Canada. In 1989 there were over 440 squadrons operating across Canada, and 30 per cent of the membership was comprised of young women.

The Belt of Orion Award for Excellence was bestowed upon the Air Cadet League of Canada in 1989.

Southern Alberta
Institute of
Technology

"For over sixty years the Southern Alberta Institute of Technology has offered courses applicable to the work of the air engineer and has contributed both provincially and nationally to the progress of aviation in Canada."

—Belt of Orion Award citation, 1990

Southern Alberta Institute of Technology (SAIT)

As early as 1922, the Southern Alberta Institute of Technology, formerly called the Provincial Institute of Technology and Art, was offering courses which were applicable to the work of the air engineer. This included electrical engineering, motor mechanics, battery and ignition, armature winding and engineering mechanics. Welding and radio were added in 1927.

The Institute's entry into a specific aviation field was casual, incidental, almost accidental when it took on the responsibility of offering ground school courses for the student pilots of the Calgary Air Club. By 1931 the Ground Courses in Aviation, as they were designated, were offered as both day and evening classes. In 1935, there were 45 enrollees in the day classes. The Institute continued to teach aeronautics up to the beginning of world War II.

With the outbreak of World War II, the Institute ceased to teach courses for future pilots and turned its attention to those whose duty it was to keep the aircraft in the air. The annual Report of the Alberta Department of Education indicates the registrations in various air engineering categories as follows:

Aircraft Engineers are as essential to the aviation industry as pilots, yet because the Aircraft Maintenance Engineer's work, in comparison to the pilot's, is unglamorous, its importance is often overlooked, even in the world of aviation itself. Pilots whose stories appear on previous pages admit freely their total reliance on their air engineers for the air worthiness of their machines.

Intake	No.1	No.2	No.3	Total
Fitters	32	21	20	73
Riggers	–	14	18	32
Electricians	–	13	–	13
Wireless Operators/ Mechanics	–	23	40	63
Total	32	71	78	181

These three intakes followed one another at seventeen week intervals.

The training courses continued throughout the war, with most of the graduates entering the Royal Canadian Air Force (RCAF) to become air engine mechanics, air frame mechanics or wireless operators. That their initial intake training was wholly adequate is indicated by the fact that two of the Institute's graduates led their intakes group in air engine mechanics at the RCAF No. 1 Wireless School in Montreal, Quebec.

During the war the Institute operated under the most trying of circumstances, in the grandstand at the exhibition grounds, as the RCAF had pre-empted their building for No. 4 Wireless School. At the end of the war they were able to move back to their own home. That year the federal Department of Transport authorized the Institute to make repairs to any aircraft, including the engines, carrying commercial or private certification.

In 1947 SAIT began to teach the final year of a three-year course leading to the examination of Associated Fellow of the Royal Aeronautical Association. The 1989 course catalogue gave the following information regarding the programs:

Aeronautical Engineering Technology:

Most courses focus on theoretical work. After completing the second year, students are eligible to receive a diploma in Mechanical Engineering Technology (Aeronautics). The third year qualifies graduates for the diploma in AET.

Graduates have successfully taken their places in engineering teams within the areas of aircraft design, manufacturing and operations.

Aircraft Maintenance Engineering Technology:

An Aircraft Maintenance Engineering Technologist is trained to maintain aircraft and components, whether structural, mechanical, or electrical. Graduates find work in all areas of the aviation industry, including fixed wing aircraft, rotary wing aircraft, general aviation, corporate aviation, engine and component overhaul facilities and heavy maintenance.

Grade XII standing is required for admission into either program.

Today, Aeronautical Engineering graduates of SAIT are active in the aviation industry not only in Alberta, but across Canada and beyond. In the field of Aircraft Maintenance Engineers Technology, SAIT's two-year program is unexcelled in Canada and unsurpassed anywhere.

The Belt of Orion Award for Excellence was bestowed upon the Southern Alberta Institute of Technology in 1990.

"The innovative thinking of the Ontario government, the pilots, air engineers and support staff has resulted in major accomplishments that have benefitted Canadian aviation." —Belt of Orion Award citation, 1991

Ontario Ministry of Natural Resources, Aviation and Fire Management Branch

One of the earliest provincial forestry aviation services was developed in Ontario, when thirteen Curtiss HS-2L flying boats were purchased in 1924. A modern waterfront structural steel hangar was built at Sault Ste. Marie, and eastern and western division bases were built at Sudbury and Sioux Lookout. A network of sub-bases were located all across Northern Ontario.

The first applications of the airplane by the Ontario Provincial Air Service (OPAS) enabled the Ontario Government's Forestry Branch to obtain an accurate inventory of the type, location and extent of its varied forest resources. With this information, it was possible to determine in which areas lumbering should be encouraged, where and when fire patrols should be made, and how fire suppression activities should be carried out. The first air-to-ground report of a forest fire was made from an OPAS flying boat in 1924, using communications equipment designed by the Air Service.

Technology and innovation related to these issues have been worked out with such consistently good results that both

operators and manufacturers of aircraft have turned to the OPAS for advice and guidance in their respective fields. The OPAS made a systematic study of essential aircraft characteristics and collaborated with manufacturers on the design of aircraft suited to northern Canada's needs. Its experience helped greatly in the design of the famous de Havilland Beaver.

OPAS pilots, flying the Beaver and working in cooperation with the National Research Council, have taken part in some outstanding experimental research projects. Excellent work was done on an aircraft ski design in the 1950's. By 1952, a ski suited to all Ontario snow conditions was approved by the Department of Transport. During that period, several other successful experiments were carried out: waterbombing as a means of fire suppression, parachuting supplies to ground parties, and the use of a radar device to assist in glassy water landings. In a different field, some original and successful research was done on aerial fish planting, with a view to stocking Ontario lakes with suitable species. In the 1940's, a Canso was adapted as a spray plane to combat wide-spread forest insect infestations.

OPAS fitted their aircraft with air-to-ground loud speakers, which were used by pilots to direct firefighters, contact lost persons and warn tourists of impending dangers.

Research and experiments in waterbombing has progressed to where smaller, specially-equipped sea planes can pick up in excess of 2,000 litres of water in a matter of seconds, attack a fire and return, time after time. These aircraft, along with the heavy waterbombers, are successful in holding the spread of fire, giving ground forces the time they need to set up and put the fire out.

Low level drops by parachute of fire pumps, hoses, fuel, shovels, axes, radio, camping gear and food enable the ground crews to complete the job. Delivery of fire crews and their equipment directly to a fire scene is a task now assigned to helicopters.

OPAS has a reputation for excellence. Over the years, personnel from its ranks went on to high levels of achievement, winning the Harmon and Trans-Canada (McKee) Trophies, becoming air vice-marshals, deputy minister, member of the Air Transport Board, and DOT inspectors. Many have been inducted as Members of Canada's Aviation Hall of Fame.

Although the name has changed to the Aviation and Fire Management Branch of the Ministry of Natural Resources, today's air service still conducts many of the same duties. Air service fixed wing and rotary aircraft are utilized in a number of additional functions, including: general and executive transport, wildlife census, photography platform, an innovative rabies bait program, fish and wildlife enforcement, flood patrol, infrared sensing, demonstrations and search and rescue.

The Belt of Orion Award for Excellence was awarded to the Ontario Ministry of Natural Resources, Aviation and Fire Management Branch, in 1991.

The 1991 fleet of the Ontario Ministry of Natural Resources, Aviation and Forestry Branch, consisted of nine CL-215 heavy waterbombing aircraft, six DHC-6 Twin Otter utility aircraft, 12 DHC-2 Turbo Beavers, two King Airs, one Navajo and six light and medium helicopters. Also maintained are the world's oldest flying Beaver, and the restored Fairchild KR-34 biplane— both reflections of a proud history.

CANADIAN OWNERS AND PILOTS ASSOCIATION

"For over forty years, COPA has used its resources to promote aviation so that Canadians may progress economically and socially through benefits that the airplane will continue to provide." —Belt of Orion Award citation, 1993

Canadian Owners and Pilots Association (COPA)

The Canadian Owners and Pilots Association is a membership-driven organization that is recognized as the voice of general aviation in Canada. COPA supports and defends the right of Canadians to enjoy the freedom to fly. The idea of forming a non-profit, democratically constituted organization to represent pilots and aircraft owners was conceived in April of 1952. Letters patent were issued over the seal of the Secretary of State for Canada in 1954.

COPA represents the collective view of pilots and private aircraft operators to all levels and branches of government, to other organizations and to the public.

One of COPA's main functions is the dissemination of aviation information to its members. In 1954, COPA began publishing a monthly COPA newsletter and a magazine titled "Canadian Flight". In 1964, COPA started a monthly newspaper called "Canadian General

The Canadian Owners and Pilots Association is governed by a board of directors, either elected or appointed. Geographical regions across Canada are represented by directors who are nominated and elected by members. Other directors are appointed to represent specialized aviation associations. Aside from essential travel expenses, COPA's directors serve without financial compensation. The head office of the organization is in Ottawa, Ontario.

Aviation News". Over the next 30 years, the newspaper expanded to become a forum for all general aviation in Canada from ultralight flying to corporate aviation. In 1994, the newspaper, which had become the largest aviation publication in Canada, was renamed "Canadian Flight". At that time, COPA began publishing its "Canadian Flight Annual", a unique directory of information for flying in Canada.

COPA provides services for specialty aviation groups. In 1957, COPA formed the first volunteer civilian search and rescue organization, called the Emergency Air Corps. In the early 1960's, COPA assisted with the formation and the initial administration of the Canadian Business Aircraft Association. In 1985, COPA agreed to supply the Ultralight Pilots Association of Canada with a monthly newspaper. COPA assumed the administration of the Canadian Seaplane Association in 1996.

A network of local chapters of COPA, called COPA Flights, was started in 1964. By 1997, there were over forty COPA Flights fostering recreational aviation in local communities across Canada. In 1995 COPA Flights became official participants in the Young Eagles Program, an Experimental Aircraft Association initiative to offer youngsters age 8 to 17 an aviation experience, including a flight.

The COPA Flight Safety Foundation, funded by member donations, was established to assist the promotion of pilot safety through seminars and a Flight Safety Bulletin published in Canadian Flight.

The COPA Special Action Fund, established in the late 1970's by long-time President Russ Beach, is also funded by member donations. This fund pays legal expenses incurred from contesting actions which are considered to be contrary to the best interests of aviation. In 1997, the fund topped $1million.

COPA is the Trustee of the Governor General's Cup. This is awarded annually

to the winner of a national amateur air rally. This rally is held in various parts of Canada, often in conjunction with COPA's annual convention.

COPA maintains a system of annual awards to recognize excellence in aviation in Canada. The association's top honour is the COPA President's Award, presented annually to the person or persons who made a significant contribution to general aviation in Canada in recent years.

COPA holds an annual convention and general meeting, giving members an opportunity to get together, learn more about aviation and to give feedback directly to the association's directors. This format is repeated at less formal regional events called COPA Rendezvous.

In 1995 COPA set up a Memorial Scholarship in Neil Armstrong's name, to be awarded to a student who has maintained a high standard of achievement and leadership. The first scholarship was presented at the COPA Annual General Meeting in Hamilton, Ontario, in 1996. Neil Armstrong was a long-time member of COPA, and one of its early Presidents. He was inducted as a Member of Canada's Aviation Hall of Fame in 1974.

The Belt of Orion Award for Excellence was bestowed upon the Canadian Owners and Pilots Association in 1993.

431 Air Demonstration Squadron—The Snowbirds

Aerobatics teams have been a part of Canada's aviation heritage for over six decades, beginning in 1929 with a biplane team called The Siskins. The year 1959 was an important year in the history of aviation in Canada: it was the 50th anniversary of powered flight, as well as the 35th anniversary of the Royal Canadian Air Force (RCAF). A Golden Anniversary aerobatics team, called the Golden Hawks, was authorized for one year. Using gold-painted F-86 Sabre 5's, the team performed 65 25-minute shows across Canada from May to the end of September. They were so popular that it was decided to continue the team, and shows were performed again, thrilling millions of people at airshows across Canada and the United States. They were acclaimed the best team in North America, and were the pride of the RCAF and heroes to the young across the country. However, they were disbanded after the 1963 shows were finished because of the high cost of maintaining the team.

Canada celebrated its 100th birthday in 1967 with a new team called the Golden

The entire 'Snowbird' squadron consists of only 24 members, including 11 pilots, 10 aircraft technicians, 1 logistics officer, 1 supply technician and a civilian secretary. The team members are all volunteers of the Canadian Forces and their tour of duty with the Snowbirds is two years. Each year, half the team members change, with the new members being taught the required skills by the second year Snowbirds.

Centennaires flying Tutor Jets. This team performed 100 air shows across Canada and the U.S., captivating audiences wherever they went.

In 1969 Colonel O.B. Philp, who had created and commanded the Centennaires, was promoted to Base Commander at Moose Jaw, Saskatchewan, operating No. 2 Canadian Forces Flying Training School, commonly known as 'The Big Two'. On his first tour of the base, he spotted several all-white CL-41 Tutors, ex-Centennaire machines, among the unpainted metal remainder.

The recent unification of the Armed Forces had created insecurity among senior Army, Navy and Air personnel, so without seeking permission, Philp encouraged 'practice' for formation demonstrations. This 'practice' was intended to maintain instructor pilots' proficiency, and their appearance across the country was hailed by the public, and gradually became an accepted fact by the top brass. In 1970 a white Tutor led the formation of four which opened the Regina football season, and at the Abbotsford Air Show that year, all four Tutors were white.

In 1971 the four became seven, a logo was developed, and a competition among school children gave the Snowbirds their name. In 1972 two solos were added to make up their present complement of nine aircraft. That year, team members were assigned to practice and performance full time.

In 1974 the aircraft were painted with the familiar red, white and blue paint scheme, and were authorized to do a fully aerobatic show. One of the reasons the shows are such crowd-pleasers is the choice of the Canadair CL-41 Tutor jet trainer as their team aircraft. The exceptional manoeuverability of this aircraft allows the Snowbirds to stay in constant contact with spectators, giving a seamless performance.

Seven years after their first show, the Snowbirds achieved full squadron status as

431 Air Demonstration Squadron, and have gradually developed into one of the world's foremost aerobatics team.

The Snowbirds' aim is to demonstrate to the North American public the skill, professionalism and team work of the Canadian Forces. Snowbirds strive for perfection in formation flight. They draw upon the spirit and example of those who have served before them. Since 1971, the team has embarked on a continuing journey as Canadian ambassadors of excellence in aerial displays.

The Belt of Orion Award for Excellence was bestowed upon 431 (AD) Squadron, the Snowbirds, in 1994.

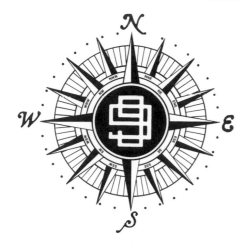

> "The spirit of fellowship of these women who share one common interest and accomplishment—flight—has been revealed in their active promotion of aviation and safety in aviation through educational, charitable and scientific activities which have been of exceptional benefit to Canadian aviation in general."
>
> —Belt of Orion Award citation, 1995

West and East Canada Sections of The Ninety-Nines, Inc. (International Organization of Women Pilots)

The Canadian Ninety-Nines are women pilots who took up flying for the joy and the challenge, and in doing so, have made significant career progress in a male-dominated field. Their purpose is "to engage in educational, charitable and scientific activities and to provide a close relationship among women pilots and unite them in any movement that may be for their benefit or for that of aviation in general."

The East and West Canada Sections were formed in 1950 and 1951, and the organization has since grown to ten Chapters with over 240 active members. They are part of an international organization, The Ninety-Nines Inc., with over 6,000 members and local chapters in 35 countries. Virtually all women of achievement in aviation have been or are presently members of the Ninety-Nines.

The Canadian Ninety-Nines organize many activities to promote safety through training and education. Members are conscious of exercising safety in flight, and all current members attempt to participate in the Annual Proficiency program. Canadian chapters have

99s are often asked how they got their name. In 1929, all licenced American women pilots were invited to assemble for mutual support and the advancement of aviation. Ninety-nine women responded, and Amelia Earhart was elected first president. Membership was immediately opened to any licenced woman pilot, and the total membership now is over 6,000 world-wide, but the name chosen at that time remained.

consistently won the 99s' International Aviation Proficiency Training Award over the years.

They organize aviation safety seminars and courses. Their popular Flying Companion Co-pilot Courses are offered to familiarize non-pilots with flying, to alleviate fear of flying, and teach fundamentals of aircraft operation and radio procedures. They are active in civilian air search and rescue training, winter survival training and sponsoring Transport Canada up-date sessions.

Ninety-Nines organize a biennial Canadian Women in Aviation Conference, and arrange speaking engagements to talk about opportunities in aviation. They reach out to schools, presenting their 'Air Bears' program for primary grade children and the 'Theory of Flight' program for grades 4 to 8. They make Career Day presentations, and work with young people in programs such as Young Eagles and Girl Guides.

They participate in many aviation events across Canada, such as major fly-ins and flying competitions. They coordinate their activities with other mutual interest groups, in particular, the Aviation Councils and the Canadian Owners and Pilots Association, where they have an appointed seat on the board of directors. Most chapters organize a 'Poker Run', a rally-type event to keep cross-country flying skills sharp, to raise funds to support scholarships and awards, and to have fun and enjoy fellowship. They have put together a precision flying team which will compete in World Precision Flying Competitions.

The Ninety-Nines recognize achievement, and grant several awards. The 99s Canadian Award in Aviation was created in 1974 to promote aviation throughout Canada, and has come to represent a special and prestigious element of the Canadian aviation community. It is awarded each year to an organization or individual whose activities improve or preserve aviation and aeronautics in Canada. The National Aviation Museum was recently honoured with the award for its upcoming exhibit 'Women in Aviation', which recognizes women who have contributed to the advancement of aviation in Canada.

Many chapters provide annual scholarships and offer Awards of Excellence to top graduating female student pilots. Amelia Earhart Memorial Scholarships for advanced flight training are awarded internationally each year.

In 1976 East Canada Section 99s began flying pollution patrols for the Ontario Ministry of the Environment. They fly ministry personnel over lakes and forests to track the source of fouled lake water and follow leads to illegal dump sites. Called 'Operation Skywatch,' the program now operates under the jurisdiction of the ministry's Investigations and Enforcement Branch.

The Canadian Ninety-Nines have made great personal achievements and received much recognition. Many 99s fly commercial aircraft, including Rosella Bjornson, first woman to fly as Captain with a major Canadian air carrier. Major Dee Brasseur (ret'd) was the world's first female CF-18 pilot. In 1992 Roberta Bondar became Canada's first female astronaut in space, and Julie Payette was selected out of 5,330 candidates to be Canada's next woman in space.

The Award of Merit is presented to a 99 who has given exceptional service to the organization. Lorna deBlicquy received this award in 1993. That same year, she was the first woman honoured to receive the Trans-Canada (McKee) Trophy. She has opened doors for all women in aviation through her successful efforts in changing government hiring policies. She became Canada's first woman Civil Aviation Inspector.

Canadian Ninety-Nines have been, or are, bush pilots, test pilots, airshow pilots, owners and operators of airlines and airports, chief flying instructors, helicopter pilots, airline pilots, air traffic controllers, civil aviation inspectors, air race participants and war-time Air Transport Auxiliary pilots. Their participation in their organization's activities paved the way to pursue careers in these, up to then, male-dominated fields.

The Belt of Orion Award for Excellence was bestowed on the West and East Canada Sections of The Ninety-Nines Inc. in 1995.

Canadian Forces— Search and Rescue (SAR)

For more than fifty years, Canadian Forces Search and Rescue (SAR) personnel have been a proud part of this country's military community. Canada's SAR program is recognized as a world leader and innovator in this essential area of humanitarian service.

In 1947 the Royal Canadian Air Force (RCAF) was given the responsibility for the provision of air resources to respond to air and marine incidents and in 1951, was tasked with the responsibility for the overall coordination of SAR in Canada.

Early aircraft and boats were not equipped with emergency radio beacons and search crews relied solely on visual indicators to locate those in distress. Later, with the invention and subsequent widespread use of Emergency Locator Transmitters (ELT's), search aircraft were able to conduct these searches electronically. In the early 1980's, a world wide satellite system, COSPAS-SARSAT, was developed jointly with the governments of France, Russia and the United States, which enabled search aircraft to respond more quickly and accurately to distress calls and greatly improved the chances of survival. Canadian Forces Base Trenton (8 Wing)

acts as the Canadian Mission Control Centre and is Canada's link to the COSPAS-SARSAT satellite-based rescue alerting system.

SARSAT stands for Search and Rescue Satellite-Aided Tracking. COSPAS is the Russian equivalent, which stands for 'the search for vessels in distress'.

The military component of Canada's Search and Rescue team is made up of more than 650 Canadian Forces personnel in three classifications: aircrew, groundcrew and air controllers. The aircrew include pilots, air navigators, flight engineers, loadmasters, and search and rescue technicians. The ground crew are composed of aviation, avionics and structures technicians. All Rescue Coordination Centre Air Controllers are experienced pilots and navigators.

An average of 1,500-2,000 missions are conducted annually by aircraft and personnel located at five primary SAR units: 103 Search and Rescue Squadron at Gander, Newfoundland, 413 Transport and Rescue Squadron at Greenwood, Nova Scotia, 424 Transport and Rescue Squadron at Trenton, Ontario, 435 Transport and Rescue Squadron at Winnipeg, Manitoba, and 442 Transport and Rescue Squadron at Comox, British Columbia. Missions are coordinated by three Rescue Coordination Centres (RCC's) located at Halifax, Trenton and Victoria.

Annually, more than 7,000 incidents are coordinated by the RCC's, which are jointly manned by Canadian Forces and Canadian Coast Guard SAR experienced personnel.

In addition to the professional military members, civilian volunteers make up a large portion of the SAR team. The Civi Air Search and Rescue Association (CASARA) and the Canadian Coast Guard Auxiliary (CCGA) are volunteer organizations which provide equipment and trained personnel to assist in SAR operations.

The Belt of Orion Award for Excellence was bestowed upon Canadian Forces Search and Rescue personnel, past and present, in 1998.

Persons who are injured or in distress need help, fast. Every hour counts if they are to survive, but they must be found first before they can be helped. In a country such as Canada, with its immense distances, rugged terrain and often harsh climate, that can be difficult. The results of studies have shown that even those persons who have survived an initial accident have less than a ten percent chance of survival in winter if the rescue is delayed beyond two days. If the rescue is accomplished within eight hours, their survival rate increases dramatically to more than 50 percent.

Fortunately, the combination of reliable communication signals and well-trained SAR personnel has resulted in many people being saved who otherwise may have died.

Glossary

AEA
Aerial Experiment Association

A.F.C.
Air Force Cross

AOS
Air Observers School (BCATP)

* (asterisk)
indicates an additional award of the same medal. It is presented in the form of a Bar added to the original ribbon, and is shown by the use of an asterisk. Eg., M.C.* shows a Bar has been added to the Military Cross.

ATA
Air Transport Association

ATAC
Air Transport Association of Canada

ATB
Air Transport Board

ATC
Air Transport Command

A/V/M
Air Vice-Marshal

B.A.
Bachelor of Arts

B.A.Sc.
Bachelor of Applied Science

BCATP
British Commonwealth Air Training Plan

B.E. or B. Eng.
Bachelor of Engineering

BGen
Brigadier General

brevet
n. a commission giving a military officer higher nominal rank than that for which he receives pay

B.Sc.
Bachelor of Science

B.Sc.F.
Bachelor of Science in Forestry

CAB
Canadian Air Board

CAF
Canadian Air Force

CAHF
Canada's Aviation Hall of Fame

CAHS
Canadian Aviation Historical Society

CALPA
Canadian Airline Pilots Association

CAPA
Canadian Aeronautical Preservation Association

CASARA
Civil Air Search and Rescue Association

CASI
Canadian Aeronautics and Space Institute

C.B.
Companion of the Most Honourable Order of the Bath

C.B.E.
Commander, Order of the British Empire

C.C.
Companion, Order of Canada

C.D.
Canadian Forces Decoration, awarded after twelve years' service

C.D.*
Clasp for the C.D., awarded after an additional ten years' service

CFB
Canadian Forces Base

CFHQ
Canadian Forces Headquarters

CGTAS
Canadian Government Trans-Atlantic Air Service

C.M.
Member, Order of Canada

C.M.M.
Commander of the Order of Military Merit

CNS
Central Navigation School (BCATP)

CO
Commanding Officer

Col
Colonel

COPA
Canadian Owners and Pilots Association

Cpl
Corporal

CSA
Canadian Space Agency

C.St.J.
Commander of the Order of St. John of Jerusalem

D.C.M.
Distinguished Conduct Medal

D-Day
Invasion of France, June 6, 1944

D. Eng.
Doctor of Engineering

DEW Line
Distant Early Warning Line

D.F.C.
Distinguished Flying Cross

DHC
de Havilland Aircraft of Canada Ltd; de Havilland Canada

DND
Department of National Defence

DOT
Department of Transport

D.S.C.
Distinguished Service Cross

D.S.M.
Distinguished Service Medal

D.S.O.
Distinguished Service Order (Companion of the Distinguished Order, instituted 1886)

D.Sc.
Doctor of Science (usually honorary)

E.D.
Canadian Efficiency Decoration (for Officers of Military Auxiliary Forces, awarded after ten years' service, with a Clasp added after an additional five years service)

EFTS
Elementary Flying Training School (BCATP)

FAA
Federal Aviation Administration (U.S.A.)

FAI
Fédération Aéronautique Internationale

F/L
Flight Lieutenant

F/O
Flying Officer; First Officer

F/Sgt
Flight Sergeant

Gosport System
system of communication in which an instructor talked through a rubber speaking tube to a student while in flight, developed at the Gosport air training centre in England during World War I

G/C
Group Captain

HMCS
His/Her Majesty's Canadian Ship

HMS
His/Her Majesty's Ship

IATA
International Air Transport Association

ICAO
International Civil Aviation Organization

IFALPA
International Federation of Air Line Pilots

IFR
Instrument Flight Rules

ILS
Instrument Landing System

INS
Inertial Navigation System

JATO
Jet Assisted Take-Off

K.C.
King's Counsel

K.St.J.
Knight of the Order of St. John of Jerusalem

LL.D.
Doctor of Laws (usually honorary)

LORAN
Long Range Aerial Navigation

Mach 1
the speed of sound, 763 mph, measured in dry air at air pressure of 29.92" of mercury and temperature of 32 degrees Fahrenheit. (From Ernst Mach, 1838 – 1916, Austrian physicist)

M.B.
Medal of Bravery

M.B.E.
Member, Order of the British Empire

M.C.
Military Cross (instituted 1915)

M.E. or M. Eng.
Master of Engineering

MGen
Major General

MiD
Mention in Despatches (denotes Royal Commendation for brave conduct)

MOT
Ministry of Transport

M.Sc.
Master of Science

N.A.M.E.
Northern Aerial Mineral Exploration

NASA
National Aeronautics and Space Administration

NATO
North Atlantic Treaty Organization

NCO
Non Commissioned Officer

NDHQ
National Defence Headquarters

NORAD
North American Air Defence System

NRC
National Research Council

O.B.E.
Officer, Order of the British Empire

O.C.
Officer, Order of Canada

O.M.M.
Officer, Order of Military Merit

OPAS
Ontario Provincial Air Service

Order of Canada
created July 1, 1967, to honour Canadians for outstanding achievement and service to the country. The post-nominals reflect the three levels of honour: 'C.C.' for Companion, 'O.C.' for Officer, and 'C.M.' for Member.

Order of Military Merit
created July 1, 1972, to recognize meritorious service and devotion to duty by members of the Canadian Forces. The levels of membership are: 'C.M.M.' for Commander, 'O.M.M.' for Officer, and 'M.M.M.' for Member.

Order of St. John of Jerusalem (Grand Priory of the Most Venerable Order of the Hospital of St. John of Jerusalem)
The Order has a long history. It became a British institution in 1858 and was confirmed by Royal Charter in 1888. It maintains two foundations—St. John Ambulance and the Ophthalmic Hospital in Jerusalem. Men and women are admitted to the Order, and the levels or grades are:
I – 'G.C.St.J.' for Bailiff or Dame Grand Cross
II – 'K.St.J.', or 'D.St.J' for Knight or Dame of Justice and of Grace
III – 'C.St.J.' for Commander, Brother or Sister
IV – 'O.St.J.' for Officer, Brother or Sister
V – 'S.B.St.J.', or 'S.S.St.J.' for Serving Brother or Sister
VI – 'ESQ.St.J.' for Esquire.

Order of the Bath (The Most Honourable Order of the Bath)
Instituted in 1725 by George I, with one level or class, the Knight, with lettering K.B. It was awarded to selected senior officers for services in action, and to civilians for political services. In 1815 the Order was extended to three classes under two branches, military and civil. The classes are the same for each of the branches: 'G.C.B' for Knight Grand Cross, 'K.C.B.' for Knight Commander, and 'C.B.' for Companion.

Order of the British Empire
Founded by George V in June 1917 for services to the British Empire, civil and military. The Classes are: 'G.B.E.' for Knights Grand Cross, 'K.B.E' for Knights Commanders, 'C.B.E.' for Commanders, 'O.B.E' for Officers, and 'M.B.E.' for Members.

O.St.J.
Officer of the Order of St. John of Jerusalem

OTU
Operational Training Unit

P/O
Pilot Officer

P&WC
Pratt and Whitney Canada

Q.C.
Queen's Counsel

RAF
Royal Air Force

RAFFC
Royal Air Force Ferry Command

RAFTC
Royal Air Force Transport Command

RCAF
Royal Canadian Air Force

RCAFA
Royal Canadian Air Force Association

RCAFFC
Royal Canadian Air Force Ferry Command

RCC
Rescue Coordination Centre

RCFCA
Royal Canadian Flying Clubs Association

RCN
Royal Canadian Navy

RCNR
Royal Canadian Navy Reserve

RCNVR
Royal Canadian Naval Volunteer Reserve

RFC
Royal Flying Corps

RMC
Royal Military College

RMS
Remote Manipulator System (Canadarm)

RN
Royal Navy

RNAS
Royal Naval Air Service

RNFAA
Royal Naval Fleet Air Arm

RNVR
Royal Naval Volunteer Reserve

RO
Radio Observer

RSFC
Return Service Ferry Command

SAE
Society of Automotive Engineers

S.A.I.T.
Southern Alberta Institute of Technology

SARSAT
Search and Rescue Satellite-Aided Tracking

SFTS
Service Flying Training School (BCATP)

SHORAN
Short Range Aid to Navigation

S/L
Squadron Leader

S.P.A.R.
Special Products and Applied Research (a division of DHC)

SST
Supersonic Transport

Suggested Reading

Index

STOL
Short Take Off and Landing

STOL/VTOL
Short Take Off and Landing/Vertical Take Off and Landing

U.K.
United Kingdom

U-boat
German submarine

USAF
United States Air Force

USAAF
United States Army Air Force

USN
United States Navy

V.C.
Victoria Cross: founded by Queen Victoria in 1856 during the Crimean War. It is described as a Maltese Cross, made of gun metal, with a Royal Crest in the centre and underneath it an escroll bearing the inscription "For Valour". It is awarded to members of any branch of Her Majesty's services for conspicuous bravery or self-sacrifice.

VFR
Visual Flight Rules

V-E Day
Victory-in-Europe Day: May 8, 1945

V-J Day
Victory-over-Japan Day: August 14, 1945

W/C
Wing Commander

WW I
World War I was started because of the assassination of Archduke Ferdinand of Austria-Hungary on July 28, 1914. The British Empire entered the war on August 4, 1914. The war ended with an armistice on November 11, 1918.

WW II
World War II began with Germany's invasion of Poland on September 1, 1939. Great Britain declared war on September 3, 1939, and Canada entered the war one week later. WW II ended May 8, 1945 in Europe, and on August 14, 1945, when Japan accepted the Allied surrender terms. The terms of Japan's surrender were signed on September 2, 1945.

Avery, Norman. *Whiskey Whiskey Papa: Chronicling the Exciting Life and Times of a Pilot's Pilot* (story of Weldy Phipps). Ottawa: Norman Avery, 1998.

Bain, Donald M. *Canadian Pacific Air Lines: Its History and Aircraft.* Calgary: Kishorn Publications, 1987.

Baker, David. *Billy Bishop, The Man and the Aircraft He Flew.* London, England: Outline Press, 1990.

Balchen, Bernt. *Come North With Me, An Autobiography.* New York: E.P. Dutton and Co. Inc., 1958.

Barris, Ted. *Behind the Glory: The Plan that Won the Allied War.* (BCATP) Toronto: Macmillan, 1992.

Beaudoin, Ted. *Walking on Air.* Vernon, British Columbia: Vernon Interior Printers, 1986.

Bishop, William Arthur. *The Courage of the Early Morning, The Story of Billy Bishop.* Toronto: McLelland and Stewart, 1965.

Canadian Aviation Historical Society. *CAHS Journal.* (Published quarterly) Willowdale, Ontario.

Collishaw, Raymond and Dodds, R.V. *Air Command, A Fighter Pilot's Story.* London, England: Wm. Kimber, 1973.

Condit, John. *Wings Over the West: Russ Baker and the Rise of Pacific Western Airlines.* Madeira Park, British Columbia: Harbour Publishing, 1984.

Corley-Smith, Peter. *Barnstorming to Bush Flying 1910 – 1930.* Victoria, BC: Sono Nis Press, 1989.

Dodds, Ronald. *The Brave Young Wings.* Stittsville, Ontario: Canada's Wings, Inc., 1980.

Ellis, Frank. *Canada's Flying Heritage.* Toronto: University of Toronto Press, 1954.

Ellis, Frank. *In Canadian Skies: 50 Years of Adventure and Progress.* Toronto: Ryerson Press, 1959.

Floyd, Jim. *The Avro Canada C-102 Jetliner.* Erin, Ontario: Boston Mills Press, 1986.

Foster, J.A. *The Bush Pilots.* Toronto: McClelland & Stewart, Inc., 1990.

Fuller, G.A., Griffin, J.A., Molson, K.M. *125 Years of Canadian Aeronautics: A Chronology 1840 – 1965.* Willowdale, Ontario: Canadian Aviation Historical Society, 1983.

Gilbert, Walter and Shakleton, Kathleen. *Arctic Pilot.* Toronto: Nelson Publishers, 1940.

Hartley, Michael. *The Challenge of the Skies.* Edmonton: Puckrin's Publishing House Ltd., 1981.

Hotson, Fred W. *The Bremen.* Toronto: CANAV Books, 1988.

Hotson, Fred W. *The De Havilland Canada Story.* Toronto: CANAV Books, 1983.

Jane's All the World's Aircraft. Series. London: Jane's Yearbooks, 1909-

Keith, Ronald A. *Bush Pilot With a Briefcase: The Happy-go-Lucky Story of Grant McConachie.* Toronto: Doubleday Canada Ltd., 1972.

Leigh, Z.L. *And I Shall Fly: The Flying Memoirs of Z. Lewis Leigh.* Toronto: CANAV Books, 1985.

Lothian, George. *Flight Deck: Memoires of an Airline Pilot.* Toronto: McGraw-Hill Ryerson, 1979.

McGregor, Gordon R. *The Adolescence of an Airline.* Montreal: Air Canada, 1970.

McCaffery, Dan. *Billy Bishop: Canadian Hero.* Toronto: James Lorimer Publishers, 1988.

McLaren, Duncan D. *Bush to Boardroom. A Personal View of Five Decades of Aviation History.* Winnipeg, Manitoba: Watson and Dwyer, 1992.

Meyers, Patricia A. *Sky Riders: An Illustrated History of Aviation in Alberta, 1906 – 1945.* Saskatoon, Saskatchewan: Fifth House Ltd., 1995.

Milberry, Larry. *Air Transport in Canada, Volumes I and II.* Toronto: CANAV Books, 1997.

Milberry, Larry. *Austin Airways: Canada's Oldest Airline.* Toronto: CANAV Books, 1985.

Milberry, Larry. *Sixty Years: The RCAF and CF Air Command 1924 – 84.* Toronto: CANAV Books, 1984.

Molson, K.M. and Taylor, H.A. *Canadian Aircraft Since 1909.* Stittsville, Ontario: Canada's Wings, 1982.

Molson, K.M. *Canada's National Aviation Museum: Its History and Collections.* Ottawa: National Aviation Museum, 1988.

Munro, Raymond. *The Sky's No Limit.* Toronto: Key Porter Books, 1985.

Nolan, Brian. *HERO: The Buzz Beurling Story.* Toronto: Lester & Orpen Dennys Ltd., 1981.

Pickler, Ron and Milberry, Larry. *Canadair: The First 50 Years.* Toronto: CANAV Books, 1995.

Pigott, Peter. *Flying Colours: A History of Commercial Aviation in Canada.* Vancouver: Douglas & McIntyre Ltd., 1997.

Pigott, Peter. *Wing Walkers, A Story of Canadian Airlines International.* Madeira Park, British Columbia: Harbour Publishing, 1998.

Ralph, Wayne. *Barker VC: William Barker, Canada's Most Decorated War Hero.* Toronto: Doubleday, 1997.

Reid, Sheila. *Wings of a Hero, Ace Wop May.* St. Catharines, Ontario: Vanwell Publishing, 1977.

Render, Shirley. *No Place for a Lady: The Story of Canadian Women Pilots, 1928 – 1992.* Winnipeg, Manitoba: Portage & Main Press, 1992.

Shores, Christopher. *History of the Royal Canadian Air Force.* Toronto: Royce Publications, 1984.

Sutherland, Alice Gibson. *Canada's Aviation Pioneers: 50 Years of McKee Trophy Winners.* Toronto: McGraw-Hill Ryerson, 1978.

Taylor, Michael J.H. *The Aerospace Chronology.* London, England: Tri-Service Press Ltd., 1989.

Ward, Maxwell. *The Max Ward Story.* Toronto: McClelland & Stewart, 1991.

Whyard, Florence. *Ernie Boffa, Canadian Bush Pilot.* Anchorage, Alaska: Alaska Northwest Publishing, 1984.

Wise, S.F., *Canadian Airmen and the First World War: The Official History of the Royal Canadian Air Force, Volume I.* Toronto: University of Toronto Press, 1980.

To Our Readers

Every effort has been made to provide accurate information in the stories about the Members of Canada's Aviation Hall of Fame. The writing of these stories depended on the amount of accurate material available in the Hall's archives and other sources. While doing the research, I often found conflicting information. When this was discovered, cross-referencing was done as far as possible.

This book is about a small group of Canadians, but they have given us a great legacy to treasure. We have done our best to represent them well. The accuracy of the contents of this book is the responsibility of everyone who has information about these people.

This is your book: if you note any errors contained in *They Led the Way*, or if you have additional information, please bring them to our attention. We depend on you to provide us with sufficient background information which will verify the sources for any changes to be made. Write to the Hall at the address given below.

We will publish these corrections in future issues of the Annual Updates. We will also publish other information about Members as it becomes available to us.

Thank you for your assistance.

Mary Oswald

—Editor

**For Your Information:
a new system for keeping you informed!**

You have obtained this book, *They Led the Way*, because of your interest in Canada's aviation heritage, and we hope you derive much pleasure and pride in the accomplishments of Canadians as you read each story. To keep you informed about new Inductees each year and to present current information on Members of Canada's Aviation Hall of Fame, we have developed an Annual Updates Binder, which is now available. It is an attractive companion to the hard-cover book, *They Led the Way*, and will automatically provide you with up-dates for the five-year period 1999 to 2003. You may use the form below to order.

Order Form

I would like to order:

_____ copies of They Led the Way @ $36.50 $_____

_____ copies of the Annual Updates Binder @ $22.50 $_____

Total: $_____

Please enclose cheque or money order, payable to Canada's Aviation Hall of Fame.

Name: _____

Address: _____

City/Town: _____ Province: _____ Postal Code: _____

Telephone: (   ) _____ Fax: (   ) _____

Mail your order to:
Canada's Aviation Hall of Fame
P.O. Box 6360
Wetaskiwin, Alberta T9A 2G1

Canada's Aviation
Hall of Fame

For more information, contact the Hall: phone (780) 361-1351 or fax (780) 361-1239.
The Hall's e-mail address is: cahf@telusplanet.net

CARLYLE CLARE 'CARL' AGAR   WILLIAM MUNROE ARCHIBALD   NEIL J. ARMSTRONG   JULIEN JOSEPH AUDETTE   JOHN

BALDWIN   RUSSELL BANNOCK   WILLIAM GEORGE 'BILL' BARKER   IAN WILLOUGHBY BAZALGETTE   ALEXANDER GRA

MARIE BJORNSON   THURSTON 'RUSTY' BLAKEY   ERNEST JOSEPH BOFFA   ROBERT WILLIAM BRADFORD   WILFRED LE

ERSKINE LEIGH CAPREOL   NICHOLAS BYRON CAVADIAS   ALFRED BEEBE CAYWOOD   LARRY DENMAN CLARKE   RAY

ROBERT LESLIE DODDS   JOHN TALBOT DYMENT   MAURICE D'ARCY ALLEN FALLOW   JOHN EMILIUS 'JOHNNY' FAUQUIE

WALTER WARREN FOWLER   THOMAS PAYNE FOX   JAMES HENRY FOY   WILBUR ROUNDING FRANKS   DOUGLAS FRA

GRAHAM   ROY STANLEY GRANDY   ROBERT HAMPTON GRAY   KEITH ROGERS GREENAWAY   SETH WALTER GROSSMITH

HISCOCKS   BASIL DEACON HOBBS   HERBERT HOLLICK-KENYON   HERBERT HOPSON   DAVID ERNEST HORNELL   H

MARLOWE KENNEDY   WILLIAM GEORGE MELVIN 'MEL' KNOX   THOMAS ALBERT LAWRENCE   WILSON GEORGE LEACH

WILLIAM FLOYD SHELDON LUCK   FRANK ARCHIBALD MACDOUGALL   ELIZABETH MURIEL GREGORY MACGILL   GERALD

MAY   FRED ROBERT GORDON MCCALL   GEORGE WILLIAM GRANT MCCONACHIE   JOHN ALEXANDER DOUGLAS MCC

MCMILLAN   ARCHIBALD MAJOR 'ARCHIE' MCMULLEN   ROBERT WENDELL 'BUCK' MCNAIR   BERT WILLIAM MEAD   ALP

ANDREW CHARLES 'ANDY' MYNARSKI   GEORGE ARTHUR NEAL   WILLIAM FRANCIS MONTGOMERY NEWSON   HAROLD

PHILLIPS   WELLAND WILFRED 'WELDY' PHIPPS   JOHN LAWRENCE PLANT   PETER GEOFFREY POWELL   ROBERT CHEETHA

FENTON 'MOLLY' REILLY   JAMES ARMSTRONG RICHARDSON   ROBERT 'DICK' RICHMOND   DONALD HOWARD ROGERS

'JOE' SCHULTZ   EUGENE HOWARD SCHWEITZER   HERBERT WALTER SEAGRIM   MURTON ADAMS SEYMOUR   JOHN GAV

SMITH   FRANKLIN ERNEST WILLIAM SMITH   ERNEST WALTER STEDMAN   ALEXANDER MACKAY 'MICKEY' SUTHERLAN

LEONARD JOHN TRIPP   JOHN HENRY 'TUDDY' TUDHOPE   WALLACE RUPERT TURNBULL   PERCIVAL STANLEY 'STAN' TU

ROLAND BURGESS WEST   ROBERT ALLAN 'BUD' WHITE   THOMAS FREDERIC 'TOMMY' WILLIAMS   ARTHUR HALIBURTON

FRANKLIN INGLEE YOUNG   JANUSZ 'JAN' ZURAKOWSKI   CANADIAN AIRLINE PILOTS ASSOCIATION   AIR CADET

CANADIAN OWNERS AND PILOTS ASSOCIATION   431 (AD) SQUADRON SNOWBIRDS   CANADIAN SECTIONS, IN